Foucault's theatres

Edited by
TONY FISHER AND KÉLINA GOTMAN

Manchester University Press

Published by Manchester University Press
Altrincham Street, Manchester M1 7JA
www.manchesteruniversitypress.co.uk

British Library Cataloguing-in-Publication Data
A catalogue record for this book is available from the British Library

ISBN 978 1 5261 3206 2 hardback
ISBN 978 1 5261 3570 4 paperback

First published 2020

Typeset by Newgen Publishing UK
Printed in Great Britain
by TJ International Ltd, Padstow

CONTENTS

FIGURES

CONTRIBUTORS

Robert Bononno is credited with the translation of over two dozen full-length works of fiction and nonfiction and numerous shorter pieces. These include René Crevel's *My Body and I* (2010) – a finalist for the 2005 French-American Foundation Prize – Hervé Guibert's *Ghost Image* (1996), and Henri Raczymow's *Swan's Way* (2002). In 2002 he received a grant from the National Endowment for the Arts to complete a translation of the nonfiction work of Isabelle Eberhardt and in 2010 he received an NEA grant for the retranslation of Eugène Sue's classic crime novel, *The Mysteries of Paris* (2018). His latest translation, Pascale Kramer's *Autopsy of a Father* (2017), was recently published by the Bellevue Literary Press.

Stuart Elden is Professor of Political Theory and Geography at the University of Warwick. He is the author of several books, including *The Birth of Territory* (2013), *Foucault's Last Decade* (2016), *Foucault: The Birth of Power* (2017), and *Shakespearean Territories* (2018). He blogs at www.progressivegeographies.com.

Tony Fisher is Reader in Theatre and Philosophy at the Royal Central School of Speech and Drama. He is author of *Theatre and Governance in Britain, 1500–1900: Democracy, Disorder and the State* (2017) and co-editor of *Performing Antagonism: Theatre, Performance and Radical Democracy* (2017), and *Beyond Failure: New Essays on the Cultural History of Failure in Theatre and Performance* (2018), both co-edited with Eve Katsouraki.

Kélina Gotman teaches Theatre and Performance Studies in the English Department at King's College London. She is author of *Choreomania: Dance and Disorder* (2018) and *Essays on Theatre and Change: Towards a Poetics Of* (2018), as well as articles and chapters in *parallax, SubStance, Textual Practice, Performance Research, About*

Performance, Choreographic Practices, and elsewhere. She is translator of Félix Guattari's *The Anti-Oedipus Papers* (Semiotext[e], 2006) and Marie NDiaye's *Les serpents* (2017).

Mark D. Jordan teaches at Harvard University in the Divinity School and the Faculty of Arts and Sciences. His recent books include *Convulsing Bodies: Religion and Resistance in Foucault* (2015).

Tracey Nicholls teaches Peace Studies and Gender Studies at Soka University in Tokyo, Japan. Previously, she was Associate Professor of Philosophy at Lewis University, in the greater Chicago area of the United States, and co-director of their Women's Studies Program. She received her PhD from McGill University, Canada. The book based on her dissertation, *An Ethics of Improvisation: Aesthetic Possibilities for a Political Future*, was published in 2012, and her work in social and political philosophy contributes to discourses in decolonisation theory, feminist theory, and peace studies.

Magnolia Pauker is Lecturer in Critical and Cultural Studies at the Emily Carr University of Art + Design on the unceded Coast Salish territories also known as Vancouver, Canada. A doctoral candidate at the Institute for Gender, Race, Sexuality and Social Justice at the University of British Columbia, she is currently writing her dissertation entitled 'Philosophy as Radical Journalism: The Public Intellectual and The Rise of the Philosopher Journalist'. She is co-editor of *Inter Views in Performance Philosophy: Crossings and Conversations* (2017).

Ann Pellegrini is Professor of Performance Studies and Social and Cultural Analysis at New York University. Her books include *Performance Anxieties: Staging Psychoanalysis, Staging Race* (1997); *Love the Sin: Sexual Regulation and the Limits of Religious Tolerance* (co-authored with Janet R. Jakobsen, 2003); and the forthcoming *Queer Structures of Religious Feeling*.

Steve Potter is Composer-in-Residence of Musarc choral collective, and Tutor in Academic Studies and Composition at Guildhall School of Music and Drama. He has presented performative works encompassing heterogeneous collections of instruments and critical theoretical texts at The Charterhouse, LSO St. Luke's, Alte Oper Frankfurt and New York City Opera VOX Showcase. His recent work for lecture, videos, prepared piano, bonang, amplified cello and violin, speaking chorus, and dancer, *Well I want it in writing, the smallest event and the secretest agency*, was created during a fellowship at Cornell University. He plays accordion occasionally in the London Improvisers Orchestra.

Dan Rebellato is Professor of Contemporary Theatre at Royal Holloway, University of London, where he teaches theatre, playwriting, and philosophy. His books include *1956 and All That* (1999), *Theatre & Globalization* (2009), *Contemporary European Theatre Directors* (2010), *Decades of British Playwriting: 2000–2009* (2013), plus numerous articles on modern and contemporary theatre. He is currently writing *Naturalist Theatre: A New Cultural History* and co-editing the *Cambridge Companion to British Theatre since 1945* and the *Cambridge Companion to British Playwriting since 1945*. He is a widely performed and published playwright for stage and radio and his plays include *Chekhov in Hell, Static, Here's What I Did With My Body One Day, Mile*

End, Beachy Head, Theatremorphosis, Outright Terror Bold and Brilliant, and *Emily Rising.* He was lead writer on the award-winning *Emile Zola: Blood, Sex & Money* for BBC Radio 4.

Mark Robson holds the Chair of English and Theatre Studies at the University of Dundee. He has published widely on drama, literature, and visual culture, as well as on modern French thought and critical theory. His most recent book is *Theatre & Death* (2019).

Joanne Tompkins is Executive Director for Humanities and Creative Arts at the Australian Research Council, seconded from The University of Queensland. She is the author of two books, co-author of three, including most recently *A Global Doll's House: Ibsen and Distant Visions* (with Julie Holledge, Jonathan Bollen and Frode Helland, 2016). She is immediate past editor of *Theatre Journal* and has also produced an interdisciplinary, innovative research tool called Ortelia to enable the analysis of theatre space through virtual reality.

Mischa Twitchin FHEA is Lecturer in the Theatre and Performance Department at Goldsmiths, University of London. He is the author of *The Theatre of Death – the Uncanny in Mimesis: Tadeusz Kantor, Aby Warburg and an Iconology of the Actor* (2016). Examples of his own performance and essay-films can be seen on Vimeo: http://vimeo. com/user13124826/videos.

Aline Wiame is Maître de conférences at Université de Toulouse – Jean Jaurès (France). Her main research interests are contemporary French philosophy (Souriau, Deleuze, Foucault, Rancière), interactions between performing arts and philosophy, and the philosophical and artistic uses of cartographical patterns. She is author of *Scènes de la défiguration. Quatre propositions entre théâtre et philosophie* (2016), and co-editor with Leonard Lawlor of a special issue on 'Deleuze, Ethics and Dramatization' in *Deleuze Studies* (2016).

ACKNOWLEDGEMENTS

We would like to express our profound gratitude to a number of people whose participation and support helped bring this book to fruition. First and foremost, we are immensely appreciative of our contributors, most of whom have been involved in the project since its inception. As with any publication of this kind, the process was a protracted one, and so we are grateful for the forbearance and generosity of all those who endured what must have seemed a genuine *longue durée*. We would particularly like also to thank Eve Katsouraki, who co-organised with us a one-day symposium at King's College London in 2015 on Foucault, theatre and performance, supported by the Theatre and Performance Research Association (TaPRA), and where the idea for the book was first gestated. We are grateful also for the financial assistance the project received from the Research Office at the Royal Central School of Speech and Drama and the Faculty of Arts and Humanities at King's College London, as well as to Sarah Thomasson for proof reading and helping us to prepare the manuscript for submission. James Rowson stepped in at the eleventh hour for indexing; thank you. Warm thanks are due, also, to Maggie Gale and Maria Delgado for their enthusiasm and support for the project. Likewise, the commitment of Matthew Frost and his team at Manchester University Press has been indispensable. The unseen work of anonymous reviewers is seldom sufficiently acknowledged in the sector, and so we would especially like to thank those colleagues who read so thoroughly the chapters in this volume, providing us with invaluable feedback. We are grateful also to Éditions Gallimard and to Michel Foucault's executors for allowing us to offer a new translation of Foucault's interview with Moriaki Watanabe, and to Robert Bononno for agreeing to provide a new version; thank you to Stuart Elden for facilitating the introduction. And thank you to Callicoon Fine Arts and to Hervé Guibert's executors for allowing us to reproduce on the cover of this volume his strikingly theatrical photograph of Foucault.

Introduction: theatre, performance, Foucault

Tony Fisher and Kélina Gotman

> I would like to do a history of the *scene* on which the true was distinguished from the false, but it is not that distinction that interests me, it is the constitution of the scene and the theatre of that distinction. It is indeed the theatre of truth that I would like to write.[1]

'Do not ask who I am and do not ask me to remain the same', Foucault wrote in *The Archaeology of Knowledge*.[2] Given such a statement, it might seem that the aim of this book falters before an immediate and insuperable paradox: to offer an account of Foucault's complex relationship to theatre and performance – for such a statement would appear to preclude our answering the very question the reader might reasonably expect us to address in this introduction: who exactly was Foucault and why does he matter to students of theatre? And yet, there is also something intriguingly theatrical in Foucault's statement that offers a substantial clue to the approach we take in the present volume. What it points to is the way Foucault himself was keenly aware of his own theatrical position as a public intellectual, lecturer, and writer; and that far from earnestly playing the role of public sage, he *played with* his interlocutors as though adopting a variety of theatrical personas. It is this 'theatrical' Foucault whom we hope to encounter in this book; and through his many personas, to explore the shifts and displacements of his own thought – the theatrical elisions and sleights of hand in his public engagements, as well as the staging of the various scenes of knowledge, power, and truth, which preoccupied him at different times in his books, interviews, and lecture courses. Not only does the book articulate theatre and performance in relation to Foucault's invigorating and highly inventive approach to questions of method and analysis, political and economic history, government and self-related practices, disciplinary knowledge and truth, but it also concerns itself with what Foucault can teach us about the practice of being a thinker and public intellectual engaged with contemporary exigencies – all of this provides the rich nexus of material upon which the various contributors to this volume have set to work.

Thus, our editorial approach has been to take Foucault at his word: not to imprison him in his own discourse, or to celebrate his work as though it constituted a vast and imposing intellectual edifice – to monumentalise him – but, on the contrary, to approach Foucauldian thought as possessing, as we hope this book demonstrates, a vital and ongoing relevance for theatre and performance today. In short, if Foucault refuses the fixity of the 'author function', as is well known, he also pressingly enjoins us to engage not in biographical or hagiographical endeavours, but in another, rather more serious, task: that of critique. For Foucault, the question of critique is essential and urgent. It demands methodological play; it compels us to spar with knowledge; it challenges us to shift our standpoints on the received wisdom of our age; it requires us to question the orthodoxies of truth, even as we are inclined to take them for granted, or at face value. In a word, it is Foucault, who challenges us to engage in the most penetrating questioning of what we think we know about our world and about ourselves. And so it is with this Foucauldian question – of what constitutes 'knowledge' for us in our present circumstances, that we begin this introduction. From there we go on to consider Foucault's continuing importance for contemporary theatre and performance scholarship, followed by a consideration of the centrality of aesthetics or style in his work – style conceived as a manner of approaching, at times circumventing, discourses of power and truth. We conclude with a brief exposition of the chapters and their position within the overall organisation of the book's argument.

Why Foucault today? – the development of a critical discourse

'*Sapere Aude!*' Wake up to the perils of the present age – and have the courage to use your understanding! This was Kant's rallying cry in 1784 in an article for the *Berlinische Monatsschrift*, at the cusp of the French Revolution of 1789 and at a time when power structures were consolidating themselves in new forms of statecraft. What emerged in Prussia, as elsewhere in Europe at the time, was a new kind of administrative state: Frederick II had declared himself King of Prussia, expanding the military apparatus of the state with appeal to theories of enlightened absolutism. He expanded bureaucratic procedures, effectively instituting one of the first centralised managerial states of the modern age. Concurrently, he permitted freedom of the press and instituted a range of other liberal reforms. All the same, when Kant suggested, in his article '*Was ist Aufklärung?*' ('What is Enlightenment?') that subjects may, indeed must, deploy their reason autonomously in order to be a little bit less governed or not quite in the same way, Frederick II retorted that his subjects may 'reason all they want to as long as they obey'.[3] In effect, Kant and Frederick II were tussling over what Foucault would call 'governmentality': if Kant was suggesting a manner of being free from conditions of tyrannical rule, Frederick II deployed the apparatus of the centralised state to ensure that a citizen may think freely as long as their thinking remained congruent with the aims of state power – with government. What was being increasingly assimilated into the discourse of state power – as Foucault reminds us in his lecture course on *The Birth of Biopolitics* (1978–79) – was the theory of reason of state (*raison d'État*). In Germany, reason of state soon developed into the form of *Polizeiwissenschaft* or the science of the state. This 'science of police' should not be confused with the contemporary English usage of the word 'police', of course; what it referred to rather was the new strategic approach taken by modern forms of government. To think and govern, in other words, by means of police was to develop governmental *policy* based on abstract and 'objective' knowledge of the state and its productive resources. Government by policy was vastly enabled with the development of statistical science (literally knowledge of the state) where statistical data permitted knowledge of the population, for instance, the health of the workforce, its birth and death rates, or levels of criminality, and so on – all of which came to be organised under the remit of governmental power.

This expansion of government's field of operations covered not just the public realm but also increasingly the private spheres of everyday life that had previously been considered to fall beyond the administrative purview of state rule. Matters of security therefore become primordially significant not just in the state's deployment of bodies and various social practices – police presence, and so on – but also in the subject's internalisation of a need simultaneously to be protected (rendered secure) by the state and to experience him or herself to be, within this new form of subjection, 'free'. The paradoxical situation of modern governmentality requires, in other words, at once a feeling of relative freedom and the security of state protection, along with its obligations. Yet, as Kant recognised, and as Foucault would later pick up, the everyday salves and distractions of this state of governmentality preclude precisely the sort of self-knowledge and care of the self that might engender a genuine autonomy of the self. This is where Foucault's thinking begins to shift towards the articulation of a concern with what it means to resist governmentality in the everyday: he begins to examine what it might mean to nurture, to cultivate a self able to desubjugate itself from internalised (as well as external) structures of power. The notion of the self, however, in Foucault needs to be carefully attended to: in key respects it is quite alien to modern modes of self-conceptualisation and self-actualisation. Christopher Lasch famously described those forms of contemporary self-obsession, prevalent under contemporary conditions of consumerism, as our modern 'cultures of narcissism'.[4] In fact, when Foucault, in a debate at the Department of History at the University of California at Berkeley in April 1983, was queried on the relationship between his own concept of the care of the self (or what he described with reference to Greco-Roman practices as knowledge of self – *gnōthi seauton* – and care of the self – *epimeleia heautou*) and Lasch's notion of narcissism (understood as an attempt to escape history and evade its responsibilities), Foucault responded that these were not only absolutely opposed but that the latter obscured the former.[5] In other words, narcissism allows one to escape oneself; whereas to embrace the possibility of cultivating a relation to oneself that is precisely not narcissistic is, for Foucault, to contemplate with simplicity and clarity a hermeneutics or knowledge of the self that is truthful. This stance towards the self, which Foucault began to evolve in the early 1980s, fundamentally challenges the Western tradition of the subject that emerged on the basis of the Christian paradigm of asceticism, by which there is a prior (sinful or 'fallen') self in need of being saved, remedied, purged, or admonished through practices of penance, mortification, and confession – and the concomitant escape from this austere cult of piety and abstinence into hedonism and narcissistic self-indulgence that is characteristic of late capitalist societies – equally a failing strategy for the desubjugation of the self.

What this entails for Foucault, in a return to Greco-Roman models, is the need to develop a renewed critical attitude, to situate the work of philosophy in a practice of life that is profoundly ethical just as it is also politically committed. What is so striking in this articulation of critique in relationship to knowledge of self and care of the self is how it enables a different sort of autonomy: not the false or superficial autonomy of consumer choices such as is offered in a liberal and (more recently) in a neoliberal paradigm (in which even the subject is constituted as a set of lifestyle choices enabling self-marketisation). Rather, this deep autonomy and culture of care articulates a relationship to self that is totally different from the culture of distractions that characterises consumerist society.

In the lecture course, *The Hermeneutics of the Subject*, given at the Collège de France in 1981–82, Foucault would ask: 'Is it possible to constitute, or reconstitute, an aesthetics of the self? At what cost and under what conditions?'[6] He suggests that this task cuts through customary and pervasive injunctions to '[get] back to oneself, freeing oneself, being oneself, being authentic, etcetera'[7] – modes of self-relation that are all too familiar to us today. By contrast, at the core of Foucault's call to renew the relation of self-to-self, is the problem of 'truth-telling' that emerges in the critical discourse of the teacher-friend or true counsellor – Foucault writes: '*Parrhēsia* [often translated as frank or fearless speech] is opening the heart, the need for the two part-ners to conceal nothing of what they think from each other and to speak to each other frankly.'[8] This requires, on the part of both parties, a willingness to hear that which is not flattering; that which does not stroke or bolster their egos – their entrenched sense of self. On the one hand, the relationship of truth-telling requires a willingness to hear that which may be hurtful or upsetting; and, on the other, in offering counsel – in telling one's friend or interlocutor a truth that may be hurtful or upsetting to them – it is to be willing to take a genuine risk; within the context of the political sphere, it is to risk speaking truth to power.

What Foucault terms an 'ethics of speech' [*éthique de la parole*][9] directly addresses the problem of governmentality, outlined above: 'an ethics of self', he writes, 'may be an urgent, fundamental, and politically indispensable task, if it is true after all that there is no first or final point of resistance to political power other than in the relationship one has to oneself [*dans la rapport de soi à soi*]'.[10] And he continues:

> if we take the question of power, of political power, situating it in the more general question of governmentality understood as a strategic field of power relations in the broadest and not merely political sense of the term, if we understand by governmentality a strategic field of power relations in their mobility, transformability, and reversibility, then I do not think that reflection on this notion of governmentality can avoid passing through, theoretically and practically, the element of a subject defined by the relationship of self to self [*de soi à soi*].[11]

What this means is that the task of the cultivation of the self – or what he otherwise refers to as an aesthetics of existence – has nothing to do with the deciphering of the self as though the subject's truth were secretly concealed from it in some arcane consciousness – what he refers to as an 'exegesis of the self'.[12] It is a task that emerges rather through what he calls etho-poiesis[13] – which is 'capable of producing a change in the subject's mode of being' such that they might resist the forms of government that would otherwise dominate them.[14]

Friendship becomes, for Foucault, therefore, a critical relation of profound equality by which subjects come to know themselves in a space of trust rather than direction or conduct, as found, for example, in the Christian pastorate that he perspicuously analysed in his lectures on governmentality. By contrast, Foucault returns philosophy's first task to that of spirituality – in this case, spirituality is fundamentally opposed to theology, which would be prescriptive rather than transformative; philosophy and spirituality here are aligned instead with the constant work of accessing a non-dogmatic and critical approach to truth, now conceived as an engine for radical questioning.[15] This renders the work of philosophy methodologically identical to the project of articulating a practice of life (opposed to the Cartesian understanding of knowledge as operating on a plane separate from material and affective being). This immanent and radical politics and ethics of self leads us to claim with Foucault that while there is no escape from governmentality at present, nevertheless, there is a way through it – a manner of navigating, perhaps, inasmuch as any voyage is not without its perils[16] – that allows us all to gain simultaneously a greater lucidity about the contingency of the present (its concepts, forms of power, structures of domination, etc.) and about the manner in which we may journey without the certainty or reassurance of a predefined end. This furthermore allows us to practise every day how to be just a little bit less governed, or governed 'not quite in that way'. Judith Butler picks up on this new critical attitude in her reading of Foucault's essay 'What is Critique?' when she suggests that the task of critique is to 'pose the question of the limits of our most sure ways of knowing'.[17] What matters thus is to query ever further, not just the foundations, but the edges of our thinking; to press perpetually beyond the limits placed on our thought by 'discourses of truth'. But how do we do this? And what is the manner of performing – or inhabiting – a critical attitude such as Butler and Foucault (after Kant) enjoin us to do? What are the practices that permit this daily work of desubjugation – of philosophical life? We submit that while there is of course no simple answer to this question, the very act of questioning in this way enables us to begin – perhaps everyday anew – to shift our critical gaze.

Why Foucault? – a question for theatre and performance studies

There is arguably no better place to practice shifting one's critical gaze than in the theatre.[18] For indeed what is theatre if it is not precisely a space for 'seeing' – for rendering objects visible, so as to reconstitute them before a critical and challenging regard, to estrange them so as to see that which would otherwise be too proximate in the field of normal vision – in short, to see the familiar anew? This use of the critical gaze with respect to theatre can be found employed throughout Foucault's work. Indeed, the term 'theatre' might be thought here in at least two related methodological senses: in the first sense, it refers to what Foucault frequently refers to as a 'grid of intelligibility'[19] – a form of theatrical optics in which certain objects, truths, ideas, discourses become visible; but also, relatedly, in his use of theatre as 'metaphor', he also draws directly on theatrical examples, indicating the level of critical practices of seeing within theatre's own history. For example, in a discussion of Racine's relation to the monarchy, in his 1975–76 lecture course 'Society Must Be Defended', Foucault describes how classical tragedy 'recomposes what court ritual establishes … [so as to] constitute the underside of the ceremony, to show the ceremony in shreds, the moment when the sovereign, the possessor of public might, is gradually broken down into a man of passion, a man of anger, a man of vengeance, a man of love, incest, and so on'.[20] In other words, the workings of power are exposed, not in an abstract sense, but through the deployment of theatre, understood as the preeminent space for rehearsing, reflecting, and showing the critical object of analysis. Theatre is not only a cultural practice Foucault lends his attention to, through his erudite readings of ancient or early modern tragedy (see Gotman and Elden in this volume), it is also a manner of reading the nexus of relationships established by all forms of representation. Whether directed to the political or aesthetic spheres, Foucault's theatrical approach is fundamentally bound to the task of exposing the spectatorial gaze of power, or what – in relation to his famous analysis of Jeremy Bentham's panopticism – he termed the 'eye of power';[21] it is also what, in his later work, is transformed into a concern with 'play' (*jeu*) and 'roles' taken in truth-telling practices. In other words, for Foucault, the display of truth – the alethurgical practices of the parrēsiast discussed above – entail theatrical structures and languages: truth is a matter of making-visible, of manifesting itself publically. Thus we discover in Foucault two related analyses: that of power that conceals truth's fictionalisations and 'manages' its truth effects, and the *parrēsia* that exposes power at some risk to the parrēsiast. This is what characterises, among other things, Foucault's profound interest in theatre as a 'grid of intelligibility' – something that enables thinking the ways in which self and other are engaged in a constant interplay of masks. Foucault, then, we argue, is a pre-eminently theatrical thinker, whether describing himself as the 'masked philosopher', drawing on spectacle in *Discipline and Punish*, or rethinking Nietzschean tragedy in *The History of Madness*.

Of course, not only does Foucault endlessly draw on the trope of the theatre in his own work, but he is also frequently referenced in theatre and performance studies. Yet despite his profound engagement with theatre, and the interest within theatre studies with Foucault's work, surprisingly, there is no book within contemporary theatre and performance scholarship that addresses the legacy of Foucault head-on – or for that matter the extensive use in his work of theatrical tropes as such. This is surprising, not least because so many Foucauldian concepts – some already mentioned – such as truth, power, bodies, knowledge, governmentality, and genealogy, amongst many others – can be found in the work of theatre scholars – although rarely are they treated as theatrical and performative problems in themselves. This is not to say that theatre and performance scholarship has failed to take Foucault seriously. Notably, Shannon Jackson thinks with Foucault 'genealogically' in her critique of the way performance becomes reified against theatre in higher education in the United States; thus Jackson draws on Foucault in order to critique 'the "institutional genealogies" of knowledge formation [within the] modern university'.[22] Likewise, Joseph Roach thinks the 'genealogies of performance' to circumvent the many 'myths' of cultural origins in his analysis of 'Circum-Atlantic Performance' – performance that recuperates and subverts colonial histories in the wake of the transatlantic slave trade. Here, Roach endeavours – in a Foucauldian manner – to think against the singularity of the body, reading performance instead through 'the reciprocal reflections [bodies] make on one another's surfaces as they foreground their capacities for interaction'.[23] In *The Player's Passion*, Roach also applies a genealogical critique of acting paradigms, rethinking the historical interaction between physiology, acting theory, and scientific concepts of the emotional and motional body.[24] There are, of course, many other ways in which Foucault's influence can be discerned in contemporary theories of performance – from Judith Butler's early work on gender constitution, which quoted Foucault, as well as her more recent work on critique, to Mark Franko's attention to a Foucauldian hermeneutics of the subject in dance studies.

Nevertheless, notwithstanding the pervasive presence of Foucault, who has shaped the contemporary critical landscape, there is as yet no research dedicated specifically to Foucault's own theatrical thinking and performative mode of address. So while Foucault's influence might be said to be ubiquitous, Foucault himself remains strangely absent from contemporary theatre and performance discourse. To be sure, aspects of his work are used expediently, almost conventionally, as an authorial citation *de rigueur* on any questions concerned with power, space, bodies, and so on. While this passing use of Foucault's name has helped to keep his work visible in the discipline, we have found that this is rarely pursued at the level of a sustained inquiry into the questions around which his work revolves. A quick survey of contemporary scholarship in theatre and performance suggests that it is obligatory to mention Foucault, but rarely to inhabit his thought: to cite and to enlist but not to engage. And, at the same time, while his work has acquired an increasingly canonical status, it also – paradoxically – has begun to appear almost passé, a relic of the failure of the poststructuralist establishment; a hangover from the time when French theory was 'in'. He is frequently cited as a foil – 'genealogical analysis by all means – but not of the Foucauldian variety!' In our post-critical climate, it is as if Foucault had not only been assimilated but

exhausted, his work reduced to vacuous catchphrases – docile bodies, discipline, punishment, and so on – less, or so it may appear, relevant to a networked world, which
Foucault did not live to experience.

Nevertheless, with the recent publication of the lectures he gave at the Collège
de France between 1970 and his death in 1984, an opportunity has arisen – and with
it a new appetite for revisiting and challenging the old shibboleths that have come
to be attached to Foucault's name. We now understand far better how incisive and
prescient his thinking was in regard to the questions raised by contemporary forms
of economics (particularly neoliberalism), the conditions and government of forms
of life (biopolitics and governmentality), the formation of subjects within a world
increasingly dominated by vast inequalities – cultural, sexual, and political (contemporary forms of subjectification). As we have been arguing, Foucault may even
be *more* salient for us today, given what some call a 'post-truth' political paradigm
nourished by mediatised fictions, given his problematising of the very concept of
'truth'. This is important when we consider that, for Foucault, truth is not a subjacent
reality or ground that can be proven or falsified. Rather, truth appears through complex discursive and performative operations – informing the very fabric of our lives.
The spaces of appearance within which a 'truth' takes effect are themselves complex
structures, where contesting forces endlessly jostle for temporary hegemony. As we
write this introduction, for example, the news cycle, since the US election of 2016,
has come to be dominated by Donald Trump. Now, we would argue that Trump is
as much the product or effect of the spaces of appearance that enable his emergence
as he is the agent of a pernicious politics that seeks to determine what counts as
true for contemporary American life. For us, what is interesting about Trump is the
way he positions himself strategically and enunciatively by claiming to speak truth
to power, through what Foucault analysed as *parrēsia* – standing up for the 'common
man' against the vested interests of corporations and a discredited liberal elite. At the
same time, Trump's example is one of what Foucault called bad *parrēsia* – a form of
'false truth-telling', which is dangerous, says Foucault, precisely because it 'imitates'
parrēsia.[25] Trump's discourse is determined, moreover, by what Foucault calls modes
of *alēthourgia* – the processes by which a truth appears or is made manifest. Truth is
not separate from these processes, but rather emerges through them as part of a wider
'discursive formation' or 'regime of truth', with material consequences in the world –
the analysis of which gives us precisely an 'ontology of ourselves' and our present.
As Foucault once reported: 'what I am trying to do, is to make a diagnostic of the
present, to tell what we are today'.[26] This 'philosophical journalism' – an expression
he used also to characterise Kant's writing – aims to embed philosophical analysis in
contemporaneity. For Foucault, there is no abstract metaphysical realm within which
something like 'truth' might be located above the fray, in all its other-worldly perfection. Truth is rather deployed as a structuring mechanism in the play of scientific,
governmental, juridical, and other discourses of veridiction and validation (terms
Foucault uses to describe the way systems of thought determine the parameters of
what is true or false, normal and normative, abnormal or pathological, etc., at a given
time). And, of course, as we have been arguing, truth is also for Foucault a lived practice of critique. In short, Foucault is not concerned with determining what is true or

false, but rather with analysing how 'truth' is deployed within the social or human sciences and aesthetic fields.

This is to say that Foucault's analysis enables ways of untangling the complex theatrical ecology within which truth comes to exist as an engine of power, operating both spatially and, we might say, dramaturgically. We would argue thus that Foucault offers a better way to understand the multi-faceted workings of 'power' in a world that for all the recent talk of 'empowerment' through 'transversal' networks (following Michael Hardt and Antonio Negri's analysis of *Empire* among others) still remains inescapably bound to relations of power. Rather than overcoming those relations, a Foucauldian reading would suggest that transversality itself points to the micro techniques of power, seen in its dispersal at the capillary level of everyday practices. Moreover, we would argue that, and as Foucault repeatedly insisted against the views of some of his critics, power is not to be grasped as a totalising macro structure belonging to a fictional monolithic and centralised entity called 'the state'; rather, power is diffused equally – or 'transversally' – across the whole social *topos*, in a dispersed, complex, and above-all relational play of forces: power is at once a 'productive' *force* – and thus an inevitable and inescapable factor in the shaping of every social relation – as much as it is an occasion that 'produces' or 'incites' or 'provokes' modes of resistance and forms of 'agonistic' struggle.[27]

Further, of immense relevance to theatre and performance scholarship today are Foucault's rich analyses of truth processes insofar as these reveal productive ways of thinking about everyday structures of subjectivation; of how subjects become implicated within the spaces of appearance that 'truth' enables. The present volume, then, seeks to engage in the following critical task: to remedy what we believe to be the neglect within theatre and performance studies of systematic engagement with Foucault's intellectual contribution to theatre and performance thinking, and to think directly about Foucault's legacy by locating Foucault at the centre of the narrative. In this sense, the volume marks a fundamental shift in the landscape of theatre and performance studies, which has today moved on beyond the first engagements with Foucault's thought in the late 1980s and 1990s; and it is the aspiration of the contributions that follow this introduction to map out emerging avenues of enquiry that speak to its ongoing importance. Simultaneously, the volume aims to open up lines of thinking across the wider field of Foucauldian scholarship: to contribute to ongoing perspectives a new performative analysis, revealing the fundamental place of theatre in his thought.

Lastly, and above all, in this volume we wish to heed Foucault's invitation to write a 'history of the present': to think in dramaturgical terms about our own contemporaneity ('*actualité*'). This 'ontology of the present [*du présent*], of contemporaneity [*de l'actualité*], of modernity, of ourselves' does not mean that we need exclusively be concerned with contemporary events, but rather that we may seek to understand how our own concepts of truth – and thus our capacity to exercise 'critique' in regard to their *grounds* – are bound up with the time in which we find ourselves.[28] This 'critique' of the present, moreover, is itself bound up with the past: on the one hand there is no writing of history that does not bear the imprimatur of the present and its contingent play of forces – it is precisely this concern, of how to connect the past to the present,

that motivated Foucault's shift from the earlier 'archaeological' studies to his later critical 'genealogies' – while on the other hand, there is no present that is not the product
of historical operations and aberrations (the task here being to make those critically
visible). Every 'history' written in the present is a history *of* the 'present' inasmuch
as it can be said to reveal concerns and ways of seeing that could only be articulated
as such at that particular moment.[29] This is precisely why for Foucault histories are
by definition only ever relative and partial; thus, contrary to the contentions of positivist historiography, Foucault's own historical practices, far from being dominated
by immutable 'epistemes' (underlying conditions of knowledge that determine what
can or cannot be spoken of or thought at a given moment), in fact embrace the fri-
ability of historiographic practices and historical knowledge. In the words of Hubert
L. Dreyfus and Paul Rabinow, Foucault's genealogical methodology, as it came to be
known, entails a 'radical shift in perspective'.[30] To write the history of the present, as
they put it, is to adopt an approach that 'explicitly and self-reflectively begins with a
diagnosis of the current situation. There is an unequivocal and unabashed contemporary orientation'.[31]

A return to Foucault's key premises, then, viewed among others in the light of
the publication of his lecture courses, centred around his genealogical enquiries,
discloses not the fixity of Foucault's thought, but its fluidity and fragility. If we seek to
re-examine Foucault's contribution to knowledge *in* and *of* the present, what becomes
most striking is his manner of compelling a fundamental rethinking of the way we
categorise knowledge: not as a set of facts or statements that can be aggregated as
independent 'findings', but in light of an ongoing and critical *practice* of thinking; and,
indeed, as we shall now discuss, it is a practice that is committed to thinking as a live
and theatrical act.

What Foucault? – The performativity of Foucault's own discourse

Perhaps no other philosopher has been so lauded, and at the same time treated with
such scepticism, as Foucault. Part of the blame for this may be placed at Foucault's door.
For a philosopher who was so concerned with method and methodology, he presents
any reader with a formidable challenge: not only is his thought ceaselessly inventive but
with it, he was also profoundly anti-methodological – his works continually turning in
or back on themselves, not unlike a Mobius strip; at the same time, with each turn –
a new challenge to think with and against what had gone before arises. Constantly
revising his working methods – almost as quickly as he had developed them – he left
even the most experienced reader with the difficult task of pinning down what exactly
his project was (perhaps one of the reasons why Foucault's legacy has seemed to stop
at a few overly familiar key words is that the sheer volume of his intellectual output
would overwhelm even the keenest student). Yet, of course, capturing change, the

evanescence of thought, or the almost ungraspable moment of rupture in knowledge was also the point. Inconsistencies and outright rejections of his own earlier writing were inevitably constitutive of the way he operated as an intellectual responding to the problems his own intellectual journey threw up. For Foucault, thought was essentially vital – never static. In reviewing his achievement in the introduction to *The Archaeology of Knowledge*, Foucault reflected on the 'cautious, stumbling manner of this text: at every turn it stands back, measures up what is before it, gropes towards its limits, stumbles against what it does not mean, and digs pits to mark out its own path'.[32] But nor did he exercise this constant innovation in an intellectual vacuum: his attentiveness to his critics displayed a keen interest in situating himself in the present moment.[33] He refused to stand outside history; just as he turned his gaze to ancient Greek and Roman sexuality, to the European Middle Ages, to the Enlightenment and political economy, so he was also engaged in current political debates – whether over the Iranian Revolution, or prison reform in France. Recalling Maurice Merleau-Ponty, Foucault wrote that the 'essential philosophical task' is 'never to consent to being completely comfortable with one's own presuppositions'; that in order to do this, 'one must have a distant view, but also look at what is nearby and all around oneself. [...] The most fragile instant has its roots'.[34] His work, then, is characterised by a penetrating intellectual curiosity, a sense of critical restlessness, political commitment – exhibiting a perpetually searching quality – while at the same time displaying an intense rigour that would earn him the respect of notable opponents such as Jürgen Habermas and Noam Chomsky.

Paradoxically, and most troubling for some critics, particularly within the Anglo-American philosophical tradition, principally committed to scientific method, this investigative quality – that cast doubt on all claims to foundation – lent his work a rather diaphanous quality that made it both frustrating and impossible to ignore. Hayden White most notably would complain that 'according to his own theory' Foucault's discourse can only derive its authority from the 'style, that characterises it'.[35] According to White, Foucault's own discourse finds no ground in truth, fact, or verifiable assertion precisely because it rejects all such notions of ground. Foucault 'seeks a space rather than a ground' and for this reason his own discourse 'unfolds seemingly without restraint, apparently without end'.[36] Worse still, its authority derives from nothing other than its rhetoric, whose form, White claims, is catachrestical in deploying rhetorical effect in order to pervert the very order of discourse:

> Foucault's style not only displays a profusion of the various figures sanctioned by this trope, such as paradox, oxymoron, chiasmus, hysteron proteron, metalepsis, prolepsis, antonomasia, paranomasia, antephrasis, hyperbole, litotes, irony, and so on; his own discourse stands as an abuse of everything for which 'normal' or 'proper' discourse stands. It looks like history, like philosophy, like criticism, but it stands over against these discourses as ironic antithesis.[37]

One cannot help but wonder, however, whether White in displaying such an astute characterisation of Foucault's work does not entirely miss the point. It is true that Foucault demonstrates extraordinary rhetorical erudition and virtuosity; but contrary to White, we do not thereby believe it discredits the work. Rather, it performs the very operation of *alēthourgia* that Foucault describes as a virtue of thought – that is to say, while there is nothing to ground thought (in the metaphysical sense), this does not mean that there is nothing to thought. For Foucault, thought has to be taken as an unfolding event. Writing of Gilles Deleuze's work in 'Theatrum Philosophicum', Foucault noted the 'decenterings' it performs; rather than substitute 'essence' for 'appearance', this 'reverse Platonism' proposes to break the link between both, in the event.[38] This points to Foucault's profound Nietzscheanism: that there is no hierarchy between truths – no essential and accidental characteristics; no means of dividing the elemental from the superficial – of distinguishing being from appearance. In working his prose rhetorically across a dizzying array of styles, tropes, and 'catechristical' operations, Foucault in fact does what he (at least according to Deleuze) says: 'I only ever wrote fictions'.[39] For the theatre or performance scholar, this refusal to distinguish between style and substance provides an immensely productive opportunity to think through the act of writing, no less than the act of speech, as being inherently performative. That is to say, for Foucault, there is no reality his language is not already intimately bound up with; and the image of 'reality' he gives us is that of a polyvalent scenography, an unfolding set of scenes. In an interview with Japanese theatre and literary scholar Moriaki Watanabe – reprinted in a new translation at the end of this volume – Foucault recognises that 'his books are indeed […] dramaturgies'; that his writing seeks 'a sort of intensification, of dramatisation of events'. What his work seeks to reveal is a 'play of gazes, the theatre of the world'; his 'scenes' describe the way men and women in the past staged, saw, and described themselves.[40] What we propose to call, light-heartedly, Foucault's 'theatr-o-retical' scenes are well known: the clinic, the ship of fools, *Las Meninas*, the asylum, the prison, the scene of execution, and so on. It is onto these scenes that critical thought trespasses and out of which it is constituted. His virtue, we believe, subsists in the critical appropriation and perversion of such scenes – rather than pretending to visit them with the detached transcendence of a critic or historian, able to deploy a neutral language, viewing them as if from 'no where', he aims to perform a 'small gesture that consists in displacing the gaze', making visible what is too close or too large to be seen; the process of course is endless.[41] In reading these philosophical scenes, Foucault probes his own manner of attending to the work of reading; to the stage of thought; and to its own edification. It thus necessitates that constant return to the 'self' that we explored in the first section of this introduction – a question (a 'problematization') that preoccupied him increasingly in later years: the Delphic *gnōthi seauton* ('know yourself'), translated into the Socratic *epimeleia heautou* ('care of the self'), consisted of philosophical attitudes and practices – a manner of being and acting or turning to others in the world, of tending one's gaze, techniques, and exercises for attending to oneself through meditation, and so on.[42]

Foucault is all too aware of the investments his language carries in the discourses unravelled by or through these scenes and so operates a series of distancing techniques – simultaneously mirroring and deflecting the 'object' of his analysis. His *ekphrastic* use of tableaus – most notably Velasquez's *Las Meninas* in the opening to *The Order of Things*, Holbein's *The Ambassadors*, or Magritte's *Ceci n'est pas une pipe* all force shifts in perspective – also throw the act of viewing back onto the viewer; a technique that will be familiar to anyone with a knowledge of Bertolt Brecht, with his deployment of alienation effects designed to enable us to question our contemporary truths and to raise the possibility of their displacement. What Foucault does in addition is to refuse the notion that we may be entirely separable from those scenes within which we are ourselves players, situating the 'critic' or 'archivist' or 'genealogist' on a continuum with the language or other material he or she scrutinises. This we believe is the great political and ethical contribution of Foucault's work. Contrary to White, then, we consider that Foucault's play with surface and spaces of appearance deeply and inextricably binds us to our presents, our pasts, and our futures. Thus again, while for White, Foucault's work is seen to be inherently indifferent to the future – even nihilistic – we believe that nothing could be further from the truth: Foucault's thought – particularly in the last phase, as we have already discussed – became profoundly concerned with questions of ethics, with forms of life, and the challenges of untangling ourselves from the entrapments of history manifest in our own time, again as we have also outlined above.

Foucault was also playful: if we agree (with White) that Foucault's thought was 'catachrestical' it is precisely because it was irreverent. In an interview from 1980, he quipped, 'I'm not an analytic philosopher. No-one's perfect'.[43] More than this, Foucault was defiantly uncategorisable. This, then, is the Foucault of our volume – who should be thought as pre-eminently a 'theatrical' Foucault: like the actor, he could assume many different roles and guises, no doubt in the process frustrating many of his critics. In fact, he actively refused various demands to conform to the expectations of either the discipline (or disciplines) or the academy, while at the same time locating himself at its very heart, as a kind of provocateur: he replaced Jean Hyppolite, for example, at the Collège de France, one of the most prestigious academic positions in the country, terming himself Professor of the History of Systems of Thought (Hippolyte was chair in the History of Philosophical Thought). What Foucault's title immediately brings to the fore is also the heterodox way Foucault's thinking occupies an 'interstitial' space, between at least two distinct disciplines: history and philosophy – while conforming to the expectations of neither. Indeed, he had an antagonistic relation to both, and herein lay the problem for many of his opponents: Foucault for some is essentially a philosopher who uses history, and for others a historian who uses philosophy. This leads to a further set of controversies: for the historian is bound to be dissatisfied with the philosopher who dabbles 'amateurishly' in history; while the philosopher is likely to dismiss Foucault's philosophical claims on the grounds that a historian has no real purchase on 'ahistorical' philosophical problems.[44] This is not to say that Foucault's work stands immune from critical scrutiny.[45] However, we would suggest that these antinomies and controversies – at least in terms of rhetoric – are for the most part reductive, and have led to the aporias that have resulted in some disengagement with the depth and complexity of Foucault's work.

Therefore, what we suggest is that Foucault is neither unintelligible, overly slippery, nor a 'post-modern' French obscurantist. His commitment to challenging our presuppositions about the organisation and institutionalisation of knowledge, and the fixed boundaries that demarcate disciplinary fields, required a language that resisted easy assimilation to institutional norms. In fact, it is the very movement of thought, its

vitality, its intricacy – its openness and its lightness – that interests us from a performative point of view, insofar as it reveals Foucault as the researcher, the lecturer, and
public speaker *as* performer – Foucault the 'masked philosopher'. In this volume, in
fact, many of the contributors draw attention to the elusive Foucault who inhabits the
margins of the more famous published works, and it is in the margins that we suggest
we can find a new or at least a different Foucault. Perhaps – most surprisingly – it is
a Foucault whose concerns are ever more germane to contemporary thought. These
include, as Wendy Brown has shown, concerns with biopolitics, governmentality,
neoliberalism, and conduct among others. Mark D. Jordan takes the lectures as an
occasion to write his own 'professorial' self into the pages of his 2015 book *Convulsive
Bodies: Religion and Resistance in Foucault* in which he attends to questions of embodiment, particularly the embodied life of reading and speaking, which we engage with in
our everyday work. It is this performative, lecturing Foucault who motivates this book,
and the many authors contributing to it.

Foucault fantasised about being unknown and about wearing a mask. In 'The
Masked Philosopher', he speaks wistfully of the anonymity that the mask provides,
'[o]ut of nostalgia for a time when, being quite unknown, what I said had some chance
of being heard'.[46] One can see why anonymity would seem so desirable of course – for
Foucault himself seems to have become a name, a sign, a function even, of the kind
he associated so famously with the 'author function'. By limiting 'Foucault' to a kind
of tropology of well-known catchphrases, we reduce his work precisely to an 'ideological figure' such as he suggests 'marks the manner in which we fear the proliferation
of meaning'.[47] Thus, in the present volume, we take this statement both as a warning
and critical injunction – aware that for Foucault, even a special issue was the sign of a
'burial';[48] instead, we hope to have presented Foucault here playfully, not as a canonical author – mobilised nominally to sanction well-entrenched ideas of an *œuvre* or
corpus – but rather as a writer whose intellectual restlessness and constant invention
invite us to imagine ever new nodal points in the counter-discourses emerging with
his work. The chapters in this book are thus concerned with extending the themes and
problematics evolved by Foucault, examining issues of truth and methodology, history
and historiography, space, disciplinarity, and power, while prolonging and at times
overturning long-held assumptions about 'knowledge' and 'authority' such as define
the Foucault we may think we know.

Foucauldian scenes: masks that Foucault wore

The present volume is attentive to several strands of Foucault's thought, but by no
means should it be read as being exhaustive – on the contrary, we hope these lines of
thinking will open up other analyses of Foucault's intimate relationship with theatrical
modes of thought, of interest to theatre and performance scholars, and to Foucault
scholarship more broadly. The book is divided into three sections, covering – broadly
stated – questions of public intellectual practices, the dramaturgies of knowledge,

and questions concerning the interplay between power, politics, and history. The first section of this book, 'Truth, Methods, Genealogies', deals with a complex of Foucauldian themes, where truth is inherently linked to the performative dispersal of the subject. In Mark D. Jordan's 'Foucault's philosophical theatres', the reader's attention is drawn to the way Foucault's writing is in itself theatrical – not inasmuch as it performs mimesis, imitating in tone or form the material it sets out to explore, but rather as an exercise in the performative practices of the self or 'arts of life'. Jordan writes: 'Theatre in Foucault is the space for writing that leads to *self*-fashioning'. Whereas Foucault's profound engagement with the work of Pierre Klossowski signalled an early 'spiralling' genre of writing attuned to Nietzschean theatricality, Foucault increasingly in his later life shifts his method and lens towards what Jordan terms 'repetitive commonplaces in archives': this 'new style', in Jordan's reading of Foucault, instantiates a move to make of history 'fiction', and so too in the latest years to '[render] as theatre the agency of minute changes'. Foucault's own concern with writing becomes an occasion to think theatrically what he had previously read as philosophical theatre in Deleuze as in Nietzsche and Klowssowski: 'style' now determines a genre of writing, just as attention to ancient practices of writing allows for the emergence of aesthetic critique. Aline Wiame furthers this line of thinking, noting that 'dramatizing' for Foucault 'is a philosophical style'. 'Foucault's writing style', she suggests, 'tries to invent a philosophical equivalent of the theatrical apparatus that "captures" an event and repeats it in order to give it all its substance'. Attentive to the way genealogical critique unfolds as a play of gazes – and to how 'history' itself is fictionalised – Wiame suggests in her chapter 'The dramas of knowledge: Foucault's genealogical theatre of truth' that his 'dramatic' style allowed Foucault to fashion a self that was performative and yet also true to the work of alethurgy or the ritual discovery of truth. Reading Foucault's relationship to theatre in the Watanabe interview (published in this volume), Wiame argues that 'Foucault develops a particular kind of writing which is not *about* theatre but which thinks *through* theatre'. For her, Foucault's genealogical method 'exaggerates, it intensifies'. As such, it highlights the 'method of dramatisation' Foucault, like Deleuze, saw in a Nietzschean 'theatrical philosophy'. Wiame argues that 'theatre, as the site of a collective *experience* that is beyond truth and falsehood, must be considered at the same time as an apparatus for a genealogical writing of philosophy and as a material practice that produces its own mode of thought' as well as 'its own complicated, non-neutral fabrication of knowledge'. Taking this line of thought on the fabrication and theatricalisation of knowledge to the site of the interview, and further thinking the relationship between writing, speech, and theatricality, Magnolia Pauker suggests that Foucault's 'interview-work' has to be taken as far more than paratextual: it should not be seen as merely a 'supplement' to his published books. On the contrary, she suggests in 'Foucault live! "A voice that still eludes the tomb of the text"', Foucault's apparently paradoxical willingness to give interviews (he notoriously refrained from revealing personal aspects of his life publicly) has to be read against the fact that he gave well over one hundred interviews, each one engaging a version of his own particular brand of self-fashioning. Simultaneously displaying his awareness of the constraints of the interview genre and the attendant expectations placed on the 'authorial voice', in his interviews Foucault practises a deliberate *détournement* of this staged position of 'authority'. For Pauker, the interviews do not just facilitate our approach to Foucault's work, then, by virtue of their at times informal and thus relatively more accessible tone; rather, they constitute 'a form of public philosophical praxis'. Kélina Gotman takes Foucault's theatrical manner of thinking to his practice of *alēthourgia*, a progressive unravelling of 'truth': oriented by an understanding of what she outlines as his self-avowedly 'anarchaeological' method – a way of doing work that is contingent and circumstantial, concerned with accident and with present givens rather than with any epistemic absolutes, she shows how his work emerges into a theatrical 'space of appearance'. In 'Foucault, Oedipus, Négritude', she demonstrates how Foucault himself in his lecture courses performed a genre of anarchaeological *alēthourgia* – what he read in the Oedipus myth as a particular sort of truth-function, a 'ritual unveiling of truth'. The ritual quality of this path towards discovery suggests a critical attention to dark spaces and to the language or discourse of 'light'. She submits that Foucault's method proceeded in this way according to a logic of poiesis, 'revealing' 'truth' through narrative juxtaposition, digressions, and asides – and that this, as she shows, coheres with Souleymane Bachir Diagne's poetic philosophy of Négritude. Foucault himself was concerned with 'magical' theatres of tyrannical power structured (among others) around Black Roman displays of truth, particularly under the emperor Septimus Severus's 'orientalising' rule. Following Diagne, Gotman argues that this genre of Négritude, which favours the rhythmic 'cut' over the straight line, suggests a philosophy as praxis of serendipity and Bergsonian intermixture: ethically, aesthetically, and politically, a co-knowledge in Diagne's terms. Engaging thus 'anarchaeologically' with Foucault's reading of the Oedipus myth, together with Foucault's dramatised scenes of Black Roman governmentality, Gotman interrogates the play of ocularism, visibility, and invisibility as a scenography of truth-telling: a dramaturgy of "showy garbs" – 'truths' manifest in partial statements, detours, and excursions revealing the contingencies and also the fragilities of power.

Section II is concerned with questions of dramaturgy, as seen from a Foucauldian perspective. With Mark Robson, in 'Foucault's Critical Dramaturgies', we return to the oft-noted scene of Foucault's encounter with the work of Samuel Beckett in Paris in the 1950s – a moment of historical and cultural rupture that, as Robson notes, marked many intellectuals at the time. For Robson, however, the Beckettian 'break' is more than just a historical encounter, described by Foucault, as an event occurring between a theatrical work and the philosophical thought that it influenced; it also suggests a whole theatrical – and indeed 'dramaturgical' – throughline in Foucault's approach to his own lectures and his writing. As Robson shows, Foucault's thinking is profoundly spatial, intimately bound up in dramaturgical scenes. 'Foucault's text is suffused with the language of the theatrical', he writes: 'scene, spectacle, figure, stage'. This proliferation of theatrical motifs has to be taken as indicative of a manner of thinking that *belongs to the theatrical*, concerned as it is with 'scenes of difference', in short, with a dramaturgical ethics open to alterity. Joanne Tompkins, in 'Heterotopia and the mapping of unreal spaces on stage' pursues this line of thinking on theatre's unique spatiality by reexamining the notion of heterotopia – perhaps Foucault's most often cited theatrical trope – to argue that it remains further open, as conceptual apparatus, to the still unfolding developments of 'postdramatic' theatre. Heterotopias do not merely indicate 'other' spaces, including theatre; rather, more complexly, thinking heterotopia in and with theatre allows us to understand the myriad ways spatiality comes to service social and political imaginaries in theatre and beyond. Foucault's thinking does not only allow us to think theatre, however; it also engages directly with theatrical texts. Stuart Elden in 'Foucault and Shakespeare: the theatre of madness' delves into particular dramatic texts and the philosophical dramaturgy they unfold: he demonstrates how Foucault's reading of Shakespeare in particular deeply informs his work on madness. As Foucault returns again and again to the Shakespearean scene, his own thinking can be read to wrestle with the dramatisation of madness, as well as the historical contingency of 'madness' as it comes to be deployed across periods and strategically across his own many writings. Here, we see madness appearing via the specific interest that Foucault had in Shakespeare's relationship to the figure of the monarch, and – through it – ultimately to the genealogical transformation and institutional articulation of power as such. Elden writes: 'Foucault argues that the transition from King's rule to doctors' rule is indicative of a different mode of political transformation'. It suggests a shift from the power of the sovereign to disciplinary power. Taking a fundamentally essayistic – and indeed dramaturgical – approach to the question of dramaturgy, and to what he calls 'Foucault's phantom theatre', Mischa Twitchin in 'Philosophical phantasms: "the Platonic differential" and "Zarathustra's laughter"' performs a dramaturgy of thinking that, after Deleuze, stages Nietzsche's 'reversal of Plato' and also problematises this staging. As Twitchin shows, Deleuze, like Nietzsche and like Foucault himself, aimed to move beyond a so-called mimetic relationship between subject and object, truth and its representation. Instead, 'reverse Platonism' instantiates what Foucault called a 'phantasmaphysical' regime that dissolves the mimetic order of representation. Phantasmaphysics is not just fantasy, but what Twitchin describes as 'a generator of images of and for the acting of thinking'. The question Twitchin asks is whether phantasmaphysics, as an image generator, might enable us to move beyond problems of representation – beyond the metaphysics of truth. As Twitchin suggests, what is in question is whether 'appearances [are] no longer defined by an opposition to truth'; rather, appearances participate in a cinematic world of montage in which truth is partial: part-fiction, part-fantasy, and, as such, dramatically unstable.

In the final section of the book, Foucault's concern with governmentality and power take centre stage. For Steve Potter, in 'Cage and Foucault: musical timekeeping and the security state', it is Foucault's interest in security – understood as the shift from a concern for the discipline of individual bodies to the government of entire populations – that provides a productive way of analysing the 'conductorless' works of John Cage. Whereas Cage has been understood alternatively as anarchic in his refusal to determine every note on the page or every position in space to be taken up by a performer, on the one hand; and as 'liberal', on the other, inasmuch as he nevertheless does regulate the conditions for the performance, Potter argues that Cage instead may be seen to announce a regime of securitisation. What this means is that Cage creates work that gives the greatest possible latitude to the performer – an essential aspect of Foucault's notion of security. The work is thus 'earthquake-proof', as Potter notes, following Cage. It can withstand risk; it is not disciplinary, in that it does not control ever-smaller increments of time, but instead opens these up through 'time-bracket' structures that are 'ductile – they can undergo significant plastic deformation before rupturing'. In a previous work, John Coltrane's free jazz improvisations provided Tracey Nicholls with an occasion to think Foucault's notion of the 'author function' against the grain of its critical function. Nicholls returns in 'Foucault and the Iranian Revolution: reassessed' to her earlier argument to reconceptualise the way Foucault's work may be thought in 'a more cross-culturally careful' way. As she suggests, reading his involvement with the Iranian Revolution in 1979, Foucault presents a political ambivalence that is powerfully, 'intellectually generative': he appears as 'a political philosopher with a radical focus on human agency'. Thus, whereas he initially became interested in a sort of 'political spirituality' – an alternative to the secular, liberal, democratic West and was chastised for failing to see how this movement would lead to repression – what is most important in the lessons to be learned from the debacles that followed Iran's revolution is the way he queried orthodoxy as such. Foucault's intellectual journey through the Iranian Revolution thus becomes for Nicholls a means of appreciating anew his passionate political commitment – one that retains, as she argues, great relevance for contemporary feminist thinking.

Foucault's interest in history and historiographical practices is, of course, essential to the development of his genealogical methodology, and the final two chapters of the volume extend Foucault's critical historiography to theatre history. Dan Rebellato's 'Sightlines: Foucault and Naturalist theatre' begins by pointing out that Foucault himself gave a lecture course on modern theatre in the 1950s, with a specific focus on Naturalist theatres; and within five years had published *The Birth of the Clinic*. Rebellato shows, through his own forensic reading of the latter, the invaluable contribution Foucault makes to the analysis of Naturalism, with the emergence of the clinical gaze – of immense relevance to the Naturalist theatre of the late nineteenth century. Just as the patient's body becomes a text without a subtext, so too, Rebellato argues, 'Naturalist theatre ... [places] onstage everything that would previously have been hidden, inferred, alluded to, or offstage'. This process of 'detheatricalisation' is not without contradiction though, as Rebellato reveals, for 'Naturalism constitutes the secret in order to abolish it'. With the final chapter of the volume, we move from Naturalist theatre to melodrama. Tony Fisher's 'Theatre of poverty: Popular illegalism on the nineteenth century stage' maps a specific theatrical form he designates the 'poor play' against a discursive analysis of nineteenth-century political economy which – he argues – constituted a 'general theatre of poverty', prescribing the ways in which the poor were to be made visible. Fisher's analysis shows how the climate set by economic discourse led to the emergence of the 'poor play', in which theatre staged what Foucault called 'popular illegalisms' (socially proscribed forms of conduct and behaviour, ranging from criminality to delinquency, associated with the popular classes). In doing so, he shows how this political, economic, cultural, and theatrical genealogy – essential to early liberalism – developed both a punitive relationship with poverty, and a mythography within which the poor were articulated or 'staged' enunciatively as an object of discourse. Fisher concludes by showing how this Foucauldian approach to theatre history can usefully be deployed as a means of problematising present political reality. At the end of his chapter, he asks: how are we to understand our present moment in terms of the discursive structures that enable us to view poverty today?

What is the moral tenor of our beleaguered welfare state, and how does this have its roots in what Foucault saw as a 'society of moralisation'? As Fisher suggests, 'we can hardly claim to have escaped the matrices of moralizing discourse, or the effects of the punitive society'.

At the end of the volume, we include a new translation of Foucault's 1978 interview with Moriaki Watanabe, 'The philosophical scene' ('*La scène de la philosophie*'), in which Foucault articulates his conception of his work as a scenography, a play of the gaze, and as a dramaturgy. As Foucault writes, the whole of his work can be seen as an attempt to write the scene on which truth and falsity have been constituted; but, as he notes, it is not that distinction that interests him, so much as the constitution of that scene and that theatre. 'It is the theatre of truth that I would like to describe', he writes. Ann Pellegrini masterfully sums up the work of this volume, attending to the centrality of the pedagogical scene in Foucault's work and enjoining us all to bring Foucault's radical pedagogy back into the classroom today. This aptly sums up the work that we have undertaken in this volume – an exploration of the manifold ways Foucault's work is at once theatrical, dramaturgical, performative, and concerned fundamentally with the scenographies of power, truth, and knowledge (*savoir*). Thus, while this trio of terms has been frequently examined from various angles, from philosophy to sociology, what we aim to do here is draw attention to the vectors of sight – the gazes and the performances – by which these discourses come to appear. These forms of visibilisation are, then, inherently theatrical: and Foucault's work, we therefore contend in this volume, must be read in this light. For Foucault, power, truth, and knowledge are always rendered theatrically, or they are not rendered at all: to see their dramaturgy – understanding 'dramaturgy' here as an analytical and an aesthetic endeavour – is thus to subject the present to what he called, in the interview published here, a diagnostic critique).

Notes

1 Michel Foucault, 'La scène de la philosophie', interview with M. Watanabe, 22 April 1978, *Sekai* (July 1978), 312–32; reprinted in Daniel Defert and François Ewald with Jacques Lagrange (eds), *Dits et écrits 1954–1988*, 2 vols. (Paris: Éditions Gallimard, 2001), 2 (1976–88): pp. 571–95 (p. 572).

2 Michel Foucault, *The Archaeology of Knowledge*, trans. A. M. Sheridan Smith (New York: Pantheon Books, 1972), p. 17.

3 Michel Foucault, 'What is Critique?', in Sylvère Lotringer (ed.), *The Politics of Truth*, trans. Lysa Hochroth and Catherine Porter (Los Angeles: Semiotext(e), 1997/2007), pp. 41–81 (p. 49).

4 Christopher Lasch, *The Culture of Narcissism: American Life in an Age of Diminishing Expectations* (New York: Norton, 1991).

5 Michel Foucault, 'Qu'est-ce que la critique?', in Henri-Paul Fruchard and Daniele Lorenzini (eds), *Qu'est-ce que la critique? Suivi de La culture de soi*, (Paris: Vrin, 2015), pp. 33–80, p. 120 (our translation).

6 Michel Foucault, *The Hermeneutics of the Subject, Lectures at the Collège de France 1981–1982*, ed. Frédéric Gros, gen. eds. François Ewald and Alessandro Fontana, English series ed. Arnold I. Davidson, trans. Graham Burchell (New York: Palgrave Macmillan, 2005), p. 251.

7 Ibid.

8 Ibid., p. 137.
9 Ibid.
10 Ibid., p. 252.
11 Ibid.
12 Ibid., p. 238.
13 Ibid., p. 237.
14 Ibid., p. 238.
15 Ibid., pp. 26–7.
16 Ibid., p. 248.
17 Judith Butler, 'What is Critique?', http://eipcp.net/transversal/0806/butler/en, accessed 28 February 2018
18 Film scholars might argue otherwise, of course, and no doubt filmmakers such as Jean-Luc Godard or Jean-Marie Straub did precisely enact a critical shift in the cinematic gaze in the 1960s and 1970s; however, we would contend that the particular sort of gaze enabled by thinking theatre as a spatial and temporal practice that is coterminous with the event of viewing enables specific sorts of engagement with the notion of critique. We hope that this conversation will open up further exchanges between Foucault scholarship and critical writing across theatre, performance, film, dance, and other fields. On film, see the wonderful collection of Foucault's own writings on film in Patrice Maniglier and Dork Zabunyan (eds), *Foucault at the Movies*, trans. Clare O'Farrell (New York: Columbia University Press, 2018).
19 A term that can be found throughout Foucault's work. For a useful discussion of this term, see Hubert L. Dreyfus and Paul Rabinow, *Michel Foucault: Beyond Structuralism and Hermeneutics* (Herefordshire: Pearson Education, 1982), p. 121.
20 Michel Foucault, *'Society Must Be Defended': Lectures at the Collège de France 1975–76*, ed. Mauro Bertani and Alessandro Fontana, gen. eds. François Ewald and Alessandro Fontana, English series ed. Arnold I. Davidson, trans. David Macey (London: Penguin, 2004), p. 176.
21 Michel Foucault, 'The Eye of Power', in Colin Gordon (ed.), *Power/Knowledge: Selected Interviews and Other Writings 1972–1977* (Essex: Pearson Education, 1980), pp. 146–65.
22 Shannon Jackson, *Professing Performance: Theatre in the Academy from Philology to Performativity* (Cambridge: Cambridge University Press, 2004), p. 5.
23 Joseph Roach, *Cities of the Dead: Circum-Atlantic Performance* (New York: Columbia University Press, 1996), p. 25.
24 Joseph Roach, *The Player's Passion: Studies in the Science of Acting* (Minneapolis: University of Michigan Press, 1993).
25 Michel Foucault, *The Government of Self and Others: Lectures at the Collège de France, 1982–83*, ed. Frédéric Gros, gen. eds. François Ewald and Alessandro Fontana, English series ed. Arnold I. Davidson, trans. Graham Burchell (Hampshire: Palgrave Macmillan, 2010), p. 182.
26 Foucault, 'Qui êtes-vous professeur Foucault?' in *Dits et Ecrits*, 1: pp. 629–48 (p. 634).
27 See for example Alan Read's use of Michel de Certeau in *Theatre and Everyday Life*, which borrows de Certeau's notion that Foucault develops a totalising vision of power in the manner of Pierre Bourdieu's concept of habitus: '[French cultural theory] in the hands of Lefebvre and de Certeau is alternative in the sense that their work resists the "panopticon" procedures and conclusions of Michel Foucault whose discourse analysis emphasised the all-pervasive influence of power over agents'. Alan Read, *Theatre and Everyday Life: An Ethics of Performance* (London: Routledge, 2005), p. 100. In 'The Subject and Power' Foucault would argue: 'The power relationship and freedom's refusal to submit cannot therefore be separated. The crucial problem of power is not that of voluntary servitude (how could we seek to be slaves?). At the very heart of the power relationship, and constantly provoking it, are the recalcitrance of the will and the intransigence of freedom'. Michel Foucault, 'The Subject and Power', in James D. Faubion (ed.), *Power*, Vol. 3, *The Essential Works of Foucault, 1954–1984*, trans. Robert Hurley and others, 3 vols. (New York: New York Press, 2001), pp. 326–64 (p. 342).
28 Daniele Lorenzini and Arnold I. Davidson, 'Introduction', in Foucault, *Qu'est-ce que la critique?*, pp. 11–30 (pp. 22–3).
29 This is in contrast to Gayatri Spivak's use of Foucault's notion of 'historical sense' which she describes as being 'much like a newscaster's persistently revised daily bulletin'. Spivak quoted in Jane Gallop, *The Deaths of the Author: Reading and Writing in Time* (Durham, NC: Duke University Press, 2011), p. 123.

30 Dreyfus and Rabinow, *Michel Foucault*, p. 109.

31 Ibid., p. 119.

32 Foucault, *The Archaeology of Knowledge*, p. 17.

33 See for an interesting discussion of Foucault's openness to engage with his critics, Knox Peden, 'Foucault and the Subject of Method', in Peter Hallward and Knox Peden (eds), *Concept and Form. Volume Two: Interviews and Essays on the Cahiers pour l'Analyse* (London: Verso, 2012), pp. 69–88.

34 Michel Foucault, 'For an Ethic of Discomfort', in Faubion (ed.), *Power*, pp. 443–8 (p. 448).

35 Hayden White, 'Foucault's Discourse: The Historiography of Anti-Humanism', in *The Content of the Form: Narrative Discourse and Historical Representation* (Baltimore, MD: Johns Hopkins University Press, 1990), pp. 104–41 (p. 114).

36 Ibid., p. 108.

37 Ibid., p. 115.

38 Michel Foucault, 'Theatrum Philosophicum', in James D. Faubion (ed.), *Aesthetics, Method and Epistemology*, Vol. 2, *The Essential Works of Foucault 1954–1984*, trans. Robert Hurley and others, 3 vols. (London and New York: Penguin and The New Press, 1998), pp. 343–68 (p. 343).

39 Gilles Deleuze, *Foucault* (Paris: Les éditions de minuit, 2004 [1986]), p. 128.

40 Foucault, 'La scène de la philosophie', pp. 571–2, 574.

41 Ibid., p. 594.

42 Foucault, *The Hermeneutics of the Subject*.

43 Foucault said this at the Howison lecture he gave at the University of Berkeley in 1980. See *Open Culture*, www.openculture.com/2013/12/michel-foucault-delivers-his-lecture-on-truth-and-subjectivity.html, accessed 12 October 2016.

44 Beatrice Han argued that Foucault should be seen as a philosopher in the transcendental tradition of Kant, while Gary Gutting argued that Foucault should primarily be seen as a historian. See Gary Gutting's review of Han's *Foucault's Critical Project: Between the Transcendental and the Historical*, *Notre Dame Philosophical Reviews*, May 2003, http://ndpr.nd.edu/news/23402-foucault-s-critical-project/, accessed 24 October 2016.

45 For an excellent critique of Foucault's use of the historical *apriori*, see Beatrice Han's *Foucault's Critical Project: Between the Transcendental and the Historical*, trans. Edward Pile (Stanford, CA: Stanford University Press, 2002).

46 Michel Foucault, 'The Masked Philosopher', in Paul Rabinow (ed.), *Ethics*, Vol. 1, *The Essential Works of Foucault 1954–1984*, trans. Robert Hurley and others, 3 vols (New York: New Press, 1997), pp. 321–8 (p. 321).

47 Michel Foucault, 'What is an Author', in Faubion (ed.), *Aesthetics, Method and Epistemology*, pp. 205–22 (p. 222).

48 Foucault, 'La scène de la philosophie', p. 572.

PART I

Truth, methods, genealogies

1

Foucault's philosophical theatres

Mark D. Jordan

Foucault often writes at the edge of some stage. He calls up stagecraft to describe violent displays of royal power or the oldest rituals of Christian temptation and repentance. Theatres help him to explicate what he means by 'heterotopia' or suggest other coinages to him ('Ubu-power', 'alethurgy'). Struck by what seems to him obvious, he can sometimes only double common terms or underline them: 'the dramatization of the drama', he writes, or 'maximum theatricality'.[1] Theatrical allusions are so frequent in Foucault, so large a part of his vernacular, that it can be hard to hear the questions they pose for his writing, especially as the questions change. Is theatre for him a set of loose terms and models, a tantalising promise of excess, or an occasion for improvising on his own?

Occasionally, Foucault reflects at some length on the theatre of his writing. Consider the piece entitled 'Theatrum philosophicum' ('Philosophical Theatre'). Published in 1970 by *Critique*, the essay presents itself as a review of two books from Gilles Deleuze. It cannot be counted a standard review-essay. It is more like a meditation on the modes of theatricality in philosophic writing. Composing the piece, Foucault takes as his most provocative conversation-partner about theatre not Deleuze but Pierre Klossowski, dramaturg of erotic-philosophical *tableaux vivants*. Foucault applies the model of a *theatrum philosophicum* to Deleuze, but he constructs it with Klossowski's help.

The essay's compositional engagement with Klossowski is partly concealed by the extravagance of the compliments it seems to pay Deleuze. Its first paragraph predicts that 'one day, perhaps, this century will be Deleuzian'.[2] Foucault uses similar constructions in other places, most famously at the conclusion of *The History of Sexuality*, Vol. 1.[3] The ambiguity of that parallel passage is already present in the prediction about Deleuze. Does Foucault foresee a historiography of philosophy that will (one day, perhaps) fully recognise the importance of Deleuze's work? Or does he commend Deleuze's writing as an already present clue or key to what can be seen around us, perhaps more clearly in other genres or authors?

Just here, it is helpful to go back one sentence in the essay's opening paragraph: 'For a long time, I believe, this work [of and in Deleuze] will turn above our heads, in enigmatic resonance with that of Klossowski, another great and excessive sign.'[4] *This work* is the Deleuzian corpus but also its task or project. It *resonates* with that of Klossowski as another *sign*. Sign of what? Of what this (European) century of philosophic writing is – of what it is becoming? If the century may one day be called 'Deleuzian', it must also be 'Klossowskian'. Foucault's diction reinforces the point. 'Resonate' is a term of art in Deleuze but even more in Klossowski. There is no simple choice between their two languages, since Klossowski intrudes so prominently on the two books by Deleuze that Foucault considers. Instead of choosing one or the other, Foucault reads Deleuze into his continuing conversation with Klossowski about how to write scripts for the *theatrum philosophicum* that the century needs.

Deleuze, Foucault, and the mime of metaphysics

Theatrum philosophicum, philosophical theatre. Foucault does not invent the title. Earlier books were published under it, including one by Jacobus Lorhard in 1613. Foucault may know Lorhard's book, since it appears in histories of philosophical terminology as an early attestation of '*ontologia*', prototype of the English 'ontology'. With many other books of the sixteenth and seventeenth centuries, Lorhard takes *theatrum* as a cognitive space in which to display the elements of some art or science. He fills the space with diagrams that map or draw the structure of philosophy in a series of binary divisions. Theatre means for Lorhard visual pedagogy through schematisation.[5] This is not Foucault's sense of the space around the resonating pair Deleuze-Klossowski. Indeed, his appropriation of the older title has to count as a pun. For Foucault, *theatrum* calls up the twentieth-century European stage. It means a succession of tableaux for the travails of thinking in the vicinity of bodies.

In Foucault's essay, theatre appears first as a topic in Deleuze's books (there too in connection with Klossowski). It is, more suggestively, a feature of Deleuze's way of thinking. Reading *The Logic of Sense*, Foucault finds an intimate exchange between two topics, personified as ancient schools. The first concerns phantasms. Ancient Epicurean accounts introduce them as intermediaries in sensation, emotion, and cognition. They require a metaphysics of incorporeal materiality, preoccupied not with God or Platonic ideas but with 'the epidermic plays of perversity'.[6] Foucault shifts the doctrine into its contemporary sequel: the transgressive atheism of Sade, Bataille, and Klossowski. The last is not named, only figured by reference to the ambivalent pose of his favourite protagonist, Roberte: she holds her 'palm upturned in a gesture of prohibition that offers itself'.[7] Roberte is the star of the *tableaux vivants* that punctuate Klossoswki's trilogy, *The Laws of Hospitality*. In the scholasticism of those novellas, she embodies many things, beginning with the doubling of No and Yes, of compulsion and freedom. Her palms are a special focus of desire and significance.

Foucault follows Roberte's gesture into Deleuzian possibilities for philosophy. The freed simulacra of our modernity cluster in two privileged scenes, psychoanalysis and theatre. (The intertwining of these two is a topic in Klossowski's first novella, *La vocation suspendue*, as well as in Foucault's *Histoire de la folie*.) Psychoanalysis and theatre are assigned, respectively, to Freud and Artaud. Indeed, Foucault describes theatre in terms that recall Artaud: 'multiplied, polyscenic, simultaneous [...] masks dance, bodies cry out, hands and fingers gesture'.[8]

Foucault's essay moves from the simulacra of Epicureans to the Stoics' preoccupation with another incorporeal materiality: the event. An event is not a concatenation of physical causes and effects. It is something fashioned on surfaces by speech, 'a point without thickness or body, that about which one speaks and as it courses over the surface of things'.[9] (An event is like a role.) At these and other points of thought, Epicureans and Stoics begin to converge. Their doctrines, their plots, enter into relations of absence and excess, which cannot be captured by knowing or judging. They must instead be *thought* in a sort of mime: 'thought has the role of producing the phantasm theatrically and of repeating the universal event in its extreme and singular point'.[10]

Near the end of Foucault's essay, theatrical language reappears decisively. He has been describing philosophy's obligation to contest not error but stupidity – the levelling of everything in purposeless monotony. The philosopher's engagement with stupidity plunges 'into this skull without candles. It is his death mask, his temptation, perhaps his desire, his catatonic theatre. [...] Once paradox has overturned the table of representation, catatonia plays the theatre of thought'.[11] Perhaps opium or LSD might help, Foucault muses. Or, better, bypass drugs bypass drugs so that so that thought can exercise unaided its capacities for ill will and ill humour. Playing with either or both, 'with this perverse exercise and this *theater*, thought awaits the issue ... Thought dawdles languidly like a perversion; it repeats itself assiduously upon a *theater-stage* ... And when chance, the *theater*, and perversion enter into resonance [...], then thought is a trance; and it is worth the effort to think'.[12] The enigmatic resonance of Deleuze and Klossowski has become a theatrical harmony of chance and perversion.

Foucault insists, across the two books under review, that Deleuze's exhausting work of composition opens the door to thinking *as* theatre. So, Foucault proceeds into a Nietzschean epilogue, ornamented with quotations from Zarathustra and Dionysus. Deleuze, he writes (again), 'is philosophy not as thought, but as theater: theater of mimes with multiple, fugitive, and instantaneous scenes, where gestures, without being seen, make signs'.[13] Then Foucault yields to his own theatrical impulses. He puts the West's contending metaphysicians onto an imaginary stage:

> Leibniz, having reached the top of the pyramid, makes out through the darkness that the celestial music is the *Pierrot lunaire*. In the sentry box of the Luxembourg Gardens, Duns Scotus places his head through the circular window; he is sporting a considerable moustache; it belongs to Nietzsche, disguised as Klossowski.[14]

The scene is worth deciphering. In Arnold Schoenberg's setting of 'Pierrot lunaire', a drunken poet wanders through drunkenness, desire, death, blasphemy, parody before returning to a home perfumed by memories. What Leibniz discerns as the cosmic score is a self-conscious musical drama. Duns Scotus has appeared in Foucault's essay as a philosopher who failed before difference. He pops up now with Nietzsche's moustache – Nietzsche being the thinker who, before Deleuze himself, did render thought in its fugitive otherness. And Klossowski – this whole scene recalls a culminating episode in his last novel, *The Baphomet*. Nietzsche appears there as an anteater, notable for an aversion to ants and a habit of tracing (eternal) circles. It names itself – because this anteater speaks – as having once been Frederick (or, let us say, Friedrich). Frederick the anteater quotes Jesus from the Gospels until he lapses into a paraphrase of Zarathustra: 'When one god proclaimed himself the only god, all the other gods died of mad laughter'.[15] Some pages later in Klossowski's novel, one of the protagonists decides to flee by riding out of the great hall on the anteater. Finding the animal nowhere, he notices instead a collared man, naked, on all fours. 'His broad forehead, turned to the ground, overhung his blazing eyes with tufted eyebrows, and his lips disappeared under an enormous mustache, brushing the flagstones'.[16] This is Hans Olde's drawing of Nietzsche just before his death, late in madness.[17] Foucault ends the essay on Deleuze by presenting a Klossowskian play in which Nietzsche appears at once naked and disguised – through the intermediary of a drawing.

All these references to theatre, beginning with Foucault's choice of title – what do they amount to? They are at least a topic in the old rhetorical sense, a source for speaking. Theatre as an occasion for philosophy to think its own writing is a topic shared by Foucault with Deleuze, Klossowski, and Nietzsche, whose youthful offering to the god Dionysus was *The Birth of Tragedy*. Foucault's 'Theatrum philosophicum' is also the space of thinking re-opened by Deleuze and Klossowski, where one can watch again Freud and Artaud, the Epicureans and Stoics. Indeed, by the end of Foucault's essay, the whole space of Western metaphysics is rendered as a theatre on the page.

The last word of Foucault's essay is the surname, 'Klossowski'. That name also appears near the opening. Foucault's reading of Deleuze is enclosed within Klossowski. Or his Deleuze is a figure in a mime directed by Klossowski. That must raise the larger question: What is the relation of Foucault's writing to Klossowski's dramaturgy? Foucault often expounds other authors by mimesis. Is he rehearsing Klossowski's scenes – or parodying them – as a most intimate form of exposition? Or does his praise hint at other ways of writing, other theatres?

These questions can best be pursued by moving both before and after 'Theatrum philosophicum'. I first turn back to some of Foucault's earliest writing on Klossowski during the 1960s. Then I jump forward to a piece from the 1980s in which Foucault describes very different genres for showing the acts of bodies. Bracketing 'Theatrum philosophicum' in this way, I hope to display more of the connections in Foucault between theatre and writing. I also turn my chapter back on itself. What do we want – for thinking, reading, or writing – when we tell such stories about Foucault?

Klossowski, Foucault, and the bathing goddess

Over decades, some readers of Foucault have noticed his relations with Klossowski. These relations are hard to ignore, since they are both textual and biographical. Still, accounts of them are often blurry. Readers confined to English can blame this up to a certain point on translation. Some of Klossowski's major works flicker in and out of English print; others have never been translated. Still, translation is neither the only nor the chief problem in bringing Klossowski into focus. He wants to elude readers, both textually and biographically. That is one reason why Foucault never attempts to capture him. Instead, he regularly helps him to escape once again. An interviewer remarks to Foucault that Klossowski is part of a 'magic constellation' that glitters over his works. (The other two stars are Bataille and Blanchot.) Foucault replies that timidity prevents him from acknowledging the extent of his debt to the three of them. He holds himself back from inscribing his own writing 'under the sign, under the epigraph of their names'.[18] Holds himself back: that describes Foucault's writing on Klossowski.

In 1964, perhaps a year after they had met in the flesh, Foucault published an essay that represented the whole of Klossowski's writing to date, across its several genres.[19] (The form and scope of this essay resemble what Foucault does for Deleuze in 'Theatrum philosophicum'.) Klossowski was charmed by the essay. Years later, he would still call Foucault his best commentator.[20] He allowed or urged Foucault to read the draft of his new novel, *The Baphomet*, and finally dedicated the book to him. Expressions of admiration did not stop there. Late in 1970 or early in 1971, a few months after the publication of 'Theatrum philosophicum', Foucault wrote to Klossowski about the newly published piece, *La monnaie vivante* (*Living Currency*). He calls it the 'highest book of our epoch' (a Nietzschean metaphor of height). Making allowance for habits of delirious praise in this circle of authors, Foucault's judgement is still striking.[21] It confirms the claim that this century, if it might become Deleuzian, is already and inescapably Klossowskian. Foucault writes: 'everything that counts in one way or another – Blanchot, Bataille, *Beyond Good and Evil* also – they lead to [your piece. ...] This is what should be thought: desire, value, and the simulacrum, – the triangle that dominates us and has constituted us, doubtless for centuries, in our history'.[22]

'The Prose of Actaeon', Foucault's 1964 essay on Klossowski, uses a small book to interpret the whole corpus. In *The Bath of Diana*, Klossowski restages Ovid's version of the myth about a hunter stumbling upon the goddess bathing in the woods.[23] For his transgression (at once erotic and theological), Actaeon is turned into a stag, with the taunt that he should now try to utter what he has seen of Diana naked. Unable to speak a word, Actaeon flees from the goddess' grotto into the jaws of his own hunting dogs, who cannot recognise him.

Klossowski's book on Actaeon and Diana fits into no single genre. On some pages, it explicates the Ovidian myth with scholarly devices. On others, it draws out the myth by improvising speeches and inventing characters. For example, Klossowski posits a Demon as the necessary intermediary between the goddess' incarnation and Actaeon's startled vision. On Foucault's reading, *The Bath of Diana* revives a long-lost experience that was silenced by official Christianity and modern philosophy since Descartes. The experience is worth retrieving because it will return in 'our' cultural future. Foucault applies to Klossowski one of Nietzsche's formulas for announcing Zarathustra: '*Incipit Klossowski*, as Zarathustra'.[24] An *incipit* is the opening of a text or melody but also – and notably in Nietzsche – of a script: *Incipit tragoedia, incipit parodia*. Echoing the phrases, Foucault associates Klossowski's book on Diana and Actaeon with Nietzsche's prophecies of the return of old gods after the demise of the God that has monopolised two European millennia. *Incipit* of a new scripture: the divine-that-comes may prefer to speak its first lessons with the insinuations of a Demon or the glistening skin of a goddess. The phrase also recalls that Klossowski's writing is always theatrical. *Incipit Klossowski*: any text by Klossowski is a script.

Foucault extends the rules of performance in Klossowski's dramas to 'our' cultural space, the desert we inhabit since the disappearance of Christian theology. On this empty, silent sand, we no longer possess either theology or myth. Yet Klossowski tries still to speak the older dramas. He is like Actaeon at the myth's end: he struggles to say what he has glimpsed of divinity even as his face is pulled into the muzzle of a speechless stag. Klossowski's writing *is* the prose of Actaeon. It depicts the lost languages of ancient theophany and heretical theology, the lost spaces in which Christians were enchanted by demons and pagans stumbled upon naked gods. The remnants of these spaces have retreated into the region we call 'literature', very much including theatre.

If Klossowski writes the prose of Actaeon, what does Foucault write? For all the deftness in reproducing *The Bath*'s images, characters, and episodes, Foucault doesn't imitate its way of setting scenes. He attends, of course, to some of the book's techniques of composition so far as they carry its possibilities for thinking. For example, Foucault describes the opening of 'a perilous space' in which 'discourses, fables, trapping and trapped ruses' can teach us 'how what is most serious in thought should find, beyond dialectic, its illuminated lightness (*légèreté*)'.[25] *The Bath* opens space for thought by re-arranging theatrical devices in the crucial scene or shifting voice from character to character, keeping an expert eye on the reader conceived as spectator.

Even as he admires these elements in Klossowski's writing, Foucault does not adopt them. He praises the style without borrowing its forms. Why isn't Foucault compelled, by his own praise, to join Klossowski in writing tableaux? If space for the bright grace of thought is opened by 'discourses, fables, trapping and trapped ruses', shouldn't Foucault find his own thinking through them?

Such questions about Foucault's choice in style often elicit two sorts of answers. Each is unsatisfying. The first supposes that Foucault felt himself somehow constrained by the genres of academic philosophy. This sort of answer ignores Foucault's record of bold writing, beginning with *The History of Madness*. The second sort of answer is that Foucault was interested in Klossowski's philosophical ideas rather than their expression. But in this essay, as in many other places, Foucault refuses precisely a distinction between form and content. 'What is most serious in thought' escapes sterile dialectics through 'discourses, fables, trapping and trapped ruses': thought finds itself through compositional devices. So, Foucault's choice to write about Klossowski's thought in genres other than Klossowski's own cannot be dismissed as trivial. A satisfying explanation of the compositional choice must show how Foucault's writing opens the theatre for thought in other ways.

The suggestion can be sharpened. In a letter about *The Baphomet*, Klossowski insists that he wrote it by transcribing the scenes before his eyes: 'The whole thing was composed very quickly, as though all I had to do was transcribe a dictation, or better yet, as though I were describing it as a play I was watching, leaving out none of the words which the actors' various poses suggested to me, so that I actually felt as though I were right there listening to them speak'.[26] A little later, Klossowski uses an interview to extend that account to all of his novels: 'my tableaux existed in my mind as such before I came to describe them in my novels'.[27] What does Foucault regard as he writes? And how does he make philosophic theatre of it?

Foucault's theatre of the self

Fourteen years after publishing 'The Prose of Actaeon', eight after 'Theatrum philosophicum', Foucault visited Japan for a series of lectures, conversations, and visits to a Zen monastery. Many readers count this year as pivotal for his writing. It marks his re-conception of the history of sexuality – pushing back from modernity at first to early Christianity, then to the broad fields of ancient moral prescription. The change of chronology and topic accompanies a change in style: Foucault appears to write more simply and directly.[28] Something of the new archive and style can be seen in the 'Tokyo lecture', which presents rather schematically Foucault's current notions about Christian pastoral power. It is as striking for its plain speaking as for any of its claims.

The day after he presented the paper in Tokyo, Foucault sat for a conversation with an old acquaintance, Moriaki Watanabe. An eminent scholar of European litera-ture and theatre, Watanabe had recently translated *The History of Sexuality*, Vol. 1 into Japanese. Unsurprisingly, he asks Foucault at once about the importance of theatre in his work. Foucault expresses pleasure at the question, then re-describes his earlier writing in theatrical terms: 'I wanted to know how one staged sickness (*mise en scène la maladie*), how one staged madness, how one staged crime [...] I want [now] to do a history of the *scene* on which one has then tried to distinguish the true and the false, but it is not this distinction that interests me, it's the constitution of the scene and of the theater'.[29]

Foucault links his persistent interest to Nietzsche, who was also fascinated by the transient event. (Here Foucault re-assigns to Nietzsche the topic he has earlier given to Deleuze.) Nietzsche was the first to define philosophy as 'the activity which serves to know what happens and what happens now'.[30] Foucault counts himself Nietzschean in this sense. Since theatre grasps the event by staging it, his own books should be read as dramaturgies. Indeed, his flaw as a writer is 'a sort of intensification, a dramatization of events about which one should speak less fervently'.[31]

Foucault's interviews are exercises in irony. Still, if only for the moment, let me remain on the surface of these remarks. Talking to this student of theatre, at least, Foucault wants to insist on the continuity of theatrical preoccupations across his work and into the foreseeable future. (He will explore the scene of true-and-false well into the 1980s.) The preoccupation with writing scenes remains. Still, Foucault's new archives and style make it harder to see what is theatrical about his forms of compos-ition. Questions in the 1960s and 1970s about the relation of his critical writing to the more theatrical elements in Klossowski (or Deleuze, Bataille, Blanchot) double or triple as a reader moves through and beyond *The History of Sexuality*, Vol. 1.

Let me trace this puzzle again. Specifically theatrical terms or models continue to appear in Foucault's works despite (real or imagined) changes of topic and tone. In *Discipline and Punish* (assigned to the old style), a sequence of scenes is deliberately staged and then analysed: the diptych of the regicide's execution and the home for young offenders; the salutary displays of Revolutionary punishments; the Panopticon; the death-bed of the penal colony's young 'saint'; Fourierist utopias.[32] Ten years later, in his lectures on the Cynics, Foucault continues to describe their radical form of life as a philosophical theatre or retells at length a drama by Euripides that marks an epoch in truth-telling.[33] Theatrical scenes are still everywhere in the 'late Foucault', closely linked to his writing of philosophy.

If the specific and substantive importance of theatre remains, what does shift is its articulation. Foucault has moved further away from the formal features he praised in Klossowski and Deleuze. The vertigo of writing recedes – the swirling simulacra, the mutating insinuations of a Demon, the bloody fangs of the hunting dogs. If his famous concern with sexuality remains, Foucault speaks less often of spectacular transgression. His gaze shifts from camp tableaux to repetitive commonplaces in archives. The returning event is no longer a gyration of Templar spirits interrupted by an anteater but the daily cycle of self-making. Describing his writing as it pivots to the 'new style', Foucault suggests at least twice that he doesn't need to write novels because he has chosen to 'fiction' history.[34] He does this, in later years, by rendering as theatre the agency of minute changes.

Foucault sketches something like this stylistic possibility in his pages on 'Self-Writing'. They offer a preliminary taxonomy of ancient Mediterranean genres for recording whatever is philosophically significant in daily life. The basic distinction is between *hypomnêmata* (memory-notes) and letters. Foucault is most interested in the letters, not least because of their illuminating contrast with certain genres of monastic writing. In Christian monasteries (at least according to Cassian), meticulous recording is part of the effort to trace certain thoughts back to their origins. A monk's continuous writing is an effort to isolate – in submission to a spiritual director – his original deviations. Even here, there are stylistic differences with some of Foucault's earlier writing on monastic temptation. Twenty years before, in an afterword to a German translation of Flaubert's *Saint Anthony*, he had treated the same space of temptation in the most melodramatic terms.[35] In 'Self-Writing', the monk's interior theatre is less extravagant, the demonic actions less lurid, though Foucault still sniffs out an inevitably melodramatic combat – overwrought warfare – in Christian obedience.

A formal alternative to monastic diagnosis appears in the philosophic self-writing of ancient letters. He emphasises how ordinary the telling is: 'recital of daily banality, recital of correct and incorrect actions, of the regime observed, of the physical and mental exercises to which one has given oneself'.[36] He quotes at length a letter from Marcus Aurelius to his tutor, Fronto. Foucault does not worry whether the letter's language grips what it is trying to describe. He does not suspect that such a record of daily events might 'graph' the life of its author as modern prison records or psychiatric case-histories can. Foucault emphasises instead how the letter helps Marcus Aurelius examine himself for the sake of change.

Is a letter to a teacher about daily routine a piece of theatrical writing? Or has Foucault in fact repented of the habit of overdramatising he confessed to Watanabe, choosing instead to paraphrase a banal archive in its very banality? The alternatives are not so simple. Foucault may not invoke theatre when he describes the self-writing of ancient letters, but he does mention theatrical functions or relations. For example, the letter is 'a certain way of showing oneself to oneself and others. [...] To write is then "to show oneself", to make oneself be seen, to make one's own face appear before the other'.[37] Ancient advice holds that the best style to accomplish this is simple, 'free in its composition, stripped down in its choice of words, because each should reveal the soul'.[38] Writing in this way reveals the self not only to the recipient but to the author. Foucault detects in these letters the beginning of a way of writing that actively relates the self to the self – though not yet in the manner of Christian surveillance or psychoanalytic cure.

Can such showing of the self be counted as theatrical? Not, I would answer, in the sense of theatre that Foucault ascribed differently to Deleuze and Klossowski. He does not credit the letters to Fronto with opening a privileged space for thinking (Deleuze) or theophany (Klossowski). Nor does he ascribe to them the creation of a demarcated heterotopia. Still, a specific sense of artful display remains.

One of its signs is the repeated recourse to categories of art and aesthetics. Foucault's remarks on the letters appear under a head-note that includes them in 'a series of studies on "the arts of oneself", that is, on the aesthetics of existence'.[39] The note refers in part to material published in *History of Sexuality*, Volumes 2 and 3. In those volumes, the conjoined words 'style, stylise, stylization, stylistics' are at the centre of the contrast between ancient bodily morality and its Christian replacement. 'Stylizing' is a basic technique for the arts of existence, those 'reflective and voluntary practices by which human beings not only fix for themselves rules of conduct, but seek to transform themselves, to modify themselves in their singular being, and to make of their life a work which carries certain aesthetic values and responds to certain criteria of style'.[40] The ancient arts of existence lost both importance and autonomy, first under Christianity, then under modern techniques for discipline. Still, they did not disappear. They flourished in the Renaissance (as Burckhardt argues). They returned in the nineteenth century – not least in the dandy and the *flâneur* (as Baudelaire tells).

Such arts of existence – of self-theatre – are still possible today. Foucault sometimes acknowledges a recent and quite particular return of the notion of a 'style' of life. During interviews about gay politics, he begins to speak of *le style de vie*, probably under the influence of the (contested) English term 'lifestyle'. In 1981, for example, he describes fighting to find a place for 'the homosexual style of life', which he then links to the notion of a 'choice of existence'.[41] More strikingly, in an interview published in *Salmagundi*, Foucault refers to 'the great problems, the great questions of the style of life'.[42] While he regrets that gay publications do not dedicate as much space as he would like to 'questions of friendship among homosexuals or the signification of relations in the absence of codes or of established lines of conduct', 'gays' have in fact begun to settle these questions for themselves. This has raised the level of political contestation, because what is most offensive to non-homosexuals is not particular sexual acts but 'the gay style of life'. Here style functions precisely as it does in *History of Sexuality*, Volumes 2 and 3 to describe the elaboration of a conduct, a form of life, beyond codes.

The arts of life, whether ancient or recent, are the theatre of Foucault's late writing. They are the final form of a lifelong preoccupation. The performance of these arts runs through all the events of a life, including fleeting bodily states and the least incidents of the daily round. They are registered in a writing that is measured less by blazing transgression than by a capacity to shift small actions. The arts of life require a theatre not for the eternal return of simulacra but for self-fashioning understood as an aesthetic – no less beautiful than the 'epidermic plays of perversity' Foucault admired in Deleuze and even more in Klossowski. Still, the contrast of form is obvious. Klossowskian self-writing issues in the phantasmagorical tableaux of a monomania, endlessly iterated scenes of multiplying simulacra and revolving phantasms. The ancient self-writing that attracts Foucault's attention in the 1980s is, by contrast, notably plain, prosaic. It may still be more powerful theatre so far as it offers real (if slow) possibilities for self-fashioning.

In 1972, Klossowski resolved to abandon writing in order to devote himself to the muteness of images. He wanted to represent more directly the tableaux always already in his mind – to move from taking spectator's notes to a sort of 'automatic' drawing, the inner scenes replicating themselves as pictures. Perhaps there is an analogous resolution in Foucault, one that took him into other writing. When Foucault composes philosophical theatre in the 1980s, he does not script phantasmagorias. Much less does he practice the documentary control dreamed of by churches and states. The philosophical theatre that interests him makes lives visible, simply, so that they can fashion themselves otherwise.

Epilogue: Foucault's *peripeties*

Some years ago now, David Halperin wrote, '[a]ll of us who write about the life or thought of Michel Foucault are embarrassed – though evidently not sufficiently embarrassed – by the implicit contradiction between Foucault's critical practice and our own'.[43] The ironic rebuke applies immediately to standard biographical narratives. To explain Foucault's thought by diagnosing his life is to disagree on every page with his critiques of biography. Halperin's remark also applies to essays that resemble my own. To trace a single concept through Foucault's 'corpus' as if it were a systematic whole is to misunderstand both his explicit lessons and his practices of writing.

In this chapter, I have not tried to trace a single concept through a unified corpus. I have wanted instead to juxtapose clusters of words across scattered writings that I regard as discrete performances. When I suggest that 'arts of life' can be traced back to Foucault's earlier remarks on theatre, or that his supposedly plain style of the 1980s might still want to accomplish what he sought in his so-called 'literary period' of the 1960s, I am not telling a biography or preparing a system. I trace a genealogy.

For me, differences among Foucault's texts on theatre and writing can become inducements to more attentive reading. They can also goad our own writing. However many things Foucault meant by the theatre of writing, he did not mean any of them as plots or concepts to be memorised and then recited. Theatre in Foucault is the space for writing that leads to *self*-fashioning. The appropriate response to his scripts is neither endorsement or rejection – as if he were trafficking in slogans. The response is to enter the space in which resonating writers continue to turn above your head: Deleuze and Klossowski – and Foucault.

Notes

1 For the theatre of royal power see, Michel Foucault, *Surveiller et punir: Naissance de la prison* (Paris: Gallimard, 1975), p. 49. For Christian practice in the exemplary case of Fabiola, see Michel Foucault, *Du gouvernement des vivants: Cours au Collège de France, 1979–1980*, ed. Michel Senellart, dir. François Ewald and Alessandro Fontana (Paris: EHESS, Gallimard, and Seuil, 2012), p. 202; Foucault, *Mal faire, dire vrai: Fonction de l'aveu en justice. Cours de Louvain, 1981*, ed. Fabienne Brion and Bernard E. Harcourt (Louvain: Presses universitaires de Louvain, and Chicago, IL: University of Chicago Press, 2012), p. 106; and Foucault, *Histoire de la sexualité* 4: *Les aveux de la chair*, ed. Frédéric Gros (Paris: NRF / Gallimard, 2018), pp. 96–8, 104–5, 141, 170–1, 229, and so on. For theatre as heterotopia see, Michel Foucault, 'Des espaces autres', in Jacques Lagrange (ed.), dir. Daniel Defert and François Ewald, *Dits et écrits* (Paris: Gallimard, 1994), 4: p. 758. For 'Ubu-power' and Alfred Jarry's *King Ubu* see, Michel Foucault, *Les anormaux: Cours au Collège de France. 1974–1975*, ed. Valerio Marchetti and Antoinetta Salomoni, dir. François Ewald and Alessandro Fontana (Paris: Gallimard and Seuil, 1999), pp. 12–13. For 'alethurgy' see, Foucault, *Du gouvernement des vivants*, p. 8. For the doubling phrases see, Foucault, *Du gouvernement des vivants*, p. 205. These citations are meant as reminders of Foucault's ongoing engagement with theatrical terms, images, devices, and paradoxes. Arianna Sforzini traces many more of them in her *Les scènes de la vérité: Michel Foucault et le théâtre* (Lormont: Le Bord de l'eau, 2017). For the sake of easy reference, I quote Foucault's shorter texts as they appear in the standard edition, *Dits et écrits* (abbreviated as *DE*).
2 Michel Foucault, 'Theatrum philosophicum', *Critique*, 282 (November 1970), 885–908, as in *DE* 2: pp. 75–99 (p. 76).
3 Michel Foucault, *Histoire de la sexualité*, 1: *La volonté de savoir* (Paris: Gallimard, 1976), p. 211.
4 Foucault, 'Theatrum philosophicum', *DE* 2: pp. 75–6.
5 For earlier notions of the theatre, see Foucault's contrast between didactic 'theatres' and the catalogue in Michel Foucault, *Les mots et les choses* (Paris: Gallimard, 1966), p. 143.
6 Foucault, 'Theatrum philosophicum', *DE* 2: p. 80.
7 Ibid.
8 Ibid. Compare Antonin Artaud, 'Sur le théâtre Balinais', in *Oeuvres complètes* (Paris: NRF/Gallimard, 1964), 4: pp. 64–81, perhaps especially pp. 65–8.
9 Foucault, 'Theatrum philosophicum', *DE* 2: p. 82.
10 Ibid., p. 85.
11 Ibid., p. 94.
12 Ibid., p. 95, my emphasis.
13 Ibid., p. 99.
14 Ibid., my translation.
15 Pierre Klossowski, *Le Baphomet* (Paris: Mercure de France, 1978), p. 188. The reference is to Friedrich Nietzsche, 'Von den Abtrünnigen', in *Also Sprach Zarathustra*, 3, sect. 2, as in *Nietzsches*

Werke: Historisch-kritische Ausgabe, ed. Giorgio Colli and Mazzino Montinari (Berlin: W. de Gruyter, 1967-), Vol. 6, part 1, p. 222.

16 Klossowski, *Baphomet*, p. 201.

17 Hans Olde, *Nietzsche*, originally published in the German magazine *Pan*, 5.4 (1899), facing p. 233, which is the beginning of an article by Nietzsche's sister on their family history – genealogy in the most narcissistic sense.

18 From Foucault's interview with Moriaki Watanabe, 'La scène de la philosophie', published in Japanese as 'Tetsugaku no butai', *Sekai* (July 1978), 312–32. I follow the French text in *DE* 3: pp. 571–95 (pp. 588–9).

19 For a summary of these contacts in the mode of standard biography, see David Macey, *The Lives of Michel Foucault* (New York: Pantheon Books, 1993), especially pp. 154–8.

20 Alain Arnaud, *Pierre Klossowski* (Paris: Éditions de Seuil, 1990), p. 190.

21 I take the phrase from Eleanor Kaufman, *The Delirium of Praise: Bataille, Deleuze, Foucault, Klossowski* (Baltimore, MD: Johns Hopkins University Press, 2001).

22 From the facsimile of Foucault's handwritten letter in *Pierre Klossowski*, ed. Anders Pfersmann, Cahiers pour un temps (Paris: Centre Georges Pompidou, 1985), pp. 89–90.

23 Ovid, *Metamorphoses*, 3, lines 138–252, following the edition of W. S. Anderson, 5th edn (Stuttgart: Teubner, 1991).

24 Foucault, 'La prose d'Actéon', *Nouvelle revue française*, 135 (March 1964), 444–59. I follow the text in *DE* 1: pp. 326–37 (p. 327). For the parallel in Nietzsche, see *Fröhliche Wissenschaft*, no. 342, as in *Nietzsches Werke: Historisch-kritische Ausgabe*, ed. Colli and Montinari, Vol. 5, part 2, p. 251.

25 Foucault, 'La prose d'Actéon', *DE* 1: pp. 328–9.

26 From a letter by Klossowski first published in Jean Decottignies, *Klossowski, notre prochain* (Paris: Henri Veyrier, 1985), pp. 137–43 (p. 138).

27 See the interview with Klossowski in *L'Ane: le magazine freudien*, 28 (October-December 1986), pp. ii–iv (p. ii).

28 Michel Foucault, 'Le retour de la morale', interview with Gilles Barbedette and André Scala, *Les nouvelles littéraires*, 2937 (28 June–5 July 1984), 36–41, as in *DE* 4: pp. 696–707 (pp. 696–7).

29 Foucault, 'La scène de la philosophie', *DE* 3: pp. 571–2, my emphasis.

30 Ibid., p. 573.

31 Ibid., p. 574.

32 For the regicide's execution and the reforming home see, Foucault, *Surveiller et punir*, pp. 9–11, 12–13. For the theatre of Revolutionary punishments see, pp. 94–100; for the Panopticon pp. 203–19; for the young saint, p. 300; for the hints at Fourierist utopia, pp. 296–9, 313–15.

33 For Cynic life as a 'visible theatre of truth' see, Michel Foucault, *Le courage de la vérité, Le gouvernement de soi et des autres II: Cours au Collège de France, 1983–1984*, ed. Frédéric Gros, dir. François Ewald and Alessandro Fontana (Paris: Gallimand and Seuil, 2009), p. 169. On Euripides' *Ion*, see Michel Foucault, *Le gouvernement de soi et des autres: Cours au Collège de France, 1982–83*, ed. Frédérique Gros, dir. François Ewald and Alessandro Fontana (Paris: Gallimard and Seuil, 2008), perhaps especially pp. 71–102.

34 See the 1976 conversation recounted by Claude Mauriac in *Mauriac et fils* (Paris: B. Grasset, 1986), p. 244, and the interview in the same year with Lucette Finas, 'Les rapports de pouvoir passent à l'intérieur des corps', *Le quinzaine littéraire*, 247 (1–15 January 1977), pp. 4–6, as in *DE* 3: pp. 228–36 (p. 236).

35 Michel Foucault, afterword to Flaubert, *Die Versuchung des Heiligen Antonius* (Frankfurt: Insel, 1964), pp. 217–51. I follow the French text in *DE* 1: pp. 293–325.

36 Michel Foucault, 'L'écriture de soi', *Corps écrit: L'autoportrait*, 5 (February 1983), 3–23, as in *DE* 4: pp. 415–30 (p. 429).

37 Foucault, 'L'écriture de soi', *DE* 4: p. 425.

38 Ibid., p. 426.

39 Ibid., p. 415.

40 Michel Foucault, *Histoire de la sexualité 2: L'usage des plaisirs* (Paris: NRF / Gallimard, 1984), pp. 16–17.

41 Michel Foucault, 'Le triomphe social du plaisir sexuel: Une conversation avec Michel Foucault', interview with Gilles Barbedette, as in *DE* 4: pp. 308–14 (p. 309). The interview was conducted in French, but first appeared in English as 'The Social Triumph of the Sexual Will', *Christopher Street* 6/4 (May 1982), 36–41.

42 Michel Foucault, 'Sexual Choice, Sexual Act', interview with J. O'Higgins, *Salmagundi* 58–59 (Autumn-Winter 1982), 10–24. I follow the French version, 'Choix sexuel, acte sexuel', in *DE* 4: pp. 320–34 (p. 333). The corresponding English reads 'the major issues and questions of life-style' (p. 21).

43 David Halperin, *Saint Foucault: Towards a Gay Hagiography* (New York: Oxford University Press, 1995), p. 127.

2

The dramas of knowledge: Foucault's genealogical theatre of truth

Aline Wiame

In an interview published in 1984, Foucault gives a surprising account of what helped him escape the intellectual horizon of the 1950s – a horizon which was so under the influence of Marxism, phenomenology, and existentialism that, Foucault says, it left him feeling suffocated. 'I was like every philosophy student at the time and, for me, the rupture came with Beckett. *Waiting for Godot* – that's a breathtaking play'.[1] Foucault goes on, in another interview published the same year, a few months before his death: 'I read in newspapers that French intellectuals ceased to be Marxists as from 1975 because of Solzhenitsyn. That's really something to laugh about. Beckett's *Waiting for Godot*, when was it?'[2] It thus appears that a theatrical event became an event in Foucault's thought, an event strong enough to open new ways of thinking, outside of the philosophical orthodoxy of the time. Beckett's theatre is for Foucault a thinking event – an event that shows another thought, an event that thinks in its own right. Nevertheless, the importance Foucault gives to Beckett in his own intellectual itinerary is quite surprising with regard to the rest of Foucault's work, which does not mention Beckett very much, and which never took theatre as a direct subject. It is even possible that Foucault is rewriting the history of his intellectual itinerary in these final interviews, as he describes events that happened thirty years before. However, the specific importance Foucault gives to Beckett's plays in 1983 and 1984 calls for a re-examination of the part theatre plays in his work and in his style of writing.

Amongst the numerous papers and interviews assembled in the *Dits et écrits* collection, only one interview directly deals with this question. Entitled 'La scène de la philosophie' ('The Stage of Philosophy'), this interview was lead in 1978 in Tokyo by Moriaki Watanabe, a Japanese specialist of French literature and theatre who initiated Foucault into Japanese forms of theatre. For some time, a first English translation of the interview was available on the *New York Magazine of Contemporary Art and Theory* website (now offline). The interview is published in a brand-new translation in this volume.[3]

While it has not been easily accessible in English before the publication of this volume, the interview is nevertheless a major resource for whoever wants to examine the connections between Foucault's thought and the theatrical apparatus. From the beginning of the text, Watanabe seems quite sure of the importance of theatre in Foucault's thought, as his very first question is: 'Why is it that the theme of the gaze and, in connection to this, the theme of the theatre consistently return in your writings, so much so that they seem to dominate the general economy of discourse?'[4] Interestingly enough, Foucault does not deny the importance of theatre in his writings, answering directly that 'this is in fact a very important question'. Foucault says 'in fact' here, but this is still a strange question, as theatre has never been a focal point in Foucault's main books. So why is the theme of the theatre in Foucault's work an important question? From the many answers Foucault gives in the interview, we can deduce two main reasons: in the first place, Foucault's style of writing is theatrical or, more precisely, dramatic. Second, Foucault uses the specificities of the theatrical apparatus to deepen his method of genealogy. Thus, Foucault develops a particular kind of writing which is not *about* theatre but which thinks *through* theatre.

Dramatising events

Regarding Foucault's style and mode of composition, Watanabe goes as far as to suggest that Foucault could be 'the last great classical writer'[5] because Foucault, just like Racine, is less interested in 'relations of meaning' than in 'relations of power'. What counts are relations of force, relations between forces, and the way they open a 'battle-field' for different tactics and strategies. Flattered, Foucault agrees that he is maybe not a philosopher in the classical meaning of the term, and that his 'dramatic' way of writing owes a lot to Nietzsche. Nietzsche, Foucault says, was the first to show the way towards a philosophy that is not interested in eternal stability but in forces that are constantly moving and becoming: Nietzsche elaborated a philosophy of the event.[6] Diagnosing those forces, diagnosing the event, requires a dramatic writing:

> It is indeed about a certain way of grasping, through the detour of philosophy, the issues theatre deals with, because theatre always deals with an event. The paradox of theatre resides precisely in the fact that this event is repeated every night since it is staged, it is repeated eternally or in any case, in an indefinite time, since it always refers to a certain previous, repeatable event. The theatre captures the event and stages it.[7]

Foucault's writing style thus tries to invent a philosophical equivalent of the theatrical apparatus that 'captures' an event and repeats it in order to give it all its substance. Historical events tend to repeat themselves as well – we 'repeat' today the modern sep-aration between madness and non-madness or the way we grasp the problem of crim-inality – so that the philosophical repetition of those historical tendencies dramatises the possibilities of our present. Hence the need for a writing which is a 'dramaturgy'[8] in Foucault's genealogical investigations into history: as drama, Foucault's genealogy is all about revisiting a past event, giving it all its intensities and revisiting all the forces that struggled to make the event what it was. Therefore, Foucault's writing also gains a very specific quality: it dramatises, even in the common meaning of the word – it exaggerates, it intensifies.

> Hence my imperfection [...] which might consist in a certain way of intensifying, of dramatizing events that should in fact be talked about with less passion. But in the end, it is nevertheless important to give the greatest opportunity to these hidden events that sparkle in the past and still continue to mark our present.[9]

Dramatising is thus a *philosophical style*: it is a way of writing and composing texts which aims at saving hidden events and the possibilities they enveloped. At this point, it is difficult to go further without noting the striking similarities between the importance Foucault gives to theatrical repetitions and dramas and Gilles Deleuze's insistence on the theatrical potentialities of contemporary philosophy in the 1960s. Deleuze's preface to his book *Difference and Repetition*, published in 1968, invokes the need for new means of philosophical expression whose quest 'must be pursued today in relation to the renewal of certain other arts, such as the theatre or the cinema'.[10] Those new theatrical means of philosophical expression require the philosophers to think as (wo)men of theatre when composing their work – as Nietzsche and Kierkegaard did when they 'staged' ideas through the characters of Zarathustra or the knight of faith.[11]

Furthermore, in 1967, when he was writing *Difference and Repetition*, Deleuze gave a lecture entitled 'The Method of Dramatization'[12] that echoes what Foucault is telling Watanabe in the interview 'La scène de la philosophie' and that could very well provide the metaphysical background of what writing philosophy in a dramatising style means. In Deleuze's lecture as well as in the pages of *Difference and Repetition* that develop the idea of 'dramatization', dramatisation is a question of relations of power. The crux of the method of dramatisation could be summed up as follows: a concept being given, look for the drama behind the logos – that is to say, look for conflicts of forces and ideas behind any still, stabilised concept. Stabilised, actual concepts are not born from evidence or from the mere rational will of a thinker; they are rather the results of a process of differentiation, of a battle of forces, of unbearable spatio-temporal determinations. Beneath 'the traditional theories of intuition and induction', the method of dramatisation finds 'the dynamisms of inquisition or admission, accusation or inquiry, silently and dramatically at work, in such a way as to determine the theoretical division of the concept'.[13]

Another component of Deleuze's elaboration of the method of dramatisation must be noted, as it strongly echoes Foucault's own stance about the dramatisation of the history of concepts: as for Foucault, Nietzsche provides the main inspiration for the emphasis Deleuze places on dramatisation. If the 'Method of Dramatization' lecture and the few pages devoted to that notion in *Difference and Repetition* are the most well-known sources on dramatisation, the first time Deleuze uses the term is in his book *Nietzsche and Philosophy*, first published in France in 1962. Here, dramatisation is immediately presented not only as *a* method, but as Nietzsche's method, and, arguably, the only proper name for Nietzsche's method. Deleuze's argument rests on the assertion that the truth cannot be looked for in any kind of neutral, 'objective', innocent manner: truth is not firstly a question of knowledge but of *will* – and the will to truth is both tragic and dramatic.[14] Deleuze writes:

> Willing is not an act like any other. Willing is the critical and genetic instance of all our actions, feelings and thoughts. The method is as follows: relating a concept to the will to power in order to make it the symptom of a will without which it could not even be thought (nor the feeling experienced, nor the action undertaken). This method corresponds to the tragic question. It is itself the tragic method. Or, more precisely, if we remove from the word 'drama' all the Christian and dialectical pathos which taints it, it is the method of dramatisation.[15]

And, a few lines below, he adds: 'The method of dramatisation is thus presented as the only method adequate to Nietzsche's project and to the form of the questions that he puts: a differential, typological and genealogical method'.[16] The reference to Nietzsche and the characterisation of his dramatic method as 'genealogical' are important here, as they are very similar to Foucault's reference to a kind of theatricality also inspired by Nietzsche. Obviously, the genealogy Deleuze is interested in is mainly metaphysical or, at least, intra-philosophical (what is the will behind the concepts we use; what forces did those concepts capture?) while Foucault's use of genealogy is primarily focused on the writing of history. However, the similarities between Foucault's and Deleuze's dramatising styles are striking. Significantly enough, after the publication of *Difference and Repetition* and *The Logic of Sense*, Foucault was the one who saw most clearly the theatrical dimension of Deleuze's philosophy, as he entitled his long book review 'Theatrum Philosophicum'.[17] Amongst references to Deleuze's 'theatrical' approach to philosophy, Foucault delivers an analysis of Deleuze's philosophy in terms of his attempt to reverse Platonism. The question of illusion, of Western metaphysics being based on a deep fear of illusion, is at the centre of Foucault's reading:

> Illusion is certainly the misfortune of metaphysics, but not because metaphysics, by its very nature, is doomed to illusion, but because for too long it has been haunted by illusion and because, in its fear of the simulacrum, it was forced to hunt down the illusory. Metaphysics is not illusory – it is not merely another species of this particular genus – but illusion is a metaphysics. It is the product of a particular meta-physics that designated the separation between the simulacrum on one side and the original and the perfect copy on the other.[18]

Hence the idea that a theatrical philosophy assumes the illusory and accepts the challenge of having to tackle the play of forces that led to the distinction between the simulacrum and the original. Moreover, a theatrical philosophy is dramatic insofar as it is determined by the genealogical sense of the term 'theatre' – as Foucault writes: 'the theater, which is multiplied, polyscenic, simultaneous, broken into separate scenes that refer to each other, and where we encounter, without any trace of representation (copying or imitating), the dance of masks, the cries of bodies, and the gesturing of hands and fingers'.[19] The ramifications of the method of dramatisation, which encompass a theatricality of philosophy, a genealogical approach, and an attempt to 'reverse' Platonism, underline the deep influence of Nietzsche on both Foucault and Deleuze. Nietzsche's influence is acknowledged many times by Foucault in his interview with

Watanabe and can help us grasp how theatre, in turn, can be seen to shape not only Foucault's style of writing but also his philosophical method.

A Nietzschean theatre

There is, indeed, a kind of theatricality inherent to Foucault's genealogical method. Let us remember that Watanabe's first question, in 'The Stage of Philosophy', is about the theme of the gaze and, correlatively, of the theatre in Foucault's work. Foucault states that he is interested in the theatrical apparatus because of the specific gaze it requires. Since Plato, and more so since Descartes, philosophy has required a type of gaze that clearly differentiates and opposes truth and falsehood, reality and illusion. However, theatre cannot function with those distinctions: asking if what I am watching on stage is true or false kills all of theatre's potentialities. Theatre – etymologically: 'the place from which you watch' – is thus radically opposed to the 'philosophical gaze'; hence either the disinterest philosophy had in theatre, or even outright opposition to it, until Nietzsche; hence, too, the great interest theatre studies can have in Foucault's genealogical method. A theatrical display of the history of concepts can indeed escape the classical gaze that ordinarily prevails when we approach those concepts, and this escape can reveal hidden components and events. In Foucault's words:

> I would like to write a history of the *stage* on which one tried to distinguish truth from falsehood; but it is not that distinction that I am interested in, but the constitution of the stage and the theatre. It is indeed the theatre of truth that I would like to describe. How the West has built itself a theatre of the truth, a stage of the truth, a stage for this rationality that has now become one of occidental imperialism's distinctive features.[20]

For Foucault, a theatrical apparatus calls for a different gaze to the one usually advocated by Western forms of rationality, allowing for a conversion of the gaze so that it can bring into the light the backstage areas of reason and its constructs – whether it is applied to the investigation into madness, medicine, or crime. Once again, Nietzsche's influence on Foucault's idea of a Western theatre of truth is patent. In a text from 1971 entitled 'Nietzsche, Genealogy, History', in which Foucault develops the concept of *Entstehung* – meaning historical 'emergence' or the arising of an event – in a theoretical frame indebted explicitly to Nietzsche's genealogical approach, he uses exactly the same theatrical lexicon that we have just encountered:

> Emergence is thus the entry of forces; it is their eruption, the leap from the wings to center stage, each in its youthful strength. What Nietzsche calls the *Entstehungsherd* of the concept of goodness is not specifically the energy of the strong or the reaction of the weak, but precisely this scene where they are displayed superimposed or face-to-face. It is nothing but the space that divides them, the void through which they exchange their threatening gestures and speeches. […] In a sense, the drama staged in this 'non-place' theatre is always the same: it is the play endlessly repeated by the dominators and the dominees.[21]

This passage is crucial to understanding what kind of theatre Foucault is thinking of when he calls for a description of the 'theatre of truth'. The genealogical, theatrical description of the emergence of the concept of goodness according to Nietzsche is neither based on the architecture of a theatre building nor on the structural writing of a play: the only thing that matters is the choreographed play of forces that genealogy stages. How does the space divide the different bodies at play; where are the voids; which gestures, which speeches are exchanged and confronted? Those are the only questions such a genealogical theatre can raise for the very reason that it is a 'non-place', formed and modulated through confrontation – a place that does not belong to anyone since the emergence of an event, as the emergence of a concept, always happens in the interstice between already formed persons and objects.

The similarities between Foucault's text about Nietzsche and his interview with Watanabe seven years later are, once again, striking. One could be tempted to believe that the history of the 'stage of the truth' Foucault wants to examine is simply another way to describe the kind of spatial analyses developed in *Discipline and Punish*. However, one of Watanabe's questions enquires whether Foucault's interest lies less in the dramaturgy of enclosed, isolated spaces in themselves (whether we talk about a stage or a prison cell) than in 'the staging and installation of a device [*dispositif*] that makes possible such a dramaturgy of space'[22] – something already suggested in Foucault's text on Nietzsche in 1971. This observation reinforces the approach that I have adopted throughout this chapter and that can now be fully formulated: theatre, for Foucault, is not a theme but an apparatus (*dispositif*). Thinking of theatre as a whole – that is to say thinking not only of what is shown on stage but of the whole construction of theatre and its staging processes, including its architecture, its backstage work, as well as the wider sociological conditions that make a performance possible – allows a drama-tisation and a genealogical method that investigates the processes by which ideas and concept are produced in their specific historical contexts, rather than looking at them as if they could only be understood as abstracted and isolated. The genealogy of our ideas needs a theatrical apparatus because it is only through the analysis of a staging that the making of the historical knowledges we develop can be 'effective' according to 'Nietzsche, Genealogy, History':

> Knowledge, even under the banner of history, does not depend on 'rediscovery', and it emphatically excludes the 'rediscovery of ourselves'. History becomes 'effective' to the degree that it introduces discontinuity into our very being – as it divides our emotions, dramatizes our instincts, multiplies our body and sets it against itself.[23]

Such a definition of knowledge as 'effective' must be taken into account when we think of the links between the production of knowledge, the writing of philosophy, and the genealogical use of a theatrical apparatus. The key point here is that, by drawing parallels between Nietzsche's genealogical method and theatre as an appar-atus, Foucault insists once again on the non-innocence, the non-neutrality of the construction and staging of our knowledge, with some forces favoured over others, with certain elements displayed and others hidden; knowledge is always negotiated through processes of inclusion and exclusion. Nietzsche had already questioned the so-called neutrality of philosophy with his concept of the will to truth in *The*

Genealogy of Morality, asking 'what meaning does *our* being have, if it were not that that will to truth has become conscious of itself *as a problem* in us?'[24] If the will to truth is a problem, if it does not rely on a 'natural', 'fluent', 'neutral' process, then conceptual writing must elaborate new means of expression to reflect this new problem. Can those means be objective when the will to truth is not? Shouldn't they develop a special connection to the porosities that characterise the boundaries between what we define as 'true' and 'false'? Hence the special kind of balance that a philosophical enquiry must find between scientific *and* artistic approaches. As Nietzsche writes: 'Great dilemma: is philosophy an art or a science? Both in its purposes and its results it is an art. But it uses the same means as science: conceptual representation. Philosophy is a form of artistic invention'.[25]

As we have already seen at the beginning of Foucault's discussion with Watanabe, theatre is an art that embodies the very essence of artistic invention by requiring us to renounce the strict separation between truth and falsehood. As such, the function of the theatrical apparatus for Foucault is one that reveals those forces at play in the elaboration of concepts – of concepts that emerge in the very event of this elaboration.

It's my life and I do what I want ... or the theatrical production of knowledge through the experience of fiction

To conclude this chapter, I will turn to an actual theatrical production in order to question further one of the main affirmations Foucault makes in the interview: the idea that theatre works with a gaze that does not differentiate truth from falsehood – and, correlatively, that this other kind of gaze can actually be useful for an alternative production of knowledge. To deal with this question, I propose we turn to a theatrical investigation into the powers of the false: the Belgian play *It's my life and I do what I want. La brève histoire d'un artiste européen du XXe siècle* [The Brief History of a European Artist of the Twentieth Century]. Conceived, written, and performed by Guy Dermul and Pierre Sartenaer, the play, created in Brussels in 2012, begins as an academic lecture about Willem Kroon, a forgotten artist of the second half of the twentieth century. Born in the Netherlands in 1944, Willem Kroon worked with many influential artists and artistic movements such as the Italian conceptual art movement *arte povera*, Polish theatre director Jerzy Grotowski (he wrote *Akropolis/ Acropolis* for him), Samuel Beckett, and the schizo writer Louis Wolfson. He also – among other things – painted like French abstract painter Pierre Soulages and, indeed, he wrote the lyrics of 'It's my life', the famous hit song by The Animals. Willem Kroon's activities are documented through numerous archives (pictures, books, flyers, newspaper articles) and his various travels across Europe are also the occasion for Dermul and Sartenaer to explain and document some obscure or less-known events in Europe's history, such as the Sudetenland crisis.[26] As the play goes on, the 'academic lecture' part is more and more interrupted by madcap re-enactments of performances created by Kroon. As an example, the two actors re-enact the performance 'The Trenches', created by Kroon in London in 1969. Based on the fact that a standard stage is the same width as the distance which separated enemy lines during the First World War, 'The Trenches' is the first 'no-man show' in history as no human actor appeared on stage. 'The Trenches' lasted for two hours, only displaying tennis balls launched from both extremities of the stage while speakers endlessly repeated the same insults from one 'trench' to another: 'Slug guts'; 'Pigheads'. At the end of the play, a bunch of bones and body pieces fell on the stage. Willem Kroon commented on the scandal that followed the performance by saying: 'In History, people took three years to realise how ridiculous and scandalous this war was. In my performance, only ten minutes were necessary to reach the same conclusion.'[27]

Of course, Willem Kroon did not and does not exist: he is a very carefully crafted pretext to revisit the history of art and the history of Europe of the last seventy years (however, the fact that Google comes up with 'artist' if 'Willem Kroon' is typed into its research tool suggests that many of the spectators who saw the play very much wanted him – and/or the play – to be true). *It's my life* … functions beyond the gaze that separates truth from falsehood. The very fact that the play is itself torn in two (is it a lecture, is it a madcap performance?) gives a good idea of the formal creativity that a gaze emancipated from the strict distinction between the true and the false can produce.

But the power that this 'true' theatrical performance about a false artist has regarding the production of knowledge can be addressed at another level, thanks to a narrative twist that occurs near the end of the play: we learn that Willem Kroon is the hidden son of Kurt Gerson, the Jewish actor and film director who was coerced by the Nazis into directing a propaganda movie about the 'humane conditions of life' Jewish prisoners were 'enjoying' in the Theresienstadt concentration camp. Gerson – whose story is totally true – was later deported along with his entire film crew and sent to the gas chambers in Auschwitz. If Gerson was historically coerced into making a forgery for ideological purposes, his imaginary, theatrical son is the object of a forgery that multiplies hidden possibilities of history and produces thereby a special kind of theatrical knowledge able to show the backstage of the production of ideology. *It's my life* therefore embodies one of the directions that a theatrical understanding of Foucault's genealogical method could take – a direction where theatre and philosophy meet and become tools to reshape the gaze we throw on our multi-layered history. Through theatrical falsehood, we are able to revisit hidden, abandoned, or forgotten historical possibilities that multiply the effectiveness of our knowledges. This effectiveness is reinforced by the multi-layered character of the theatrical apparatus, as the theatrical gaze, which supposes a suspension of the distinction between the true and the false, is inhabited by a fiction that pretends to be true and looks for effects that are beyond the simulacrum/original distinction. Actually, by doing so, *It's my life* can shed light on an essential trend in Foucault's writing of philosophy and history.

In several texts and interviews, Foucault refers to the writing of his books (the *History of Madness*, *The Order of Things*, *Discipline and Punish*) as a production of fiction: the choices he makes as a 'genealogist' do not reflect what was, but create a kind of fiction that will only 'become' true and produce true effects through the experience the reader makes of them. In a 1978 interview with Duccio Trombadori, Foucault says: 'People who read me, even those who appreciate what I do, often say to me, laughing: "but in the end you realize the things you say are nothing but fictions!" I always reply: of course, how could it be anything but fiction?'[28] He continues this reflection in regard to the reception of the *History of Madness*, which was considered as a virulent attack against psychiatry a few months after its publication (while psychiatrists were quite curious about the book when it was published, Foucault says, they then turned hostile towards the book, as they came to regard it as a manifesto for antipsychiatry).[29] Foucault underlines how a book such as the *History of Madness* is a very specific kind of 'fiction' that produces an experience:

> So here is a book that functions as an experience, much more than as the demonstration of a historical truth. I return to the discourse on 'truth': it is evident that in order to have such an experience through a book like *The History of Madness*, it is necessary that what it asserts is somehow 'true', in terms of historically verifiable truth. But what is essential is not found in a series of historically verifiable proofs; it lies rather in the experience which the book permits us to have. And an experience is neither true nor false: it is always a fiction, something constructed, which exists only after it has been made, not before; it isn't something that is 'true', but it has been a reality.[30]

Foucault then mentions the case of *Discipline and Punish*: despite the fact that the scope of the book ends around the year 1830, it was received as a depiction of modern society, as an experience of contemporary life – with prisoners reading the book aloud to each other in their cells. Fiction, here, produces true effects because it has been experienced. How can this 'experience', this production of experience through fiction, be characterised? Foucault gives four defining traits:

1   'There does not exist a theoretical background which is continuous and systematic';[31]
2   A direct personal experience must be implied in the writing;
3   A direct, individual experience is not sufficient; it is necessary to clear the way for a metamorphosis;
4   This metamorphosis has a collective component; it must be connected 'to a collective practice and to a way of thinking'.[32]

This characterisation of the writing of a 'fiction' book towards a collective experience is profoundly akin to the theatrical experience that can only be made through a specific gaze. In theatre too, there is no continuous and systematic background, but only the involvement of a personal experience, and its metamorphosis, which produces a collective experience and a specific way of thinking. Maybe *It's my life*, with its duplication of fiction, expresses the very theatrical production of knowledge that Foucault wanted to underline when reflecting on his own writing. In that regard, theatre, as the site of a collective *experience* that is beyond truth and falsehood, must be considered at the same time as an apparatus for a genealogical writing of philosophy and as a material practice that produces its own mode of thought and its own complicated, non-neutral fabrication of knowledge. Theatre's genealogical powers of the false thus echo a Nietzschean aphorism that Foucault loved to quote, stating that the study of history makes one 'happy, unlike the metaphysicians, to possess in oneself not an immortal soul but many mortal ones'.[33]

Notes

1 Michel Foucault, *Dits et écrits, 1976–1988*, ed. Daniel Defert, François Ewald, and Jacques Lagrange, Vol. 2 (Paris: Quarto-Gallimard, 2004), p. 1427, my translation.
2 Ibid., p. 1469, my translation.
3 Michel Foucault and Moriaki Watanabe, 'La scène de la philosophie', in ibid., pp. 571–95. The English translation, which I used – and sometimes modified – throughout when writing this chapter, was available as Michel Foucault and Moriaki Watanabe, 'The Stage of Philosophy', trans. Rosa Eidelpes and Kevin Kennedy, *New York Magazine of Contemporary Art and Theory*, 1.5 (2011), www.ny-magazine. org/PDF/The_Stage_of_Philosophy.html, accessed 12 December 2016, URL no longer active. Further mentions in the endnotes refer to the French version.
4 Foucault and Watanabe, 'La scène de la philosophie', p. 571.
5 Ibid., p. 572.
6 Ibid., p. 573.
7 Ibid.
8 Foucault himself uses the word to qualify his writing in ibid., p. 574.
9 Ibid.
10 Gilles Deleuze, *Difference and Repetition*, trans. Paul Patton (New York: Columbia University Press, 1994), p. xxi.
11 Ibid., p. 9.
12 Gilles Deleuze, 'The Method of Dramatization', in David Lapoujade (ed.), *Desert Islands and Other Texts*. trans. Michael Taormina (Los Angeles: Semiotext(e), 2004), pp. 94–116.
13 Ibid., p. 99.
14 Deleuze's distinction between what is 'tragic' and what is 'dramatic' is different from the categories used in theatre studies. For Deleuze, 'dramatic' is used to characterise a general 'theatrical' process, while 'tragic' indicates that this theatrical process implies forces surpassing any human, psychological will.
15 Gilles Deleuze, *Nietzsche and Philosophy*, trans. Hugh Tomlinson (New York: Columbia University Press, 1983), p. 78.
16 Ibid., p. 79.
17 Michel Foucault, 'Theatrum Philosophicum', in James D. Faubion (ed.), *Aesthetics, Method and Epistemology*, Vol. 2, *The Essential Works of Foucault 1954–1984*, trans. Robert Hurley and others, 3 vols (London and New York: Penguin and The New Press, 1998), pp. 343–68.
18 Ibid., p. 347.
19 Ibid., p. 348.
20 Foucault and Watanabe, 'La scène de la philosophie', p. 572, original emphasis.
21 Michel Foucault, 'Nietzsche, Genealogy, History', trans. Donald F. Bouchard and Sherry Simon, in Paul Rabinow (ed.), *The Foucault Reader* (New York: Pantheon, 1984), pp. 76–100 (pp. 84–5), slightly modified translation.
22 Foucault and Watanabe, 'La scène de la philosophie', p. 575.
23 Foucault, 'Nietzsche, Genealogy, History', p. 88.

24 Friedrich Nietzsche, *On the Genealogy of Morality*, ed. Keith Ansell-Pearson, trans. Carol Diethe (Cambridge: Cambridge University Press, 2006), p. 110, original emphasis.

25 Friedrich Nietzsche, *Philosophy and Truth. Selections from Nietzsche's Notebooks of the Early 1870's*, ed. and trans. Daniel Breazeale (Atlantic Highlands: Humanities Press, 1979), p. 19.

26 The Sudetenland crisis refers to the 1938 annexation by the Nazis of border zones of Czechoslovakia that were mainly inhabited by Sudeten Germans.

27 My translation from the text of the play, kindly provided by Guy Dermul and Pierre Sartenaer.

28 Michel Foucault, *Remarks on Marx: Conversation with Duccio Trombadori*, trans. R. James Goldstein and James Cascaito (New York: Semiotext(e), 1991), p. 33; modified translation.

29 See ibid., p. 35.

30 Ibid., p. 36.

31 Ibid., p. 38.

32 Ibid., p. 39.

33 Friedrich Nietzsche, 'The Wanderer and His Shadow', in Oscar Levy (ed.), *Complete Works of Friedrich Nietzsche*, trans. Robert Guppy (New York: Gordon Press, 1974) quoted in Foucault, 'Nietzsche, Genealogy, History', p. 94.

3

Foucault live! 'A voice that still eludes the tomb of the text …'

Magnolia Pauker

This is not philosophy as thought, but as theatre.[1]

Culture, alive and at work in a play of differences, can be tracked only in the series of the many figures that orient and frame knowledge.[2]

Michel Foucault notoriously disdained publicity and yet he also engaged – and staged – a striking number of more and less mediatised interviews between the publication of *Histoire de la folie* in 1961 (translated in 1964 as *Madness and Civilization*) and his death in 1984.[3] In fact, his biographer, David Macey, counting interviews between two interlocutors only, has identified more than one hundred such interviews in over eighty publications during the course of those twenty-three years; these ranged from televised debates to cultural and literary magazine features and Q&As.[4] Edward Said describes Foucault as 'a master of the interview as a cultural form'.[5] Gilles Deleuze notes that 'Foucault's interviews form an integral part of his work'.[6] And Mitchell Dean describes the interviews as 'a kind of art-form [… that] exemplify the open possibilities of speech as a practice that constructs an impossible intersubjectivity'.[7] Biographer James Miller likewise recognised that Foucault's interviews 'played a defining role in [… the] public enactment of his thought'.[8] Yet the interviews are – by and large – read as paratext,[9] marketing devices assumed to produce little more than a publicity-function, or – in the more sympathetic accounts – as pedagogical devices, what may be termed supplement[10] to the written work. Whether understood through Genette's notion of the paratext or Derrida's supplement, Foucault's interviews function as the hyper-visible yet simultaneously invisibilised infrastructure for the books. The written word meanwhile maintains its place centre stage, occupying what Avital Ronell describes as the preeminent 'philosophical venue'.[11]

Paradoxically, Foucault's interviews have been decisive in terms of the reception and popularisation of his work, inasmuch as they have been treated as written language. The first English-language collections of Foucault's work were predomin-antly comprised of interview texts. Yet, the theorisation of Foucault's engagement with the interview form remains surprisingly underdeveloped. Thus, this chapter seeks to respond to a critical history that largely reads the interviews as essential for accessing his work, yet at the same time as being *merely* paratextual. Resisting the inclination to establish a concrete *œuvre* – something Foucault himself cautions against[12] and, I suggest, actively resists in interview – I read the interviews in relation to the written work, the books and essays, as well as the lecture courses (themselves ambivalently paratextual and yet central to a new corpus of writing) to propose that Foucault's interview-work exceeds the function of the paratextual, constituting a distinct domain of his practise as a philosopher and public intellectual.

In fact, Foucault's interview practice is, according to Deleuze, of primary import-ance to understanding his work overall: '[t]he complete work of Foucault […] cannot separate off the books which have made such an impression on all of us from the interviews which lead us towards a future, towards a becoming: the underlying strata of the present day'.[13] For, in the interviews, Foucault 'was able to trace [… the] lines [of power, knowledge, and subjectivity] leading to the present which required a different form of expression from the lines which were drawn together in his major books'.[14] Time and again Foucault addresses the question of the present (and its presence) in interviews. As Deleuze notes:

> *If Foucault's interviews form an integral part of his work*, it is because they extend the histor-ical problematization of each of his books into the construction of the present problem, be it madness, punishment, or sexuality. What are the new types of struggle, which are trans-versal and immediate rather than centralized and mediatized? What are the 'intellectual's' new functions, which are specific or 'particular' rather than universal? What are the new modes of subjectivation, which tend to have no identity? This is the present triple root of the questions: *What Can I do, What do I know, What am I?*[15]

Deleuze's analysis of the interview-work here converges with the diversity of Foucault's methodological practice, attuned as it is to differential modes of engagement and ana-lysis in accordance with the material context. As Foucault remarks with regard to his deployment of the television interview:

> for someone like me, someone who has plenty of opportunities for self expression, it seems to me to be indecent to come and talk about my book. So much so that, when I go on tele-vision, *it is not to substitute for or to duplicate what I have said elsewhere*, but *to do something that may be useful and to say something that the viewers don't know about*.[16]

Affirming this, Deleuze notes, 'Foucault is not content to say that we must rethink certain notions; he does not even say it; he just does it, and in this way proposes new co-ordinates for praxis'.[17] For, 'it is praxis that constitutes the sole continuity between past and present, or, conversely, the way in which the present explains the past'.[18] Thus, Deleuze identifies Foucault's interview-work as a form of public philosophical praxis.

In my reading, the performative scene of the interview offers a particular oppor-tunity for counterhegemonic analysis. As I have written elsewhere:

> 'The interview' in its dominant form is […] an apparatus of repetition, a theatrical produc-tion (re)enacting *The Endless Return of the Same* – the same questions, the same answers,

answers posing as questions: politics as usual. I suggest that it is the *critically queer* conjunction of these two command performances – of philosophy and the journalistic interview – that together present the conditions for subversion of, and indeed, *as* quotidian
norms and forms. A conventional mode of knowledge production, the ubiquity of 'the
interview' as a naturalized form across multiple domains of everyday life – journalism
and media, politics, education, etc. – stages an opportunity for critical intervention and
invention.[19]

The oft-accepted understanding of 'the interview' as a dialogic(al) form rooted in a
dialectical epistemology of Q&A does not and cannot account for all that happens at
the scene of the interview (and this assertion extends beyond an analysis of Foucault's
interview-work). Sociologists Paul Atkinson and David Silverman define this hegemonic mode of interview as one that 'affirms the speaking subject, with an authenticity
guaranteed as the author of his or her own life', and of which 'the confessorial voice is
thoroughly characteristic', something that we know Foucault abhorred.[20] As Foucault
maintains in a 1977 interview, 'Truth and Power':

> Each society has its regime of truth, its "general politics" of truth; that is, the types of dis-
> course which it accepts and makes function as true, the mechanisms and instances which
> enable one to distinguish true and false statements, the means by which each is sanctioned
> [...] the status of those who are charged with saying what counts as true.[21]

Relying on Foucault's theorisation of knowledge, power, and the production of truth,
we may come to see the interview as a discursive apparatus wherein author- and truth-
functions intersect and merge in the (re)production of a 'regime of truth'.

Foucault's conception of 'the politics of truth' and the configuration of the relations
between knowledge and power are taken up at length in an interview with journalist
and writer Pierre Boncenne – longtime editor of the literary magazine *Lire* as well
as Bernard Pivot's partner in the production of *Apostrophes*, a popular literary talk
show that aired during primetime on Friday evenings in France from 1975 until 1990.
Conducted in 1978, the interview was not published until two weeks after Foucault's
death in 1984, and then, only segments were printed in the weekly news magazine,
L'Express. Foucault maintains that the exercise of power is imbricated in the production of knowledge, noting that:

> Philosophers or even, more generally, intellectuals justify and mark out their identity by
> trying to establish an almost uncrossable line between the domain of knowledge, seen as
> truth and freedom, and the domain of the exercise of power. What struck me, in observing
> the human sciences, was that the development of all these branches of knowledge can in no
> way be dissociated from the exercise of power.[22]

Might we in fact say that the figure of 'the intellectual' is produced as a subject at the
very nexus of lines of power and knowledge in accordance with the Foucauldian tri-
umvirate: knowledge, power, subjectivity? The interview in which the above lines are
drawn opens with a retrospective question asking that Foucault situate his first book,
Histoire de la folie, in relation to his larger body of work and explain his interest in 'the
problem of madness'.[23] Foucault offers a 'few memories', stating that writing was never
his calling, but rather that the book arose due to 'a series of circumstances – studying
philosophy, then psychopathology, then training in a psychiatric hospital and being

lucky enough to be there neither as a patient nor as a doctor'.[24] While appearing to proffer biographical information, none of it is in fact 'personal' or even particularly unique to Foucault. Rather, he positions himself as a *subject* specifically situated to do this work and thus presents himself not as a universal, but as a 'specific intellectual', a concept that I shall return to shortly. Foucault articulates his position not as a unique individual, but as a subject whose place can be occupied by another. Such is the performance of a philosophical mode of trans-subjectivity whose activity in interview models a potentiality that is not *essentially* unique, but subjectively specific. Foucault refuses to position himself as a universal intellectual, a Sartrean leader of the people or a 'great man of history' whose 'genius' defines and qualifies him to speak on all matter of things. Instead Foucault elucidates the circumstances leading to his work thereby effectively demystifying the status of the philosopher and the intellectual. Here, I suggest, we witness a performance of Foucault's theoretical injunction 'to operate a decentering that leaves no privilege to any centre'.[25]

When Boncenne presses Foucault to distinguish between the social and the so-called 'hard' sciences, Foucault responds by offering a specific example – that of the correlation between chemistry and 'the development of industrial needs' – of how science, in maintaining rigorous protocols and disciplinary norms, 'also exercises power'.[26] 'Science', Foucault tells us, 'has become institutionalized as a power through a university system and through its own constricting apparatus of laboratories and experiments'.[27] Boncenne's follow-up question – 'Doesn't science produce "truths" to which we submit?' – elicits the following response from Foucault:

> Of course. Indeed, truth is no doubt a form of power. And in saying that, I am only taking up one of the fundamental problems of Western philosophy when it poses these questions: Why, in fact, are we attached to the truth? Why the truth rather than lies? Why the truth rather than myth? Why the truth rather than illusion? And I think that, instead of trying to find out what truth, as opposed to error, is, it might be more interesting to take up the problem posed by Nietzsche: how is it that, in our societies, 'the truth' has been given this value, thus placing us absolutely under its thrall?[28]

Through his insistence on the productivity of power in the constitution of knowledge, Foucault asks that we question the epistemological underpinnings of the Western philosophical and scientific traditions. 'Truth' in Foucault's estimation, is a motive force, a method, an ethos, and an episteme orienting, perhaps even constituting, the production of knowledge and with it, the subject. 'Techniques of truth', a concept that Foucault elaborates elsewhere, are equally the purview of the scientist, the philosopher, and the intellectual. In this, Foucault does not offer a pronouncement, but rather effects a problematisation, as a method of analysis,[29] highlighting the question of the constitutive relations among various domains of knowledge production and their subjects.

Boncenne shifts the conversation to a consideration of Foucault's delineation between the 'universal intellectual' and the 'specific intellectual', asking 'Would you like to say something about this distinction?'[30] While such a topical shift may seem abrupt, or even fortuitous in terms of the way in which it seemingly anticipates what has often been misread as a shift towards thinking the subject in Foucault's later work,

Boncenne's question indicates an understanding that in Foucault's thought, power and the subject are already bound together – a question that relies, at least in part, on his reading of Foucault's 1977 conversation with Deleuze, later published in English as 'Intellectuals and Power'.[31] Here, Foucault responds to Boncenne's question by defining intellectual labour as 'an essentially critical work'.[32] He maintains that the specific intellectual is constituted through 'a critical examination, a critical questioning' of the present and their own orientation to it.[33] Thus, Foucault holds that the 'specific intellectual' – a figure with whom he identifies – must engage a 'struggle against the forms of power that transform him into its object and instrument in the sphere of "knowledge", "truth", "consciousness", and "discourse"'.[34] I contend, then, that the scene of the interview imposes precisely such an objectifying form – hence Foucault's resistant engagement.

Reading this well-known and much-cited interview, 'On Power', as an exchange rather than a monological address emphasises the interlocutory structure of the text, allowing us to see how the scene of the interview itself stages and structures a responsive mode of philosophical praxis. The two interlocutors collaboratively (though this does not entail a relationship of 'equality' or conviviality by any means) produce a text in which questions both disclose and foreclose the conditions within which Foucault reflects upon his work, his thinking, and the situation of the present. Thus, I would like to suggest that this interview, as it moves from a consideration of the apparatus of truth production in the sciences to an evaluation of the role of the intellectual, is neither a conversation nor a transcript, but rather an intertextual script in which Foucault, situated as a public intellectual, reflects upon the conditions of his subjective position from within the apparatus of the interview, whose structuring constraints both figure and (re)present the intellectual as an object of interest. It is, of Foucault's many interviews, one in which his performance may be viewed as perhaps more accommodating to the form than is sometimes the case. Even so, I maintain that this interview deserves to be read as more than a straight documentary in that it demonstrates how even a relatively obliging engagement constitutes a distinctly public mode of philosophical praxis shifting the disciplinary demarcations of the philosophical field.

Foucault's interview-work presents an exemplary means through which he practices his refusal to fully abide by standard modes of knowledge production in the domains of media, public intellectual culture, and the tradition of Western philosophy, preferring instead to alter the terms of engagement. To be clear, I am not claiming that Foucault's refusal is complete, like that of his mentor, Georges Canguilhem who did not participate in a single interview.[35] Rather, I hold that Foucault's resistant though proliferous engagement comprises a technique of performance through which he draws attention to the implicit commands of the form, a critical gesture which is emblematic to his various works. As Foucault maintains in 'What is an Author?': 'the task of criticism is not to reestablish the ties between an author and his work or to reconstitute an author's thought and experience through his works [...] criticism should concern itself with the structures of a work, its architectonic forms, which are studied for their intrinsic and internal relationships'.[36]

The performative scene of the interview configures what Dina Al-Kassim describes as a 'politics of address' in which Foucault is positioned not as a mono-logical sovereign, but as a 'deliberating subject' through interlocution with the other.[37] The notion of address implicitly orients speech in relation to its destination, acknow-ledging from the outset that it is always-already a social act. In the 'interlocutory scene' of 'the interview', an interviewee's mode of address is at once fundamentally responsive and explicitly relational – oriented as it is towards an interlocutor and, by extension, an audience.[38] Foucault's performance of a critical 'politics of address' refuses to occupy 'the knowing position of sovereign speech'.[39] Thus, the – and perhaps, *his* – perform-ance cannot be accounted for if approached as a series of 'sovereign speech act[s]'.[40] As Shannon Jackson reminds us, 'the non-unity of discourse is […] for Foucault, a principle [sic] operating assumption'.[41] Here, the non-unity of the subject, 'Foucault', is, I submit, discursively staged at the scene of the interview where theory and practice intersect in the formation of the 'critical attitude'.[42]

But just what constitutes this 'critical attitude'? And how might a questioning orientation figure therein? In his 1978 lecture, 'What is Critique?' Foucault tells us that the 'critical attitude' is 'a certain way of thinking, speaking and acting, a certain rela-tionship to what exists, to what one knows, to what one does, a relationship to society, to culture and also a relationship to others'.[43] It further requires recognition of one's position within structures of power and finally, a desire to effect change.[44]

As Foucault famously remarks in the introduction to *The Archaeology of Knowledge*:

> What, do you imagine that I would take so much trouble and so much pleasure in writing, do you think that I would keep so persistently to my task, if I were not pre-paring – with a rather shaky hand – a labyrinth into which I can venture, in which I can move my discourse, opening up underground passages, forcing it to go far from itself, finding overhangs that reduce and deform its itinerary, in which I can lose myself and appear at last to eyes that I will never have to meet again. I am no doubt not the only one who writes in order to have no face. Do not ask who I am and do not ask me to remain the same.[45]

Not uncharacteristically, the ambiguity of Foucault's response here is framed under the auspices of clarification: a single footnote tells us that the introduction is written as a reply to questions that were previously put to him. And Foucault scripts his text as an interaction in the form of an interview, placing the text inside speech marks, a formal convention designating authenticity as the author appears to be quoting himself – a choice that was surely more than coincidental. The (ventriloquised) questions eliciting Foucault's comments cited above deserve full quotation as they represent the typology of inquiry in interview:

> Aren't you sure of what you're saying? Are you going to change yet again, shift your position according to the questions that are put to you, and say that the objections are not really directed at the place from which you are speaking? Are you going to declare yet again that you have never been what you have been reproached with being? Are you already pre-paring the way out that will enable you in your next book to spring up somewhere else and declare as you're now doing: no, no, I'm not where you are lying in wait for me, but over here, laughing at you?.[46]

But why, in the introduction to *The Archaeology of Knowledge*, does Foucault deploy the interview as a formal device through which he 'discusses' his methodological persistence towards change and the resistance with which it has been received? How is this choice related to his theorisation of the archaeology of knowledge? Does the interview form itself somehow enable him more than that of the monological address, to articulate change?

Unfolding these connections reinscribes and reasserts the explicitly political dimension enfolding Foucault's methodological insistence on opacity, which Nicholas de Villiers terms a 'queer tactic', with his theoretical commitment to structural analysis.[47] Refusing to abide by current 'techniques of interpretation', Foucault elucidates and intervenes in the disciplinary norms underpinning contemporary knowledge production in the West.[48] The interview-work as philosophical praxis takes shape through the 'complex interplay between what replicates the same process and what transforms it'.[49] Thus, I read his engagement of the form as mode of critical appropriation or *détournement* constituting a strategic intervention in what Butler names 'the tacit performativity of power'.[50] In Foucault's lexicon, it is a practice of problematisation as 'the development of a domain of acts, practices, and thoughts that [...] pose problems for politics'.[51] Disrupting the normative demands and expectations inherent to 'the interview' as a scene of confession, Foucault performs precisely what he advocates for as critique: 'the desubjugation of the subject in the course of what we would call [...] the politics of truth'.[52] This does not mean that there is no Foucauldian subject to be found in interview, but rather that the subject emerges, as Butler notes, 'within the context of a set of norms that precede and exceed the subject', that the subject is both constrained and enabled by the infrastructural supports in which it acts, and that the subject is always-already multiple.[53]

In the final section of her book, *Giving an Account of Oneself*, Butler presents a detailed analysis of Foucault's 'account of himself' proffered in the interview published under the title: 'How Much Does It Cost for Reason to Tell the Truth?' The account offered is, according to Butler, 'not one that identifies causes and elaborates consequences'.[54] She reminds us that it is an account formed through the conditions of its emergence in interview. For, 'the account cannot be understood outside of the interlocutory scene in which it takes place'.[55] Butler asks that we consider what this account might tell us about the relationship between Foucault's 'practice' in interview and, specifically, 'the theory of truth-telling that he devises in his later years'.[56] Should the account be read as an interrogation, a confession? And, if so, how so?

Butler's elaboration of Foucault's concept of confession suggests that it is a kind of performance that is not necessarily – in fact, *necessarily not* – representative of a deeper or inner 'truth'. In Butler's words: 'a certain performative production of the subject within established public conventions is required of the confessing subject and constitutes the aim of confession itself'.[57] The performance of truth, rather than its veracity is what is at stake here. Butler's analysis is imbricated in Foucault's conceptualisation of the scene of confession, in which he explains that the 'madman' must admit to his 'madness'. Whether he believes his own confession is incidental according to Foucault's retelling of psychiatrist François Leuret's description of 'therapeutic confession'.[58] Similarly, in Butler's account, the act of truth-telling 'does not "express" a pre-existing self but takes its place' leading to the question: *what* and not '*who*' is this Foucault that performs in interview?[59] In other words, not '*who*', but *what* is the speaking subject? And *what* is being presented as a 'publicized mode of appearance'?[60] Can this performance be read as that of the Foucauldian subject itself as the one *who* or, rather, *that*, as Butler advises, 'cannot fully furnish the grounds for its own emergence'?[61] In other words, criticality proceeds from the understanding that one cannot be perfectly critical, that one cannot ever fully know, even – perhaps especially – oneself.

As Al-Kassim explains, '[i]n an audacious suggestion that picked up a thread from his lectures of the 1970s, Foucault argued that indeed practices of freedom may not proceed from clear and sovereign intelligibilities'.[62] Further, the 'suggestion that the critical attitude owes its existence not to rational clarity but to the murky depths and a speech not bound by reason's law and order resonates with another theme of the late work': Foucault's (hotly contested claim made in interview), shortly before his death, that his objective from the outset of the 1960s was 'to create a history of the different modes by which in our culture, human beings are made subjects'.[63] I submit, then, that Foucault's resistant engagement with the interview presents a mode through which his desire to create alternative histories is put into practice. Here the Foucauldian performance comprises an alternative history of the 'specific intellectual' as critical subject. This is, I suggest, also a genealogical practice that may be described in Foucault's own words, in that: 'it disturbs what was previously considered immobile; it fragments what was thought unified; it shows the heterogeneity of what was imagined consistent with itself'.[64]

In the 1977 roundtable interview, 'The Confession of the Flesh', Foucault is asked repeatedly to give an account of his work, and, in a sense, of his *self*.[65] While the conditions through which the account is given may not be overtly punitive, they are somewhat hostile: Foucault is being rather severely questioned (and critiqued) by a panel of Lacanian psychoanalysts. In the context of the interview, the 'I', whose place is held by Foucault (in this instance), is the 'I' of the critic/philosopher/public intellectual. As Butler explains, '[t]he "I" is always to some extent dispossessed by the social conditions of its emergence'.[66] Here, at the scene of the interview, these conditions are put in place through the relations established with the questioning others. Thus, the narrative of the 'I' is already, as Butler maintains, 'also the story of a relation – or set of relations – to a set of norms'.[67] The relations, in this context, are staged by the interview form as an 'interlocutory scene'; the norms are at once formal and historical (that is, related to the disciplinary production of knowledge in a specific time and place). Again, as Butler suggests, if dispossession is the condition for the emergence of the 'I', it is therefore also the condition for the emergence of both giving an account (of oneself) and of critique. In fact, in Butler's reading of Foucault,

> critique finds that it cannot go forward without a consideration of how the deliberating subject comes into being and how a deliberating subject might actually live or appropriate a set of norms. Not only does ethics find itself embroiled in the task of social theory, but social theory, if it is to yield nonviolent results, must find a living place for this 'I'.[68]

I propose that Foucault's interview-work performs this 'consideration' of how the 'deliberating subject' is constituted as a subject-in-relation to pre-existing norms, while strategically acting on those norms. The scene of 'the interview' presents precisely the stage upon or through which a deliberating subject comes into being as a public intellectual; for the relations structured therein are not only between those who are present, the lines of power/knowledge radiate outward, in anticipation of an audience, a 'public'. Note, as Butler does, that Foucault understands 'codes of morality' as 'codes of conduct' and further, that '[f]or Foucault, reflexivity emerges in the act of taking up a relation to moral codes'.[69] Foucault himself maintains that in a 'dialogue situation' such as an interview, the 'search for truth and the relation to the other' reveals 'morality' as a form of responsiveness in contradistinction to polemical engagement.[70] Indeed, in Foucault's interview-work, his performance is of the critical subject *par excellence*.

We are witnessing, in Foucault's interview-work, a mode of self-making (*poïesis*) as 'an aesthetics of the self that maintains a critical relation to existing norms'.[71] The critique performed by Foucault in interview *acts out* the unmaking or the undoing of the subject at and simultaneously with the scene of its very constitution. Here, I am thinking in particular of Foucault's choice to interview anonymously as 'The Masked Philosopher'.[72] Or, recall how, in 'The Confession of the Flesh', Foucault jokes (or so he claims) and feigns not knowing the Lacanian axiom 'that there is no sexual relation'.[73] These performances playfully demonstrate Foucault's 'cultivation of a self [...] as the art of existence'[74] – what he articulates elsewhere in terms of 'technologies of the self'[75] – as a practice whose effects involve undermining the normative coercions of both (full-)disclosure, 'truth' production, and the authority of his own position as philosopher.[76]

In the interview, 'The Concern for Truth' with François Ewald, Foucault is again asked to give an account of his work and specifically of the methodological linkages among his works, a demand that Foucault is not always and elsewhere willing to oblige.[77] The interview is one of Foucault's last and was published in 1984 in *Le magazine littéraire*, a national publication with a wide readership in France and beyond. Near the end of it, Ewald asks: 'On this occasion you will certainly be expected to answer the question: what must we do, what must we want?'.[78] The question elicits another of Foucault's much-referenced responses, which I will here cite at length:

> The role of an intellectual is not to tell others what they must do. By what right would he [sic] do so? [...]. The work of an intellectual is not to mold the political will of others; it is, through the analyses that he does in his own field, to re-examine evidence and assumptions, to shake up habitual ways of working and thinking, to dissipate conventional familiarities, to re-evaluate rules and institutions and starting from this re-problematization (where he occupies his specific profession as an intellectual) to participate in the formation of a political will (where he has his role as citizen to play).[79]

Foucault's conception of intellectual labour along with his understanding of the changed role of the intellectual involve both a questioning *of* and a response *to* his present, in the context of profound social and political transformations effected by the student movements of the late 1960s, France's changing status as a colonial power, and, in no small part, due to the impact of poststructuralist critique with which French intellectual culture was grappling during this time. The intellectual is no longer the (pre)modernist master who leads the 'masses', but rather a 'citizen' who must 'participate in the formation of a political will'. As Al-Kassim points out:

this statement borrows from radical political aims as well as republican values – neither a Marxist dogma nor a liberal profession of faith, this political practice of the intellectual refuses to position itself as vanguard while also retaining the power, goal, and duty to dissipate convention.[80]

In the context of a shifting and polarised intellectual climate, Foucault develops a notion – and I maintain, a praxis – of a 'public intellectual' that refuses to engage in polemics, a refusal that insists upon the dissipation of convention, not only in theory, but through practice.[81] The intellectual's participation in the formation of a public and political will comprises what Foucault terms 're-problematization'. In Foucault's case, theory and practice intersect at the scene of the interview, thereby posing a problem for politics as usual.

Furthermore, the distinction that Foucault elaborates between the modern(ist) intellectual as leader of the people and the intellectual as a critical subject is inextricably bound up with his identification of the two critical traditions emanating from Kantian philosophy.[82] As Foucault details, in lecture, the very question of the relationship between the intellectual and the(ir) public is constituted historically through Kant's philosophical legacy, which he credits with having 'founded the two great traditions which have divided modern philosophy'.[83] According to Foucault, the first is 'that tradition of critical philosophy which *posed the question* of the conditions of possibility of a true knowledge'.[84] The second 'critical tradition' turns its attention towards the present. As Foucault maintains:

> *it asks the question*: What is present reality? What is the present field of our experiences? What is the present field of possible experiences? Here it is not a question of the analytic of truth but involves what could be called an ontology of the present, of present reality, an ontology of modernity, an ontology of ourselves.[85]

Evidently, Foucault aligns himself with this second tradition wherein the 'question' and the structure of its orientation introduce a 'mode of critical questioning' as a new form of philosophical expression and engagement.[86]

Leo Bersani explains that Foucault's elaboration of a 'new relational mode […] put us on the path of a new relationality' wherein the 'analytic dialogue would be the accidental, or contingent, indicator'.[87] I propose that Foucault's notion of relational innovation requires further elaboration as a structural articulation that is inscribed in the very form that relationality takes – through the encounter with an other – in interview. Crucially, Bersani notes that 'new relational modes […] usually sustain and even reinforce old ones'[88] – explaining, in part, the dominant, and so-tired, reading of the interview-work as paratext. While Foucault's engagement of the interview form is at times novel and potentially subversive – notably with regards to his staunch refusal to respond to identity demands and confessional exhortations – readers and specialists rarely remark upon the ways in which the form itself structures the conditions of possibility for what may and may not be said, and, for what and how, Foucault says what he says and does not say. Expanding on this criticism, I posit that Foucault's interview-work sets the stage for a critical intervention where theory and practice (e)merge as praxis – what Foucault himself terms 'the art of voluntary insubordination'.[89] Foucault's performance of the 'critical attitude' in interview thus presents a complex mode of problematisation wherein, as Butler maintains, 'ethical deliberation is bound up with the operation of critique'.[90] Following Butler, I maintain that Foucault's creative and resistant engagement of 'the interview' form comprises a philosophical praxis whose enactment is constituted through the dynamic interplay between performativity and performance therein. Mobilising the interview-work as *mere* paratext often relies on a 'straight reading', itself bound up in the disavowal of the ways in which philosophy is always already a performance and philosophical texts – treatises, meditations, aphorisms, and so on – are themselves performative. I see the marginalisation of Foucault's interview-work as part and parcel of the increasingly problematic division between 'the Academy' and 'the public'. A careful consideration of the contingencies of the form will illuminate a critical performance of an interview subject that is neither 'authentic' nor 'authoritative'. Instead, we may come to see Foucault's performance in interview as a mode of self-fashioning where 'the author' is no longer figured as a concrete entity, but rather posed as 'an open question',[91] thus opening 'the philosophical venue' into the public realm.

Ultimately, a reading of Foucault's interviews *as* and through the optic of performance complicates the popular delineation between 'the early' and 'the late' Foucault – much of which hinges on what was said in interview. It also displaces the certainty with which Foucault's *œuvre* has been codified and canonised. Foucault's description of Deleuze's work in *Difference and Repetition* (1969) and *The Logic of Sense* (1969) may be effectively brought to bear upon his own interview practice: 'This is philosophy not as thought, but as theatre: a theatre of mime with multiple, fugitive, and instantaneous scenes in which blind gestures signal to each other'.[92] As Foucault once responded to the questions: 'Who are you? What are you doing?' defined by Michel de Certeau as an oft-repeated 'identity request ...': 'Who am I? A reader'.[93] Or as Roland Barthes anticipated: 'The birth of the reader must be at the cost of the death of the author'.[94] Through its (re)configuration of a mode of address that is essentially responsive and potentially response-able, the interlocutory scene of 'the interview', offers a frame – indeed a stage – through which Foucault comes into view as a public intellectual, understood not as a sovereign but as one whose deliberations are bound to the interlocutory scene, and through it, to the presence of the other.

Notes

1 Michel Foucault, '*Theatrum Philosophicum*', in Donald F. Bouchard (ed.), *Language, Counter-Memory, Practice: Selected Essays and Interviews*, trans. D. F. Bouchard and S. Simon (Ithaca, NY: Cornell University Press, 1977), pp. 165–96.

2 Dina Al-Kassim, 'The Face of Foreclosure', *Interventions: International Journal of Postcolonial Studies* 4.2 (2002), 168–75 (p. 171).

3 The title for this chapter intentionally invokes the title for the most complete English translation of Foucault's interviews, Sylvère Lotringer (ed.), *Foucault Live: Collected Interviews 1961–1984* (New York: Semiotext(e), 1996) and draws from Michel de Certeau's analysis of Foucault's 'irritated retort' to the oft-repeated 'identity demand' as 'a live voice that still eludes the tomb of the text', Michel de Certeau, *Heterologies: Discourse on the Other*, trans. Brian Massumi (Minneapolis: University of Minnesota Press, 1986), pp. 193–4.

4 David Macey, 'The Foucault Interviews', *Nottingham French Studies* 42.1 (2003), 77–86 (p. 79).

5 Edward Said, 'Michel Foucault, 1926–1984', in Jonathan Arac (ed.), *After Foucault: Humanistic Knowledge, Postmodern Challenges* (New Brunswick: Rutgers University Press, 1988), pp. 1–11 (p. 3).

6 Gilles Deleuze, *Foucault* (Minneapolis: University of Minnesota Press, 1988), p. 115.

7 Mitchell Dean, *Critical and Effective Histories: Foucault's Methods and Historical Sociology* (New York: Routledge, 1994), p. 3.

8 James Miller, *The Passion of Michel Foucault* (New York: Simon & Schuster, 1993), p. 388.

9 Gerard Genette, *Paratexts: Thresholds of Interpretation* (Cambridge: Cambridge University Press, 1997).

10 Jacques Derrida, *Of Grammatology* (Baltimore, MD: Johns Hopkins University Press, 1974), pp. 141–64.

11 Anna Street, Julien Alliot, and Magnolia Pauker (eds), *Inter Views in Performance Philosophy: Conversations and Crossings* (Basingstoke: Palgrave Macmillan, 2017), p. 33.

12 Michel Foucault, 'Nietzsche, Genealogy, History', in Bouchard (ed.), *Language, Counter-Memory, Practice*, pp. 139–64 (p. 118).

13 Gilles Deleuze, 'What is a dispositif?', in Timothy J. Armstrong (ed.), *Michel Foucault: Philosopher* (New York: Routledge, 1991), pp. 159–68 (p. 166).

14 Ibid., pp. 165–6.

15 Deleuze, *Foucault*, p. 115, original emphasis.

16 Michel Foucault, 'On Power', in Lawrence Kritzman (ed.), *Politics, Philosophy, Culture: Interviews and Other Writings 1977–1984* (New York: Routledge, 1988), pp. 96–109 (p. 108).

17 Deleuze, *Foucault*, p. 30.

18 Ibid., p. 115.

19 Magnolia Pauker, 'The Philosophical Interview: Queer(y)ing Performance', in Street, Alliot, and Pauker (eds), *Inter Views in Performance Philosophy*, pp. 23–36 (p. 25), original emphasis.

20 Paul Atkinson and David Silverman, 'Kundera's *Immortality*: The Interview Society and the Invention of the Self', *Qualitative Inquiry* 3.3 (1997), 304–25 (pp. 315, 313).

21 Michel Foucault, 'Truth and Power', in Colin Gordon (ed.), *Power/Knowledge: Selected Interviews and Other Writings 1972–1977* (New York: Pantheon Books, 1980), pp. 109–33 (p. 131).

22 Foucault, 'On Power', p. 106.

23 Ibid., p. 96.

24 Ibid.

25 Michel Foucault, *The Archaeology of Knowledge and the Discourse on Language*, trans. A. M. Sheridan Smith (New York: Pantheon, 1972), p. 205.

26 Foucault, 'On Power', p. 107.

27 Ibid.

28 Ibid.

29 Foucault, 'Nietzsche, Genealogy, History', pp. 185–6.

30 Foucault, 'On Power', p. 107.

31 Michel Foucault and Gilles Deleuze, 'Intellectuals and Power', in Bouchard (ed.), *Language, Counter-Memory, Practice*, pp. 205–17.

32 Foucault, 'On Power', p. 107.

33 Ibid., pp. 107–8.

34 Foucault and Deleuze, 'Intellectuals and Power', p. 207.

35 Macey, 'The Foucault Interviews', p. 78.

36 Michel Foucault, 'What is an Author?', in Bouchard (ed.), *Language, Counter-Memory, Practice*, 113–38 (p. 118).

37 Dina Al-Kassim, *On Pain of Speech: Fantasies of the First Order and the Literary Rant* (Berkeley, CA: University of California Press, 2010), pp. 1–60; and Judith Butler, *Giving an Account of Oneself* (New York: Fordham University Press, 2005), p. 8.

38 Butler, *Giving an Account*, p. 8.

39 Al-Kassim, *On Pain of Speech*, p. 35.

40 Judith Butler, *Excitable Speech: A Politics of the Performative* (New York: Routledge, 1997), p. 77.

41 Shannon Jackson, *Professing Performance: Theatre in the Academy from Philology to Performativity* (Cambridge: Cambridge University Press, 2004), p. 4.

42 Michel Foucault, 'What is Critique?', in Sylvère Lotringer (ed.), *The Politics of Truth*, trans. Lysa Hochroth and Catherine Porter (New York: Semiotext(e), 1990), pp. 41–81 (p. 42).

43 Ibid.

44 Ibid., p. 45.

45 Foucault, *The Archaeology of Knowledge*, p. 17.

46 Ibid.

47 Nicholas de Villiers *Opacity and the Closet: Queer Tactics in Foucault, Barthes, and Warhol* (Minneapolis: University of Minnesota Press, 2012).

48 Michel Foucault, 'Nietzsche, Freud, Marx', in James D. Faubion (ed.), *Aesthetics, Method and Epistemology*, Vol. 2, *The Essential Works of Foucault 1954–1984*, trans. Robert Hurley and others, 3 vols (London: Penguin, 1998), pp. 269–78 (p. 269).

49 Foucault, 'What is Critique?', p. 65.

50 Butler, *Excitable Speech*, p. 159.

51 Michel Foucault, 'Polemics, Politics and Problematizations', in Paul Rabinow (ed.), *Ethics: Subjectivity and Truth*, Vol. 1. *The Essential Works of Foucault 1954–1984*, trans. Robert Hurley and others, 3 vols (London: Penguin, 1997), pp. 111–19 (p. 114).

52 Foucault quoted in Butler, *Giving an Account*, p. 17.

53 Butler, *Giving an Account*, p. 17.

54 Ibid., p. 112.

55 Ibid.

56 Ibid.

57 Ibid., p. 113.

58 Michel Foucault, 'About the Beginning of the Hermeneutics of the Self: Two Lectures at Dartmouth', in Jeremy R. Carette (ed.), *Religion and Culture* (New York: Routledge, 1999), pp. 158–81 (p. 158).

59 Butler, *Giving an Account*, p. 114.

60 Ibid.

61 Ibid., p. 116.

62 Al-Kassim, *On Pain of Speech*, p. 2.

63 Ibid.

64 Foucault, 'Nietzsche, Genealogy, History', p. 147.

65 'The Confession of the Flesh' was to have been the title for the fourth volume of *The History of Sexuality*, which has recently (2018) been published in France as *Confessions of the Flesh* despite Foucault's contrary instruction in his will. The interview was originally published in French as '*Le jeu de Michel Foucault*' ('The game of Michel Foucault').

66 Butler, *Giving an Account*, p. 8.

67 Ibid.

68 Ibid.

69 Ibid., p. 16.

70 Foucault, 'Polemics, Politics and Problematizations', p. 111.

71 Butler, *Giving an Account*, p. 17.

72 Michel Foucault, 'The Masked Philosopher', in Lotringer (ed.), *Foucault Live*, pp. 302–7 (p. 302).

73 Michel Foucault, 'The Confession of the Flesh', in Gordon (ed.), *Power/Knowledge*, pp. 194–228 (p. 213).

74 Michel Foucault, *The Care of the Self*, Vol. 3, *The History of Sexuality*, trans. Robert Hurley (New York: Random House, 1986), p. 43.

75 Michel Foucault, 'Technologies of the Self', in Luther H. Martin, Huck Gutman, and Patrick H. Hutton (eds), *Technologies of the Self* (Amherst: University of Massachusetts Press, 1988), pp. 16–49.

76 As Gayatri Chakravorty Spivak has observed in her analysis of the Foucault-Deleuze interview, 'Intellectuals and Power', Foucault's performance is of a specifically Eurocentric mode of power and privilege that is both highly gendered and racialised, an insight that deserves further discussion, but which I cannot take up in the context of this chapter. Gayatri Chakravorty Spivak, 'Can the Subaltern Speak?',

in Cary Nelson and Lawrence Grossberg (eds), *Marxism and the Interpretation of Culture* (Urbana and Chicago: University of Illinois Press, 1988), pp. 271–313 (p. 279).

77 See Foucault, 'The Masked Philosopher' and Foucault, 'What is an Author?'.

78 Michel Foucault, 'The Concern for Truth', in Lotringer (ed.), *Foucault Live*, pp. 455–64 (p. 462).

79 Ibid., pp. 462–3.

80 Dina Al-Kassim, personal email to author, 30 June 2015.

81 Foucault, 'Polemics, Politics and Problematizations'.

82 Michel Foucault, *The Government of Self and Others: Lectures at the Collège de France 1982-1983*, ed. Frédéric Gros, gen. eds. François Ewald and Alessandro Fontana, English series ed. Arnold I. Davidson, trans. Graham Burchell (New York: Palgrave MacMillan, 2008), p. 19.

83 Ibid., p. 20.

84 Ibid., my emphasis.

85 Ibid., pp. 20–1, my emphasis.

86 Michel Foucault, 'Pour une morale de l'inconfort', in Daniel Defert, François Ewald, and Jacques Lagrange (eds), *Dits et Ecrits II, 1976–88*, Vol. 2 (Paris: Quarto-Gallimard, 2004), pp. 783–4 (p. 783), my translation.

87 Leo Bersani, *Intimacies* (Chicago, IL: University of Chicago Press, 2008), p. 4.

88 Ibid.

89 Foucault, 'What is Critique?', p. 46.

90 Butler, *Giving an Account*, p. 8.

91 Foucault, 'What is an Author?', p. 113.

92 Michel Foucault, 'Theatrum Philosophicum', in Bouchard (ed.), *Language, Counter-Memory, Practice*, pp. 165–96 (p. 196).

93 De Certeau, *Heterologies*, pp. 193–4.

94 Roland Barthes, 'The Death of the Author', in *Image-Music-Text* (London: Fontana Press, 1977), pp. 142–8 (p. 148).

4

Foucault, Oedipus, Négritude

Kélina Gotman

> I would like to finish with Oedipus [today]. I am not very sure that the ultra-aggressively and bluntly positivist interpretation I am giving you is entirely true. I see at last a sign of it in the fact that I have just left my copy of *Oedipus* at home and [so] there are things that I will not be able to tell you. Too bad. Punished![1]

This chapter seeks to read Foucault's lectures on *Oedipus the King*, delivered in the first four weeks of his course 'On the Government of the Living' at the Collège de France in 1979–80, in a manner that performs *alēthourgia*, the ritual unveiling of truth; but this is not mere 'performance', mere show. It enacts the work of thinking where thinking and truth-telling operate a shared logic – a manner of play.[2] The stakes are high: not only is what comes to play, in this, a way of conceptualising the work of critique as aesthetic figuration; the whole apparatus of 'truth' is revealed as an act of revealing, a theatrical and dramaturgical act. This suggests we are worrying the edges of the discourse on 'truth' – a discourse concerned with the scenographies of thought.[3] As I was writing this chapter, I encountered, fortuitously, a book; the contingency of this 'revealed', to use an encumbered term, a whole set of contiguities that struck me: writing of masks and of African philosophy, Souleymane Bachir Diagne in *African Art and Philosophy: Senghor, Bergson and the Idea of Negritude* suggested a rhythmic manner of reading which aligned itself with a version of Négritude not concerned with essentialism, but with dialogue, 'co-naissance', mixture, intermingling.[4] This, I saw, reading Foucault at the same time, was also what Foucault was doing: arriving-towards 'truth' by way of digressions, juxtapositions, asides. This poetic logic – *illogical* inasmuch as it does not proceed from propositions lined up in a causal progression – operates by way of the partial movement, the gesture that offers an *aparté*. What I propose here, then, is at once to do *alethurgical* thinking – I hope what this means will become clearer as I go – and to reflect, by this, on the ways in which Foucault's philosophy is aligned with an articulation of Black radical thought that favours the rupture, the break, and, as in jazz, improvisation.[5] Fred Moten has called this a 'syncopated' aesthetic, 'asymmetrical' and 'off', when talking about Sigmund Freud's notion of the drive; this 'erotics' 'of the cut', 'of arrangement', rethinks the way we think and write of and with difference, desire; encounter.[6]

I hope in what follows to offer partial through lines, in fact lines that do not go *through* at all but that are arranged, cut, ruptured, syncopated; and that suggest a manner of doing the very thing Foucault does too and yet which is rarely noted: that is, to think in the rivulets that run alongside zones of thought arising in furtive events of co-temporality – to inhabit the erogenous mysteries so often elided from the ostensive work of bringing 'truth' to 'light'. This is, in other words, to conceptualise 'critique' as that which comes – nearly an uninvited guest – in tatters, rooting, often half-blind, in the dark; it is in fact the very work of probing and piecing that Foucault, reading the Greeks, calls *alēthourgia*, and which happens, he notes, in *Oedipus*, as well as in the hall of the African-born Roman emperor Septimus Severus whose story he also, with this, tells. This is not to say that thinking is always or necessarily a casual affair, mere happenstance. In theorising thinking as common, open to others, unfinished, too, what we find is dramatic contingency and contiguity – that is to say, a passionate and patient weaving, a manner of coming-to-be together with thought as it emerges; as it becomes unravelled.

Thus, we arrive at a commingled site of a sort, a Greek-African place of 'origin' that is not and never was one; and in that gesture towards a fictitious return we find other angularities, other ways to write the *anarchaeology* of movement-towards 'truth'. 'Anarchaeology', Foucault wrote, in the same lecture course, consists of just the sort of 'secret' space of contingency within which 'knowledge' appears: a contingent space and time that refuses the neat closures of 'theory'. Indeed, there is a moment in this course 'On the Government of the Living' when Foucault muses nearly in passing that what he is in fact proposing is 'a sort of anarcheology'; parenthetically, he gestures towards Paul Feyerabend's *Against Method* (1975), which he notes was just translated into French that year (1979). This book, he says, poses 'something interesting on the problem of anarchy in knowledge', and he closes this parenthesis almost as soon as it is opened: anarchaeology – never elaborated on much further – suggests, however, Foucault says, a 'type of study' that

> consisted in taking the practice of confinement [for example] in its historical singularity, that is to say in its contingency, in the sense of its fragility, its essential non-necessity, which obviously does not mean (quite the opposite!) that there was no reason for it and is to be accepted as brute fact.[7]

Confinement, like many other structures Foucault works through (madness, etc.), both is and never was 'necessary'; thus, to study the conditions, the manners, perhaps the theatre of its (un)intelligibility – is that towards which anarchaeology tends, which is to say, this is a manner of thinking 'negative theory', for Foucault.[8] It is not *how we got here* but *how we arrived, nearly accidentally, to this place; and we found this, too, nearly accidentally.* This 'negative theory' is in itself contingent, a form of thinking that embraces concurrence without shying away, without pretence to universal or objectivising certainty or totality. It arrives thus at what we may term the 'present', in its ontological entanglements, its accidental conjunctions – and anarchaeology in this is thus a form of thinking the way discourses, structures, *dispositifs* are *in this way* contingent too; arrangements. Attention to these overlapping contingencies is the object (and subject), the method, of anarchaeological analysis, a study that looks at prior formations, engaged in genealogical arrivals, and that situates itself within the broader work of critique; but that also, in this, sees obliquely, refusing – just – to suggest historical inevitabilities. Thus, we may be a little bit less governed, as Foucault writes of the aims of critique – not because we confront 'truth' head-on, in the light, but precisely because of these crevices and cracks; these are the openings that may be pried apart and within which other worlds begin to appear.[9] For Foucault, 'knowledge' consists of swerves, lines, forks, deviations, encountered with appetite, not generally following a grand plan; he writes,

> for me theoretical work – and I am not saying this out of pride or vanity, but rather with a profound sense of my inability – does not consist in establishing and fixing the set of positions on which I would stand and the supposedly coherent link between which would form a system. My problem, or the only theoretical work that I feel is possible for me, is leaving the trace, in the most intelligible outline possible, of the movements by which I am no longer at the place where I was earlier.[10]

This is 'something like a sort of secret':[11] the fragility of anarchaeological practice shows an *un*disciplined or a-disciplined, 'anarchic' arrival towards knowledge – as towards 'truth'. This is not to say there is no 'truth' or 'knowledge' – and no discipline to this adisciplinarity – or nothing that should perform that role; but that these discursive dramaturgies constitute the present as *lived unfoldings*. What's more, this work of unfolding or unravelling – these forays along contingent discursive paths – leaves traces that nevertheless reveal *some sort of* truth; and it is that partial and unnecessary truth that shows so vividly what 'critique', the practice of knowing the present, here, now, affords. Attention to the frame of thinking; to the work (the labour and play) of thought does not merely suggest there is a hiccup in thought's forward march, but that this very figure of the march is at stake, replaced with an openly, irreverently, roguishly, elliptical journeying; and that this is what thought – what knowledge-forming, knowledge-finding (knowledge foraging) – is. This is, perhaps in other terms, the dramaturgy, the set of rhythms and co-temporalities, and the languages of reading, that show an anarchaeological manner of doing intellectual work in a radically open, non- or even anti-dogmatic and improvisatory way: Foucault shows us how he inhabits – himself – the half-mask. In this self-conscious play of lecturing/thinking, in these interstices, we find glimmers of noticing that operate as sets of refractions and diffractions, recombinations, reorganisations. To follow a line of thought through and to break off; in that moment of surprise, there is another event, another sliver of 'truth', that appears – and in that space of appearance, this partial truth glints. This chapter thus thinks with Foucault's play of light and dark, spaces and paths, as they reveal a dramaturgy within which arrival towards the contingent 'light' of 'truth' is performed as a ceremonial unfolding – one that remains always half-shadowed, always shared and in parts.

In these lectures, thus, among the very few to deal at any length specifically with a dramatic play text, Foucault articulates a theory of the relationship between power and knowledge hinging on what he calls the 'ritual of manifestation of the truth', a form of truth-saying (and truth-making) articulated through 'rituals, ceremonies, and various operations of magic, divination, and the consultation of oracles, of gods'.[12] These 'verbal' and 'non-verbal procedures' enable a way of dramatising truth's appearance on the civic stage in such a way as to remove the bringer of this truth – the speaker, and enactor – from the speech and action.[13] This mysticalises the process of truth's appearance as given from beyond the human realm, and further belonging to an extra-human realm, from which the 'mere' human extracts him or herself. In shifting the discursive analysis of power to the mythical and mystical realm of theatre as dramatic ritual, Foucault invites us to think in performative terms about the way in which power comes to be constituted as if extra-mundanely. The very privileged space and time of theatrical, ritualised truth-shaping, I argue, enables a negotiation and renegotiation of power strictures beyond the discourse of the state, as if to inform and to protect it. It is the 'as if' that matters: the theatre of this magicalisation – this theatre of appearance (as if) out of the dark.

Further reading Foucault's analysis of *Oedipus the King* in line with his near-contemporaneous introduction to the English translation of Gilles Deleuze and Félix Guattari's *Anti-Oedipus*, which appeared in 1983, this chapter seeks to bring discussion of Foucault's work on power into greater direct engagement with the ethics and aesthetics of philosophical writing, as writing not only meant to describe the 'why' of everyday life, power and desire, but also the 'how' one is meant to upturn it.[14] Understood as a theatrical logic by which hierarchy comes to be *deconstrued*, unravelled, Foucault's, like Deleuze and Guattari's, thinking sets itself at the 'foot' of an edifice – that of Freud and Marx (and, via Freud, Oedipus) – knocked down through a process of shifting the light. I argue that by bringing attention to the dark spaces around which and under which such edifices are built, Foucault like Deleuze and Guattari enables a different sort of philosophical labour, which we can properly conceive as taking place politically, ethically, philosophically 'in the wings'. This inhabitation of a dark space, the darkened space of the auditorium, shifts the coordinates of the theatron, the seeing-place, so that with Deleuze, speaking of Foucault in his lectures at the Université de Vincennes, Paris VIII, we may understand the work of deep, archaeological, as well as anarchaeological and choreographic thinking to undo the grounds and walls of thought and speech. Foucault, Deleuze says, brings to light not just a history of behaviours (*comportements*), but of speech and seeing – the principles by which behaviours come to take place. Ways of seeing and ways of speaking enable birth, marriage, death, eating, sex, and so on; but these deeper analyses show a whole complex of enunciations and, as Deleuze says, 'coordinates' by which the entire structure and *emplacement* or situation of the universe can be understood.[15]

With his own reading of *Oedipus the King*, Foucault – beginning with a brief exergue on the Roman emperor Septimus Severus, who had the astrological omen announcing his access to power grafted on the wall of his palace in the form of the night sky as it was at the hour of his birth – announces Oedipus's envelopment in 'fate', and in truth, with an entirely other sort of set of coordinates, his feet. Oedipus did not have a night sky by which to tell the story of his proceeding through life, his banishment, his passage *extra-muros* (by his own decree), but feet, which marked him just as he marked the soil with them, in passing.[16] With Foucault, the *emplacement* of power as omen, as sign (even if it is strictly illegible to him who bears it) is in a certain respect less significant than its illegibility, its invisibility to sight. In other words, whereas in much of Foucault's work, as Deleuze points out, the process of uncovering prior archaeological strata in the history of thinking, being, in the structures of power that have almost imperceptibly saturated our notions and experiences of society and self, comes to take place in reading the way the world is seen and spoken about, here, we have another, perhaps reverse process. The *Oedipus* story shows that what matters – what is powerful – is often what is *not seen* and strictly *cannot be seen* by those bearing it. In other words, power is not a secretive thing, a secret and hidden agency, known only to sovereign rulers, but on the contrary it is a thing that cannot be known to them. This paradox underlines a whole process of truth-guarding more ambivalent than the structures of the panopticon or other disciplinary enclosures allow, but instead a structure of safe-keeping *in spite of* power, and which allows it to be maintained.

Power then is enacted not in action – not in gestures made – but in the tenuous space *between* a body and a sign it carries, at least in the Oedipus myth. What Foucault argues is that the dark space, the invisible, unintelligible and murky zone of indiscernibility he otherwise construes as being characteristic of 'madness' before it comes to be discursivised or 'sex' before it is spoken about (or rather, before a whole series of beliefs, actions, and attitudes come to be written together into 'madness' or 'sex') *takes the place of* power, holds and guards it. Being in power then is a state of blindness. Power is granted upon one only when one does not know it. But also, this is not exactly power; this is a sort of powerlessness constitutive of power, by which those entrusted with rulership are themselves constantly undermined by hidden things, codes they cannot properly see. These are contained, in Oedipus's case, in places to which one has little or no access: his feet bear the imprint of his doom, his end, his *telos*, that towards which everything in the tragic narrative conspires, even as it will continue to surpass, to move beyond it. Yet, as Foucault also points out, there is another secret agent in this story, another holder of truth, hidden away in the wings: the shepherd who witnessed the young Oedipus's secreting away, and who will later on reveal him. Foucault's repeated use of the term 'witnessing' (*témoin*) suggests ethical bystanding; not (yet) a regime of surveillance or control. 'This slave arrives as a witness, as final witness', Foucault writes, 'he who was hidden, who had hidden himself away in his hut for so many years so as not to tell the truth. He is brought onto the stage and it is he who is indeed forced to attest that Oedipus had been handed over to him to be exposed'.[17] The procedure of showing – revelation – conjugates a series of *appearances*: first, the shepherd-slave, forced out of hiding; then, Oedipus *as* Oedipus, as he who is coming into the light, though only the slave (as last remaining witness) is the one to come *onto* the stage. In a 'real' (masked) performance, the slave's arrival signals a witnessing already done, and which the audience are 'indeed forced' to witness again *for themselves*: for those still (dramatically, dramaturgically) in the dark (though they would have been watching this under a hot sun).

So we have a structure of power by which agency is held marginally, in the extremities and in the wings, the dark and dirty spaces of civic life; this is not the 'capital' Foucault described in another set of lectures, *Security, Territory, Population. Lectures at the Collège de France, 1977–1978.*[18] The capital, arising in the seventeenth and eighteenth century as a centralising, organising force, designed to connect and to integrate disparate lines of communication, making visible a centrality that by its very connectedness enabled administrative and bureaucratic procedures to function smoothly and efficiently at the outer edges of a territorial space, serves to hold together, to concentrate. With *Oedipus*, power takes place in spite of the sovereign ruler, who is also sovereign over himself, that is to say, who has no sovereignty at all. A sovereign, we may be given to understand by this counterexample, can only rule over others; as soon as he is ruled upon, by secret agents, he is already doomed. Power in this regard occurs inasmuch as it is open, potentially infinitely; even in a representative democracy, the possibility of re-election at a later stage makes the ruler's power representative, symbolic, and potentially infinitely extendable; even the most careful constitutional means do not hold a ruler back in principle – not absolutely. Laws do not hold ends the way signs do.

There always was, Foucault provisionally concludes, an anti-Oedipus, playfully taking a stab back at his friends, whose own playfulness he alludes to in his preface; a playfulness moreover central, he argues, to the way that their writing methodologically, procedurally, upturns forms of knowing that are fascistic, invested in power. Anti-Oedipus in Foucault's reading is the surplus, the excess, the hidden, offstage space, the corner of the sky Septimus hides in his private dwellings, that marking the time of his end; the shepherd off in the margins of Oedipus's story, in the fields. That anti-Oedipal principle is not just what comes *prior* to disclosure (and closure), end, or the termination of the exercise of power; but also it is the necessary other force, which comes always already to check power that appears absolute. It is in that regard anti-hegemonic, where 'hegemony' means, in the contemporary sense, all-powerful rule *over*; but also where it means, as in the Greek sense Foucault alludes to, a process of leading others. Yet, Foucault remarks, in order to lead – to conduct the conduct of – others, there must be a principle of making truth *appear*. This does not mean verifying the truth of one or another's right to rule, but the ritual theatricalisation of a principle unquestioned by virtue of the theatre of its appearance. Paradoxically, the 'truth' of – for example – the African-born Septimus's rule is made manifest in the painting of the sky which he sets above his head and those of subjects who may come into the sphere of his palace; and the 'truth' of Oedipus's rule (and impending ruin) is made manifest not in scientific, experimental knowledge, veridiction or validation, but in the whole process of *appearing* by which 'truth' comes to be known, that is, made visible. Foucault – borrowing from Heraclitus – calls this *alēthourgia* – a fictional construction denoting the manifestation of truth (the making-appear) out of dark, uncertain, illegible, or as Foucault puts it 'false, hidden, inexpressible, unforeseeable, or forgotten' aspects of the everyday.[19]

Given that Foucault's primary example of the Roman sort of *alēthourgia* is Septimus, an African emperor infatuated, taken, as Foucault notes, by Oriental mysteries, mystical and magical cults very much at odds with the Stoic rule of government implemented by his recent predecessors; and given that Oedipus's story is also riddled with – precisely – riddles, magical appearances, and improbable fictions and fabrications, it seems noteworthy that the notion of truth-making should be allied with just this sort of confabulation. The procedures of power are fundamentally dramatic and performative: they take as their prime mode of operation the work of theatre. They *make visible*. They do, significantly, nothing more nor less. Power becomes itself by virtue of 'truth' which is rendered *seen*.

The frame and the framework for this seeing is of course complex. Seeing is not just, as all of Foucault's *œuvre* argues, a process of looking with eyes; it is not merely an organic function, a process of coming literally into the light. Rather, seeing operates (and operates as) a whole machinery of what we may call *visibilisation*, and which I am further submitting must be understood as a theatrical process by which an object comes to *appear* as *standing for* truth. This slippage: the *standing for* enabling a *standing*, that is, the representation of power enacting the power's coming-to-be, constitutes what I argue is the 'magic' of theatre and, concomitantly, here, of the state.

Michael Taussig has written elsewhere of this 'magic', as a process of *making-appear*. Diseases, Taussig argues, become things written about (and spoken about) inasmuch as a whole complex of principles, practices and the rest are reified, made into a thing that can be seen as a disease. The work of *appearance* is magical inasmuch as it coordinates a complex of unseen things being seen *as such*; but significantly, the unseen things were not ever exactly unseen. They too constituted a regime of seeing through metaphorically (occasionally literally) other eyes. The eyes of power – like the feet of power – are those whose coordinates *become* aligned with 'truth', *alētheia*, as it appears as the 'manifestation of truth', *alēthourgia*. Truth is not a stable entity, but becomes itself through its manifestation, its being submitted to theatricalisation, its being brought to light. The process, the act and space of bringing is theatrical. Power then cannot be conceived except as theatre; but simultaneously, power requires the theatrical machinery to disappear. The making-visible must appear as if without theatre; as if the process of becoming visible had never taken (a) place.

In this sense, the past is erased; and power inhabits a continuous present – the present of its visibility. The 'ritual' transformation effected in the theatre then is a magical, alchemical formula by which truth becomes as if it had always been such; something in a process of becoming appears as if always already and stably there. Anti-Oedipus then is the surplus lurking in the margins or in the corner; that which reminds us that what appears always already powerful contains within it a secret space of undoing, a zone of indeterminacy that is precisely determining of another 'truth', another reality before or beside this one.

But does that just substitute one form of teleology for another? Beside this power, does there lie an alternative? How does such a model enable the radical destabilisation of a whole system of seeing, so that we are precisely *not* just taking one potentate for another, but instead arriving at real anarchy, arriving at an anti-system by which even the marginal space of disturbance elides reintegration, containment, recuperation into power's central fold? Foucault argues that there are two principles by which contemporary state politics, contemporary modes of governmentality or *raison d'État* operate, really or symbolically, and that is via (in Rosa Luxemburg's analysis) a lack of total knowledge about the truth and (in Solzhenitsyn's analysis), on the contrary, total knowledge about the truth. In the first case, a utopic, anarchic one, if people were to know what was actually going on, they would revolt totally and irrecoverably. Power could not hold; it could not keep its place. In the second, a more cynical, perhaps, but also a far more chilling view, socialist power remains in place precisely because *everybody knows*. It is the fact of knowing the extent of corruption, surveillance, and the rest, that keeps the system intact. The system operates according to a logic of fear, of terror; because you know that everything is bugged, that there are gulags, you keep your mouth shut; you do not, because you cannot, adequately revolt.[20]

The procedures of governmentality are then hinging centrally, in Foucault's analysis, on varying degrees of *appearance* (or, in his terms, manifestation) of 'truth'. This reorganises his earlier writing on the knowledge-power dyad, so that 'governmentality' comes to signal a whole complex of ways in which people are organised, not just administratively, bureaucratically, but around axes – coordinates – making 'truth' come to light. This includes, clearly, scientific and other academic endeavours designed to help the state (the *raison d'État*) articulate truth-values *qua* truth, so that the more saturated with 'truths' a system may be, the less individuals need to be forcibly governed. What Deleuze would call the 'society of control' effectively brings this to its logical conclusion: in a society of control, Deleuze writes, individuals (subjects) no longer need to be disciplined or punished, but come to control themselves through deeply and widely saturated principles of self-surveillance and self-censorship.[21] This takes Solzhenitsyn's observation of the socialist state to another level, where not only has the impossibility of rebellion become internalised, but the possibility of imagining a rebellion that would be short-circuited by power is itself extenuated, short-circuited. In a 'society of control', we do not even (hardly) remember that there is perhaps a possibility of rebellion that would be thwarted through insidious processes of surveillance; we have become mute, aligned. We believe that we want, that we are not threatened by, the constantly watching eye. It is not even Big Brother's eye anymore, but an eye imagined as being *just like* our own. It is disembodied, ubiquitous. We do not seek 'truth' because 'truth' is no longer distinguishable from anything else; the shadow (between truth and non-truth) has vanished. In Alenka Zupančič's terms, the shadowless 'noon' that figures so prominently (and enigmatically) in Friedrich Nietzsche's writing signals just this impossibility of turning back. Where the thing 'throws its shadow upon itself', 'the one becomes two'. As she writes, '[w]hen the sun is at its zenith, things are not simply exposed ("naked", as it were); they are, so to speak, dressed in their own shadows'. This is the point at which movement appears for a second – not even a second – to stall.[22] (There is, it appears, no *eternal recurrence*, no becoming self-same by a process of constant *displacement* – constant movement forward, sideways, or back in space and in time. Yet inevitably, the sun shifts, the shadow emerges again.)

In Foucault's analysis of *Oedipus the King*, mystical power supplants the administrative, bureaucratic, rational exercise of governmental power before this could even take hold, as Oedipus operates as a king who banishes himself. There is no machinery of ministers and academics to sanction or prevent him from acting; instead, he becomes the truth he decrees. This theatrical doubling enables him to become the person he imagines outside himself; he meets his future along the way. And in that uncanny space of doubling, that space outside the home, his own power dissolves; but not that of the oracle. With Oedipus, we have an institution of power beyond the sovereign, and which the sovereign only temporarily, and almost unknowingly, safeguards. Power has already become extracorporeal, extra-individual. Power is already constituted as that which cannot be known and, significantly, may never entirely come to light. The process of making-visible is fundamentally partial. There is no power where there is not also anti-Oedipus.

Yet, Foucault argues, the structure of *Oedipus the King* requires a whole set of partial truths to come together, like *sumbola*, symbols, shards, each bringing part of the story, until the puzzle makes truth come to light. In this 'game' of truth (as Foucault calls it), there are many types of players; most arresting, for their complementarity and utter difference, are gods and slaves. Gods, Foucault notes, instantiate, silently hold, truth; what they say is true, though it may not be known to men. Slaves, on the other hand, bear witness to events. Their 'presence' on the 'scene of the truth' is accidental, but essential for the truth's unfolding: for its manifestation. They are, Foucault writes, 'powerless spectators', at once in the scene and on its sidelines, midwives to truth – instrumental in its arrival – but yet always beside it.[23]

The status of the 'slave' in this dramatic ontology, this procedure for making truth *appear* spectacularly – ocularly and oracularly[24] – is one of seemingly vacuous subjecthood. The slave is a vessel in this conception, enabling the god's truth to appear; the slave speaks, but the words are his only by the virtue of circumstance, only incidentally – to him. Paul Gilroy describes radical music – specifically jazz – as a process of midwifery, as if musicians 'catch' a baby (the music) as it comes into the world.[25] But they are custodians of that delicate, vulnerable life. Slaves here become temporarily custodians of a truth they do not own, but only temporarily safeguard. And yet, if we draw this figure of truth-fashioning out further, we discover that in the work of being 'present' at a scene of truth, and saying what one saw there, the slave effectively brings truth to the light, and so acts as a greater *agent* of change than any king does. For while Oedipus, like Jocasta, also hold pieces of the puzzle – they each, Foucault reminds us, recall a story of a murder at a crossroads (each seeing it from a different, nearly incompatible perspective) – that story, that truth does not become verified, and does not verify. It only holds temporarily the figurative centre of a narration that takes place, in its *truth-manifestation*, its alethurgical process, in the wings. The (combined, collaborative) act of making truth come to light is performed by all those who have no part to play in the action but to see and to say it.

This reveals a vision of truth (and slavery) by which the slave subject speaks only to bring (unwittingly) ruin to her master, in a design not her own, but yet which she midwives. The slave is not accidental, not surplus, but agential and central to a narrative in which 'truth' becomes what had been safeguarded by another. The passage from darkness to light is also concomitantly a passage from another (false) light to the deepest darkness of all: in Oedipus's case, total banishment, despair and destruction leading ultimately to death.

But what do we make of this dramaturgy? Foucault reads the *Oedipus* story as a drama, taking place on the page; there is no consideration of the bodied beings that *play* at this 'game' of truth; that *make appear* the contradictions and the many halves which another sort of spectator sees – the spectator literally seated in the audience of this play. What's more, Foucault later notes, Oedipus himself comes to appear as *surplus*; he is in effect the *only* surplus in the play; that which must be gotten rid of for the town to be rid of the plague.[26] This means that the *Oedipus* story is not just a story of truth-finding, but of medicine, and law.[27] The work of deciphering signs is the work, Foucault argues, of *gnōmē*, a kind of knowing that opines, rather than certifies; a kind of knowing that occurs *around*, *about* a disappearing (nearly unintelligible) centre, the centre of power, the *turannos* at the heart of the play – Oedipus's own relationship to (singular) power. The process of *gnomic* knowing, then, if we may play on words here, is one in which knowledge occurs through a sort of feeling-through, a feeling-for, in dramatic terms, a kind of blind groping, the sort Tiresias, the blind seer, also inevitably represents. Oedipus does not exactly instantiate the sort of blind knowing-by-groping that Tiresias portrays, but a sort of knowing in the empty middle between Tiresias's cryptic, seer-like prophecy, and Creon's power as representative of the people (as Foucault notes, Creon is remarkable for being *both* a figure of power *and* – unlike Oedipus – not responsible for the exercise of this power; he is simultaneously an *archon*, at the forefront of civic life, and a go-between, ultimately not responsible for civic decisions). Oedipus then is blind, but in a position of power (of decision-making). His singular occupation of this space renders him *turannos*, tyrannical, not in the sense that he exercises power unjustly, but rather that he exercises a singular sort of rule, from which he himself is not exempt, it is so total. In effect, the story of *Oedipus the King* is that of Oedipus's extraction of himself from power, his own elimination, the liquidation of himself as surplus.

Oedipus then becomes a principle of disappearance, enabled by slave narratives and the difficult-to-decipher gods' power. As a ruler between slaves and gods, he vanishes, at the point where speech meets truth. In other words, his rule can only take place where there is a hovering and indeterminacy between truth and lies. Power only occurs – it only takes place, it can only be enacted, inhabited, played out – where there is a zone of indeterminacy by which truth and lies are in a process of negotiation. As soon as the certainty of truth comes to light, by a magical sort of alignment of slave-speech and god-utterance, power vanishes. It is shown only to have been an effigy, a mirage, a temporary zone of indeterminacy, never autonomous. The *turannos* is a slave to circumstance. Though Oedipus insists that he himself came from nowhere – he was (he thought) a foundling – and rose to power by virtue of the gods' good will, he ends up even less than a foundling. He has doubled back on himself, and unbecome the ruler, by his own decree. Yet it was not his decree, he himself yet again only decreed what a physician would to rid the town of plague, by virtue of divine prophecy. He was an agent in a series of operations, never a free agent, hardly a spectator, but spectated from the wings. He continues to be spectated as the play unfolds, and we see him following a course of action that could (it seems) only have been so, and yet which enacts a whole series of contingencies by which aspects of truth – and falsehoods, fabrications, fictions – are brought together into light. The puzzle appears *as puzzle*, that is, as something that had to have been put together, for another set of events to emerge. This other set of events is the same set of events that had always (it seems) been there to unfold, yet which were not visible as such.

So the story of Oedipus is a story of truth evacuating itself, and its unwitting bearer. The power of the ruler is temporary; it is a vessel. The king is a midwife. He never knows what he births, nor is he a creative principle. Creation itself is a combination of forces, and factors, and modes of speech. There remains the question of the slave. If Oedipus himself, as Foucault notes, is surplus, the slave, Foucault adds, is instrumental in the confirmation of the gods' cryptic proclamations. The slave is clarity, prosaity, speech devoid of ornamentation or poetry; speech that says what it sees. The slave's speech is pure speech, speech devoid of innuendo, or falsehood. The slave represents the total symbiosis of seeing and saying, and so too of *alētheia*. This is not the *alēthourgia* of truth's appearance (as process) but the arrival into the light of truth; of truth as arrival. Truth, with the slave's speech, is not masked; it is not mask or unmasking. Truth with the slave is (in Souleymane Bachir Diagne's terms) a process of *co-naissance*, or knowledge born together, born simultaneously; a perfect summation of 'eye-reason' and 'embrace-reason', further borrowing from Leopold Sédar Senghor, for whom, following vitalist philosopher Henri Bergson, knowing is a process of intermixture by which the Dionysian and the Apollonian, the rational and the intuitive, meet, to birth 'truth' as something simultaneously seen and felt.

If we stretch at the edges of Foucault's reading of truth processes in the Oedipus story, we arrive at a concept of Négritude as articulated by Senghor, further reflected upon by Diagne, by which masking implies a certain rhythm and rhythmicity, the adjacence of parts, the congruence of lines (or vectors of seeing, hearing, feeling) – ultimately and profoundly aesthetic, but as such also philosophical – by which parts of the world come together as mixture. What this means is that knowledge emerges, contrapuntally, contiguously, when parts of a mask are shown to be aligned rhythmically, in other words to engage a temporal and spatial relationship that transcends or supersedes, that steps to the side of linear, logical processes of veridiction. The *gnomic* knowledge which Oedipus engages in order to arrive, obliquely, at the truth he was unable to see frontally, full-on, face-forward, but to arrive at from the sidelines, as it were, contrasts dramatically, dramaturgically, with the technical knowledge, the 'art of arts' or *tekhnē tekhnēs* that, Foucault submits, comes to define political power as power of bureaucratic procedure, veridiction by way of calculation, accounting, government over others (rather than around oneself).

With Oedipus, then, we have a contrast between a sort of knowledge of oneself, what truly interests Foucault (the *self*-knowledge engaged in the autotelic process of veridiction, and of *alethurgy*), which takes place by dancing around the centre, the disappearing cone of power; and a knowledge over others, which is – we must understand it this way – always blind, always unable to see what it rules over, and therefore mobilises whole contingencies of others, a whole (Oedipal) machine by which veridiction will take place as bureaucracy, as government. Governing, then, we must be given to understand, takes place – as power – blindly, where the truth of the governing person is something that has to arise in the dark, in the wings, circuitously, in solitude, piecing together what one cannot otherwise arrive at, paradoxically, in the light.

The process of knowledge is always a process of arriving-at, in Bergsonian terms, an intuition that tends-towards and is therefore a vital process, a process of life becoming what it has the potential to be. For Senghor, this was the duality between

poet and statesman that would enable him to become on the one hand a writer of
Négritude and on the other – not contradictorily – a proponent of the fluidity and
mixture, of the movement of thought and of bodies that enables recognition, Diagne
notes, that all cultures – Greek included – are also Black, also mixed, also intercultural
and interracial.[28] That any myth of purity exceeds this understanding, and must be
evacuated as surplus; that the cultural life of nations is mixed, moving. And that a
state, to be a state, must also be a recipient of and host to others, a space of circulation, of darkening and lighting; and that it has always been this way. The idea that
there would have been an Oedipus not defiled is the myth that has to be evacuated for
another order of things to take place, an order in which we are given to understand – as
spectators – that truth-making appears by way of vectors of sight shifting, so that none
merely takes the place of another. There is not one Oedipus, then another Oedipus; nor
is there solely a singular Oedipus. Rather, Oedipus is a doubling, chasing after his own
shadow, the knowledge of himself that came before and catches up to where he is now.
The evanescence of noon. The whole order of the world is to be engaged in a constant
process of surrogation and displacement, even while new hegemons are being put into
place to stand in for the old, never entirely standing in for them; always displacing the
notion of hegemony in the process.

Foucault writes in 'The Masked Philosopher' that he prefers a world in which
no one is named; he prefers the fantasy of writing without reputation, without that
which came before.[29] To be, in a sense, always present; always in a process of *appearing*,
of coming into the light; of *alēthourgia*. Making truth is a more dynamic and vital
process than holding truth and proclaiming it (or being believed to be proclaiming
it). The actual work of philosophy in this regard is theatrical: it is to be masked; and
for the language to reveal itself in spite of one's persona, one's face. Foucault argues
that this is the very process of truth-revealing that characterises nearly all cultures, in
which truth is revealed in dreams: precisely, the revelation is important – it is believ-
able – paradoxically when it does *not* come from the (waking) mouth (or mind) of
the person to whom it arrives. In other words, truth is a process that arrives circuitously, as through a prophetic vessel. It might be a dream; it might be a witness; what
matters is that the word, the message, comes as if in spite of the person bearing it. That
person recognises and receives the truth, though he or she is not always able to interpret it. Truth, then, is a series of operations according to which linguistic and symbolic
displacements move knowledge along until it can come properly to light as such. The
theatre, in this perspective, is a machine for making truth appear through the mouths
of others. The theatre then is Oedipal; or, Oedipus is theatrical; both instantiate a series
of displacements whose being-toward-truth is to hide and shift and move, in short to
choreograph a set of dislocations by which something else can appear, something that
is not properly singular or even human.

So what then is this 'truth' that appears through and in spite of the many masks
worn by characters, none of whom holds the truth, but only shards, *sumbola*,
pieces of the whole? It is an empty middle, the black hole around which power is
organised.

Here then is where Négritude – as a philosophy of purity *and* intermixture – and
anarchism – as a philosophy of self-organisation *and* chaos – comes to stand in for

the vacuum left in power's wake. As a philosophy of convergence, bilingualism, and displacement, in Senghor and Diagne's terms (different, of course, from the essentialist philosophies by which Négritude has come more often to be known), Négritude signals a process of dislocation, translation, and rearticulation by which Africa comes to mean something alongside of, contemporaneous with, and co-knowledgeable of (*co-naissant*, in Diagne's terms) ancient Greece, the 'West', Europe, America, all these places and principles that nineteenth-century anthropology submitted as *knowing of* the unknowable, dark, and absent other, 'primitive' Africa as a place before speech or reason. Négritude, then, as a force of recombination, sheds light on whole processes of intermixture – reason and emotion, rhythm and line – according to which knowing is also art-making, and this art, Diagne argues, signals an aesthetic philosophy that articulates vital principles, movement and flux. Art is not a representation of something else; masks are not ethnological objects to be apprehended as other; but rather, the representation of 'art' in and as African philosophy, Diagne submits, enables a concept of self, society, history, by which – in Bergsonian terms – movement-towards knowing implies a constant shift in perspective. If we take this as a premise for all knowing, as the circuitous – the choreographic – route by which one arrives at something, together (*co-naissance*), one is born with another; then Africa is not prior to Greece; nor is Greece prior to Africa. Oedipus is not prior to himself. Jean-Paul Sartre, who wrote paternalistically of Négritude in his notorious preface to Senghor's era-defining *Anthologie de la nouvelle poésie nègre et malgache: de langue française* (*Anthology of New Negro and Malagasy Poetry in the French Language*) (1948), is not explaining Négritude in terms of communist revolt, the people's international movement, workers' rights; but rather, he is presenting a view of his time *with* that of Senghor's, as its (paternalistic, appropriating, overwriting) participant.[30] Jean-Paul Sartre's piece of the (Oedipal) puzzle is to write himself in as having a certain knowledge, knowledge in this case of his own (supposed) distance, superiority, ability to synthesise and to explain. At the same time, in writing this piece of the story – this *sumbolon* – Sartre is opening up a space of dislocation, as Senghor, Aimé Césaire, and others would emerge telling another, contrary and complementary story, in which Africa is not catching up to Europe, nor prior; neither of the song and the body, nor of another, learned literature (a French that is borrowed); but rather co-creating, co-temporally a version of reality that shifts the entire era, entering into a new ocular and oracular relation to truth and language, art and history. Pablo Picasso would shift the perspective of faces on his canvases, rendering them just like masks; Gertrude Stein would appear herself as a recomposed character in Picasso's work; Guillaume Apollinaire, Arthur Rimbaud, and others would all in different ways borrow from, reconfigure, and speak back to rhythms, shapes, narratives, fantasies, just as Senghor, Césaire, and others on the Left Bank in Paris rewrote themselves in relation to the philosophies and literatures they encountered. This does not deny a history of violent oppression, of colonialism, and of the sort of paternalism that marks Sartre's preface to Senghor's work. But seeing the history of cultural intermixture from the perspective of a disappearing centre, an Oedipal black hole, a set or series of enigmas, a process of *alethurgy* according to which 'truth' only *appears* procedurally through interlocking mechanisms, we can begin to reconfigure the standard narrative according to which the history of the West is troubled, enriched, shifted, or expanded by its encounter with a version of Africa in the twentieth century, for example; or Africa is mimicking, catching up to, or in some way contaminating some mythically pure white European West. Instead, as Susan Buck-Morss notes of Hegel's intimate intellectual engagement with the history of the Haitian revolution at the time of his writing on phenomenology, the master-slave dialectic, and the rest, histories are co-constitutive, unthinkable without the other, and unrecoverable without whole series of operations by which various forms of thinking and seeing *come to light* – even if they remain, for centuries, obscured.[31] What this means with regard to Foucault's notion of Oedipus – a notion, as he puts it, playfully, self-mockingly, 'ultra-aggressively and bluntly positivist', a positivism he punishes himself for, unwittingly, by forgetting, as he says, his copy of *Oedipus* at home on the last day of his series of lectures on this play – is that Oedipus signals a transcultural moment of encounter and reinscription. Oedipus is not 'Greek' but African, Oriental, Western, and none of these things. The notion of *Oedipus* is a notion that puts into play a whole set of procedures for knowing and speaking about something that seems to be of the 'West', for example; of messages, crypticism, but that is also, as I argued at the start of this chapter, full of the sort of magic, the hidden knowledge, the symbolism and the many voices characteristic of a polyvocal, pluralistic, and pre-logocentric (or alter-logocentric) version of knowledge it is nonetheless meant, so often, to represent.

Oedipus then stands as a cypher, something to be decrypted; something that is in itself a code. It appears to be the ultimate sign of Western tragedy, and psychoanalysis; of power and fate. But the story only comes to take the place of a set of epistemological operations by which we can come to know a version of ourselves – whoever that 'ourselves' may be. And this is precisely the point. Reading *Oedipus* forces consideration of whole sets of emanations by which this story comes to stand in for an asepticised version of the West that takes it as its ur-sign. Yet in coming angularly, ocularly and oracularly, rhythmically, and perhaps choreographically to read it again, with oblique and circuitous reference to other works, other worlds, we may come to see that *Oedipus* is a cypher for epistemic procedures that elude linearity, genealogy. We must read *Oedipus* at an angle, taking a side route; through other eyes; as a clue to finding straight speech and impossible, unintelligible utterances. This is not because *Oedipus* holds the key to all *alēthourgia*, all making-appearing of truth; but because in the set of operations by which we may come to read in this case Foucault's reading of *Oedipus*, we are given to look at ourselves reading along, as spectators.

Foucault speaks his lectures, and these are written. He gestures towards the banality of his example, the tired way in which *Oedipus* is so predictable, yet so productive to work with. He apologises for this. And yet in order to mobilise *Oedipus* as a story by which he will work through processes of bureaucratic rationalisation, governmentality by theatrical procedures of truth-making (and truth-making-to-appear, i.e. relative falsification of truth for the purposes of a public narrative), he needs to appear as an amateur reader engaging in the story the play tells for the sake of some other truth, that of thinking about how truth comes to be fashioned then, and so too obliquely now. In this way, working through a dramatic-historical example enables Foucault circuitously to arrive at self-knowledge, which is to say knowledge of the present, as it casts a particular eye on the 'past': a past that is always displaced, fictionalised in its *appearance*. Because what appears on the page of Foucault's transcribed lectures is a reading that brands itself 'ultra-aggressively' 'positivist' and yet in spite of seeming to proceed, frontwards, on a path towards the deployment – the revelation – of an argument – enables the showing of another sort of epistemic procedure. With Foucault, the working-through reveals thinking as a *gnomic* process. The entire history of his lectures is to be always lecturing about something other than what he claims. But in order to arrive at biopolitics, 'the government of the living', or what have you, he takes paths that angularly, rhythmically take him into other relations with the material ostensibly at hand. In this way, Foucault enacts a philosophical process that we may characterise as *paratactic*: it is always moving aside, moving the argument to the side. This is anarchaeological; anti-methodical; anarchic – a proliferation of '*ans*', just as the 'an' is itself displaced through and with the 'para'.

The argument is always putting itself into exile. It proclaims that it requires truth, to banish the plague of non-knowledge, but in doing so it goes on a search for itself, requiring itself to become unknown, shifted, seen from other perspectives. It goes down other paths. And Foucault follows this, becomes as if the midwife to the argument, asking of his audiences for responses they do not give (as he grumbles, confronted with a mountain of tape recorders but no live interlocution). He becomes engaged in a cryptic game of seeking puzzles, but the journey is long and winding; it seems to appear in the light, but it takes place in the dark, a darkness in which he finds himself, but only to extract himself from the equation in the end. He has punished himself, by forgetting his book; by speaking regardless. He wants only to be masked, to disappear – as Foucault. To become no longer Foucault, but something else entirely, without name. Diagne writes of Senghor's drama that he posited a racialism that he then negated entirely; this constituted his originality, also. To be paratactic with regard to oneself, to be rhythmically (like an African mask) at an angle with one's own arguments and prejudices, to be simultaneously positivist and gnomic, that is to enact a drama of truly anarchic thought, thought that has no stable referent, no hegemonic source of or end to power. That is to be *not* at the front, as *archon*, but constantly looking behind and moving aside.

The choreography of this epistemic procedure is crab-like; and endless. It does not vanish on a horizon, but keeps going, keeps shifting. In this way, it is *anti-Oedipus*. There is no way for it to die; there is no surplus that will be expurgated, and the plague ended. And so it is also *Oedipus*; because Oedipus too goes on, his story moves to other planes, other generations. He is intergenerationally, intertribally locked and interlocked. The opposite of Oedipus is not anti-Oedipus, but something else, interstitially. Even between the dialectic of the master and the slave, there is another set of dialectics; these are not just smaller, but utterly other; they move things according to relationships of masking and unmasking, but also (in Diagne's terms, after Senghor) of being the rhythm of the mask; being-with the dance.

Deleuze's lectures on Foucault reveal one thing, among others. Just as Foucault reveals to us (his deferred auditors, his readers) that he left his book, his copy of *Oedipus*, at home, thereby – this is his sign to himself, which he reads for us, to

us – punishing himself, for his positivism, leaving aside – back home – signs that
will never be read, in the 'sign' of this omission, this forgetting, summarised in the
verbal shrug of the shoulders, 'Too bad', Deleuze ventures an observation about a
book Foucault likewise never produced for the public. Foucault, Deleuze tells his
audience, burned the manuscript of a book on Manet, one that might have revealed
an aesthetic philosophy like his book on Magritte (*Ceci n'est pas une pipe*) did, surprising and marginal – to the side – relative to the rest of his *œuvre*. But in these
signs, these proliferations of signs (and asides), there is also a reflection on the surplus of thought, and of thought as surplus. Foucault leaves his book at home. 'Too
bad. Punished!' The thought can go on. This is not necessary thought; these are
not clues, signs, thoughts intrinsic to the lecture taking place. The lecture can, in
effect, continue to take place; it takes (a) place. Borrowing here from Julia Kristeva's
short essay on Stéphane Mallarmé, 'Modern Theater Does Not Take (a) Place' ('Le
théâtre moderne n'a pas lieu'),[32] what I am seeking to underline is the extent to which
Foucault performs his coming-to-be of thought, his alethurgical process, as a process in which there are no necessary signs, only a gnomic space of reflection around
which thinking steps gingerly, even if it parades in the costume, the garb, the mask
of positivism. Because Foucault is never positivist in his reading, even as he cloaks
himself in this self-reference. He does not seek to display a provable answer, a verifiable reading, but instead shifts the locus of reading constantly, over to Septimus, first
of all; then back to governmentality, by way of Luxemburg, Solzhenitsyn, fleetingly;
he is always talking of 'showy garbs', the 'showy garb' of power; power engaged in
the 'play of light and shadow, truth and error, true and false, hidden and manifest,
visible and invisible'.[33]

Foucault himself offers his thinking as such a play of contrasts, in effect just what
Diagne, after Senghor, calls the aesthetic philosophy of the African mask: not because
there is an essential being to the mask, something behind it – prior, more primitive,
which it would reveal – some 'essence towards which masks and sculptures point',
indeed some 'Africanity to be retrieved and examined'.[34] Instead, combinations of
lines, parts and limits, jostling on the surface of the (African) mask, produce enjoyment, 'enjoyment [...] derived [...] from an experience of limits and from the trans-
mutation of the fear of seeing unity lost [...] into the surprise of sensing that the work
has found "means to weld the contrasting themes together by some note common to
both"', in the words of Paul Guillaume and Thomas Munro, whose work on *Primitive
Negro Sculpture* (1926, translated into French in 1929 as *La sculpture nègre primitive*) Senghor read closely.[35] The aesthetic enjoyment trumps – but in effect also
becomes – the work of philosophy, of meaning-making, of truth-forging, as a play of
lines, rhythms, contrasts, meetings that appear about to fall off course, but that come
together, affirming more unity in this disunity than any ostensibly harmonious play
of proportions might. Because what is harmony here? Harmony is a set of valleys
and dips, a 'complete visual music', in Guillaume and Munro's terms, again; a play of
distribution, shocks, ridges, roughened hollows, alternating with smoother intervals;
a play of repetitions, brought together under the unity of design which appears as
such almost as an afterthought and an aftershock, as if it had to be this way, yet the

serendipity of the parts is equally overwhelming.[36] The craft appears to be no craft at all. If the 'Hellenic' is a myth, and the Dionysian and the Apollonian, for Senghor, are equally Hellenic and African; equally emotional and rational; then *Oedipus the King* instantiates just such a mysterious play of intermixture, of lines meeting and failing to meet, then appearing to become united, inevitably, masterfully, as if in after-thought … and aftershock … as if by design, but the design is not god-given, it is of the moment, of the craftsman, of a *tekhnē tekhnēs* (an art of arts) that is not bureau-cratic, procedural, governmental, operational, but contingent, serendipitous, nearly impulsive, intuitive, *life-forming*; it is of the aside and the street corner; of the café, the agora, rather than the cell block, though it may also take place in a cell block, where an encounter is formed, furtively, even under the watchful eye of the guard, a guard who may himself later take part in the process of speaking, of saying and seeing, not because he has knowledge, but because – as a slave himself – he is given to see, and the set of signs that are pieced together according to a whole series of contin-gent effects makes it appear *as truth*, a violent truth often, inasmuch as it aligns with nothing more than itself, its own position as the prose corresponding to the enigmatic (lawful) utterance of the 'god'. This violent, apparently casual, speech act – speech as if only speaking – articulating a whole series and set of shapes and colours operating as if temporary custodians of the truth, is properly tyrannical. I have sought to show this theatre of *holding* truth – as if off to the side – constitutes the masked face(s) of power, by which power operates, interstitially, between fictions of truths and fictions of lies. The lie revealed as such is only a process of truth-appearing (an alethurgical process) itself: it shows that this is a lie, and that, and that; but that showing (that theatre) deploys only the power of alignment. As a midwife to truth, a temporary cus-todian, the guard stands to the side of what comes to be represented as a path – as the *only possible path* – just as he instantiates the process of framing it, of ascertaining its viability (and its validity), of verifying that by which it procedurally comes to 'light'. Tragically, paradoxically, that by which it does so is the act of *walking down it only*. Truth appears when one walks down a path that is lighted by those who see for (in the feet of) others. *Oedipus = swollen feet*. His eyes are not lacking, it is his feet that suffer from their own surplus, their own excess of 'sign'. He is forced to share the task of walking *along*.

This very old notion of philosophy – the recovery of something prior – conjugates poorly with Deleuze and Guattari's notion of philosophy as a creation of concepts, an aesthetic act, a formation of a new life.[37] Yet as we have seen, as I hope to have shown, concept formation itself is dramatic and dramaturgical; it proceeds along an uncertain path, as if to discover the design that had always already been there, but whose ritual making-bare (whose *alēthourgia*) it is the audience's particular pleasure to enjoy in the unfolding.

The masked philosopher treads like Oedipus uncertainly; but we watch his walking, his dance. In that, we are complicitous; we are his (unwitting) guards. Our eyes are to his feet what Oedipus himself is to his city: too much, the book that was better left at home. Foucault said it: 'Punished!' The 'tragedy' is only that he will (have to) keep walking along. In his stumbling, he will find another patch of half-light.

Notes

1 Michel Foucault, *On the Government of the Living: Lectures at the Collège de France, 1979–1980*, ed. Michel Senellart, gen. eds. François Ewald and Alessandro Fontana, English series ed. Arnold I. Davidson, trans. Graham Burchell (Basingstoke: Palgrave Macmillan, 2014), p. 47.

2 Gregory L. Ulmer, 'The Object of Post-Criticism', in Hal Foster (ed.), *The Anti-Aesthetic: Essays on Postmodern Culture* (New York: The New Press, 1998 [1983]), pp. 83–110.

3 See Kélina Gotman, 'Foucault, *Aufklärung* and the Historical "Scene"', *parallax* 24.1 (2018), 45–61.

4 Souleymane Bachir Diagne, *African Art and Philosophy: Senghor, Bergson and the Idea of Negritude*, trans. Chike Jeffers (London: Seagull, 2011 [2007]).

5 Brady Heiner has offered a thorough analysis of Foucault's close involvement with the Black Panther Party (BPP) in Brady T. Heiner, 'Foucault and the Black Panthers', *City* 11.3 (2007), 313–56. Interestingly, Heiner sees Foucault's move from archaeological analysis to genealogical critique as influenced by the BPP, much as Behrooz Ghamari-Tabrizi argues that Foucault's radical move from genealogy to critique was influenced by his formative encounter with the 1979 Revolution in Iran – and the painful critical debacle that ensued – in *Foucault in Iran: Islamic Revolution after the Enlightenment* (Minneapolis: University of Minnesota Press, 2016). In both these cases, Foucault's work is seen to operate contrapuntally with and in relationship to political and ethical histories and relationships taking place in the backstage spaces and 'scenes' of everyday life, at times just off the critical stage, yet saturating it fundamentally. It is the dramaturgy of this broader 'context' (or scenography) that I engage with here. On Iran, see Nicholls (this volume) and Gotman 'Foucault, *Aufklärung* and the Historical "Scene"'.

6 Fred Moten, *In the Break: The Aesthetics of the Black Radical Tradition* (Minneapolis: University of Minnesota Press, 2003), pp. 28–30.

7 Foucault, *On the Government of the Living*, p. 79.

8 Ibid., p. 76.

9 Foucault writes that 'the first definition of critique' would be this: 'the art of being not so governed' ('Et je proposerais donc, comme toute première définition de la critique, cette caractérisation générale: l'art de n'être pas tellement gouverné'). In Michel Foucault, 'Qu'est-ce que la critique?', in Foucault, *Qu'est-ce que la critique? suivi de La culture de soi*, ed. Henri-Paul Fruchaud and Daniele Lorenzini (Paris: Vrin, 2015), pp. 33–80 (p. 37).

10 Foucault, *On the Government of the Living*, p. 76.

11 Ibid.

12 Ibid., p. 6. In fact Foucault began his reflection on the Oedipus story at the end of his 1970–71 series of lectures at the Collège de France, *Leçons sur la volonté de savoir* (Lectures on the Will to Know), and returned to it periodically in the decade following. See, for example, 'Le savoir d'Œdipe', in Michel Foucault, *Leçons sur la volonté de savoir. Cours au Collège de France, 1970–1971. Suivi de Le savoir d'Œdipe*, ed. Daniel Defert, gen. eds. François Ewald and Alessandro Fontana (Paris: Seuil/Gallimard, 2011), pp. 225–51; and 'La vérité et les formes juridiques' ('Truth and Juridical Forms') in *Dits et Écrits, vol. II, 1976–1988*, ed. Daniel Defert and François Ewald with Jacques Lagrange (Paris: Gallimard, 2001), pp. 538–646. For a detailed account of Foucault's returns to the Oedipus story in his writing on knowledge and governmentality, see *On the Government of the Living*, p. 43n2. Whereas Foucault's writing on the (psychoanalytic) Oedipus complex, and to some extent Gilles Deleuze and Félix Guattari's anti-Freudian reading of the Oedipus complex in *Capitalisme et schizophrénie* have received some scholarly attention, Foucault's writing on the Oedipus drama remains uncharted. On Foucault's reading of the psychoanalytic Oedipus complex as a continuation of (psychiatric) disciplinary power in the institution of the modern bourgeois family, see, for example, Mauro Basaure, 'Foucault and the "Anti-Oedipus movement": Psychoanalysis as Disciplinary Power', *History of Psychiatry* 20.3 (2009), 340–59.

13 Foucault, *On the Government of the Living*, p. 6.

14 Michel Foucault, 'Preface', in Gilles Deleuze and Félix Guattari, *Anti-Oedipus: Capitalism and Schizophrenia*, trans. Robert Hurley, Mark Beem, and Helen R. Lane (Minneapolis and London: University of Minnesota Press, 1983), pp. xi–xiv (p. xii).

15 'La voix de Gilles Deleuze enligne', www2.univ-paris8.fr/deleuze/article.php3?id_article=403, accessed 29 April 2016.

16 Foucault, *On the Government of the Living*, pp. 1–3.

17 Ibid., p. 30.

18 Foucault, *Security, Territory, Population: Lectures at the Collège de France, 1977–1978*, ed. Michel Senallert, gen. eds. François Ewald and Alessandro Fontana, English series ed. Arnold I. Davidson, trans. Graham Burchell (New York: Palgrave McMillan, 2007), pp. 15–23.

19 Foucault, *On the Government of the Living*, p. 7.

20 Ibid., p. 15.

21 Gilles Deleuze, 'Postscript on the Societies of Control', *October* 59 (1992), 3–7.

22 Alenka Zupančič, *The Shortest Shadow: Nietzsche's Philosophy of the Two* (Cambridge, MA: MIT Press, 2003), p. 27.

23 Foucault, *On the Government of the Living*, pp. 37–8.

24 Ibid., pp. 36ff.

25 Paul Gilroy, *The Black Atlantic: Modernity and Double Consciousness* (Cambridge, MA: Harvard University Press, 1993), p. 76.

26 Foucault, *On the Government of the Living*, pp. 66–7.

27 Ibid., p. 57.

28 See especially Diagne, *African Art as Philosophy*, pp. 196–8. See, for example, Léopold Sédar Senghor, 'Grèce antique et Négritude', in *Liberté 5: Le Dialogue des Cultures* (Paris: Éditions du Seuil, 1993), pp. 43–5.

29 Michel Foucault, 'The Masked Philosopher', in Foucault, *Ethics: Subjectivity and Truth*, ed. Paul Rabinow, trans. Robert Hurley and others (New York: The New Press, 1997), pp. 321–8.

30 Jean-Paul Sartre, 'Orphée noir', in Léopold Sédar Senghor, *Anthologie de la nouvelle poésie nègre et malgache: de langue française* (Paris: Quadrige/PUF, 1948), pp. ix–xliv. See also Diagne, *African Art as Philosophy*, pp. 21–32ff.

31 Susan Buck-Morss, *Hegel, Haiti, and Universal History* (Pittsburgh, PA: University of Pittsburgh Press, 2009).

32 Julia Kristeva, 'Le théâtre moderne n'a pas lieu', *34/44 Cahiers de recherche de S.T.D., Spécial Théâtre* 3 (1977/1978) Université Paris VII, 13–16. Published in English as Julia Kristeva, 'Modern Theater Does Not Take (A) Place', trans. Alice Jardine and Thomas Gora, *SubStance*, Vol. 6/7, no. 18/19 (1977/1978), 131–4.

33 Foucault, *On the Government of the Living*, p. 17.

34 Diagne, *African Art as Philosophy*, p. 58.

35 Ibid., pp. 56ff, 67. See Paul Guillaume and Thomas Munro, *Primitive Negro Sculpture* (New York: Harcourt, Brace, 1926).

36 Diagne, *African Art as Philosophy*, p. 67.

37 Gilles Deleuze and Félix Guattari, *Qu'est-ce que la philosophie?* (Paris: Les éditions de minuit, 1993).

5

Foucault's critical dramaturgies

Mark Robson

What does it mean to think of the work of Michel Foucault in terms of what I am calling here critical dramaturgy? There might appear to be a certain redundancy in underlining the critical, since from as early as Lessing's *Hamburgische Dramaturgie* (1767–79), the critical dimension of dramaturgy has been insistently reinforced. For Lessing, it is necessary not only to think through the ways in which a piece of theatre is structured and achieves its effects, but also to examine the context for the piece, including the wider social role of theatre itself. It is not accidental that the most frequent reference in Lessing is to Aristotle, and one of the aims of the *Hamburg Dramaturgy* is essentially philological, namely, to defend Aristotle from the classical French theatre and a conception of tragedy that claims the *Poetics* as its theoretical underpinning.[1] Dramaturgy in Lessing's terms involves a double movement, then, in which a given theatrical performance has to be viewed critically, but equally theatre might possess a critical social function of its own. What Lessing's project reveals most clearly is the division at its heart, figured in the playing off of one interpretation of Aristotle against another, each claiming critical and creative validity.

If dramaturgy is in part conceived as a critique of particular theatrical works and their context, then it equally necessitates a thinking of the nature of theatre and theatricality. What I am interested in here is both the kind of analysis that dramaturgy is or might be, and how it may be translated into ways of thinking and forms of explanation that draw upon conceptions of theatre for their articulation. What, for example, is the force of the recurrent invocations of theatre, theatricality, stage, scene, act, and so on, within critical thought? It is not clear that these uses are simply metaphorical, and neither is there anything simple about the relation between theatre and metaphor.

I am intrigued to see how Foucault's work – while being susceptible to a dramaturgical analysis – might also offer the opportunity to rethink aspects of dramaturgy itself. What happens to conceptions of dramaturgy when placed alongside Foucault's adoption of an investigation into the 'history of systems of thought', the title he chose for his Chair at the Collège de France, for example? The insistence that there are systems of thought, but equally that these systems are necessarily contingent, might offer routes into thinking the potentiality that is always both actualised and never exhausted by a specific production. Following Foucault, looking at the specific configuration of a performance can be a way of opening it up to its wider systemic ramifications. The model here might be Foucault's analysis of the 'work', exemplified in this comment on authorship:

> It is a very familiar thesis that the task of criticism is [...] to analyse the work through its structure, its architecture, its intrinsic form, and the play of its internal relationships. At this point, however, a problem arises: 'What is a work? What is this curious unity which we designate as a work? Of what elements is it composed?'[2]

This opening out of the structural analysis of the object to a questioning of the onto-logical status of the work might also be related to what Foucault says in *The Archaeology of Knowledge*:

> the *œuvre* itself, will not be the same in the case of the author of *Le Théâtre et son Double* (Artaud) and the author of the *Tractatus* (Wittgenstein), and therefore when one speaks of an *œuvre* in each case one is using the word in a different sense. The *œuvre* can be regarded neither as an immediate unity, nor as a certain unity, nor as a homogeneous unity.[3]

In both of these quotations, it is unity that is at stake, and it is clear how far this is from the Aristotle of the classicists.

Alternatively, one might take Foucault's definition of power in *The History of Sexuality*. Famously, Foucault dethrones a model in which sovereign power is exercised from above, imposed by an act of will and reinforced through violence, such as the spectacles of torture in *Discipline and Punish*. In its place, Foucault offers a description in which power is relational, involving every element in the system as productive, and as such:

> Power is everywhere [*Le pouvoir est partout*]; not because it embraces everything [*il englobe tout*], but because it comes from everywhere [*il vient de partout*] [...] power is not an institution, and not a structure, neither is it a certain strength we are endowed with [*une certaine puissance dont certains seraient dotés*: the English misses the restriction here in the French, referring to a potency that only some of us – *certains* – might possess: Foucault's point is that all are implicated]; it is the name that one attributes to a complex strategical situation in a particular society'.[4]

In both cases here, an apparently unified structure – whether the work or sover-eignty – is shown to be riven by an internal division or self-differentiation. This con-cern for division rather than unity is already apparent in Foucault's earliest work. In his introduction to Foucault's *History of Madness*, Jean Khalfa speaks of the nature of Foucault's move from phenomenology to structuralism, seeing his treatment of madness as indicative of that methodological shift. Unlike the majority of those who have tackled madness as a topic, says Khalfa, Foucault does not write the history of a disease:

Rather, in order to grasp what is no longer directly accessible, it is the history of the gesture of *partage*, division, separation, through each of its moments, incarnations or *figures*, to use the Hegelian vocabulary so present throughout the book (and still so dominant in French philosophy at the time of its writing) to describe a process of division through which a reality splits into radically different parts until a new realisation takes place, a synthesis which in itself is a new reality.[5]

The usefulness of the term *partage* lies precisely in its contradictory senses, at once indicating division, separation, and so on, and, on the other hand, sharing and sharing-out, the common, the intra-subjective (which can also mean the non-subjective). In Khalfa's description of the project of Foucault's *History of Madness*, *partage* becomes the means by which reality transforms itself in a movement of dialectical synthesis that rests on exclusion. Reality may be divided into radically different parts in an unstable relation that demands to be repeatedly remade, since the new reality that emerges is itself determined by and as an exclusion, even if what is excluded from this new reality, or the mode by which an exclusion is repeated, differs. Read in this way, says Khalfa, the project retains a Hegelian structure, even if Foucault is certainly not wedded to a notion of spirit, historical determinism, or essentialism. Foucault's later sense of his own work is of one focused not on conceptual determination (as in Hegel) or material determination (as in Marx), but instead on the structures of particular practices as contingent.[6] As he puts it in the interview published as 'Questions of Method', his historical work is centred on *singularity* rather than continuity, and its primary targets are, first, that which is presented as self-evident and, second, explanations that assert a necessity to the structures that emerge. For Foucault, there were and must remain other possibilities. Analysis of any 'regime of practices' depends on seeing practices as 'places where what is said and what is done, rules imposed and reasons given, the planned and the taken-for-granted meet and interconnect' ('*les pratiques étant considérées comme le lieu d'enchaînement de ce qu'on dit et de ce qu'on fait, des règles qu'on s'impose et des raisons qu'on se donne, des projets et des évidences*').[7] In the displacement of the subject, there is also a parallel refusal to anthropomorphise necessity under the name of 'history', logic, nature, and so on. The term *partage* is useful here, I would suggest, because it is analogous to the structures of dramaturgy, allowing for the recognition of the disparate elements that are woven together in a production but without producing a false sense of unification and totality. Contemporary dramaturgies stress the dispersal of a privilege of the text, without forging a false reconciliation of the elements of the mise-en-scène.[8]

I am not the first to think of Foucault's texts as guided by a form of dramaturgy, and the word is explicitly used by Daniel Defert in his contextualisation of the *Lectures on the Will to Know*.[9] First he refers to a 'secret dramaturgy' organising the lectures and then speaks of Foucault 'abandoning the Hegelian dramaturgy with its share of negativity'.[10] If Hegel still haunts *The History of Madness*, then by the end of the 1960s Foucault has lost the drive towards synthesis.[11] Defert insists on the importance of Deleuze's *Difference and Repetition* for the shaping of Foucault's thinking at this time (broadly 1969–71). Foucault writes two reviews of the book, the most well-known being 'Theatrum philosophicum' (which also reviews *The Logic of Sense*), and in addition produces the long essay 'Nietzsche, Genealogy, History'. Defert reads these texts as a sequence of translations by Foucault of Deleuze's thought into his own terms, which at this point is genealogical. As Defert notes, notions of origin are replaced by *Entstehung* or emergence. Defining emergence, Defert calls it 'the placeless theater where the same play of dominators and dominated *is repeated*' ('*c'est le théâtre sans lieu où se répète la même pièce des dominateurs et des dominés*').[12] Defert's characterisation picks up on a language of theatre that imposes itself through Foucault's own texts on Deleuze.

In 'Theatrum philosophicum', for example, Foucault suggests that Deleuze's work plays itself out on two stages, metaphysics reconceived in the figure of psychoanalysis, and the theatre. If metaphysics is framed in terms of psychoanalysis, then Foucault's sense of theatre is similarly specified. But specified doesn't necessarily mean clarified. It is worth comparing a couple of existing translations of what Foucault says here, since the French passage raises several problems of interpretation that the attempt to render it in English makes manifest. The translation given in *Aesthetics* runs: 'the theater, which is multiplied, polyscenic, simultaneous, broken into separate scenes that refer to each other, and where we encounter, without any trace of representation (copying or imitating), the dance of masks, the cries of bodies, and the gesturing of hands and fingers'.[13] A modified translation by Graham Burchell is given in *Lectures on the Will to Know*: 'theater, multiplied, polyscenic, simultaneous theater broken up into scenes that ignore each other and signal to each other and where, without any representing (copying, imitating), masks dance, bodies cry, and hands and fingers gesticulate'.[14]

Two obvious divergences in the translations present themselves. First, there is the question of how scenes relate to each other. In one version they refer to each other; in the other, they both ignore and signal to each other. The second variance concerns representation. In the first translation 'we' 'encounter' dances, cries, and gestures without 'any trace' of representation. In the second, there is no need for this 'encounter' nor for this 'we', since the agency is given to the masks, bodies, hands, and fingers, which variously dance, cry, and gesticulate seemingly without an observer.

The text given in *Dits et Écrits* reads: '*le théâtre, le théâtre multiplié, polyscénique, simultané, morcelé en scènes qui s'ignorent et se font signe, et où sans rien représenter (copier, imiter) des masques dansent, des corps crient, des mains et des doigts gesticulent*'.[15] The issue about the relation of scenes rests on the verb *s'ignorer*, which is usually used to indicate a lack of self-knowledge or something unconscious. *Faire signe* might plausibly lead us to referring, since it is often used to say gesture, nod, beckon, and so on, in the literal sense of giving or making a sign. The sentence pulls in two directions as *s'ignorent* and *signe* echo each other in their separation.

For the sentence on representation, it would be preferable to think in terms of nothing (*rien*) being represented – so, 'without representing anything' – rather than with no trace of representation. What Foucault seems to be suggesting here, through the underlining of copying or imitation, is that what he has in mind is *mimesis*. In its multiplicity and fragmentary simultaneity, what is being rejected is any Aristotelian sense of dramatic unity, as well as the (self-)consciousness upon which the unities depend.[16] Just as the work or power are not unified, neither is what Foucault calls theatre.

In part, Foucault is simply drawing on the vision of theatre given by Deleuze, who plays off a 'theatre of repetition' against a 'theatre of representation'.[17] Later in the review, Foucault resonantly suggests that in Deleuze's texts: 'This is philosophy not as thought but as theater – a theater of mime with multiple, fugitive, and instantaneous scenes in which blind gestures signal to each other. This is the theater where the laughter of the Sophist bursts out from under the mask of Socrates'.[18]

My point here is not to highlight possible shortcomings in the existing translations, but rather to indicate that the difficulties of translation at this point are the sign of a broader difficulty in getting the measure of Foucault's conception of theatre. In 'Theatrum philosophicum', Foucault gives this vision of theatre a name: Artaud.[19] It is not difficult to find masks and bodies, cries and gestures in the essays that make up The Theatre and its Double. The name of Artaud is one that appears frequently in Foucault's work, but if this provides a theoretical sense of what theatre might be, there is also a formative theatrical experience.

A country road. A tree. Evening.

In his biography of Jean Genet, Edmund White suggests that: 'For the young Michel Foucault, [Samuel Beckett's Waiting for] Godot was the turning point of his intellectual life […]. Certainly it was the most prestigious intellectual event in Paris in the early 1950s'.[20] The event that White is referring to is Roger Blin's staging of Beckett's play, first performed on 5 January 1953 at the Théâtre de Babylone. The initial reception for the play was somewhat more mixed than White's comments suggest, including fighting among audience members, but it broke box-office records for the Babylone.[21] Roland Barthes writes in the France-Observateur of 10 June 1954 about the extraordinary trajectory of Beckett's play, from supposedly avant-garde piece with a 'natural public of intellectuals and enlightened snobs' to its status at that point as an example of Parisian 'popular theatre'. Barthes states that by mid-1954, Godot had been played around 400 times to a total audience close to 100,000.[22] Barthes also notes how young that audience is, unsurprised because, he says, 'Godot carries within it the specific properties of its time'.[23] Clearly Foucault saw this production rather than knowing the play through the printed text: in 1984, he would refer to it in an interview as 'a breathtaking performance [spectacle]'.[24]

David Macey observes that in the early 1950s Foucault's taste for Beckett – like his admiration for Maurice Blanchot or Friedrich Nietzsche – carried a certain political charge, and was severely at odds with any affiliation to the French communist party (PCF), an association with which he had in fact already become uncomfortable.[25] Foucault was aware of the absurdity of trying to be a 'Nietzschean communist'.[26] Despite his admiration, Foucault was never to write a text centrally devoted to Beckett, but he would echo one of Beckett's prose texts, Molloy, in his inaugural lecture 'L'ordre du discours' at the Collège de France in 1970.[27] In 'Archaeology of a Passion', however, Foucault suggests that the impact of Beckett was not simply a matter of a memorable night at the theatre, and nor was it a question of personal taste, saying that 'J'étais comme tous les étudiants de philo à cette époque-là, la rupture est venue avec Beckett'

('I was like all the philosophy students at that time, the break came with Beckett').[28] Certainly Alain Badiou also testifies to encountering Beckett for the first time in the 1950s, although in his case it seems to have been the prose rather than the theatre works that struck him in an 'incalculable' way.[29]

The 'rupture' arrived for Foucault in a specific context, then, and it was a particular but not personal configuration that Beckett's play disturbed; Foucault belonged, as he puts it himself, to a generation of students who had been enclosed within a certain view of the world. That worldview was composed of a combination of elements of Marxism, phenomenology, and existentialism ('etc.', he says in French, a supplement that drops out of the English version). Similarly, Badiou describes himself at that time (around 1956) as 'a perfect Sartrean'.[30] That intellectual horizon, Foucault suggests, however interesting its elements may have been, also produced in the students immersed in it a feeling of being stifled. It prompted, as Foucault puts it, '*le désir d'aller voir ailleurs*'.[31] This change of perspective, a change not only of what is seen but also of how one sees, is what *Godot* seems to have offered to a generation of Parisian philosopher-spectators.

If Foucault found in Beckett an alternative to the presiding intellectual configuration in Paris, there is an obvious irony in the fact that Beckett quickly became associated with an 'absurd' existentialist worldview, most clearly by Martin Esslin in *The Theatre of the Absurd*, but also noted in Adorno's influential 1958 essay on Beckett's *Endgame*.[32] As Martin Puchner notes, Beckett 'becomes the playwright who captured the absurd without a single philosophical speech – if one discounts Lucky's "thinking" rant in *Waiting for Godot*'.[33]

Foucault's response to theatre cannot be attributed to the experience of seeing Beckett alone. Foucault was also an admirer and later friend of Jean Genet, for example, and became close to Hélène Cixous at Vincennes.[34] Foucault did not write very much directly on theatre and performance, but the theatrical metaphor and the notion of what theatre might stand for (that is, how it can be used as an example or an index of a particular relation) become key to his later texts. I will be looking in particular at the movement towards the idea of the spectacle that will become so central to *Discipline and Punish* (published in 1975), but the traces are already present in his reading of Deleuze.

So what is it that made Beckett's play so striking? One way of answering that would be to rehearse again the by now familiar narratives of Beckett's place in the theatrical culture of post-war Europe. We might look to Harold Pinter's suggestion that it was Beckett rather than John Osborne who took a 'singular' theatrical leap in the 1950s, in particular through the use of a certain kind of theatrical image; Pinter's example is precisely the tree in *Waiting for Godot*.[35] It is equally possible to speculate about the potential appeal of its cyclical structure, its refusal of the dynamics of Aristotelian 'action', its humour coupled with its linguistic flatness, its insistence on the material and the bodily, its refusal to ennoble human suffering, and so on. In light of Foucault's work on prisons, it is striking to recall that Esslin's book on the absurd begins with an account of a performance of Beckett's play at San Quentin prison in 1957 and its extraordinary effect on its more than usually captive audience.[36] Even if Beckett's work represented a break with drama (and literature) as it was conventionally understood in the 1950s, it nonetheless comes in response to that tradition, and the trace of that relation remains readable. It is not an accident that when Hans-Thies Lehmann offers a brief recapitulation of the postdramatic in a recent book, the first example he chooses is Beckett:

> Time and again, it has become clear that theatrical forms and texts which are no longer dramatic operate before the backdrop of dramatic tradition (and this is why they should continue to be discussed as post-*dramatic*). For example, Beckett's pieces abound in references to classical dramatic schemata and neoclassical theatrical conventions.[37]

The trace of tradition at their core is perhaps what makes Beckett's works acceptable both to those seeking the avant-garde and those more attuned to the popular. Beckett's work finds a strange resonance with a generation of philosopher-spectators who would come to desire a philosophical practice that did not remain enclosed within the university and its disciplinary boundaries, who sought and to some extent found a place in the streets as well as in the lecture halls (like Badiou, encouraged by the persona of Sartre, if not ultimately by his thought). The philosophical and the popular come together in the theatre in a double movement of renewal and interruption that might be captured in the divergent senses of the word 'instauration'. I will come back to this later.

'un éclat d'autre'

One thing that Foucault seems to take from theatre is a privilege for what Michel de Certeau identifies as an 'optical style'. Foucault's texts, de Certeau says, are 'cadenced by scenes and figures. *Madness and Civilization* opens with the image of the ship of fools; *The Order of Things*, with Velasquez's "Las Meninas"; *Discipline and Punish*, with the narrative of the torture of Damiens, and so on'.[38] These are images that 'institute' the text, they are 'scenes of a difference', says de Certeau, that is, they are not merely decorative but instead act in a specific way upon the reader-spectator:

> Forgotten systems of reason stir in these mirrors. On the level of the paragraph or phrase, quotes function in the same way; each of them is embedded there like the fragment of a mirror, having the value not of a proof but of an astonishment – a sparkle of other [*un éclat d'autre*]. The entire discourse proceeds in this fashion from vision to vision.[39]

This fragmented mirror is a glittering surface that reveals the astonishment of the reader as spectator, but perhaps not without a certain violence: *un éclat* is both a sparkle and a shard, a splinter, even a burst or a roar (of laughter, as in de Certeau's title), to be *en éclats* is to be shattered, in pieces. These mirror-scenes disrupt two moments, or better, the two moments become juxtaposed and resonate: our astonishment at the strangeness of the past reveals the order of the present, but it also shows the past's ability to resist our vision of and our desire for it. This is not the encroachment of an outside but the anamnesis of a repressed element within our thinking, these astonishing thoughts have been 'forgotten'; they cannot accurately be thought of as 'new' even as they burst through the present. As de Certeau himself asks, is this self-conscious textual staging not odd from a philosopher as attuned to the problems of the visual, of the panoptic, as Foucault? Yes. Yet, he continues,

> the visible constitutes for Foucault the contemporary theater of our fundamental options. It is here that a use of space for policing purposes is confronted by a vigilance attuned to what else happens there. [...] Two practices of space clash in the field of visibility, the one ordered by discipline, the other based on astonishment.[40]

Discipline and astonishment: two forms of vision confront one another in a contemporary theatre marked by a failed unity, attuned to the 'what else'. Is this a metaphor? If so, this recourse to the theatrical figure appears to be something that de Certeau finds in Foucault, as if immanent, imposing itself on de Certeau as a self-reading inscribed in Foucault's texts. The suggestion that this is a matter of spatial practices is one that can be better understood if it is approached through Foucault's thinking on space in terms of utopia and heterotopia.[41]

From representation to spectacle?

> To make a parenthetical remark, I recall having been invited, in 1966, by a group of architects to do a study of space, of something that I called at that time 'heterotopias', those singular spaces to be found in some given social spaces whose functions are different or even the opposite of others. The architects worked on this, and at the end of the study someone spoke up – a Sartrean psychologist – who firebombed me, saying that space is reactionary and capitalist, but history and becoming are revolutionary. This absurd discourse was not at all unusual at the time. Today everyone would be convulsed with laughter at such a pronouncement, but not then.[42]

The Sartrean psychologist-architect embodies precisely the horizon of thought (Marxist-phenomenologist-existentialist) from which Foucault had wished to escape in the 1950s. In 1984, Foucault authorised the publication of this talk, first given on 14 March 1967 to the Cercle d'études architecturales. The lecture 'Des espaces autres', translated as 'Different Spaces', was written in Tunisia during the first months of 1967, and was based on ideas first presented as two radio broadcasts in December 1966.[43]

Foucault begins by differentiating between the nineteenth-century 'obsession' with history (that is, with time), and his own moment: 'The present age may be the age of space [...]. We are in an era of the simultaneous, of juxtaposition, of the near and the far, of the side-by-side, of the scattered'.[44] Like the conception of theatre in 'Theatrum philosophicum', the age of space is multiple, simultaneous, and based on juxtaposition and the side-by-side rather than on unity. This immediately leads Foucault into a definition of structuralism as a species of dramaturgical analysis, that is, as 'the effort to establish, between elements that may have been distributed over time [*répartis à travers le temps*], a set of relations that makes them appear juxtaposed, opposed, implied by one another, that makes them appear, in short, like a kind of configuration'.[45] This spatial configuration has its own specificity, and space is understood not as an abstract concept or category, but as itself having a history.

Contrasting his approach to phenomenology's supposed concern with 'internal' space, Foucault is interested in what he calls 'the space outside', *l'espace du dehors* (so both of and from the outside). He suggests that:

> The space in which we are living, by which we are drawn outside ourselves, in which, as a matter of fact, the erosion of our life, our time, and our history takes place, this space that eats and scrapes away at us [*nous ronge et nous ravine*], is also heterogeneous space in itself. In other words, we do not live in a kind of void, within which individuals and things might be located [*on pourrait situer des individus et des choses*].[46]

Different emplacements have different relations, and these are susceptible to description and analysis. But, he suggests, there are some emplacements that are related to all the others, even as they are at variance with them, and these he names as utopias and heterotopias. He proposes that:

> Utopias are emplacements having no real place [*sans lieu réel*]. They are emplacements that maintain a general relation of direct or inverse analogy with the real space of society. They are society perfected or the reverse [*envers*] of society, but in any case these utopias are spaces that are fundamentally and essentially unreal [*irréels*].[47]

Utopias are unreal, no-places, but they are also models of perfection. In this, Foucault observes both of the possibilities offered by Thomas More's ambiguous term: U-topia is both ideal community (*eu-topos*) and no-place (*ou-topos*). But utopias are stepping stones in his argument, and Foucault continues:

> There are also, and probably in every culture, in every civilization, real places [*lieux réels*], actual places [*lieux effectifs*], places that are designed into the very institution of society, [*et qui sont des sortes de contre-emplacements*, and which are types of counter-emplacements (my translation, subclause missing from *Aesthetics*)] which are sorts of actually realized utopias in which the real emplacements, all the other real emplacements that can be found within the culture are, at the same time, represented, contested, and reversed [*inversées*], sorts of places that are outside all places, although they are actually localizable. Because they are utterly different [*absolument autres*] from all the emplacements that they reflect or refer to, I shall call these places 'heterotopias', as opposed to utopias.[48]

Heterotopias are 'outside' all places, absolutely other emplacements, but localisable.

Foucault offers both a list of places that function as heterotopias and a set of principles for their identification, but one example in particular is relevant here. In exemplifying his third principle, that 'Heterotopias are not unified or internally coherent', he says:

> The heterotopia has the power to juxtapose several spaces in a single real place, several emplacements that are in themselves incompatible. Thus the theatre brings successively onto the rectangle of the stage a whole series of places that are foreign to one another [*étrangers les uns aux autres*].[49]

The places staged are placed in relation, but this does not mean that they are synthesised. Foucault suggests that there are two main forms of this relation:

> Either the heterotopias have the role of creating a space of illusion that denounces all real space, all real emplacements within which human life is partitioned off, as being even more

illusory [...]. Or, on the contrary, creating a different space, a different real space as perfect, as meticulous, as well-arranged as ours is disorganized, badly-arranged, and muddled. This would be the heterotopia not of illusion but of compensation.[50]

A hasty gloss on this passage might be: all the world's a stage, or else, life aspires to the condition of art. But Foucault perhaps intends something much closer to a collapsing of the distinction between world/stage or life/art upon which such a gloss might depend.

Foucault suggests a third term which embodies this complication of the opposition he has established: the mirror. For Foucault:

The mirror, after all, is a utopia, since it is a placeless place [*un lieu sans lieu*]. In the mirror, I see myself where I am not, in an unreal space that opens up virtually behind the surface; I am over there, there where I am not, a kind of shadow that gives me my own visibility, that enables me to look at myself there where I am absent: utopia of the mirror. But it is also a heterotopia, to the extent that the mirror really exists, where it has a sort of return effect on the place that I occupy; due to the mirror, I discover myself absent at the place where I am, since I see myself over there. Due to the look that, in a way, falls on me, from the depth of this virtual space which is the other side of the glass, I come back to myself and I begin once more to direct my eyes towards myself and to reconstitute myself there where I am; the mirror functions as a heterotopia in the sense that it makes this place I occupy at the moment I look at myself in the glass at once both absolutely real, connected with the entire space surrounding it, and absolutely unreal, since it is obliged, in order to be perceived, to go by way of that virtual point which is over there.[51]

The mirror opens up an unreal space while occupying a real space, virtualising the real space in which I stand by allowing me to see myself in a space I know not to be real. (Hamlet's understanding of theatre as a mirror up to nature prefigures this thinking.) I return to myself by seeing my virtual self seeing me in real space. The heterotopic element retains a critical function in relation to the 'real' world precisely by making awareness of the real a function of a return made possible by a passage through the unreal of the utopic. The effect is either to heighten consciousness of the irreality that structures the real – in which the real is revealed as being as illusory as the unreal – or to provide a perfected version of the real, but a version that is only available as a fiction.

This might usefully be read against one of the scenes identified by de Certeau, namely the reading of 'Las Meninas' that opens *The Order of Things*.[52] In describing Velasquez's canonical painting, Foucault's text is suffused with the language of the theatrical: scene, spectacle, figure, stage; he comments on 'the spectacle [that the figures in the painting] are observing,'[53] on 'the other side of the scene,'[54] he tells us 'we must move down again from the back of the picture towards the front of the stage,'[55] and repeatedly the one who views the painting is called 'the spectator'. He concludes that: 'The entire picture is looking out at a scene for which it is itself a scene'),[56] ('*Le tableau en son entier regarde une scène pour qui il est à son tour une scène*').[57] The spectator thus becomes the 'real centre of the scene.'[58] Foucault chooses this painting because it stands in for more than itself, it is the exemplary example. But what it exemplifies is not tied to what it represents alone – if by that we mean its manifest 'content' – but is instead a question of the painting's relation to its own visibility, and thus its relation to its 'spectator'. Foucault speculates:

> It may be that, in this picture, as in all representations of which it is, as it were, the manifest essence, the profound invisibility of what one sees is inseparable from the invisibility of the person seeing – despite all mirrors, reflections, imitations, and portraits.[59]

The painting is and is not like the mirror, that is, it seems to be a mirror that contrives to be both utopic and heterotopic. The play of visibility and invisibility is already a question of where one stands, but where one stands is unplaceable. The illusory depth that the mirror embeds in the scene is projected into the real space of the spectator, but impossibly, since the spectator is unable to become the one who can see herself staring out from that depth. The circle of representation is interrupted, unable to close itself. The attributes that Foucault finds in the painting are those that he finds in theatre, as the insistence in his reading on scene, spectacle, and spectator shows.

Maskwork

In February 1965, Foucault appeared for the first time on French television. The occasion was an interview with a lycée teacher of philosophy who had at that time published a novel, but had yet to make much of a mark on the French philosophical world. The interview was part of a series of educational programmes on philosophy, aimed at a mainstream audience, particularly teachers, but making few concessions to non-specialists. In the course of the discussion, Foucault rehearses ideas which will find fuller expression in *The Order of Things*, published the following year.

In his biography of Foucault, David Macey gives a vivid description of this television performance. It is, says Macey, 'remarkable mainly for the flight of fantasy with which it ends'. Macey's account is as follows:

> Asked what he would teach a philosophy class in a lycée about psychology, [Foucault] said that his first step would be to buy a mask. He would adopt a different voice, 'like Anthony Perkins in *Psycho*', so that 'nothing of the unity of my discourse would be apparent'. He would then give a lucid account of current developments in psychology and psychoanalysis, before abandoning his mask, adopting his usual voice and giving a class on philosophy which would demonstrate that psychology was 'a sort of absolutely inevitable and absolutely fatal impasse in which western thought found itself in the nineteenth century'.[60]

At this point, the film cuts to shots of the Sorbonne, and the end titles begin. There is no record of the reaction of Foucault's interviewer to this unconventional pedagogical proposal, but we can assume that the encounter was largely positive for both participants; five years later, Foucault would select the interviewer, Alain Badiou, as one of the founder members of the newly formed philosophy department at the experimental university, Paris VIII, first established at Vincennes.

So much might be said here about the performative aspects of Foucault's approach to teaching, beginning with the normalisation of philosophy as opposed to a discourse on psychology and psychoanalysis that presents itself masked and with a disguised voice, a voice that Foucault himself compares to that of a fictional cross-dressing psychotic. At this point, Foucault apparently identifies himself primarily as a philosopher of sorts, even if his account of psychology is framed as a historical narrative concerning 'thought' that cannot simply be identified with philosophy. His commentators have subsequently struggled to situate him.[61] Foucault's answer to Badiou's question raises the notion that – contrary to the transdisciplinary and generic insistence of university training courses for new lecturers which empty out disciplinary concerns in order to effect an atomisation of the student body into 'learning styles' at the individual level – different areas of knowledge might require different teaching methodologies. Or rather, that different modes of knowledge demand different modes of staging.[62]

An actor or an acrobat

This sense that teaching might possess a theatrical dimension was not one that Foucault always saw in positive terms. In the text of *L'ordre du discours*, the published version of the inaugural lecture that he gave at the Collège de France on 2 December 1970, Foucault expresses the need to 'fix the terrain [*lieu*] – or perhaps the very provisional theatre – within which I shall be working.'[63] But in a piece published in *Le nouvel observateur* in 1975, the journalist Gérard Petitjean quotes Foucault expressing dissatisfaction with the format that his Collège de France lectures have taken on, in large part due to their popularity:

> It should be possible to discuss what I have put forward. Sometimes, when it has not been a good lecture, it would need very little, just one question, to put everything straight [*pour tout remettre en place*]. However, this question never comes. The group effect in France makes any genuine discussion impossible. And as there is no feedback [*canal de retour*], the course is theatricalized [*se théâtralise*]. My relationship with people there is like that of an actor or an acrobat. And when I have finished speaking, a sensation of total solitude.[64]

There is already a sense of dramaturgy here in the desire *pour tout remettre en place*, the desire for an ordering of space and of relation. But here to be theatricalised is negative, it implies a closure or enclosure, a mediation that ruptures any rapport between lecturer-performer and audience. The philosopher-performer is less comfortable than the philosopher-spectator with the presence of a crowd. The rupturing mediation is literal. Petitjean describes the rush to the front of the lecture hall when Foucault stops. The students descend on the podium, however, not to speak to Foucault but instead to collect their cassette recorders.[65] This reinforces the peculiar situation of the Collège de France. In effect, there are no students at the lectures, only auditors, and there is less concern among those who attend for the co-presence with Foucault than for a 'textual' remainder of that (missed) event. Such, at least, is the sense conveyed by Petitjean's presentation of Foucault's feelings.

There is a curious echo of this scene in Hans-Thies Lehmann's *Postdramatic Theatre*, which ends with an epilogue that draws out some conclusions from his claim that the dramatic impulse in Western culture has been exhausted to the point of disappearance. Lehmann suggests:

> It is apparent that the decline of the dramatic is by no means synonymous with the decline of the theatrical. On the contrary: theatricalization permeates the entire social life, starting with the individual attempts to produce or feign a *public self* [öffentliches Ich] […]. If we add advertising, the self-staging of the business world and the theatricality of mediated self-presentation [*Selbstdarstellung*] in politics, it seems that we are witnessing the perfection of what Guy Debord described as emerging in his *Society of the Spectacle*. It is a fundamental fact of today's Western societies that all human experiences (life, eroticism, happiness, recognition) are tied to *commodities* or more precisely their consumption and possession (and not to a discourse). […] The totality of the spectacle is the 'theatricalization' of all areas of social life.[66]

Foucault's concern about the theatricalization of his teaching expresses precisely the fear that it has become simply a commodity, mediated into a form in which no event worthy of the name is possible. That Lehmann explains his own sense of theatricalization through Debord is telling: *Society of the Spectacle* was first published in 1967, the same year as Foucault's lecture on utopic and heterotopic space. Foucault's discomfort with becoming merely a performer, staging his thought in a mediatised and alienated form that risks reducing the performance of philosophy to philosophy as 'mere' performance, opens the scene of his thinking to the more literal violence that he puts at the heart of the notion of spectacle developed in *Discipline and Punish*. If, in Beckett and Deleuze, Foucault can find a way for thought to be theatre, then what theatre means has to be understood as a space of division, of disunity, of *partage*, in which questions can be posed and where the closure of representation is interrupted by juxtaposition, by the multiple, by the simultaneous.

If there is to be a truth in theatre as thought or thought as theatre, then it is by virtue of a critical dramaturgy that insists that there is no truth in a false unity, that truth is always defined by its relation to that which it cannot tame. In a passage that appears in the manuscript of Foucault's final Collège de France lecture but which he did not have time to deliver, he says: 'there is no establishment [*instauration*] of the truth without an essential position of otherness; the truth is never the same; there can be truth only in the form of the other world and the other life (*l'autre monde et de la vie autre*)'.[67] Truth is instituted, then, through a kind of instauration. In its Latin root, instauration carries a sense of restoration and renewal as much as initiation, just as avant-garde theatrical works such as Beckett's must reawaken the tradition that they interrupt. Borrowing de Certeau's terms, this instauration is instantiated in Foucault's work through 'scenes of difference': theatre and its 'metaphors' (scene, stage, mirror, and so on) open the relation to otherness, to the other world, to the other life, in a critical dramaturgy without which truth cannot find its place.

Notes

1 See, for example, §80 (5 February 1768). G. E. Lessing, *Hamburgische Dramaturgie*, ed. Klaus L. Berghahn (Stuttgart: Reclam, 1999), pp. 407–12.

2 Foucault, 'What is an Author?', trans. Josué V. Harari, in *The Foucault Reader*, ed. Paul Rabinow (Harmondsworth: Penguin, 1991), pp. 101–20 (p. 103). Foucault cites Beckett on the first page. A significantly different French text appears as 'Qu'est-ce qu'un auteur?', in *Dits et Écrits 1954–1988*, ed. Daniel Defert and François Ewald, 2 vols, Quarto (Paris: Gallimard, 2001), 1: 817–49. Hereafter referred to as *DE*.

3 Michel Foucault, *The Archaeology of Knowledge and the Discourse on Language*, trans. A. M. Sheridan Smith (New York: Pantheon, 1972), p. 24.

4 Michel Foucault, *The History of Sexuality*, Vol. 1, *An Introduction*, trans. Robert Hurley (Harmondsworth: Penguin, 1990), p. 93. *Histoire de la sexualité 1: La volonté de savoir* (Paris: Gallimard, 1976), pp. 122–3.

5 Foucault, *History of Madness*, ed. Jean Khalfa, trans. Jonathan Murphy and Jean Khalfa (Abingdon: Routledge, 2009), p. xv.

6 See 'Interview with Michel Foucault', *Power*, in *Essential Works of Foucault 1954–1984*, ed. James D. Faubion, gen. ed. Paul Rabinow, 3 vols (Harmondsworth: Penguin, 2000), 3:239–97, on his anti-Hegelianism and rejection of phenomenology's philosophy of the subject, citing Bataille and Blanchot as influences, both of whom wrote significant pieces on Beckett (p. 241).

7 Foucault, 'Questions of Method' in *Power*, pp. 223–38 (p. 225); *DE* 2:841.

8 For a summary, see Christel Weiler, 'Dramaturgie', in Erika Fischer-Lichte, Doris Kolesch, and Matthias Warstat (eds), *Metzler Lexikon Theatertheorie* (Stuttgart: Metzler, 2014), pp. 84–7.

9 Foucault, *Lectures on the Will to Know: Lectures at the Collège de France 1970–1971 and Oedipal Knowledge*, ed. Daniel Defert, gen. eds. François Ewald and Alessandro Fontana, English series ed. Arnold I. Davidson, trans. Graham Burchell (London: Picador, 2013). *Leçons sur la volonté de savoir: Cours au Collège de France 1970–1971 suivi de Le savoir d'Œdipe*, ed. François Ewald, Allessandro Fontana, and Daniel Defert (Paris: Seuil/Gallimard, 2011).

10 Foucault, *Lectures on the Will to Know*, p. 263, *Leçons sur la volonté de savoir*, p. 258; Foucault, *Lectures on the Will to Know*, p. 265, *Leçons sur la volonté de savoir*, p. 261. See also two fascinating interviews, both of which attempt explicitly to link Foucault's work to theatre. See 'Le savoir comme crime' and 'La scène de la philosophie', in *DE* 2:79–86 and 571–95.

11 Foucault's understanding of Hegel is marked by that of his teacher Jean Hyppolite, and especially Hyppolite's *Logique et Existence: Essai sur la Logique de Hegel* (Paris: PUF, 1953). See Foucault's tribute in *DE* 1:807–13, in which he describes *Logique et Existence* as '*un des grands livres de notre temps*' ('one of the great books of our time'), p. 813. Foucault took over the position at the Collège de France that had been held by Hyppolite as the Chair of the History of Philosophical Thought.

12 Foucault, *Lectures on the Will to Know*, p. 274, *Leçons sur la volonté de savoir*, p. 271.

13 See Michel Foucault, *Aesthetics*, in *Essential Works of Foucault 1954–1984*, ed. James D. Faubion, gen. ed. Paul Rabinow, 3 vols (Harmondsworth: Penguin, 2000), 2:343–68 (p. 348). This translation by Donald F. Brouchard and Sherry Simon has been 'slightly amended' by the editor of the volume, James Faubion.

14 Foucault, *Lectures on the Will to Know*, p. 280.

15 Foucault, *DE* 1:948.

16 Foucault may have in mind here Louis Althusser's essay, 'The "Piccolo Teatro": Bertolazzi and Brecht', in *For Marx*, trans. Ben Brewster (London: Verso: 1990), pp. 131–51. First published in *Pour Marx* (Paris: Maspero, 1965).

17 Gilles Deleuze, *Difference and Repetition*, trans. Paul Patton (London: Athlone, 1994), pp. 5–11. First published as *Différence et Répétition* (Paris: PUF, 1968).

18 Foucault, *Aesthetics*, p. 367; *DE* 1:967.

19 In *The Discourse on Language*, Foucault names three 'signposts for all our future work': Artaud, Nietzsche and Bataille (p. 220). See Jean-François Favreau, 'Artaud mis en scène par Foucault: une "fiction critique"', *Les Temps modernes*, 687–8 (2016), 178–206.

20 Edmund White, *Genet* (London: Picador, 1994), p. 496.

21 See James Knowlson, *Damned to Fame: The Life of Samuel Beckett* (London: Bloomsbury, 1996), p. 387; George Craig and others (ed.), *The Letters of Samuel Beckett 1941–1956* (Cambridge: Cambridge University Press, 2011), p. 355. Knowlson suggests the play should have opened on 3 January 1953.

22 Roland Barthes, *Écrits sur le théâtre*, ed. Jean-Loup Rivière (Paris: Seuil, 2002), pp. 87–90 (p. 87), my translation.

23 Ibid., p. 90.

24 See 'Archaeology of a Passion'. Printed as the afterword to Michel Foucault, *Death and the Labyrinth: The World of Raymond Roussel*, trans. Charles Ruas (London: Continuum, 2004), pp. 171–88 (p. 176). First published (Paris: Gallimard, 1963).

25 See David Macey, *The Lives of Michel Foucault* (London: Hutchinson, 1993), p. 41.

26 See 'Interview with Michel Foucault', *Power*, p. 249.

27 Macey, *The Lives of Michel Foucault*, p. 242.

28 Foucault, *DE* 2:1427, my translation.

29 Alain Badiou, *Beckett: L'increvable désir* (Paris: Hachette, 1995), pp. 5–6.

30 Ibid., p. 7.

31 Foucault, *DE* 2:1427.

32 Martin Esslin, *The Theatre of the Absurd*, 3rd edn (London: Methuen, 2001 [1961]). Theodor W. Adorno, 'Trying to Understand *Endgame*', in *Notes to Literature*, trans. Shierry Weber Nicolson, 2 vols (New York: Columbia University Press, 1987), 1, pp. 241–75.

33 Martin Puchner, *The Drama of Ideas: Platonic Provocations in Theater and Philosophy* (New York: Oxford University Press, 2010), pp. 149–50. I am grateful to Kélina Gotman for pointing out the significant framing of what counts as philosophy that Puchner makes here.

34 Cixous comments: 'I met Ariane [Mnouchkine, the artistic director of the Théâtre du Soleil] in 1972 in overdetermining and prophetic circumstances: I went to see her and took along my friend Michel Foucault to get her involved in the work of the Groupe Information Prison which Michel Foucault had founded'. Hélène Cixous, 'Enter the Theatre', in *Selected Plays of Hélène Cixous*, ed. Eric Prenowitz (London: Routledge, 2004), pp. 25–34 (p. 27).

35 In Richard Eyre, *Talking Theatre: Interviews with Theatre People* (London: Nick Hern, 2009), pp. 168–77 (p. 169).

36 Esslin, *The Theatre of the Absurd*, pp. 19–21.

37 Hans-Thies Lehmann, *Tragedy and Dramatic Theatre*, trans. Erik Butler (Abingdon: Routledge, 2016), p. 6.

38 Michel de Certeau, 'Le rire de Michel Foucault', *Le Débat* 41 (1986), 140–52; Michel de Certeau, 'The Laugh of Michel Foucault', in *Heterologies: Discourse on the Other*, trans. Brian Massumi (Manchester: Manchester University Press, 1986), pp. 193–98 (p. 196).

39 De Certeau, 'The Laugh of Michel Foucault', p. 196.

40 Ibid., pp. 196–7.

41 For an intriguing account leading Foucault back towards phenomenology, see Carl Lavery, *The Politics of Jean Genet's Late Theatre: Spaces of Revolution* (Manchester: Manchester University Press, 2010).

42 Michel Foucault, 'Space, Knowledge and Power', in *Power*, pp. 349–64 (p. 361).

43 Michel Foucault, 'Different Spaces', trans. Robert Hurley, in *Aesthetics*, pp. 75–85. Published in *DE* 2:1571–81, and as Foucault, *Le corps utopique, Les hétérotopies*, ed. Daniel Defert (Paris: Lignes, 2009).

44 Foucault, 'Different Spaces', p. 175.

45 Ibid., p. 175; Foucault, *DE* 2:1571.

46 Foucault, 'Different Spaces', pp. 177–8; Foucault, *DE* 2:1573–4.

47 Foucault, 'Different Spaces', p. 178; Foucault, *DE* 2:1574.

48 Foucault, 'Different Spaces', pp. 178–9; Foucault, *DE* 2:1574–5.

49 Foucault, 'Different Spaces', p. 181, translation modified; Foucault, *DE* 2:1577.

50 Foucault, 'Different Spaces', p. 184.

51 Ibid., p. 179, translation modified; Foucault, *DE* 2:1575.

52 Michel Foucault, *The Order of Things: An Archaeology of the Human Sciences* (London: Routledge, 1994); Michel Foucault, *Les Mots et les choses* (Paris: Gallimard, 1966).

53 Foucault, *The Order of Things*, p. 10.

54 Ibid.

55 Ibid., p. 11.

56 Ibid., p. 14.

57 *Les mots et les choses*, p. 29.

58 *The Order of Things*, p. 15.

59 Ibid., p. 16.

60 Michel Foucault, 'Philosophie et psychologie', in *Dossiers pédagogiques de la radio-télévision scolaire*, 15–27 February 1965, p. 20. See Macey, *The Lives of Michel Foucault*, p. 158. The video is easily accessible on YouTube from a number of sources.

61 Todd May, for example, even in a book entitled *The Philosophy of Foucault* (Chesham: Acumen, 2006), chooses to describe his thought as 'philosophically oriented' rather than strictly philosophical (p. 1).

62 Mark Robson, 'Impractical Criticism' arrives at similar conclusions from a different angle in Philip W. Martin (ed.), *English: The Condition of the Subject* (Basingstoke: Palgrave Macmillan, 2006), pp. 168–79.

63 Michel Foucault, *L'ordre du discours: Leçon inaugurale au Collège de France prononcée le 2 décembre 1970* (Paris: Gallimard, 1971), p. 10; Michel Foucault, 'The Discourse on Language', trans. Rupert Swyer, in *The Archaeology of Knowledge*, pp. 215–37 (p. 216).

64 Gérard Petitjean, 'Les Grands Prêtres de l'université française', *Le Nouvel Observateur*, 7 April 1975. Cited in the Foreword reproduced in each volume of the Collège de France lectures, in both French and English editions.

65 It is ironic, perhaps, that these recordings have been used extensively in reconstructing the lectures for publication.

66 Hans-Thies Lehmann, *Postdramatic Theatre*, trans. Karen Jürs-Munby (Abingdon: Routledge, 2006), p. 183. Hans-Thies Lehmann, *Postdramatisches Theater* (Frankfurt am Main: Autoren, 1999), pp. 466–7.

67 Michel Foucault, *The Courage of Truth (The Government of Self and Others II): Lectures at the Collège de France 1983–1984*, ed. Frédéric Gros, gen. eds. François Ewald and Alessandro Fontana, English series ed. Arnold I. Davidson, trans. Graham Burchell (Basingstoke: Palgrave Macmillan, 2012), p. 340. Michel Foucault, *Le courage de la vérité (Le gouvernement de soi et des autres II): Cours au Collège de France 1984*, ed. Frédéric Gros, gen. eds. François Ewald and Alessandro Fontana (Paris: Seuil/Gallimard, 2009), p. 311.

PART II

Dramaturgy

6

Heterotopia and the mapping of unreal spaces on stage

Joanne Tompkins

I completed a study of heterotopia which culminated in *Theatre's Heterotopias: Performance and the Cultural Politics of Space* in 2014.[1] Building on Michel Foucault's description of heterotopia in 'Of Other Places', I explicated a method for understanding the spatiality of performance, outlining the constructive connections between stage space on the one hand, and spatial practice in the world outside a performance location on the other. At its simplest, heterotopia is a vehicle for comparing and contrasting our experiences of different aspects of the world. Heterotopias are spaces that are alternative to the world at large: Foucault includes museums, institutions, cemeteries, theatres, which are sites that are set off from the actual world, but, significantly, sites that resonate with that actual world. In being part of the world at large, cemeteries, gardens, museums, and so on, serve necessary functions but in being set off from the world – through fences, rules, and/or entry points – they create their own realities, what Foucault calls a 'counteraction'[2] that may blur the boundaries between 'real' and 'unreal'.[3] The concept of heterotopia, which can assist in the understanding of the relationships between spatial structures in a culture, has not been explored to its full potential in theatre (or in other contexts that he itemises in his essay). My book aimed to provide theatre practitioners, scholars, and audiences with a map, as it were, to imagine and mobilise the glimpses, snapshots, or brief indications depicted in performance of how spatial structures enacted in the theatrical experience might create a context for changes in the world outside the venue. Heterotopias have the capacity to reveal insight into structures of power and knowledge: in theatre, they offer a chance to understand theatre's spatial arrangements in far greater detail and their potential implications for the world at large.

This chapter revisits Foucault's articulation of theatre as heterotopic in 'Of Other Spaces' against a more theatre-specific understanding of performance, to update it, and to incorporate other forms of spatiality that are regularly represented in theatre and performance. My book project used Foucault's argument as a springboard but this chapter engages with his work more deeply and specifically – with and through the theories of other critics – to enhance the potential for heterotopia in investigating and even performing theatre today. Foucault was first and foremost a thinker of spatiality (arguing that 'the present epoch will perhaps be above all the epoch of space'[4]). Following Foucault, I find spatiality to be fundamental to an understanding of theatre.[5] Yet while space (architecture, design, and imaginative locations) remains a major underpinning feature of theatre, the means of analysing it are limited. The effects of this are, all too often, a partial exploration of this key feature of the form in criticism.

My point here is to demonstrate that the exploration of the spatiality in theatre and performance has not yet taken advantage of Foucault's concept, perhaps because of its elliptical description: it is seldom used in theatre criticism, and when it is, it is usually superficially applied and/or misunderstood. I expand the potential for heterotopia in theatre by focusing on different types of alternate spaces – mythic and unreal spaces – to argue for a re-evaluation of heterotopia to better articulate the role of theatre and its social context. I also endeavour to highlight the tensions between 'real' and 'unreal' in this concept. I return to Foucault via two other spatial theorists: Gaston Bachelard (who predates and influenced Foucault) and his perception that we are shaped by the earliest space(s) we remember, and Yi-Fu Tuan (who follows Foucault) and his exploration of mythic space.[6] I briefly examine a historical and a contemporary play, each addressing a location that is not 'real' but that is equally 'not unreal' which accords with Tuan's description of mythic space: '[w]hen we wonder what lies on the other side of the mountain range or ocean, our imagination constructs mythical geographies that may bear little or no relationship to reality'.[7] The function of theatre is, to some extent, the exploration of those geographies because, Tuan maintains, '[h]uman places become vividly real through dramatization. Identity of place is achieved by dramatizing the aspirations, needs, and functional rhythms of personal and group life'.[8] Richard Brome's *The Antipodes* (first performed 1638) deploys such mythic space, while debbie tucker green's 2015 play, *hang*,[9] provides an opportunity to address the fundamental changes to spatiality that are characteristic of theatre in the late twentieth and the twenty-first centuries. I conclude with the implications of such a historicised, spatial, Foucauldian perspective[10] for theatre and performance generally.

First, a brief reprise of heterotopias which are other spaces that, by their contrasting nature, are helpful in understanding the world at large. As Foucault outlines in 'Of Other Spaces', utopias and heterotopias 'have the curious property of being in relation with all the other sites, but in such a way as to suspect, neutralize, or invert the set of relations that they happen to designate, mirror, or reflect'. These sites 'are linked with all the others' and 'contradict all the other sites'.[11] Heterotopias tend to have boundaries, admission points, rules, and, in some cases, they present a world in miniature. Foucault was notoriously ambiguous in his descriptions of heterotopias, so in addition to delving deeper into his essay, it is perhaps useful to look to other critics' interpretations. Peter Johnson helpfully defines heterotopias as a set of relations that are not separate from dominant structures and ideology, but go against the grain. [...] They offer no resolution or consolation, but disrupt and test our customary notions of ourselves. These different spaces, which contest forms of anticipatory utopianism, hold no promise or space of liberation. [...] [H]eterotopias glitter and clash in their incongruous variety, illuminating a passage for our imagination.[12]

Singling out theatre as an example, Foucault notes that a 'heterotopia is capable of juxtaposing in a single real place several spaces, several sites that are in themselves incompatible. Thus it is that the theater brings onto the rectangle of the stage, one after the other, a whole series of places that are foreign to one another'.[13] Such locations on the stage that shift from scene to scene are juxtaposed to one another but also, in Foucault's understanding of theatre as heterotopic, the whole theatrical experience is juxtaposed to the world at large, the world beyond the venue. Of course Foucault's aim in 'Of Other Spaces' was not to demonstrate a full knowledge of theatre – or any others of his examples – but the effect of a suggestion of theatre as a generic, metaphoric building and art form has tended to preclude a detailed application. Foucault's own engagement with performance is known to have been broader than a proscenium experience, but the brief mentions of it in 'Of Other Spaces' do not on their own easily give scope to a wide range of performance traditions. While other chapters in this volume demonstrate that Foucault's deep engagement with theatre crossed genres and intersected with the social, political, and theatrical shifts of the 1960s, his brief account of heterotopia in theatre in his essay leaves room for the development of spaces in theatre as disruptive. My argument builds on Foucault's to explore how his formulation of heterotopia may be expanded upon to accommodate a more detailed understanding of theatre, an understanding that can develop as new forms of performance arise.

My book deploys Foucault's articulation of heterotopias from 'Of Other Spaces' in conjunction with the work of Kevin Hetherington, who himself built on Louis Marin's *Utopics*, as a way of augmenting Foucault's brief descriptions.[14] My account enables a fuller awareness of the multiple interpretations of spatiality, interpretations and meanings that are essential for analysing theatre. It reads 'place' through the action that occurs on the stage in the worlds that are created there, as well as leaving room to explore the relationship between those places and the larger social experience or culture which contains the performance. Briefly, I found that using heterotopia as a lens for analysis requires enumerating the range of 'spaces' and 'places' that are depicted and suggested on stage via a text, the architecture of the venue in which it is staged, and the set design. From a collection of such spaces, it is sometimes possible (although not in all productions) to discern a heterotopia between the locations of constructed space and of abstracted space: this is a physical location that emerges in performance and that offers an alternative (even if transient or fleeting) to the status quo, or the current dominant paradigm(s). My heterotopic model then explores the intersections between three component parts of space – constructed space, abstracted space, and heterotopic space – to account for what they and their interrelationships might mean in a broader cultural context. Foucault's essay provides only the beginning of a sense of how one might understand the interconnections between the set of relations that heterotopia puts into dialogue. I took it as my task to explore how that may take place, spatially, in theatre that aims not to simply 'entertain' or reinforce norms but rather that which sets out to intervene in those norms and/or provoke change. This experimental zone offers, for me, a proving ground to test out spatial alternatives that might prompt audiences to think (and act) differently in the world at large about the possible spaces they have seen generated on stage.

In writing the book, I realised that there were many other forms of theatrical space that intersected with heterotopia that required investigation: while I had no room to discuss them, equally I could not let them go. I am less interested here in applying the methodology I describe in the book to new examples than I am in attempting to broaden our understanding of heterotopia against a deeper awareness of theatre, performance, and spaces. Foucault maintained that '[s]pace is fundamental in any exercise of power',[15] with which it is hard to disagree: I address the specifics of how this pertains to theatre, beyond 'just' a venue-based or architectural analysis. A helpful step is to turn to Deirdre Heddon who breaks down space's fundamental role in the theatre and its capacity to shift and change through the ages and across different genres or forms of theatre. She argues that '[p]lace and self are deeply imbricated and implicated, and both are contingent, shifting, always becoming',[16] a state that is even more pronounced in the places and spaces of the theatre than other art forms. I focus here on one specific spatial context to facilitate a broader deployment of heterotopia: the ways in which unreal or mythic spaces might be understood through heterotopic terms, to demonstrate some of the shifts in theatre as an art form, shifts that don't appear to be accommodated in Foucault's heterotopia.

While my earlier study favoured different performance contexts over geographical spaces,[17] this chapter focuses on geographical locations in the first instance, albeit sites that are not as well marked out or established, as a means of articulating the significance of geographical and site 'analysis' in theatre. If the unreal or mythic can be read to articulate spatial meaning, then it is far more likely that locations able to be understood as heterotopic will have the capacity to be transformative. Bachelard's and Tuan's spatial ideas come into play here: the mythic and unreal, spatial contexts that are necessarily geographic and yet at the same time not able to be located on a map. Heterotopia in theatre enables the comparison of that which takes place against what else *might transpire* such that the 'unreal' spaces that comprise a theatrical experience can propose concrete effects for audience members as they negotiate the potential for porosity in the walls that mark off 'theatre' from 'the larger culture outside the venue'. Mythic and unreal spaces may be 'unpindownable' spaces or lands long ago and far away, Arcadian landscapes, fantastical spaces, geographies as yet unmapped, or the unanchored place that could be here, or a time in the future, or somewhere else altogether. Both Tuan and Bachelard suggest the importance of the intimate, the interior, and, more importantly, the connection of the familiar with the public or the world beyond the interior. Beyond the mirror, Foucault does not discuss the intimate and the imaginary,[18] but I see the need to draw out these relationships for the concept's application to theatre in the same way that Bachelard understands that 'intimate space and exterior space keep encouraging each other'.[19]

My first example, Richard Brome's *The Antipodes*, is set explicitly in an unreal landscape. Staging London in a Jonsonian manner, via an imagined perception of the eponymous land that had, at that point, not been explored to any depth by Europeans,

The Antipodes connects Bachelard's psychic location with Tuan's unreal one. A doctor pretends to transport Peregrine, a young man under the thrall of a fourteenth-century book that purports to be a travel narrative, *The Voyages and Travailes of Sir John Mandeville, Knight*,[20] to the Antipodes, a land that is the opposite of London. He is in fact simply given a sleeping potion that makes him think he has taken the eight-month long sea voyage. His doctor 'sends' him on this journey to cure his illness in which he is so infatuated with Mandeville's (made-up) travels that a fantasy life has taken over his own, and he fails to consummate his marriage. A group of actors perform as the people of the Antipodes (in a play within a play, also titled *The Antipodes*), assisted in the ruse by Peregrine never having been to a play. The doctor prepares him, explaining

> The people through the whole world of Antipodes,
> In outward feature, language and religion,
> Resemble those to whom they are supposite:
> They under Spain appear like Spaniards;
> Under France, Frenchmen; under England, English
> To the exterior show; but in their manners,
> Their carriage, and condition of life,
> Extremely contrary. (I.vi.106–113)

The actual mythic/unreal unknown land is set up as a type of utopia, although it becomes clear that all manner of disruptions can occur in 'Anti-London' as well as in London. Ann Haaker notes the place of the inversion in representing the 'topsy-turvy conditions of the time'[21] but the play also presents a heterotopia in situating the 'cure' and the way to read London in the interstices between the London of the day and the Antipodes that is presented: in the space between the 'real' and the 'pretend' as Peregrine explores a location that is other to both. The mythic space of the Antipodes is realised through the play-within-a-play structure, the experience of which disrupts Peregrine's 'Mandeville madness' (IV.xi.45) as well as the audience's thinking; it ultimately presents a place from which to understand the order and chaos of the play and of the world. Haaker argues that

> [c]lever manipulation of the play within the play enables Brome not only to merge two worlds of illusion into a third world of reality, but also to demonstrate concentrically the relative ratio between social consciousness and harmony: the greater the bounds of social consciousness, the greater the harmony and happiness.[22]

The audience watches Peregrine in the midst of the play within a play, occasionally taking part (even 'unscripted' according to the hapless actors of the play within the play who are forced to respond to his not-always-passive observation), while his family watches his exploits as an additional onstage audience. There are, then, at least three layers of audience: Peregrine, his worried father and others from London of 1638, and the paying audience at the theatre.

Bachelard's space of interiority provides a means to understanding the effects of Brome's layering of audience and viewing positions, as well as to a consideration of heterotopia and theatre more generally, even though Foucault distinguishes his project from Bachelard's. In *The Poetics of Space* Bachelard describes the significance of the space of home that we first remember and that produces, at times, a visceral response; home (whether fraught or lost) is, of course, a common location for theatrical narratives. He suggests that we retain memories of a specific location in an early home (for instance, a room or part of a room), memories which determine much in our subsequent relationships with other spaces. This physical interiority generates a psychic space and place that Foucault appears to reject in 'Of Other Spaces'.[23] Theatre as a form needs to be able to address interiority such as psychic spaces (including Bachelard's topoanalysis, the 'study of the sites of our intimate lives'),[24] as a play like *The Antipodes* exemplifies. Further, in theatre, internal space cannot necessarily be separated from external space, suggesting that the concept needs to accommodate both. In fact Bachelard alludes to this when he comments that '[t]he space we love is unwilling to remain permanently enclosed. It deploys and appears to move elsewhere without difficulty; into other times, and on different planes of dream and memory'.[25] This elasticity of space is significant to theatre where contemporary theatre practice has moved away from a rigid reflection of a culture on stage. Theatre depends on that kind of reverie and an emotional response to space in order to draw its audiences into its narrative through its interpretive, often affective responses. Finally, whereas Foucault suggests an ordered procession of different spaces in his characterisation of theatre (the juxtaposition of on 'the rectangle of the stage, one after the other, a whole series of places that are foreign to one another', cited above), theatre is not always orderly in its intertwining of different types of space, both actual and imagined, as *The Antipodes* illustrates in its multiple locations and relatively fluid movement from Peregrine's psychic space to London.

This play also clarifies that the crucial 'unreality' of the setting is not simply a psychic location but also a geographical one, that of the Antipodes, even if it was then an imaginary space. I return to Tuan's use of mythic space which helps extend the understanding and impact of heterotopia in the context of theatre today. The first of Tuan's two-part definition of mythic space is 'a fuzzy area of defective knowledge surrounding the empirically known' or 'a conceptual extension of the familiar and workaday spaces given by direct experience'.[26] The second is 'the spatial component of a world view, a conception of localized values within which people carry on their practical activities';[27] this conception is linked to 'a world view or cosmology' which is 'a people's more or less systematic attempt to make sense of environment'.[28] Mythic space 'persist[s] because for individuals as well as for groups there will always be areas of the hazily known and of the unknown, and because it is likely that some people will always be driven to understand man's place in nature in a holistic way'.[29] Theatre frequently negotiates locations that are imaginary: playwrights, actors, and designers generate a fictional space/place that is often related to perceptions of contemporary space/place in the world outside the theatre, as Brome does here. The audience's receptivity to that fictional space comes about because of our understanding of mythic space. There is an unreality to mythic space, given its uncertainty – or at least its unlikelihood of being fixed on a map. Tuan's mythic space behaves similarly to metonymic space: '[i]n mythical thought the part can symbolize the whole and have its full potency';[30] this aligns with theatre where a very limited range of signs (props, lighting, gestures) can generate in performance a magical realm or a particular time and space, or even 'history' itself.

This play's staging of an unknown land (using the upside-down-world device) permits the exploration of the foibles of the day but there is more here than simply an inversion of the world at large. In a move that Tuan (and Bachelard) would appreciate, Matthew Steggle argues that 'Brome is fascinated by the dynamic possibilities of space and place, and the ways in which geography can be contested and manipulated.'[31] For Brome, 'realist techniques are being used in the service of representing the flagrantly unreal.'[32] Given the era (and the need for theatre to 'perform' multiple social functions following a long period of plague in London), *The Antipodes* ends with the harmony represented by a dance, and all being restored: the main characters 'return' from the mythic Antipodes, its function as other having generated a clearer sense of the world that the audience will return to beyond the theatre's walls.

The Antipodes was performed at Shakespeare's Globe in 2000, directed by Gerald Freedman in a manner that did not create a vastly different spatial world on stage, reinforcing Brome's implicit point about the similarity between the two worlds.[33] The production, which used period costumes and simple props/scenery, introduced a low (250 cm) metal fence all the way around the stage, and set about 250 cm in from the edge. In the way of Foucault's heterotopias, the stage was marked off from the audience as much as the theatre's walls separate it – only just – from its surrounding social context, the pretend barrier serving to call attention to itself. David Jays explains that '[w]hile most Globe productions dissolve boundaries between stage and pit, here, a low rail around the stage maintained the succession of frames for the play-within-the-play.'[34] This staging accentuated the script's in-built heterotopia, with the relationship *between* London and Anti-London generating a heterotopia of restoration and restitution through this additional space. The heterotopia assists audiences with navigating the world (whether actual, psychic, or unreal locations) that overarches the theatre, one that may appear joyless; understood through such locations, the play provides an alternative means for the audience to rethink their own land and their place in it.

The importance of staging such a mythical world is less to map *that* world than it is to *re*map the one in which we live; this could also be said to be the point of heterotopias which assist us in understanding our culture(s). That this play links audience and actors so closely contributes to its message: Peregrine's family watch him watch the Antipodean world, as the audience watches the whole thing. *The Antipodes* traces how theatre creates and manipulates space, here generating and performing both an imagined and an interior space in the guise of a 'real' one. It articulates theatre's world-making, turning the unknown or unreal into something of substance, even if temporarily; it demonstrates how theatre merges illusion and reality, whether through an evocation of 'real' locations or imagined ones. An unreal/mythic space, then, helps define a re-imagined 'real' place, in this context London. In so doing, it enables a nuancing of Foucault's heterotopia that better suits application to theatre. Theatre illustrates that its spaces are always to some extent unreal and it is their very unreality that provides the mechanism for it to communicate the material connection to the world at large.

My second example, debbie tucker green's *hang*, builds on the nature of unreal/psychic locations in theatre while also demonstrating the shifts in theatrical world-making that have occurred in the four centuries since Brome's play. To make this leap,

I turn away briefly from heterotopia towards utopia. Some of the locations I have proposed as unreal spaces may appear superficially to be utopian, but I see them as distinctly heterotopian.[35] Foucault explains that '[u]topias are sites with no real place. They are sites that have a general relation of direct or inverted analogy with the real space of Society. They present society itself in a perfected form, or else society turned upside down, but in any case these utopias are fundamentally unreal spaces'.[36] More than simply unreal, utopias are also too ordered to act in the same way as heterotopias.[37] Utopias, Johnson notes, are, for Foucault, ordered in their unreality, even if classified as other, whereas the ways in which heterotopias cut across the grain of order render them a more exciting concept.[38]

This is particularly important to theatre because Foucault's characterisation of utopias as unreal introduces a problem for theatricality, not because utopias are essential to theatre but because the delineation of the 'unreal' represents a challenge for theatre which generates 'unreal spaces' as a matter of course, and makes them real, at least to a perceivable extent for the duration of a performance. To negotiate the gap between the real and unreal, I turn to Richard Schechner's description of theatre's use of 'not-not' which is 'the peculiar but necessary double negativity that characterizes symbolic actions'.[39] For Schechner,

> [a] performance 'takes place' in the 'not me ... not-not me' between performers; between performers, texts and environment; between performers, texts, environment and audience. [...] The field [of the 'between'] is the embodiment of potential, of the virtual, the imaginative, the fictive, the negative, the not not.[40]

This well-quoted concept, which helps to isolate what theatre accomplishes in a cultural context, is inevitably more than Foucault identifies in his partial description but I think it is in keeping with Foucault's depiction of heterotopias as 'other spaces'.

While Schechner initially explored the 'not me' in relation to actors, the 'not not' in theatre can extend to spatiality. One need only look to Shakespeare's setting of numerous plays in European cities to see how this works with geographical places textually. Venice, for instance, functions in *Othello* as a city that has associations with the city in Italy but is used for multiple representational purposes, and rarely as an actual 'map' of the location. *Othello*'s Venice is not necessarily the same as the city in Italy at the time or today, but it is also not-not those Venices. The two are connected even if Shakespeare's version of the city deviates from geography, history, and culture; such locations can be 'versions' of themselves, recognisable geographically, but also more. Their relationship to the actual city is akin to theatrical props and locations being a theatrical conceit that is not the 'thing' but that stands in for the thing: see Keir Elam's description of the stage chair acquiring quotation marks.[41] Further, even the most elaborate of stagings will only provide a hint or a glimpse of a location, a setting that will be removed to make way for the next production. Shakespeare's plays, then, accommodate the not-not in the description and function of 'known' cities, with the design of particular productions extending this not-not further when additional geographical (or historical, temporal, political) locations are called upon. Mythic or unreal locations contain an element of reality, which provides the means for them to make sense to an audience; *hang* provides that link between its different worlds of reality and unreal locations.

But before turning to *hang* I want to briefly note that while examining the staging of mythic and/or unreal spaces enhances the significance of heterotopias, extending the scope for 'real' versus 'unreal' is even more important to accommodate the shifts and changes that performance has witnessed in the decades since Foucault's death: the nature of theatre – and even of set design – has shifted so much that the 'reality' of mapped or actual geographical space cannot really be a defining feature of theatre. To pick up one example, theatre design has in recent decades altered quite substantially to present a very different framing of the world, incorporating non-specific and minimalist settings and equivalent stage designs, and these transformations are particularly useful to explore through a heterotopic lens given their visual rethinking of spatiality, of the relationships between different times and places and humans' interactions with them. From the time of Edward Gordon Craig, much design has become pared back to more symbolic representations of locations and states of being. Even today's productions of Henrik Ibsen's narratives, which mostly take place in living rooms, generally break out of a naturalistic frame to extend interpretation.[42] Christopher Baugh has encapsulated this shift in design in the context of postdramatic theatre when he quotes Hans-Thies Lehmann on dramatic and postdramatic theatre:

> [t]he dramatic theatre, in which the scene stands for the world, can be compared to perspective: space here is both technically and mentally a window and a symbol, analogous to the reality 'behind' [...,] equivalent to the scale of the world, a metaphorical likeness obtained through abstraction and accentuation.[43]

Baugh explains what this means to contemporary scenography: he argues that the frame metaphor 'with its parallel and colonial conceit of providing the superior vantage point of a "window on the world" that [eighteenth-century painter and stage designer Philip James de] Loutherbourg sought has been replaced by the quintessential relativism and ephemerality of contemporary performance'.[44] Building on Nick Kaye, Baugh notes 'that the paradigm of theatrical performance may be structurally alien to *any* quest for certainty and stability',[45] a context which has the potential to radically change the notion of the self, space, and the self in place. Taking this towards digital performance, he argues that '[w]ithin digital dramaturgies and within virtual theatres of performance, the virtual actor, the avatar, may be brought into existence and may walk upon an entirely new space and within a completely re-functioned scenography of performance'.[46] It is, then, increasingly commonplace for contemporary theatre to be set in unreal or mythic spaces, or, in postdramatic theatre, a non-specific place that stands in for many different potential abstract or ill-defined locations that underpin the work of writers like Sarah Kane, Martin Crimp, and many other writers.

[H]*ang* exemplifies the different relationship that such a non-specific setting generates with an audience. Performed at the Royal Court's Jerwood Downstairs, *hang* stages three characters: named One, Two and Three. One and Three are female; Two can be either a male or female. One and Two are 'of any race. Character Three is Black'.[47] The time is '[n]early now'.[48] The audience learns over the 70-minute performance that Three and her family have been victims of a terrible, unspecified crime, the effects of which have taken an incalculable toll on her, her husband, and two young children. One and Two are authority figures of some sort who have received a letter from the perpetrator of the crime. Three visits their office not just to receive the letter but to mete out punishment: it is her choice which form of execution the perpetrator will receive (the title revealing her decision).

The time is '[n]early now' but the set suggests an office now, even though no specific geographical location is discernible: the Royal Court production staged an anonymous staff room or interview room with worn institutional furniture, and an adjacent corridor. The inadequacy of the vaguely-defined bureaucracy is clear in the set: while Three is expected, One and Two are not prepared for the meeting (the glass-ware to offer her a drink of water is absent, several of the chairs upended). Susannah Clapp describes this uninviting, ugly meeting room set (designed by Jon Bausor) as 'a black tunnel lit by long rows of fluorescent tubes that pulse at prime moments'; she calls it a 'terrifying space'.[49] There are two other features to the set. Victoria Sadler describes the first:

> the walls are reflective plastic sheets that shake and tremble ever so slightly, giving the impression of a world that could be real, could be just an apparition. A dream – or a night-mare – of what could come to pass. A nightmare that if you were to reach out to touch it, could melt away and evaporate.[50]

These walls (assisted by the pulsing lights) shift the atmosphere of the room's other-wise naturalistic feel. They lend 'a Kafkaesque nightmare feel to the whole scenario',[51] a situation that Sadler describes as a 'warning' such that the 'play feels like it is set in the future but not that far away. Possibly only tomorrow'.[52] In heterotopic terms, the walls create the abstracted space that intersect – and conflict – with the constructed space of the meeting room.

While the reflective, trembling walls collide with the naturalistic set, there is also another 'space' on stage, that of a void that forms a second feature to push the meeting room out of a realistic moment into a realm of unreal or mythic. This void was 'located' adjacent to the meeting room. The corridor that the actors used to get to the meeting room (both raised quite significantly) snaked around the void, suggesting that the meeting room was not a public space in this agency. The actors' seemingly long walk around it drew attention to it so that it seemed essential to the action to me. The cor-ridor formed its perimeter, effectively defining it. This void is not obvious in any of the production's images but its presence – perhaps because of its awkwardness – was the most notable feature of the set for me (its significance becoming clear to me from my seat in the last row of the raked venue).[53] In a Schechnerian way, it was not used by the actors during the performance but it was not-not used, being left there as a visual marker of the unknown, an indication of this unreal location, a location that could all too quickly become very real. It was used at the conclusion of the performance during the curtain call when one of the actors broke the 'frame' and jumped down from the stage to the void's lower level to make a quicker exit and re-entrance. This void represented for me the possibility of the location for the narrative: will this 'nearly now' be unrealised or will the void become all too real?

Even though a non-specific location is common in much contemporary perform-ance which displays a deliberate reluctance to present a recognisable, modern location in which to set a narrative dilemma, the reviews of the play suggest that some critics found the absence of detail and the unspecified location, events, and time confusing and even a shortcoming.[54] That lack of specificity is, of course, the play's achievement, serving to make audiences feel uncomfortable. The very realistic, nervous conversation of the officials and Three's anger and grief are contrasted to the scarily-familiar normality of the uninviting room.

[H]ang could be construed to be set in a futuristic place (only just) or a 'here but not here'. More broadly, Deirdre Osborne calls tucker green's work 'trans-geographical'.[55] Both depictions reinforce the play's fundamental challenge to our perceptions of space – in that it is possibly 'here' and now – through the narrative of the macabre events *and* through the staging of those events. Arguing from a different perspective, Elaine Aston writes that tucker green 'brings together the epic and the domestic, the terrifying feeling of a world lost to a global tide of dehumanizing values'.[56] This collapsing of different types of space (both real and unreal) is helpful to examine the events of the play, as well as epitomising a feature of contemporary performance. Such only-just-futuristic locations in *hang* are too common to overlook in contemporary performance; having a means to investigate them fully through a concept like heterotopia offers a more significant method for analysing spatial practice.

Being able to recognise how heterotopia intersects with *hang*'s real/not-real location (the 'nearly now' and the effect that seems like it is now, and the potential to ensure that it won't *be* now) opens up the possibility for heterotopia to be an effective method for exploring other locations that are frequently performed in contemporary theatre.[57] One such example occurs in David Greig's recent work. His 2010 *Dunsinane* takes on what has become a 'mythic' space of the Scottish location from *Macbeth* but, when restaged in Basra, Iraq, the play also accommodates an actual contemporary location of war and loss, more immediate than whatever narrative *Macbeth* retells.[58] This is a deeper engagement with a multi-layered and symbolic geography (as well as the significance of place in theatre) than simply rendering fictional space on stage. The imagined/imaginary is, through shifts in geography, history, and current events, 'made' real or given a more concrete (often politicised) meaning.[59]

A mythic or unreal space becoming real on stage has potential for the staging of classic narratives to have more nuanced spatial dimensions, as well as in the mapping of psychic landscapes, which can be so personal. Given the spatial underpinning of theatre as a form, any place that is staged (whether overtly and physically or psychically) begs to have the relationships between it and other spaces (including other spaces that have been created on the same stage) explored as a means of constructing meaning, whether those locations are charted on a Mercator map or in a mythic location. It is through the formation of places and the description, classification, performing of places (whether real or imagined) that we understand the places we do inhabit and might inhabit and can use that understanding to shape our worlds and to think about how we can transform them – for the better.[60] Expanding upon and deploying Foucault's concept helps us keep pace with the shifts in theatre and performance, shifts that have continued to be staged in provocative ways. The concept can be applied to a more nuanced, dynamic, and evolving understanding of performance. Theatre layers real, not-real, and 'real' places (imaginary or temporary) to intersect with each other and resonate well beyond 'just' the performance. Ironically, looking at unreal and mythical places helps us think about maps and the staging of 'real' places and spaces and how theatre conceptualises not just the significance of spatiality at micro and macro levels.[61] By broadening the potential applicability and frame of reference that Foucault provides to theatre through heterotopia, we enhance the effects of both heterotopia and theatre. The wealth of interpretational possibilities in 'Of Other Spaces' suggests that Foucault's other writings on spatiality would also find value for theatre scholars similarly captivated by mapping the form's locations.

Notes

1 Thanks to Diana Looser, Sarah Thomasson, and the volume's editors for their comments on various stages of drafts of this chapter. Joanne Tompkins, *Theatre's Heterotopias: Space and the Analysis of Performance* (Basingstoke: Palgrave Macmillan, 2014).
2 Michel Foucault, 'Of Other Places', *Diacritics* 16 (1986), 22–7 (p. 24).
3 These are notoriously difficult terms to deploy. Foucault distinguishes between 'real' and 'unreal' only obliquely in 'Of Other Spaces', in the context of utopias (unreal) versus heterotopias (real) (ibid., p. 24). The mirror, which is both, is the bridge between them. As this chapter argues, the exploration of locations on stage that are palpably unreal is necessary to understand the possibility of heterotopic effects in performance.
4 Foucault, 'Of Other Spaces', p. 22.
5 This importance is reinforced and influenced by the work of Henri Lefebvre. See Henri Lefebvre, *The Production of Space*, trans. Donald Nicholson-Smith (Oxford: Blackwell, 1991) and Henri Lefebvre, *The Urban Revolution*, trans. Robert Bononno (Minneapolis: University of Minnesota Press, 2003).
6 Gaston Bachelard, *The Poetics of Space*, trans. Maria Jolas (Boston, MA: Beacon Press, 1994); Yi-Fu Tuan, *Space and Place: The Perspective of Experience* (Minneapolis: University of Minnesota Press, 1977). I have recently deployed Bachelard and Tuan in a different theoretical context in a chapter co-authored with Kim Solga on the staging of 'home' in modern theatre. Kim Solga and Joanne Tompkins, 'The Environment of Theatre: Home in the Modern Age', in Kim Solga (ed), *A Cultural History of Theatre in the Modern Age*, Vol. 6 (London: Bloomsbury Methuen Drama, 2017), pp. 75–94.
7 Tuan, *Space and Place*, p. 86.
8 Ibid., p. 178.
9 Richard Brome, *The Antipodes*, ed. Ann Haaker (Lincoln, NE: Regents, 1966 [1640]); debbie tucker green, *hang* (London: Nick Hern Books, 2016). My analysis is based on the performance directed by tucker green: *hang*, Jerwood Downstairs, Royal Court Theatre, London, 2015. Note that tucker green uses lower case letters for her name and the play title.
10 These adjectives may well seem tautologous since history and space are central to Foucault's thought, regardless of the focus, but by articulating them thus, I draw attention to the specific facets of Foucault's work that are central to my argument.
11 Foucault, 'Of Other Spaces', p. 24.
12 Peter Johnson, 'Unravelling Foucault's "Different Spaces"', *History of the Human Sciences* 19.4 (2006), 75–90 (p. 87).
13 Foucault, 'Of Other Places', p. 25.
14 Hetherington takes up Marin's separation of 'utopia' into its two constituent parts: 'eu-topia' and 'ou-topia' (which translate to 'good place' and 'no place'): it is in this considerable conceptual gap that he sees heterotopic space situated in a location that differs from the actual world. Kevin Hetherington, *The Badlands of Modernity: Heterotopia and Social Ordering* (London: Routledge, 1997); Louis Marin, *Utopics: The Semiological Play of Textual Spaces*, trans. R. A. Vollrath (New York: Humanity Books, 1984 [1973]). See also Tompkins, *Theatre's Heterotopias*, pp. 24–6.

15 Michel Foucault, *Power/Knowledge*, ed. Colin Gordon (London: Harvester, 1980), p. 252.

16 Deirdre Heddon, 'One Square Foot: Thousands of Routes', *PAJ* 86 (2007), 40–50 (p. 42).

17 These included how site-specific performance intersects with our understanding of the relationship between performance site and the 'real' world; the effects of performance from a theatre company, the National Theatre of Scotland, that seeks to establish a specific spatial and historical relationship with its audiences; how to think about the 'relevance' of performance in Shakespeare's Globe, a theatre that seems to have a specific, predetermined historical and geographic definition; and how multimedia performance affects our understanding of place and space in performance and its relationship with the world beyond the venue.

18 Johnson characterises Foucault's intentions – at least as far as heterotopia – as opposing a relationship with intimacy: '[I]n describing generally the space in which we live, as opposed to Bachelard's inner space, Foucault refers to that which "draw us out of ourselves". This is crucial. Heterotopias draw us out of ourselves in peculiar ways; they display and inaugurate a difference and challenge the space in which we may feel at home. [...] In a sense, they do not fully function except in relation to each other. But their relationships clash and create further disturbing spatio-temporal units. Lefebvre's brief formulation of heterotopy captures this but with Foucault there is no inevitable relationship with spaces of hope. It is about conceiving space outside, or against, any utopia framework or impulse'. Johnson, 'Unravelling', p. 84.

19 Bachelard, *The Poetics of Space*, p. 201.

20 Mandeville's influential travels ostensibly took place in the fourteenth century. See McInnis for more on Mandeville and Brome's selection of this text. David McInnis, 'Therapeutic Travel in Richard Brome's *The Antipodes*', *SEL* 52.2 (Spring 2012), 447–69 (pp. 457–9).

21 Ann Haaker, 'Introduction', in Richard Brome *The Antipodes*, ed. Ann Haaker (Lincoln, NE: Regents, 1966 [1640]), pp. xi–xxi (p. xviii).

22 Ibid., p. xix.

23 Foucault does include the mirror, ironically both a utopia and heterotopia, but even in its being 'a placeless place', the mirror's reflected image remains actual, unlike psychic space which I interpret to be more complex. Foucault, 'Of Other Spaces', p. 24.

24 Bachelard, *Poetics of Space*, p. 8.

25 Ibid., p. 53. For an elaboration on Bachelard's point in theatre, see Lawrence Bradby and Carl Lavery who note in a different context that '[f]or Bachelard, reverie is what makes us care for space, what gives it a sense of duration. To occupy a place, we need, he suggests, to enchant it'. Lawrence Bradby and Carl Lavery, 'Moving Through Place: Itinerant Performance and the Search for a Community of Reverie', *Research in Drama Education* 12.1 (Feb 2007), 41–54 (p. 49).

26 Tuan, *Space and Place*, p. 86.

27 Ibid.

28 Ibid., p. 88.

29 Ibid., p. 86.

30 Ibid., p. 100.

31 Matthew Steggle, *Richard Brome: Place and Politics on the Caroline Stage* (Manchester: University of Manchester Press, 2004), p. 9. He further notes that 'Mandeville's own identity is famously unstable, problematizing the distinction between truth and fiction in all directions'. Ibid., p. 109.

32 Ibid., p. 111.

33 Gerald Freedman, dir. *The Antipodes* by Richard Brome, Master of Clothing and Properties, Jenny Tiramani. Shakespeare's Globe, London, 2000. This account is based on a video of the 2 pm performance on 18 August 2000, watched at the Shakespeare's Globe archive.

34 David Jays, 'Monsters and Medicine', *Around the Globe*, 15 Autumn 2000, pp. 10–11 (p. 10).

35 For a more detailed analysis of utopia in performance, see Dragan Klaić's *The Plot of the Future: Utopia and Dystopia in Modern Drama* (Ann Arbor: University of Michigan Press, 1991). See also Jill Dolan's use of utopia in *Utopia in Performance: Finding Hope at the Theater* (Ann Arbor: University of Michigan Press, 2005).

36 Foucault, 'Of Other Spaces', 24.

37 As Johnson notes, Foucault's preference for heterotopias over utopias was related to his fascination with the account of Borges' being dumbfounded by the classifications in a Chinese encyclopaedia,

an anecdote he used in *The Order of Things*. Peter Johnson, 'History of the Concept of Heterotopia', *Heterotopian Studies*, December 2015, p. 1 www.heterotopiastudies.com/wp-content/uploads/2012/05/2.1-History-of-Concept.pdf, accessed 4 July 2017.

38 Ibid. The space of the negative or the 'no place' is as popular as more concrete examples of location. See Marc Augé's concept of a non-place which can be isolated on stage in *A Sense for the Other: The Timeliness and Relevance of Anthropology*, trans. A. Jacobs (Stanford, CA: Stanford University Press, 1998 [1994]), p. 97. See my *Unsettling Space* for more on this concept and its applicability to theatre. Joanne Tompkins, *Unsettling Space: Contestations in Contemporary Australian Theatre* (Basingstoke: Palgrave Macmillan, 2006), pp. 94–5.

39 Richard Schechner, *Between Theater and Anthropology* (Philadelphia: University of Pennsylvania Press, 1985), p. 117.

40 Ibid., p. 113.

41 Keir Elam, *The Semiotics of Theatre and Drama*, 2nd edn (London: Routledge, 2002), p. 8.

42 It must be noted that the non-'reality' of setting a living room on stage is part of a pact (the willing suspension of disbelief) that audiences make with performers. We know that what appears on stage as a home is not a 'real' house or even one that has been resized and reordered to suit a theatrical endeavour. We know that even the fully rendered box set on stage for a play by Ibsen does not resemble any 'home' off-stage, well beyond its temporary status.

43 Christopher Baugh, *Theatre, Performance and Technology: The Development and Transformation of Scenography*, 2nd edn (Basingstoke: Palgrave Macmillan, 2014), p. 221.

44 Ibid.

45 Ibid., p. 222; original emphasis.

46 Ibid.

47 tucker green, *hang*, p. 5.

48 Ibid.

49 Susannah Clapp, 'Marianne Jean-Baptiste's Terrible Choice in a Terrifying Space', Rev. of *hang*, *Observer*, 21 June 2015, www.theguardian.com/stage/2015/jun/21/hang-review-marianne-jean-baptiste-debbie-tucker-green, accessed 4 July 2017.

50 Victoria Sadler, Rev. of *hang*, *Huffington Post*, 18 June 2015, www.huffingtonpost.co.uk/victoria-sadler/hang-royal-court-theatre_b_7606006.html, accessed 4 July 2017.

51 Sarah Hemming, Rev. of *hang*, *Financial Times*, 19 June 2015, www.ft.com/content/fc523ff8–159f-11e5-be54–00144feabdc0, accessed 4 July 2017.

52 Sadler, Rev. of *hang*.

53 Sadler's review picks up on it obliquely: '[t]he incident at the heart of the debate is never explained. And, of course, what fills this void is the feverish leaps of the audience's imagination'. Ibid.

54 See reviews by Michael Billington, Susannah Clapp, and Sarah Hemming, among others. Michael Billington, 'Marianne Jean-Baptiste Looks Back in Fury', Rev. of *hang*, *Guardian*, 17 June 2015, www.theguardian.com/stage/2015/jun/17/hang-review-marianne-jean-baptiste-justice-capital-punishment, accessed 4 July 2017.

55 Mojisola Adebayo and Valerie Mason-John, in conversation with Deirdre Osborne, '"No Straight Answers": Writing in the Margins, Finding Lost Heroes', *New Theatre Quarterly* 25.1 (Feb 2009), 6–21 (p. 18). Aston notes that another tucker green play, *Stoning Mary*, delimits that 'the fictional world of the play should be located in whichever country it is being staged in' so that it 'dis-illusions audiences of the "luxury to look down on others" by bringing home the lack of caritas, our inability to care genuinely for others'. Elaine Aston, 'Feeling the Loss of Feminism: Sarah Kane's *Blasted* and an Experiential Genealogy of Contemporary Women's Playwriting', *Theatre Journal* 62.4 (2010), 575–91 (p. 589, quoting Stjepan G. Meštrović). About a production of *Stoning Mary* at the Royal Court, Aston notes that 'the intimate hostilities of the couple were juxtaposed with the vastness of the playing space (the auditorium was adapted to create a gladiatorial styled arena), bringing an epic quality to a personal, domestic quarrel'. Ibid.

56 Aston, 'Feeling the Loss', p. 588. This combination of locations echoes Kane's *Blasted* for Aston which, she explains, quoting Heidi Stephenson and Natasha Langridge, stages 'a common rape in Leeds … [and at the same time] mass rape as a war weapon in Bosnia'. Ibid., p. 584.

57 The narrative in *hang* suggests a dystopia, the inverse to utopia, and Trish Reid discusses the play in a dys-
topian context (Trish Reid, '"Killing Joy as a World Making Project": Anger in the Work of debbie tucker
green', *Contemporary Theatre Review* 28.3 (2018), 390–400 (p. 391)), but the staging of the Royal Court's
production retained a heterotopic possibility for this audience member. There is something very concrete about tucker green's locations, as Reid also notes: '[a]s we watch *hang*, and as tucker green accounts
rationally for her imagined world, we are obliged to consider the connections as well as disconnections
between that world and our own'. Ibid.

58 See Andrew Dickson, 'How Playwright David Greig Discovered Birnam Wood in Basra', *Guardian*, 24
January 2015, www.theguardian.com/stage/2015/jan/24/how-david-greig-discovered-birnam-wood-
in-basra, accessed 4 July 2017.

59 See also Greig's production of Aeschylus's *The Suppliant Women* and the discussion of his play, *The
Events,* for further explorations of this performance of real/unreal locations, both from today and from
historical narratives. Mark Fisher, '*The Suppliant Women* Five-Star Review – An Epic, Feminist Protest
Song', *Guardian*, 6 October 2016, www.theguardian.com/stage/2016/oct/06/suppliant-women-review-
royal-lyceum-edinburgh, accessed 4 July 2017.

60 Greig further explains that for him, 'a world doesn't exist until it's been made into fiction. Our experience
doesn't exist until it's been made into fiction. A way of experiencing the world doesn't exist until it's been
made into fiction. So somehow the act of making a play is a kind of restoration to the real of something
which exists but which is not yet a map'. Quoted in Verónica Rodríguez, '*Zāhir* and *Bātin*: An Interview
with David Greig', *Contemporary Theatre Review* 26.1 (2016), 88–96 (p. 89).

61 Tuan even argues that '[s]pace is historical if it has direction or a privileged perspective. Maps are ahistorical, landscape paintings are historical'. Tuan, *Space and Place*, p. 122.

7

Foucault and Shakespeare: the theatre of madness

Stuart Elden

The names of Michel Foucault and William Shakespeare are linked in many ways. Following the influence of new historicism, Foucault has had a significant impact in Shakespeare studies. Many themes in Foucault's work, from power, sexuality, madness, disease, and government, resonate with aspects of Shakespeare's plays. The potential for using Foucault to examine Shakespeare's plays is a topic for another time. But it is only slowly becoming clear just how important Shakespeare was to Foucault. Foucault was interested in Shakespeare's plays from the beginning to the end of his career. Shakespeare is used as an illustrative example in Foucault's first publications on mental illness in 1954; he has a small but significant role in *The History of Madness*; he is an occasional reference point in the lecture courses at the Collège de France, especially those concerning the transition from sovereign to disciplinary power; and in his final lecture course Foucault provides a poignant reading of the opening scene of *King Lear* as a test of *parrēsia*. This chapter explores those different readings, tracing the significance of Shakespeare for Foucault. In all of these readings Foucault is intrigued by the relation between the theatre as a representation and theatre as a 'tear in the fabric of the world'.[1]

Figures of madness

The dominant focus of Foucault's early work was the question of mental illness. Initially he was interested in psychology and especially the *Daseinsanalysis* of Ludwig Binswanger and his colleagues. This interest dominates his first publications, written in the early 1950s. In the mid-late 1950s, Foucault's focus develops into the research that will shape his first major book, *History of Madness*. It was perhaps inevitable that he would turn to Shakespeare on this theme, given the several figures of madness who appear in plays such as *King Lear, Hamlet,* and *Macbeth.* One of Foucault's first publications was a long introduction to Binswanger's *Dream and Existence,* published in French translation in 1954.[2] The jury is out as to whether it was his first publication or was preceded by *Maladie mentale et personnalité,* which also appeared that year. In the introduction Foucault suggests that 'the dream, as with Macbeth, murders sleep'.[3] He cites two speeches from Shakespeare's play to illustrate this point. Both speeches follow the murder of Duncan, and both touch on the relation between sleep and death. The first speaks of Macbeth's concern for the deed's consequence:

> Methought I heard a voice cry, 'Sleep no more.
> Macbeth does murder sleep' – the innocent sleep,
> Sleep that knits up the ravelled sleave of care,
> The death of each day's life, sore labour's bath,
> Balm of hurt minds, great Nature's second course,
> Chief nourisher in life's feast –[4]

This is a passage of stark contrast, from the violence of the murder and the death of sleep, to the beautiful phrasing of the healing power of sleep in ordinary circumstances. The idea of sleep tying up the frayed, loose ends of our troubles, a bath, a balm, a nourisher is a calming gentle one of rest; though the idea of sleep being a death to 'each day's life' leads the praise back to the violence. A 'sleave' is a slender filament of silk (OED), though the homonym 'sleeve' is surely also meant.[5] Following a question from Lady Macbeth, Macbeth continues in this manner: 'Still it cried, "Sleep no more" to all the house; "Glamis hath murdered sleep, and therefore Cawdor/Shall sleep no more. Macbeth shall sleep no more".[6] Yet as we later discover in the play, it is actually Lady Macbeth who is unable to sleep peacefully, and who paces the castle's rooms at night, trying to rid her hands of the blood she imagines still stains them. As the Doctor suggests, this is 'a great perturbation in nature, to receive at once the benefit of sleep and do the effects of watching', something he describes as a 'slumbery agitation'.[7]

Binswanger was a Swiss psychologist, influenced by Sigmund Freud but also by German thinkers such as Edmund Husserl and, most significantly for his later work, Martin Heidegger. Foucault had been asked to collaborate on the translation by an old family friend, Jacqueline Verdeaux. Asked by Verdeaux for a good first piece to translate, Binswanger had suggested the essay 'Dream and Existence', which he thought was a good introduction to his mature work. While Verdeaux was an accomplished translator and clinician, she felt a need to consult an expert on the existential philosophy which shapes so much of the text. A recent graduate in philosophy and psychology, Foucault knew the specialised vocabulary and had ideas of how to render it in French. Indeed, so little of Heidegger was translated into French at the time that Foucault and Verdeaux are to a large extent shaping the vocabulary themselves, rather than being able to make it consistent with existing works in French. Having completed the translation, Verdeaux suggested that Foucault might like to introduce it. The result was a long, sprawling text, longer than the essay it introduced.[8]

In this introduction, Foucault makes a second reference to Shakespeare. This is the passage where Banquo, Malcolm, and Donalbain are awoken by Macduff from their 'downy sleep, death's counterfeit' to 'look on death itself'.[9] Shakespeare has

Macduff continue to compare the sight to 'the great doom's image', and implores the king's sons to 'As from your graves rise up, and walk like sprites/To countenance this horror'.[10] This sense of the relation between sleep and death, and disrupted sleep with madness is a recurrent theme in the play – from Macbeth's famous hallucination of the dagger shortly before the murder, to his suggestion that 'Now o'er the one half-world/ Nature seems dead, and wicked dreams abuse/The curtained sleep'.[11] The sense, surely, is that the natural order of things sleeps, appearing dead, and that wicked and unnatural dreams take over. 'Curtained' is both a direct relation to a four-poster bed, but also the idea of a veil or shroud over a sleeping body.[12] As Ross later says in conversation with an old man:

> By th' clock 'tis day,
> And yet dark night strangles the travelling lamp.
> Is't night's predominance, or the day's shame,
> That darkness does the face of earth entomb
> When living light should kiss it?[13]

The old man replies that it is 'unnatural', like the crime, and gives the example of a falcon attacked by a 'mousing owl' – a lower flying, and lower ranking, bird killing a higher one.[14] While Foucault does not draw on all these resources in *Macbeth* to make his point, his discussion is also notable because it is the one place that he talks about Shakespeare's *Julius Caesar*. His focus is specifically the dream of Calpurnia which 'foretells the death of Caesar: a dream which speaks no less of the entire power and freedom of the *imperator* who shakes the world – in the interpretation of Decius – than of the risks he runs and his imminent assassination, in Calpurnia's own interpretation'.[15] Calpurnia is Caesar's wife, and her dream is a crucial moment in the play, though one perhaps overshadowed by the Soothsayer, in anticipating what will come to be. The Soothsayer tells Caesar, famously, to 'beware the Ides of March'.[16] Caesar recalls that in the night Calpurnia called out 'Help ho: they murder Caesar'.[17] When she recalls the dream, she tells him:

> Caesar, I never stood on ceremonies,
> Yet now they fright me. There is one within,
> Besides the things that we have heard and seen,
> Recounts most horrid sights seen by the watch.
> A lioness hath whelped in the streets,
> And graves have yawned and yielded up their dead.
> Fierce fiery warriors fight upon the clouds
> In ranks and squadrons and right form of war,
> Which drizzled blood upon the Capitol.
> The noise of battle hurtled in the air,
> Horses do neigh, and dying men did groan,
> And ghosts did shriek and squeal about the streets.
> O Caesar, these things are beyond all use,
> And I do fear them.[18]

The idea of 'standing on ceremonies' has become a well-known phrase. But its familiarity masks that the term 'ceremonies', here, has a more technical sense, both of formalities but also of 'a portent or omen drawn from a rite' (OED).[19] When Decius

Brutus arrives, Caesar says that he will not leave home to go to the Senate, because of his will. But pressed, he reveals that Calpurnia's dream included a vision of his statue:

> Which, like a fountain with an hundred spouts,
> Did run pure blood; and many lusty Romans
> Came smiling and did bathe their hands in it.[20]

While Calpurnia takes this as a literal premonition, Decius says that rather it was a positive 'vision, fair and fortunate', and the spouting blood that the people rushed to 'signifies that from you great Rome shall suck/Reviving blood'.[21] Caesar accepts this information, and heads to the Senate. As Caesar says to the Soothsayer: 'The Ides of March are come', to which comes the reply: 'Ay, Caesar, but not gone'.[22] He is, of course, stabbed by each of the conspirators a few moments later.

Foucault elaborates a little on both *Macbeth* and *Hamlet* in the *History of Madness*, the 1961 book publication of his doctoral thesis. There he provides brief readings of the madness of two women: Ophelia and Lady Macbeth. Foucault mentions the madness of 'the last song of Ophelia'; and notes that 'the delirium of Lady Macbeth reveals to those who "have known what [they] should not" words long uttered only to "deaf pillows"'.[23] The fuller passage from *Macbeth* which Foucault is quoting is revealing in the terms outlined above. The Doctor tells Lady Macbeth's servant that 'Foul whisperings are abroad. Unnatural deeds/Do breed unnatural troubles. Infected minds/To their deaf pillows will discharge their secrets/More needs she the divine than the physician'.[24] Here we have the relation between disrupted sleep and the unnatural; the revelation of truth in madness; and the suggestion that the disease is spiritual rather than physical.

However, in the *History of Madness* Foucault is interested predominantly in 'the bittersweet dementia of King Lear'.[25] Foucault relates Shakespeare's work to Miguel de Cervantes's *Don Quixote*, published in two parts in 1605 and 1615. Shakespeare and Cervantes famously died on the same day: their literary works, while of quite different forms, are contemporaneous. Foucault suggests that

> The madness to be found in the work of Shakespeare leads to death and murder, while the forms we see in Cervantes are linked rather to presumption or the compensations of the imagination. But they are the high models that imitators inflect and weaken. Both in all probability still bear witness to the tragic experience of madness born in the fifteenth century more than they reflect the critical or moral experience of unreason that is nonetheless a product of their era. Through time, they connect with a kind of madness that is in the process of disappearing, and which will live on only under the cover of darkness. But a comparison between their work and what it maintains and the new forms to be found in their contemporaries or their imitators will show what is happening in this early part of the seventeenth century, in the literary experience of madness.
>
> In Cervantes and Shakespeare, madness occupies an extreme position in that it is invariably without issue. There is no going back to truth or reason. It opens only onto a tear in the fabric of the world [*le déchirement*], and therefore onto death. Madness, in its empty words, is not vanity: the void that fills it is a 'disease beyond my practice' as the doctor says of Lady Macbeth, and it is already the plenitude that death brings, a madness that does not need a doctor, but divine forgiveness. The sweet joy that Ophelia finds at the end has little to do with happiness, and her senseless song is as near the essential as 'the cry of women' announcing in the corridors of Macbeth's castle that 'the Queen is dead'.[26]

This is a powerful passage, certainly, and while Shakespeare and Cervantes work for Foucault as the two parallel literary examples of a specific period, and a hint of a period that precedes them, the contrasts between their conceptions are also intriguing. The madness of Don Quixote is delusional, an excess of imagination, whereas Lady Macbeth's madness is spiritual, generated by the crime she and her husband had planned and completed. The specific form her madness takes leads to the doctor's comment that the disease is beyond his practice. When we come to the wonderful phrase 'a tear in the fabric of the world', we actually need to thank his translators, Jonathan Murphy and Jean Khalfa. Foucault simply says madness is a tear or rip, *le déchirement*, without specifying what that rupture is within. In the earlier translation of an abridged version of the text, *Madness and Civilisation*, Richard Howard translates the phrase as 'it leads only to laceration and thence to death'.[27]

In a contemporaneous interview Foucault underlines the point that Lady Macbeth only begins to speak the truth when she is mad.[28] She is overheard saying such things as 'who would have thought the old man to have so much blood in him',[29] which is part of the reason behind the doctor's statement that 'infected minds/To their deaf pillows will discharge their secrets'.[30] Yet these citations are to set up a contrast to the period Foucault thinks we entered in the seventeenth century, suggesting that '[b]ut early on, madness leaves these extreme regions where Cervantes and Shakespeare had placed it'.[31] As he concludes the chapter on 'The Great Confinement':

> Madness was denied the imaginary liberty that still allowed it to flourish at the time of the Renaissance. Not so long ago it was still visible in the light of day, as in *King Lear* or *Don Quixote*, but within the space of half a century it found itself a recluse in the fortress of confinement, bound fast to Reason, to the rules of morality and their monotonous nights.[32]

Foucault's point about madness is intriguing in relation to Shakespeare, because he sees him as writing at a pivotal moment at the shift from the medieval world to the modern one. *King Lear* was first performed in 1606, and published in a quarto text in 1608; shortly after the first part of *Don Quixote*. *Macbeth* was similarly first performed in 1606, but not published until the first folio of 1623. As with his understanding of other phenomena of his time, Shakespeare is writing with one eye on the historical past, and one eye to the present or future. He thus helps us to see the way that things were conceived at the moment of a crucial transition: where they are not so familiar that we cannot imagine things otherwise. I have made the same argument about his understanding of territory.[33]

In *History of Madness*, Foucault's reading is principally influenced by André Adnès's study *Shakespeare et la folie*.[34] Since Foucault wrote the *History of Madness* much discussion has followed in his footsteps, and it would be an unusual analysis of madness which did not relate in some way to his researches.[35] As Richard Wilson elaborates, Foucault 'read Shakespearean theatre as a battleground between the modern state and the dreamers, lunatics, suicides and vagrants who escape its discipline, an evasion he identified especially with Shakespeare's fools'.[36] Of course, some of Foucault's critics have challenged him for his too easy equation of dramatic, fictional representations and historical fact. His use of the idea of a ship of fools has been especially disputed. Here, Foucault elaborated from Sebastian Brant's book of that title, and Hieronymus Bosch's painting, to suggest the actual existence of these vessels.[37]

Foucault regularly returns to *King Lear*, but often repeats similar points.[38] In a radio lecture from 1963 he presents a long passage from the play, but does not say a great deal about what he sees as significant in it.[39] The passage is Lear in the storm, beginning with the famous words:

> Blow winds, and crack your cheeks! Rage! blow!
> You cataracts and hurricanes, spout
> Till you have drenched our steeples, drowned the cocks!
> You sulphurous and thought-executing fires,
> Vaunt-couriers of oak-cleaving thunderbolts,
> Singe my white head! And thou, all-shaking thunder,
> Strike flat the thick rotundity o'the world,
> Crack nature's moulds, all germens spill at once
> That make ingrateful man![40]

Foucault continues reading the scene for several more lines, including the dialogue with Lear's fool and with the disguised Duke of Kent. He describes this as 'the great scene of madness in the play, the scene on the heath'.[41] In his radio address he seems to think that this passage largely stands without commentary, and so we are not given the kind of line glosses that might have been revealing, especially for a French audience hearing this in translation. Foucault uses the 1959 Gallimard translation from the Pléiade edition; his notes now archived at the Bibliothèque Nationale include a transcription of this passage from the 1942 Camille Chemin bilingual edition.[42] For the benefit of his listeners it might have been helpful to explain that the winds Lear invokes are from the sky and the sea, that the cocks are weathercocks on the steeples, and that 'vaunt-couriers' are forerunners. Cracking 'nature's moulds' would be the end to natural forms, a way of describing the end of the world; as would the idea of all seeds, 'germens', spilling at one moment.[43] Yet while he seems reluctant to take on the role of an exegete, Foucault is unstinting in his praise of the play:

> *King Lear* is, without doubt, the very rare, the very solitary portrayal of a fully and completely tragic expression of madness. It's without equal, without equal in a culture like our own because our culture has always taken care to keep madness at a distance and consider it from a somewhat remote, and always justified, point of view, in spite of the occasional indulgences of comedy.[44]

While *King Lear* therefore functions for him as an exemplar of a lost age, he occasionally sees it as an example of wider theatrical device. For example, in a 1970 lecture in Japan he suggested:

> In the traditional European theatre – I imagine the same thing is true in Japan – the fool assumed a central role, from the Middle Ages to the eighteenth century. The madman made the spectators laugh, for he saw what the other actors did not see, and he revealed the ending of the plot [*dénouement de la trame*] before they did. That is, he is an individual who reveals the truth with spirit. Shakespeare's *King Lear* is a good example. The king is a victim of his own fantasy, but at the same time he is someone who tells the truth. In other words, in the theatre the madman is a character who expresses with his body the truth that the other actors and spectators are not aware of, a character through whom the truth appears.[45]

Lear himself plays that role later in the play, where he takes on the mediation of truth between the action and the spectators. But earlier in the play this mediating role is taken on by Lear's fool. The fool regularly makes comments that had they been made by any of Lear's other followers would have led to banishment or death. The tolerance of his chiding of Lear is in clear contrast with the way that Lear treats the Duke of Kent in the opening scene. Following her refusal to join her sisters in their praise of their father, Cordelia is condemned by Lear, and disinherited. Kent comes to Cordelia's defence and suggests that Lear should 'revoke thy doom'.[46] In a related manner of the risk of truth-telling, Cordelia's refusal to make the obsequious display of love that her sisters had is a mad gesture of the truth. She too, like Kent, the only figure who comes to her defence, is disowned and expelled. The disappearance of the fool in the play, for reasons which are only textually hinted at in the final scene with the line 'and my poor fool is hanged', has been much debated.[47] Foucault's suggestion perhaps gives one rationale: once Lear himself is taking on this mediating role, there is no need for the fool anymore.

Indeed, it is with this very question of truth in mind that Foucault returns to *King Lear* late in his career in his final lecture course *The Courage of Truth*.[48] Now he reads Lear again as 'no doubt the highest expression of this theme of the king of derision, the mad king, and the hidden king'.[49] But the analysis goes beyond this, bringing in the theme of *parrēsia*, fearless or frank speech:

> After all, *King Lear* begins with a story of *parrēsia*, a test of frankness: who will tell the king the truth? And King Lear is precisely someone who is unable to recognize the truth that was there. And on the basis of this failure to recognize the truth, he in turn is unrecognized. Unrecognized as king, he wanders through the world, accompanied by those who protect him and do what is good for him, without him being aware of this, until the end which covers all at once the death of his daughter, Cordelia, his own death, and the fulfilment of his wretchedness [*misère*], but a fulfilment which is at the same time the triumph and res-toration of the truth itself. I think that Cynicism has played a large role in this, as it were, political imaginary of the unrecognized monarchy.[50]

This reading continues some of the themes of the earlier treatment, but refocuses it in the light of Foucault's concerns with the question of *parrēsia* in these, his last public words. This discussion comes in the penultimate lecture of his final course, delivered just three months before his death, and there is often a poignancy to his remarks on his subject matter, from the death of Socrates to that of Lear.

Political power

Foucault's other references to Shakespeare in works he published in his lifetime are brief. He mentions the neglect of Shakespeare in the classical age in his essay 'Nietzsche, Genealogy, History',[51] and Shakespeare is perhaps an inevitable refer-ence in his discussion of the question of authorship and naming.[52] He suggests that

Raymond Roussel owes something to Shakespeare in his study of the French writer.[53] Aside from these, the other discussions in his published books and essays are largely around the question of madness and can be seen as illustrations of the conflict between the individual and the mechanisms of discipline. Those themes have been the focus of this chapter.

However, there is another reading of Shakespeare which comes through in Foucault's Collège de France lecture courses. Foucault suggests that 'a part of Shakespeare's historical drama [*théâtre historique*] really is the drama of the *coup d'État*'.[54] The majority of Shakespeare's shifts in power are from one king to another – the deposition of Richard II by Henry Bolingbroke; the killing of Duncan by Macbeth; the machinations of Richard, Duke of York on his way to the throne. Foucault recognises this, and suggests that the *coup d'État* is a necessarily theatrical act. It leads him to some intriguing reflections on the relation between theatre and politics. In his 1975–76 course '*Society Must be Defended*' Foucault suggests that 'tragedy was one of the great ritual forms in which public right was displayed and in which its problems were discussed'.[55]

Indeed, as well as the French dramatists Corneille and Racine, Foucault singles out Shakespeare for insisting on this:

> Shakespeare's 'historical' tragedies are tragedies about right and the king, and they are essentially centered on the problem of the usurper and dethronement [*déchéance*], of the assassination of kings and the birth of the new being who is constituted by the coronation of a king. [...] Shakespearean tragedy is, at least in terms of one of its axes, a sort of ceremony, a sort of re-memorialization of the problems of public right.[56]

Nonetheless, when Foucault is searching for an example of shift in political power he turns away from Shakespeare. In the 1973–74 lecture course, *Psychiatric Power*, one of Foucault's striking examples is of a monarch who lived and died long after Shakespeare's time, George III (1738–1820). Foucault takes the account from Philippe Pinel – a key figure in the *History of Madness* – who himself based it on the account by the King's doctor, Sir Francis Willis.[57] Here the mad king is effectively deposed by his doctors. In contrast to Shakespeare's plays, with the shift from one sovereign to another, Foucault argues that the transition from this King's rule to his doctors' rule is indicative of a different mode of political transformation:

> Deposition [*destitution*] and therefore the king's fall; but my impression is that it is not the same type of fall as we find in, say, a Shakespearean drama: this is not Richard III threatened with falling under the power [*puissance*] of another sovereign, nor King Lear stripped of his sovereignty and roaming the world in solitude, poverty and madness. In fact, the king's [George III] madness, unlike that of King Lear, condemned to roam the world, fixes him at a precise point and, especially, brings him under, not another sovereign power [*un autre pouvoir souverain*], but a completely different type of power [*pouvoir*] which differs, term by term, I think from the power of sovereignty. It is an anonymous, nameless and faceless power; it is a power that is distributed between different persons. Above all it is a power that is expressed through an implacable regulation that is not even formulated, since, basically, nothing is said, and the text actually says that all the agents of this power remain silent. The silence of regulation takes over, as it were, the empty place left by the king's dethronement.[58]

In these early Collège de France courses, Foucault was continually searching for examples where sovereign power is replaced by a different kind of power, what he at this time calls discipline. In France, with the Revolution, a king had been executed and the first republic founded. However, political thought had, Foucault suggested, not kept up with this development. Instead of following the practice where power became more dispersed and not concentrated in a single place, Foucault felt that the political thought of his time was still in thrall to that earlier model of power. This is the reason behind his famous claim that 'in political thought and analysis we still have not cut off the head of the king'.[59] The *Psychiatric Power* course predates *Discipline and Punish* – Foucault had drafted a version before its delivery, and finalised the revisions only a few months after its completion – but its focus is rather different. In a sense, the course is an expansion and development of claims made in the closing parts of *History of Madness*, especially the chapter on 'The Birth of the Asylum', in the light of the new concepts of power and discipline Foucault had been developing in his early 1970s lecture courses.[60] For Foucault, the treatment of a mad figure in hospitals or asylums is emblematic of the conflict between the individual and the mechanisms of discipline. That this figure is a king merely reinforces the point of a shift in strategies of power. At this time the Shakespearean *coup d'État*, where a king is replaced by another king, seems to be less interesting to Foucault than a moment where a sovereign is replaced, not with another sovereign, but with a different, more anonymous, form of power.

Nonetheless, even as he highlights the contrast, Foucault still utilises the language of ritual, ceremony, and procedure to make his point. He claims that the treatment of George III is an example of

> basically, a ceremony, a ceremony of deposition [*destitution*], a sort of reverse coronation [*sacre à l'envers*] in which it is quite clearly shown that it involves placing the king in a situation of complete subordination; you remember the words: 'all trappings of royalty having disappeared', and the doctor, who is, as it were, the effective agent of this dethronement, of this deconsecration, explicitly telling him that 'he is no longer sovereign'.[61]

The reading of George III developed here is thus more appropriate to the model of power that Foucault is developing. Foucault also explicitly relates it to the discussion of madness in his earlier writings.

> So this is not a case of one sovereign power falling under another sovereign power, but the transition from a sovereign power – decapitated by a madness that has seized hold of the king's head, and dethroned by the ceremony that shows the king that he is no longer sovereign – to another power. In place of this beheaded and dethroned power, an anonymous, multiple, pale, colorless power is installed, which is basically the power that I will call discipline.[62]

Elsewhere I have pursued this question of ceremony in relation to Foucault and Shakespeare in much more detail. The political reading is, as I have suggested, potentially productive in a wider inquiry into the ceremony in Shakespeare. Several Shakespeare plays, especially his histories and tragedies, show the political role of ceremony and ritual; and their performance is a political theatre which is itself a kind of ceremony. Yet as I show in that piece, it is striking that many of the ceremonies in Shakespeare's plays are ones which are contested, disputed, censored, repeated, refused, or parodied.[63]

Foucault in Münsterlingen

The extent of Foucault's interest in theatre, Shakespeare, and madness is only slowly being revealed. We have long known of the importance of theatre generally, such as the performance of Samuel Beckett's *Waiting for Godot* which he saw in 1953 and said had a profound impact on him.[64] Much of the more political reading of Shakespeare comes from his lecture courses, and the work on madness can be revisited in the light of new documentary sources. These include some recent archival publications, drawn from the extensive collection of Foucault's materials at the Bibliothèque National de France, as well as transcriptions of lecture and other recordings. One of these is the radio address where he read the passage from *King Lear*. At the beginning of that programme he suggests a contrast between his view and that of the radio host, Jean Doat, who he describes as a 'man of the theatre'. Foucault suggests that his view is somewhat different:

> I have the impression that theatre turns its back on festival [*fête*], turns its back on madness, that it tries to attenuate their powers, to control their force and subversive violence in favour of the beauty of representation. The theatre, ultimately, destroys the participants, the participants of the festival, to bring to life the actors on one side and the audience on the other. In place of the mask of festival, which is a mask of communication, it substitutes something made of cardboard or plaster, something more subtle but which conceals and separates.[65]

Robert Bonnono renders the French *fête* as 'celebration', but this risks missing the importance of the festival, a carnivalesque celebration discussed by, among others, Mikhail Bakhtin and Henri Lefebvre in their readings of François Rabelais.[66] Foucault is doubtless thinking of a more concrete reference, however. As a direct result of his translation work with Verdeaux, Foucault made several visits to Binswanger's Kreuzlingen sanatorium, where he met Binswanger and Roland Kuhn. On one of the visits, in 1954, Foucault went to nearby Münsterlingen on Lake Constance. There he attended a 'fête des fous', a carnival of the mad, a festival with roots back to the Middle Ages.[67] One of the most intriguing publications from the archive recently has been *Foucault à Münsterlingen*, a documentary and photographic report of that visit.[68]

The ceremony had the patients, along with their doctors and nurses, in costumes and elaborate, over-sized masks. The masks obscured their identities, as well as representing a carnivalesque attitude. For the style of the masks, think Punch and Judy rather than a masked ball. All paraded from the hospital to the local village hall, led by the figure of Carnival. At the end of the evening they burnt the effigy of Carnival and the masks in a large bonfire.[69] Foucault only spoke of this event a couple of times in discussions of a film – the *Histoire de Paul*. He made the contrast between the film and the festival in impersonal terms. Here he describes the *fête des fous* that took place in some Swiss psychiatric hospitals and I think in certain areas of Germany: the day of the carnival, the mad disguised themselves and went into town, of course not the ones who were gravely ill; they acted out a carnival where the population watched from a distance and with some trepidation, and it was ultimately rather terrible that the only day they were permitted to go out together *en masse* was the day they had to disguise themselves and literally act mad, like how non-mad people act mad.[70]

Only with the publication of *Foucault à Münsterlingen* are we really able to connect this invocation with the events Foucault witnessed, and which seems to have had a significant impact on his early work. Foucault's first two major publications appeared in 1954: *Maladie mentale et personnalité* and the introduction to the Binswanger translation.[71] After 1954 Foucault published very little until the *History of Madness* in 1961. Even his two 1957 essays on psychology were likely written before he left for a post in Uppsala in 1955.[72] While in Uppsala Foucault's work shifted from what he describes as a history of psychology – and for which he signed a book contract with La Table Ronde – to the work that he submitted as his primary doctoral thesis, which was published as *Folie et déraison* – better known in English by the first half of its subtitle: *History of Madness*. This was a book which took a very different approach to these questions than his publications of the 1950s. Indeed, when the publisher wanted to reissue *Maladie mentale et personnalité* Foucault tried to prevent it, but eventually compromised by rewriting some of the first part and the whole of the second part, leading to a book under the title of *Maladie mentale et psychologie* which appeared in 1962.

Through this period the use of literary examples, and Shakespeare in particular, endures. My own ongoing research looks in detail at this period of Foucault, and the transition from the 1954 texts to the *History of Madness* and related writings.[73] It is a period in which questions of madness dominate, but the recurrent role of Shakespeare suggests the important role that theatre plays throughout Foucault's writing.[74]

Notes

1 Michel Foucault, *Histoire de la folie à l'âge classique* (Paris: Gallimard, 1976), p. 50; Michel Foucault, *History of Madness*, trans. Jonathan Murphy and Jean Khalfa (London: Routledge, 2006), p. 38. The French is a little more restricted than the English here; a point to which I will return.
2 Ludwig Binswanger, Le rêve et l'existence, trans. Jacqueline Verdeaux, Introduction and Notes by Michel Foucault (Paris: Desclée de Brouwer, 1954).
3 Michel Foucault, 'Introduction', *Dits et écrits 1954-1988*, ed. Daniel Defert and François Ewald, 4 vols (Paris: Gallimard, 1994), 1:94. Hereafter referred to as *DE*; Michel Foucault, 'Dream, Imagination and Existence', in Ludwig Binswanger and Michel Foucault, *Dream and Existence*, trans. Forrest Williams, ed. Keith Hoeller (Atlantic Highlands, NJ: Humanities Press, 1985), p. 54.
4 William Shakespeare, *Macbeth*, ed. Sandra Clark and Pamela Mason (London: Bloomsbury Arden Shakespeare, 2015), Act II, scene ii, 37–41. The first two lines are not directly cited by Foucault.
5 Clark and Mason, note to *Macbeth*, p. 181.
6 Shakespeare, *Macbeth*, II.ii.42–4.
7 Ibid., V.i.9–11.

8 This story is recounted in both Didier Eribon, *Michel Foucault*, trans. Betsy Wing (London: Faber, 1991), pp. 43–9 and David Macey, *The Lives of Michel Foucault* (London: Hutchinson, 1993), pp. 59–62.
9 Shakespeare, *Macbeth*, II.iii.75–7; see Foucault, 'Introduction', pp. 94–6; Foucault, 'Dream, Imagination and Existence', pp. 54–5.
10 Shakespeare, *Macbeth*, II.iii.78–9.
11 Ibid., II.i.49–51.
12 Clark and Mason, notes to *Macbeth*, pp. 175–6.
13 Shakespeare, *Macbeth*, II.iv.6–10.
14 Ibid., II.iv.10–13.
15 Foucault, 'Introduction', 1:95; Foucault, 'Dream, Imagination and Existence', p. 55. Calpurnia is the classical spelling, in, for example, Plutarch, and the one that Foucault uses. Calphurnia is the spelling in the Folio, and many editions of the play.
16 William Shakespeare, *Julius Caesar*, ed. David Daniell (London: Arden Shakespeare, 1998), I.ii.18.
17 Ibid., II.ii.2–3.
18 Ibid., II.ii.13–26.
19 Daniell, note to *Julius Caesar*, p. 219.
20 Shakespeare, *Julius Caesar*, II.ii.76–9.
21 Ibid., II.ii.87–8.
22 Ibid., III.i.1–2.
23 Foucault, *Histoire de la folie*, pp. 49–50; Foucault, *History of Madness*, p. 37; Shakespeare, *Macbeth*, V.I.46, 73.
24 Shakespeare, *Macbeth*, V.i.71–4.
25 Foucault, *Histoire de la folie*, p. 49; Foucault, *History of Madness*, p. 37.
26 Foucault, *Histoire de la folie*, pp. 49–50; Foucault, *History of Madness*, pp. 37–8. 'This disease is beyond my practice' – Shakespeare, *Macbeth*, V.i.59; 'The Queen, my lord, is dead' – Ibid., V.v.16.
27 Foucault, *Madness and Civilization: A History of Insanity in the Age of Reason*, trans. Richard Howard (London: Routledge, 1971), p. 31.
28 Foucault, 'La folie n'existe que dans une société', in *DE*, 1:169; Michel Foucault, 'Madness Only Exists in Society', *Foucault Live (Interviews, 1961–1984)*, ed. Sylvère Lotringer, trans. Lysa Hochroth and John Johnston (New York: Semiotext(e), 1996), pp. 7–9 (p. 9).
29 Shakespeare, *Macbeth*, V.i.39–40.
30 Ibid., V.i.72–3.
31 Foucault, *Histoire de la folie*, p. 50; Foucault, *History of Madness*, p. 38. See Foucault, *Maladie mentale et psychologie* (Paris: PUF, 1962), p. 79; Michel Foucault, *Madness: The Invention of an Idea*, trans. Alan Sheridan (New York: Harper Perennial, 2011), p. 111.
32 Foucault, *Histoire de la folie*, p. 91; Foucault, *History of Madness*, p. 77.
33 See Stuart Elden, *Shakespearean Territories* (Chicago, IL: University of Chicago Press, 2018). The reading of *King Lear* has been published as 'The Geopolitics of *King Lear*: Territory, Land, Earth', *Law and Literature*, 25.2 (2013), 147–65.
34 André Adnès, *Shakespeare et la folie: Étude médico-psychologique* (Paris: Librairie Maloine, 1936).
35 In a large literature, see the recent work of Lynne Huffer, *Mad for Foucault: Rethinking the Foundations of Queer Theory* (New York: Columbia University Press, 2009) and Kélina Gotman, *Choreomania: Dance and Disorder* (Oxford: Oxford University Press, 2018).
36 Richard Wilson, *Shakespeare in French Theory: King of Shadows* (London: Routledge, 2007), p. 9. Some of the chapters in this book, especially chapter 2, show the influence of Foucault on his work. Wilson principally uses the works published in Foucault's lifetime, rather than the lecture courses, largely due to the dates of their publication. The same is true of his earlier *Will Power: Essays on Shakespearean Authority* (London: Harvester-Wheatsheaf, 1993), which like many works of new historicism takes inspiration from Foucault's work.
37 Richard Wilson, 'Ship of Fools: Foucault and the Shakespeareans', *English Studies*, 94.7 (2013), 773–87; revised version in Jennifer Ann Bates and Richard Wilson (eds), *Shakespeare and Continental Philosophy* (Edinburgh: Edinburgh University Press, 2014), pp. 195–209.

38 There is a brief mention of the mad in Shakespeare in a recently published lecture: Michel Foucault, 'La literature et la folie', *Critique*, 835 (2016), 965–80 (p. 966).

39 Michel Foucault, *La grande étrangère: À propos de literature*, ed. Philippe Artières, Jean-François Bert, Mathieu Potte-Bonville and Judith Revel (Paris: Éditions EHESS, 2013), pp. 29–32; Michel Foucault, *Language, Madness, and Desire: On Literature*, trans. Robert Bonnano (Minneapolis: University of Minnesota Press, 2015), pp. 8–11.

40 William Shakespeare, *King Lear*, ed. R. A. Foakes (London: Arden Shakespeare, 1997), III.ii.1–9.

41 Foucault, *La grande étrangère*, p. 29; Foucault, *Language, Madness, and Desire*, p. 8.

42 Editor note to Foucault, *La grande étrangère*, p. 29n.2; Bibliothèque Nationale de France, Fonds Michel Foucault, NAF28730 (34a), Folder 2, p. 1. The editions are William Shakespeare, *Œuvres complètes*, trans. Pierre Leyris and Elizabeth Holland (Paris: Gallimard, 1959); and William Shakespeare, *Le roi Lear*, trans. Camille Chemin (Paris: Aubier, 1942).

43 See Foakes, notes to Shakespeare, *King Lear*, p. 263.

44 Foucault, *La grande étrangère*, p. 32; Foucault, *Language, Madness, and Desire*, pp. 10–11.

45 Foucault, 'La folie et la société', in *DE*, 2:133; Michel Foucault, 'Madness and Society', in *Aesthetics, Method and Epistemology: Essential Works Volume 2*, ed. James Faubion (London: Penguin, 1998), pp. 335–42 (p. 340).

46 Shakespeare, *King Lear*, I.i.165, following the Quarto text.

47 Ibid., V.iii.304. Cordelia has herself been hanged, and there is a therefore a question of whether this line applies only to her, to perhaps to the character of the fool as well.

48 For a fuller discussion of Foucault's work on *parrēsia*, see Stuart Elden, *Foucault's Last Decade* (Cambridge: Polity, 2016), especially chapter 8.

49 Michel Foucault, *Le courage de la vérité: Le gouvernement des soi et des autres II: Cours au Collège de France (1983–1984)*, ed. Frédéric Gros (Paris: Gallimard/Seuil, 2009), p. 263; translated as Michel Foucault, *The Courage of Truth (The Government of the Self and Others II): Lectures at the Collège de France 1983–84*, trans. Graham Burchell (Basingstoke: Palgrave Macmillan, 2011), p. 286.

50 Foucault, *Le courage de la vérité*, p. 263; Foucault, *The Courage of Truth*, p. 286. See Arianna Sforzini, 'The Role of Parrhēsia', in Catherine M. Soussloff (ed.), *Foucault on the Arts and Letters: Perspectives for the 21st Century* (London: Rowman and Littlefield International, 2016), pp. 135–46.

51 Foucault, 'Nietzsche, la généalogie, l'histoire', in *DE*, 2:152; Foucault, 'Nietzsche, Genealogy, History', in *Aesthetics, Method and Epistemology*, pp. 369–91 (p. 384).

52 Foucault, 'Qu'est-ce qu'un auteur?', in *DE*, 1:797; Foucault, 'What is an Author?', in *Aesthetics, Method and Epistemology*, pp. 205–22 (p. 210).

53 Michel Foucault, *Raymond Roussel* (Paris: Gallimard, 1963).

54 Michel Foucault, *Sécurité, Territoire, Population: Cours au Collège de France (1977–1978)*, ed. Michel Senellart (Paris: Seuil/Gallimard, 2004), p. 271; Michel Foucault, *Security, Territory, Population: Lectures at the Collège de France 1977–1978*, trans. Graham Burchell (Basingstoke: Palgrave Macmillan, 2008), p. 265.

55 Michel Foucault, *'Il faut défendre la société': Cours au Collège de France (1975–1976)*, ed. Mauro Bertani and Alessandro Fontana (Paris: Seuil/Gallimard, 1997), p. 155; Michel Foucault, *'Society Must Be Defended'*, trans. David Macey (London: Allen Lane, 2003), pp. 174–5.

56 Foucault, *'Il faut défendre la société'*, p. 155; *'Society Must Be Defended'*, pp. 174–5.

57 Philippe Pinel, *Traité médico-philosophique sur l'aliénation mentale* (Paris: Brosson, 1801), pp. 192–3, 286–90; *Report from the Committee Appointed to Examine the Physicians who have Attended his Majesty during his Illness, touching the Present State of his Majesty's Health* (London: J. Bell, 1789). For the fullest account, see Ida Macalpine and Richard Hunter, *George III and the Mad-Business* (London: Allen Lane, 1969).

58 Michel Foucault, *Le pouvoir psychiatrique: Cours au Collège de France (1973–1974)*, ed. Jacques Lagrange (Paris: Seuil/Gallimard, 2003), p. 23; Michel Foucault, *Psychiatric Power: Lectures at the Collège de France 1973–1974*, trans. Graham Burchell (Basingstoke: Palgrave Macmillan, 2006), p. 21.

59 Foucault, *Histoire de la sexualité I: La Volonté de savoir* (Paris: Gallimard, 1976), p. 117; Foucault, *The History of Sexuality*, Vol. 1, *The Will to Knowledge*, trans. Robert Hurley (London: Penguin, 1978), pp. 88–9.

60 For a fuller discussion see Stuart Elden, *Foucault: The Birth of Power* (Cambridge: Polity, 2017), chapter 4; on the writing and arguments of *Discipline and Punish*, see chapter 5.

61 Foucault, *Le pouvoir psychiatrique*, p. 22; Foucault, *Psychiatric Power*, pp. 20–1.

62 Foucault, *Le pouvoir psychiatrique*, p. 23; Foucault, *Psychiatric Power*, pp. 21–2.

63 Stuart Elden, 'Foucault and Shakespeare: Ceremony, Theatre, Politics', *Southern Journal of Philosophy*, 55, Spindel Supplement S1 (2017), 153–72. Several of the quotations from Foucault in this section are also analysed in that piece, along with readings of a number of Shakespeare plays and a discussion of the first half of Foucault's *Théories et institutions pénales: Cours au Collège de France 1971-1972*, ed. Bernard E. Harcourt (Paris: EHESS/Gallimard/Seuil, 2015).

64 Foucault, 'Archéologie d'une passion', in *DE*, 4:608. For a discussion, see Marisa C. Sánchez, 'Foucault's Beckett', in Soussloff (ed.), *Foucault on the Arts and Letters*, pp. 121–33.

65 Foucault, *La grande étrangère*, p. 28; Foucault, *Language, Madness, and Desire*, p. 7.

66 Mikhail Bakhtin, *Rabelais and His World*, trans. Helen Iswolsky (Bloomington: Indiana University Press, 1984); Henri Lefebvre, *Rabelais*, 2nd edn (Paris: Anthropos, 2001 [1955]).

67 Eribon, *Michel Foucault*, pp. 46–7; Macey, *The Lives of Michel Foucault*, pp. 61–2.

68 Jean-François Bert and Elisabetta Basso (eds), *Foucault à Münsterlingen: À l'origine de l'Histoire de la folie* (Paris: Éditions EHESS, 2015); see Elisabetta Basso, 'Complicités et ambivalences de la psychiatrie: Münsterlingen et le carnaval des fous de 1954', *Médecine/Sciences*, 33.1 (2017), 99–104.

69 See also Eribon, *Michel Foucault*, p. 42; Macey, *The Lives of Michel Foucault*, pp. 61–2.

70 Foucault, 'Sur "Histoire de Paul"', in *DE*, 3:62; 'The Asylum and the Carnival', in Michel Foucault, Patrice Maniglier, and Dork Zabunyan, *Foucault at the Movies*, translated and edited by Clare O'Farrell, New York: Columbia University Press, 2018, 151; see 'Faire les fous', in *DE*, 2:804–5; 'Paul's Story: The Story of Jonah', in *Foucault at the Movies*, 138.

71 Michel Foucault, *Maladie mentale et personnalité* (Paris: PUF, 1954).

72 Foucault, 'La psychologie de 1850 à 1950'; 'La recherché scientifique et la psychologie'; both reprinted in *DE*, 1:120–37, 137–58.

73 See Stuart Elden, *The Early Foucault* (Cambridge: Polity, forthcoming).

74 On this theme see also Arianna Sforzini, *Les scenes de la vérité: Michel Foucault et le theatre* (Lormont: Éditions Le Bord de l'Eau, 2017).

8

Philosophical phantasms: 'the Platonic differential' and 'Zarathustra's laughter'

Mischa Twitchin

What changes in our understanding of 'theatre' if it is qualified as 'philosophical'? That is, when theatre is addressed not in terms of its own historical practices – as, for example, literary or visual; dramatic or 'post-'; actors' theatre or directors' theatre; immersive or even invisible – but as something conceptual? Besides the recycling of metaphors, when Foucault reviews Gilles Deleuze's two major works of 1969 – *The Logic of Sense* and *Difference and Repetition* – under the title of 'Theatrum Philosophicum',[1] how does either term distinguish the other; not least, with respect to the history of practices and personae which it names for itself? Following the Latin idiom of Foucault's title, perhaps the most obvious distinction here would not be between the terms (theatre and philosophy) themselves, but rather with the metaphorics of the *Theatrum mundi*, that 'world' (or, in its changing meanings, 'globe') with which we think ourselves familiar.

The Platonic relation of philosophy to the world – one of abstinence, asceticism, abstraction (even in Socrates' or Seneca's exemplary deaths) – was famously overthrown by Friedrich Nietzsche, just as perhaps he himself was overthrown in Turin, 3 January 1889. In Maurice Blanchot's wonderful evocation: 'We see Nietzsche collapse at the point where Dionysus, the pagan revelation of the divine, collides in him against the affirmation of the Crucified'.[2] Here the traditional sense of philosophy as a preparation for death, the thoughtful consolation for mortality, implies that the world is its double, where death is a proof of immanence, not a realisation of transcendence. The *Theatrum mundi* is thus displaced by the sense of theatre as an exemplary trope (albeit disavowed) of philosophy's relation to itself as a *Theatrum philosophicum*. This sets the scene, when thinking with Foucault, of a phantasmaphysics displacing metaphysics.

Especially in the work of mourning, the testimony of friendship is a significant aspect of the history of philosophy. Addressing the concerns of this chapter, for example, Deleuze's little book on Foucault[3] offers a condensed reflection on a yearlong seminar (1985–86) devoted to what Foucault has still to say to us after his death.[4] Although the focus here is, indeed, on Foucault and Deleuze, with their shared discussion of Nietzsche, it is also important to remember that this is a Nietzsche presented in the work of Pierre Klossowski. Arguably, the exemplary 'philosophical theatre' in Foucault's reading is that of Klossowski's novel *Diana at her Bath* and we may note again the tragic scene of Nietzsche's collapse in Foucault's short essay on the 'prose of Acteon' (1964), evoking 'the Nietzschean interplay of Dionysus and Christ (since they are each, as Nietzsche saw, a simulacrum of the other)'.[5] Similarly, Acteon's dream of possession of Diana becomes his own death, distinct from that familiarity – or identification even – with thought that is the legacy of Descartes. Here philosophical theatre becomes a play of phantasms emanating from the death mask of thought.[6]

When Plato cites an analogy that was already ancient when he used it in the *Philebus* (47D-50E) – discussing (or, rather, disdaining) the everyday mixture of pleasure and pain in the soul – it is clear that neither the comic nor the tragic mask becomes philosophy. For Plato, philosophy should be the purification of such affects as anger, envy, and jealousy, which provide the principal motives of both life and drama. Transposing the former into the latter – the apparent arbitrariness of emotion into the ideal type of 'character' – Aristotle identifies plot as a technique for the purifying of such affects through catharsis. In the name of a *poetics*, he sought thereby to save theatre for philosophy. Paradoxically, as discussion remains caught in continued reference to the Ancients, it often seems that translations of Plato appear more contemporary than those of writers historically closer to us. While the implications of Nietzsche's drawing parody out of tragedy,[7] for instance, marks a modern resetting of the theatrical question for philosophy, it remains common place – especially in obituaries – to ascribe an 'exemplary' genre (whether tragic *or* comic) not only to the events of a person's life, but to that life itself. Here the question remains as to how the difference between the *Theatrum mundi* and the *Theatrum philosophicum* is conceived of by either, not least in defining the other.

Symptomatic of new fault lines in the historical stratification of society, Renaissance humanists, when addressing the ambiguities of the passions, would admit a hybrid genre as more appropriate to the human condition: dramatising the tragicomedy of life. Here, for example, Montaigne proposes: 'For while it is true that most of our actions are but mask and cosmetic, and that it is sometimes true that *Hœredis fletus sub persona risus est* [*Behind the mask, the tears of an heir are laughter*], nevertheless we ought to consider when judging such events how our souls are often shaken by conflicting emotions'.[8] It is in this sense of a 'conflicting' genre (as, precisely, one of the so-called 'problem' plays) that Shakespeare offers us the example, in *Measure for Measure*, of such judgement in the characters of Angelo and Isabella (in contrast, for instance, to Tarquin and Lucretia). With Shakespeare we enter, as spectators, the very Globe, passing beneath the motto of its theatre: *Totus mundus agit histrionem* – 'All the world's a stage/ And all the men and women merely players', as it is so famously glossed in *As You Like It*. If such a theatre is not philosophical (at least, in Platonic terms), does Foucault's twentieth-century evocation suggest, then, something necessarily anti-Platonic? And what might be the consequences for thinking through the difference – literally more Greek than Latin – between the theatrical and the philosophical?

Here we are engaged with a paradox. For the humanist world of theatrical analogy, with its metaphysically grounded ethical concerns with relations between face
and mask, nature and artifice, itself conforms to a Platonic dramaturgy. This mundane
theatre adheres to an interpretative metaphysics that distinguishes between reality and
appearance, as if between truth (the honest character) and lie (the dissembling character). It even relegates to a derivative interest its own reproduction of appearances
in terms of masks and actors, as if adopting for itself the traditional philosophical
denigration of such role play as simulacra or phantasms. Indeed, the dramatic canon
is full of plays that make this their very subject, whether in the name of 'dreams' or
the 'absurd'. For all that modernists tried to revalue this scenario in terms of professional training (as if an art or technique would save acting from 'mere' artifice), from
the point of view of the philosophical guardians the theatre-going *hoi polloi* remain as
happy to mistake reality for fiction as fiction for reality.

Resisting the lures of resemblance that would have us refer understanding back
to originary models or meanings, Foucault indeed calls theatre 'philosophical' in an
anti-Platonic sense. What we might think is meant by 'theatrical' in the everyday
is displaced conceptually as, precisely, a matter – or, rather, an event – of thinking;
indeed, by its avowed dis-simulation as philosophy. 'If the role of thought', Foucault
writes, 'is to produce the phantasm theatrically and to repeat the universal event in
its extreme point of singularity, then what is thought itself if not the event that befalls
the phantasm and the phantasmatic repetition of the absent event?'[9] In Foucault's echo
of Descartes' *larvatus prodeo*, the philosopher here goes out into the world wearing
a mask.

Understood in the specifically modern sense of what, after Nietzsche (following
Heidegger's reading), is called the 'reversal of Platonism',[10] the mask is now conceived
of as 'freed from the constraints of similitude'.[11] As both Foucault and Deleuze
note, this 'reversal' is, however, already Platonic in its very inception; at least, when
considering the example of Plato's own difficulty in saving Socrates from the sophists.
'What philosophy has not tried to overturn Platonism? If we defined philosophy at
the limit as any attempt, regardless of its source, to reverse Platonism then philosophy
[…] begins with Plato himself, with the conclusion of the *Sophist* where it is impossible
to distinguish Socrates from the crafty imitators'.[12] It is this paradoxical recognition
that provides what Foucault calls a 'Platonic differential',[13] as an index of the return of
Platonism within what is opposed to it. Contemporaneously, Deleuze even offers an
example of this 'reversal' as 'dramatization',[14] when making a parallel with the sense of
differentiation (distinct from dialectics) – where the question *of* philosophy is understood, in its Nietzschean transformation, as a question *for* philosophy. 'Given any concept', Deleuze proposes, 'we can always discover its drama' as soon as the question is
no longer 'what is the true?' but 'who wants the true?'[15]

Before returning to the 'theatre' (or 'drama') of this philosophy, we might also
recall its relation to art history. Perhaps the most familiar example of the mask of difference (as an appearance of indifference) comes from Pop Art, with which Foucault's
'philosophical theatre' was historically contemporary. Andy Warhol (for all his Catholic
piety) famously provides us with a silk-screened veronica of this emancipated mask,
not least in the guise of a self-portrait: 'If you want to know all about Andy Warhol, just

look at the surfaces of my paintings and films and me, and there I am. There is nothing behind it'.[16] Needless to say, for each Warhol candle there are many more fifteen-minute artist-moths. Here one might also reflect on the co-creation of sculpture and spectator entailed by Robert Morris's *Untitled (Mirrored Cubes)*, first presented in 1965 (of which Tate Modern has a sanctioned 'remake', 1976).[17] The edifying 'presence' of art shows its apparent subject quartered into a mirrored *abyme* that is, precisely, all surface and no depth. Famously, art and theatre here become the simulacrum of performance; not least, in the latter's phantasy of 'presence'.

But if the reverse-Platonic performance art of the 1960s concerns the 'mask of these masks',[18] what kind of mask or persona might become the 'worldly' philosopher – traditionally distinct from both artist and actor (Nietzsche notwithstanding) – as a figure of and for their 'voice'? Is it possible to 'translate' the philosopher, as with the great Ass's Head of worldly theatre, without the measure of a Platonic differential? As no longer an Angel to a Faery Queen or a Bottom to mere mortals, for example? What relation might now hold between a gay science and a philosophical theatre; or a symposium and an asses' festival (with Zarathustra's laughter at men who would be gods)?[19] Foucault's own answer was to advocate the mask of anonymity, taking the question 'who?' (rather than 'what?') and replying – with Beckett – by proposing this as 'one of the fundamental ethical principles of contemporary writing'.[20]

In Foucault's phantom theatre, the many deaths of Plato are ritually enacted by the philosophers in a pantomime of repetition, like a parody of *Julius Caesar*, beginning (as already noted) with Plato himself in the attempt to decide between the mask of Socrates and the Sophist. The cast also includes Duns Scotus – who appears 'sporting an impressive moustache [...] belong[ing] to Nietzsche, disguised as Klossowski'.[21] Indeed, amongst Foucault's philosophical personae, it is this particular disguise that provides a synopsis of all that came before in the understanding of what follows. The epilogue, meanwhile, is provided by Deleuze's staging of Nietzsche's 'reversal of Plato' (in the translation by Klossowski). This is not simply 'untimely' in its question of modernity, but becomes a question of which century we, the spectators of this 'world', might imagine ourselves to be living in, whether as this concerns nihilism or 'progress'.

For all the continuing academic industry of Deleuze studies, certain aspects of his century have, perhaps, proved rather short-lived, especially when mistaken for something that used to be called 'post-modern' – distinct from the enduring anachronism of its past futures. Nonetheless, what Foucault – in his thinking 'theatrically' – suggests 'most urgently needs thought in this century'[22] is not just in and of its own time. In 'this' century (the Deleuzian one), Foucault writes: 'The philosophy of representation – of the original, the first time, resemblance, imitation, faithfulness – is dissolving; and the arrow of the simulacrum [or phantasm] released by the Epicureans is headed in our direction. It gives birth – rebirth – to a "phantasmaphysics"'.[23] In terms of a concern that is recurrent in Deleuze, this involves a philosophical search for a 'new image of the act of thought, its functioning, its genesis in thought itself'.[24]

Does 'phantasmaphysics' – as a generator of images of and for the act of thinking (as its 'theatre') – undo the Platonic differential of metaphysics? Does it, thereby, transform the sense of a philosophical 'theatre' after Nietzsche? Is 'phantasmaphysics' an atavism of the 'pre-philosophical', like the 'primitivism' that is amongst the proudest inventions of modernism? Is it an echo of that return of tragedy, of Dionysus contra Socrates, explored by different participants in the College of Sociology? Is there, perhaps, an echo of philosophical laughter in this old-new knowledge (or 'science') of phantasms, at least in its difference from phenomenology?

The repressed of metaphysics has taken many names, so that now 'phantasmaphysics' itself seems to have as little recognition as its near homonym, 'pataphysics'. The knowledge of phantasms (in both senses of the genitive) becomes here a question of appearances no longer defined by an opposition to truth. Amongst the emblematic statements of this, we might recall Nietzsche's artful appeal to lived (rather than transcendental) experience: 'We no longer believe that truth remains truth when the veils are withdrawn; we have lived too much to believe this'.[25] And it is, precisely, the *Gay Science* (with the posthumously published notes, following Colli and Montinari's text) that, in 1967, Deleuze and Foucault together presented – again in Klossowski's translation – as the first volume of the new Gallimard edition of Nietzsche.[26]

Whether the distinction between phenomenology and phantasmaphysics is itself more (or less) than apparent is another question, however; one that could well be explored through Deleuze's philosophical parody, adducing Heidegger's relation to Jarry.[27] But, beyond the metaphysical guignol of the history of philosophy, the theatre of 'phantasmaphysics' is not simply a problem of and for understanding (or thinking) itself. It offers an orientation to help problematise much else that 'needs thought in *this* century' – in broaching, for instance, the decolonisation of such thinking. How might this philosophical theatre contribute to what Latour has called an 'anthropology of the moderns',[28] for example, through an enquiry not only about – but with – the phantasms that possess modernity in its very denial of them? In this 'theatre', the 'primitivism' that was once thought to distinguish modernity from its Other has long been recognised as a distinction within modernity itself, as the effect of cracks in the mirror of its claimed 'universality'. The theatre of phantasmaphysics offers manifold senses of 'possession' – and dispossession – that would be key to exploring worlds which modernity has sought to define in its own image (conceived through its Platonic differential rather than Zarathustra's laughter).

Between the philosophical and the theatrical (in the miming of the one by the other), we might then wonder how phantasms become *personae*; not least, when something in the voice invites a change in hearing. Whether in Turin or in Rodez, the potential of laughter – that scream of the enlightened – is not reducible to the genre masks of sacred tragedy *or* profane comedy. In the echo of laughter, if the metaphor of 'unmasking' is itself unmasked by phantasmaphysics, what might it mean to 'face the truth'? What becomes of an all-too-human face, with no divine model, in the claims of – and for – a modernity that is as murderous as it is emancipatory?

In Zarathustra's account, the pagan gods died laughing at the pretension of one amongst them who jealously proclaimed himself to be the *only* one;[29] one who would later have to be killed by his worshippers, who would then look amongst themselves for the victims of a new holocaust. It is hard now to hear the echo of the gods' laughter in the vertigo of masks, where those who have killed their (one) god no longer have any sense of sacrifice in common. In modernity, the sense of each as the other's potential victim – in the image of a god – no longer bears any meaning of 'purification'.

Despite 'this century's' appeal to a 'rebirth' of phantasms, perhaps we remain afraid of not being able to distinguish the former gods from future madmen? This question is a red thread in the post-Nietzschean dramas of Stanislaw Witkiewicz, for instance; while the suspicion is now widespread as to whether the personae of a 'post-Platonic' theatre can offer any resistance to cynicism.

In Deleuze's attempt to save the eternal recurrence from the principle of the (Platonic) Same (to which difference is otherwise subordinated), what are the consequences (or, at least, the implications) of turning the question of theatre from that of imitation (or representation) to that of simulation (or masquerade) – as if metaphysics were, indeed, 'overcome'? What is the temporality of this 'reversal', which offers an unmasking not of the face but of the mask itself? The figure of 'reversal', after all, no more means that modernity is 'post-Platonic' than that it is defined by anti-Platonism. Here one might substitute any number of actors in this 'theatre', wearing the very masks of these same prefixes. Such instances of dramatisation (and their recurrence) engage with the historically relative claims for what needs thinking: the post-colonial, for instance, as the desired consequence of anti-colonialism. If, then, the Platonic differential provides a diagnosis (which, in another philosophical register, could be called a 'pharmacology'), perhaps the symptom of an impossible cure for metaphysics remains Zarathustra's laughter?

Amongst the exemplary simulacra of and for Eurocentric, metaphysical reason is the 'fetish' and its corollary theatre of possession by forces that rationality calls 'primitive'. While we might think here of Artaud's celebration of the Marx brothers,[30] Peter Brook preferred, for his planned 'theatre of cruelty' season, to share with his company a film by Jean Rouch entitled *Les Maîtres Fous* (or *The Master Madmen*).[31] This film has had a complex (and controversial) reception and one might wonder whether a phantasmaphysical theatre might allow us to think through this example without simply repeating its historical reception, as if it 'unmasked' the interest of the film. Of what then might the entangled reception of Rouch's film be symptomatic, at least amongst its 'Western' audiences, including those in Niger where it was filmed? Whatever Rouch's film may or may not tell us about the Hauka, whose cult of spirit possession it presents (commissioned, indeed, by two of its priests), what does its reception tell us about its European viewers – within a phantasmaphysical ethnography of 'the moderns'? How do colonial phantasms appear in the neo-colonial metropolis, screened (literally) by the image of others; when, unlike the 1960s (the decade of Independence), the post – as in the post-colonial (or even the post-modern) – is no longer a promise of the future? Here we return to the question as to which century we might imagine ourselves to be living in 'philosophically' – surrounded by the phantasmata of our consumerist fetishism.

In contrast to Foucault's own example of LSD-induced 'trance' (like Pop Art, emblematic of its time),[32] Rouch's film focuses (as it were) on a theatre of transformation that profoundly interrupts modernist expectations of perception; especially where the face becomes its own mask, with bulging eyes and contorted mouth. Crucially, the West African Hauka cult adopted various European colonial officials into the spirit pantheon of traditional Songhay rituals of possession. Phantasmaphysics invites us to consider that such possession is not explained (still less purified or exorcised) simply in Platonic terms as a question of model and imitation – as between the colonial figure (or image) and the colonised imagination (or body) – but invents new images of and for a historical understanding of modernity's necropolitics.[33]

While the temptation to speak of ceremonial mask and naked violence seems almost inevitable with respect to the colonisers themselves, does this not simply reproduce the metaphysical theatre that, in the colonial phantasy, would distinguish itself from a 'pre-modern' atavism or 'primitivism' of possession? The difference between the metaphysical and phantasmaphysical might, indeed, appear to be that between acting and possession; as if the one projected a 'model' that the other introjected. But given that most theories of acting contradict this, it is perhaps the very structure of the opposition here that fails to account for the difference. This is precisely the conceptual scenario that Foucault's philo-sophical theatre invites us 'urgently' to consider; even as the Platonic schema is perhaps implied in Rouch's own commentary on the Hauka, which provides a pharmakon or theoretical 'cure' of the otherwise delirial impression of their practices.[34]

Crucially, the point is not so much a cure of the dissociation manifested in the possession states but, precisely, a cure of dissociation by the possession states – as manifesting an integration of psychic disturbance with a social practice. Here the question of mimesis returns for a European philosophical theatre of 'difference and repetition', a review of which precisely provided the occasion for Foucault's *theatrum philosophicum*. The possession by phantasms is a mode of mimesis that is not simply an identification, but a technique of acting with identification for which theatre offers an occidental metaphor.

In Hausa the word *hauka* means crazy or mad;[35] but here the question of trans-lation is not simply of a word but the contexts through which its meaning – for whom? – is in question. It is a moot point, after all, whether this (anti-) Platonic 'cure' of and by phantasmatic possession serves for the Hauka themselves, who are seen in everyday life outside the confines of the colonial psychiatric hospital (not to mention the cinema, as in the contrasting example of Jean-Pierre Bekolo's film, *Aristotle's Plot*); or for the European viewers, who see no mastery, only madness in the inverted image of their own identification with the phantasms of the screen, possessed by an atavism that they claim to know only in others.[36]

Perhaps in terms of phantasmaphysics we could reflect otherwise on the conster-nation, if not the racist anxiety, with which *Les Maîtres Fous* has been typically viewed, with its 'modern' audience – who might also be spectators at the Globe, going to see actors embody that dreamwork of colonialism, *The Tempest* – unwilling, or unable, to relate to the Haukas' colonial mimicry (at least as film), especially when it foams at the mouth. For the unsuspecting, this expression of the spirit possession appears as a kind of *informel* transgression of the 'civilised' demarcation of the cultural from the natural – a scenario (like the eating of dog meat) that refers itself to the conventions that constitute a taboo. But this excessive saliva is also an example of technique, just as with all aspects of possession and its 'visibility'.[37] These masters of colonial madness, in their parody of Prince Philip as much as their exorcism of Mr Kurtz, mix both horror and humour, presenting a simulacrum of European colonial violence as coeval with its primitivist (capitalist) 'reason'.[38]

The Hauka demonstrate the contemporaneity of 'tradition', the continually developing meaning of the past in the present (through the chiasmic relation of the present in the past), where the phantasm is also a phantom, not reducible to an 'anti-theatrical' opposition between world and representation. In Paul Stoller's research with the Hauka since the 1970s (in the decades after Independence), we seem to return to the question of 'mixed genre' in worldly theatre, when he calls their rituals of possession – as a mode of cultural resistance to European power in Niger – an 'horrific comedy'.[39] Again, what if this 'horrific comedy' were to be thought of in terms of a philosophical theatre? Rather than recalibrating a trad- itional philosophical differential – between simulacrum and truth – what if our understanding did not try to curtail or contain the laughter (or the fear) which it mimetically incites? What if the question of a 'mixed genre' here concerned the senses rather than the poetics of plot? A haptic vision, a hearing eye, an unset- tling of the separation between active and passive? How different this would be from the recuperation offered, for instance, by the wish to see in spirit possession something 'authentic' in relation to 'alienated' modernity, something 'really real' (as Mattijs van de Port describes it),[40] which carries over into the curiously Platonic 'intensities' of so much discussion of performance art? These paradoxes are par- ticularly manifest when de Port discusses 'the theatre metaphor' in the example of Candomblé – reflecting on the incorporation of the tourist gaze into the circuit of authentication of what is 'inexplicable' in the ceremonies.[41]

Of course, the Hauka masquerade is not one that European museums choose to show when 'animating' their formalist displays of African masks – whether these are understood as ethnographic artefacts or as examples of 'world art'. The Hauka are not recognised as part of the standard contextualisation in terms of perform- ance for these museum encounters (or 'contact') with what has been imagined in the 'West' as 'pre-modern'. One might say that this reticence concerning phantasms is due to obvious reasons concerning the violence of their appearance. But how and why something is deemed to be 'obvious' – especially with respect to vio- lence – may not itself be so obvious. The appearance of masks and the symbol- isation of violence in critical examples of African cinema – for instance, the very different poetics of Sembène's *Moolaadé* or Bekolo's *Aristotle's Plot* – is not part of this museum encounter either. African futures, as transforming European pasts, are again appropriated by these institutions' new investment in contemporary art, as if the global art market offered answers to questions of museum anthropology that have ceased even to be asked.

With respect to the supposed evidence of film, modernity is so enthralled by the phantasms of the screen that image industries are now devoted to promoting 'immer- sive experiences' of commoditised vision, including within the so-called 'interactive museum'. Is this not another global colonisation of imagination through the tech- nology of 'spirits' and their exploitation of affect – now 'purified' simply in terms of reducing resistance to consumption? In the 'war of dreams',[42] the sense that thinking about phantasmata involves a return of thinking with or through such phantasms – that, indeed, reflection on film or cinema might be oriented by what has still to be learnt from cultures of spirit possession, rather than simply by projection upon them – is, as Foucault said, 'urgent'.

Perhaps the vaunted digital emancipation of simulacra or phantasms – especially in terms of a commodified reality that wants to be called 'augmented', 'immersive', and (*ad absurdum*) '3-D' – has not made the ancient theatrical metaphor of 'the world' philosophically redundant, after all. The digital economy, afraid of a reality that may yet limit its powers of exploitation, remains chained to what it still advertises as an experience of the 'real thing'. Here the possibility for thinking through relations between the colonial museum and global imaging technologies in phantasmaphysics broaches an anthropology of mediated consciousness beyond the old disciplinary walls. Exploring the manifold senses in which 'we have never been modern',[43] Deleuze's evocation ('after' Foucault) of 'control societies' reflects on an image of thought that could indeed be called a 'philosophical theatre'. The subject of research would follow the shift (advanced by Deleuze and Foucault, after Nietzsche) from determining the 'what' of exhibitionary or curatorial power to questions of the 'dramatization' (or agency) differentiating that power. Such a research opens itself up to the possibilities of the phantasmatic, rather than simply the perceptual; to the dynamic, rather than simply the descriptive.

Paradoxically perhaps, in less histrionic (or perhaps more stoical) terms, Foucault's turn to a hermeneutics of the self, to an aesthetics or technique of the mask, suggests a more than superficial reading of philosophical survivals, including laughter. The authentic is not a return to origins but an ongoing invention, as the very artifice that is traditionally condemned as inauthentic and unoriginal. Whether in Eleusis or in Kreuzlingen, the question of truth is not what it appears; and here, perhaps, reference to Foucault's 'theatre' of thought is not only historical but necessary. Between difference and repetition (or between mimesis and alterity), this philosophical theatre offers an interpretation of life and death quite distinct from the networked Fitbits that translate desires and anxieties into marketable data. This latest digital short-circuiting of reflection, with its inverted claims of 'self-control', contrasts with the corporeal interruption of reflection – or, indeed, its 'possession' – by the 'eternal return' of laughter. At stake in both is an understanding of mortality, which (as Foucault reminds us) the Stoics conceived of, in an *art* of philosophical performance, as a practice of individuation in correspondence with others.

From the circle of Klossowski's Nietzsche again, Blanchot too offers an example of this, in a reading of the phantasmaphysical play of the subject becoming its own differentiation: '[E]verything has still not been said definitely; for if the gods die laughing, it is no doubt because laughter is the movement of the divine, but also because it is the very space of dying – dying and laughing, laughing divinely and laughing mortally, laughter as Bacchic movement of the true and laughter as mockery of the infinite error passing incessantly into one another'.[44] What may be said here is not said ' "once and for all" but, rather, "yet again" '.[45] And is it not such an art of spacing – that of dying and laughing, as that of writing and reading – that returns in Foucault's own practice of critical research? That is, when it invites us to think with – as much as about – what has already been said concerning philosophical phantasms?

Notes

1 Michel Foucault, 'Theatrum Philosophicum' (1970), in Michel Foucault, *Language, Counter-memory, Practice*, ed. Donald Bouchard, trans. Donald Bouchard and Sherry Simon (Ithaca, NY: Cornell University Press, 1986), pp. 165–96.

2 Maurice Blanchot, 'Cruel Poetic Reason', in *The Infinite Conversation*, trans. Susan Hanson (Minneapolis: University of Minnesota Press, 1993 [1969]), pp. 293–7 (p. 296).

3 Gilles Deleuze, *Foucault*, trans. Sean Hand (London: Bloomsbury, 2013 [1986]).

4 Gilles Deleuze, *Seminar on Foucault*, 1985–86, www2.univ-paris8.fr/deleuze/rubrique.php3?id_rubrique=21, accessed 14 January 2018.

5 Michel Foucault, 'The Prose of Acteon' (1964), in Pierre Klossowski, *The Baphomet*, trans. Sophie Hawks and Stephen Sartarelli (Colorado: Eridanos Press, 1988 [1965]), p. xxviii.

6 This constellation of claims about and for authorship amongst a close coterie of writers in the late 1960s is explored by Eleanor Kaufman in her book *The Delirium of Praise* (Baltimore, MD: Johns Hopkins University Press, 2001).

7 Friedrich Nietzsche, *The Gay Science*, trans. Walter Kaufmann (New York: Vintage Books, 1974), p. 38.

8 Michel de Montaigne, *How We Weep and Laugh at the Same Thing*, trans. M. A. Screech (London: Penguin, 2015), p. 2.

9 Foucault, 'Theatrum Philosophicum', p. 178.

10 'Reversing Platonism' (1967) was the title of the first version of what was later published as 'Plato and Simulacrum', in Gilles Deleuze, *The Logic of Sense*, trans. Mark Lester with Charles Stivale (London: Athlone Press, 1990 [1969]).

11 Foucault, 'Theatrum Philosophicum', p. 177.

12 Ibid., p. 166.

13 Ibid.

14 Gilles Deleuze, 'The Method of Dramatization' (1967), in Gilles Deleuze, *Desert Islands*, ed. David Lapoujade, trans. Michael Taormina (Los Angeles: Semiotext(e), 2004 [2002]), pp. 94–116 (p. 94).

15 Ibid., p. 98. As Deleuze summarises this (in reply to a question about 'dramatization'): '[W]hen Nietzsche asks *who*, or *from what perspective*, instead of *what*, he is not trying to complete the question *What is this?*, he is criticising the form of this question and all its possible responses. When I ask *what is this?*, I assume there is an essence behind appearances, or at least something ultimate behind the masks. The other kind of question, however, always discovers other masks behind the mask, displacements behind every place, other "cases" stacked up in a case'. Ibid., p. 114, original emphasis.

16 Quoted in Hal Foster, *The First Pop Age* (Princeton, NJ: Princeton University Press, 2012), p. 7.

17 'Robert Morris', *Tate Liverpool*, www.tate.org.uk/whats-on/tate-liverpool/display/dla-piper-series-constellations/phase-one-1960-now/robert-morris, accessed 14 January 2018.

18 Foucault, 'Theatrum Philosophicum', p. 196.

19 Friedrich Nietzsche, 'Thus Spoke Zarathustra', trans. Walter Kaufmann, in *The Portable Nietzsche* (London: Penguin, 1978), pp. 425–9.

20 Michel Foucault, 'What is an Author?' (1969), in Michel Foucault, *Language, Counter-memory, Practice*, ed. Donald Bouchard, trans. Donald Bouchard and Sherry Simon (Ithaca, NY: Cornell University Press, 1986), pp. 113–38 (p. 115).

21 Foucault, 'Theatrum Philosophicum', p. 196.

22 Ibid., p. 180.

23 Ibid., p. 172.

24 Gilles Deleuze, 'On Nietzsche and the Image of Thought' (1968), in Gilles Deleuze, *Desert Islands*, ed. David Lapoujade, trans. Michael Taormina (Los Angeles: Semiotext(e), 2004 [2002]), pp. 135–42 (p. 140).

25 Nietzsche, *The Gay Science*, p. 38.

26 Michel Foucault and Gilles Deleuze, 'Michel Foucault et Gilles Deleuze veulent rendre à Nietzsche son vrai visage' (1966), in Michel Foucault, *Dits et écrits*, Vol. 1 (Paris: Gallimard, 1994). The gist of their

co-written, brief introduction (reprinted as Michel Foucault and Gilles Deleuze, 'Introduction générale' (1967), in Michel Foucault, *DE*, Vol. 1 (Paris: Gallimard, 1994)) is given in the translation of an interview with Gilles Deleuze, 'Nietzsche's Burst of Laughter' (1967), in Gilles Deleuze, *Desert Islands*, ed. David Lapoujade, trans. Michael Taormina (Los Angeles: Semiotext(e), 2004 [2002]), pp. 128–30.

27 Gilles Deleuze, 'How Jarry's Pataphysics Opened the Way for Phenomenology', in *Desert Islands*, ed. David Lapoujade, trans. Michael Taormina (Los Angeles: Semiotext(e), 2004 [2002]), pp. 74–6; Gilles Deleuze, 'An Unrecognised Precursor to Heidegger: Alfred Jarry', in *Essays Critical and Clinical*, trans. Daniel Smith and Michael Greco (Minneapolis: University of Minnesota Press, 1997), pp. 91–8.

28 Bruno Latour, *An Enquiry into Modes of Existence: An Anthropology of the Moderns*, trans. Catherine Porter (Cambridge, MA: Harvard University Press, 2013).

29 Nietzsche, 'Thus Spoke Zarathustra', p. 294.

30 Antonin Artaud, *Theatre and its Double*, trans. Mary Caroline Richards (New York: Grove Press, 1958), pp. 142–4.

31 The film *Les Maîtres Fous* is accessible on Youtube (with Portuguese subtitles), www.youtube.com/watch?v=Z8uHE2oIARk&list=PLqMCEvP8dVMU1FlpfCVaS0nbshilFyvj5&index=2, accessed 2 December 2018.

32 Foucault, 'Theatrum Philosophicum', pp. 190–1.

33 We could compare this with Fanon's Hegelian dialectics of freedom and alienation, especially in its idealisation of combatant masculinity in the anti-colonial struggle in North Africa. See Françoise Vergès, 'Chains of Madness, Chains of Colonialism: Fanon and Freedom', in Alan Read (ed.), *The Fact of Blackness* (London: Institute of Contemporary Art, 1996), pp. 46–75.

34 The image of power adopted by post-independence dictators, supported by the neo-colonial powers (who also participated in local politics through the murders of Lumumba, Sankara, Cabral, and others), is another aspect of this scenario – the most egregious example of which is perhaps the self-proclaimed 'Emperor' Bokassa.

35 Paul Stoller, *The Cinematic Griot: the Ethnography of Jean Rouch* (Chicago, IL: University of Chicago Press, 1992), p. 145.

36 It would be interesting here to engage also with Manthia Diawara's 1995 film *Rouch in Reverse*.

37 Jean Claude Muller, 'Review of *Les Maîtres Fous* by Jean Rouch', in *American Anthropologist*, New Series, 73.6 (December 1971), 1471–3 (p. 1472).

38 Indeed, it is curious how avant-gardist Marxism also appeals to this scenario from which (in the name of change, or revolution) it otherwise wishes – often ruthlessly – to distinguish itself. In an interview, Thomas Sankara observed that: 'You cannot carry out fundamental change without a certain amount of madness. In this case, it comes from nonconformity, the courage to turn your back on the old formulas, the courage to invent the future. Besides, it took the madmen of yesterday for us to be able to act with extreme clarity today. I want to be one of those madmen ... We must dare to invent the future'. Interview in Ouagadougou, January–June 1985, quoted in Jean-Pierre Bekolo, 'Haunted by the Future', in Lien Heidenreich-Seleme and Sean O'Toole (eds), *African Futures* (Bielefeld: Kerber Verlag, 2015), p. 125.

39 Stoller, *The Cinematic Griot*, p. 160.

40 Mattijs van de Port, 'Circling Around the *Really Real*: Spirit Possession Ceremonies and the Search for Authenticity in Bahian Candomblé', *Ethos*, 33.2 (2008), 149–79 (p. 153).

41 Ibid., p. 174.

42 Marc Augé, *The War of Dreams*, trans. Liz Heron (London: Pluto Press, 1999 [1997]).

43 Bruno Latour, *We Have Never Been Modern*, trans. Catherine Porter (Cambridge, MA: Harvard University Press, 1993).

44 Maurice Blanchot, 'The Laughter of the Gods', in *Friendship*, trans. Elizabeth Rottenberg (Stanford, CA: Stanford University Press, 1997 [1971]), pp. 169–82 (p. 182).

45 Ibid., p. 181.

Cage and Foucault: musical timekeeping and the security state

Steve Potter

From discipline to security

John Cage (1912–92) was an American composer, performer, writer, and visual artist, whose development of writing and performance processes that allow performance elements to be decided by chance established him as a leading figure of musical and theatrical avant-gardes from the 1950s up to the present day. In this chapter I argue that John Cage's musical practice should be seen in terms of a general aesthetic economy that governs relationships among writer, text, conductor, performers, and audience in a distinct way. Furthermore, this general aesthetic economy is ambivalent in the way that it governs, which we can observe by noting its parallels to two techniques of power that Foucault, in the first three lectures of his 1977–78 series at the Collège de France, *Security, Territory, Population*, suggests should be distinguished from one another – those of security and discipline.[1] Musicologist Benjamin Piekut is virtually alone in drawing connections between Foucault's richly diverse characterisations of liberal power arrangements and Cage's various experimental strategies for governing ostensibly free performers. Piekut has applied multiple moments in Foucault's thought to the analysis of Cage's practice, notably discussing the New York Philharmonic's reluctant 1964 performance of *Atlas Eclipticalis* in terms of disciplinary control and liberalism, and renegade cellist Charlotte Moorman's irreverent performances in the 1960s and 1970s of *26'1.1499" for a String Player* in terms of discipline and the care of the self. While I find his analyses productive, I suggest that his evaluation of Cage is too damning overall, and that we can achieve a richer understanding of Cage's work by attending to Foucault's distinctions between security and disciplinary, as well as juridico-legal, techniques of power.

I will argue that there are kinships between the way Cage's musical scores govern groups of musicians and the mechanisms of power that Foucault analyses. In taking this approach I share Jon McKenzie's drive in *Perform or Else: From Discipline to Performance*, to build obliquely on Foucault's reading of mechanisms of power while recognising, with Gilles Deleuze, 'the transience of [the disciplinary] model';[2] however, whereas Deleuze and McKenzie, writing before the publication of *Security, Territory, Population*, thematise contemporary power formations in their own terms – 'societies of control' and 'the performance stratum', respectively[3] – I see significant potential in examining Foucault's own revision to his famous thematisation of discipline with the formulation of apparatuses of security.

Cage described the bulk of his orchestral works as models of anarchist communities. He conceived these works without a conductor and wrote their sheet music in such a way that each performer must make decisions regarding what exactly and/or when exactly to play. Piekut argues in 'When Orchestras Attack', the first chapter of his 2011 book, *Experimentalism Otherwise*, that Cage's practice, while perhaps suggestive of utopian anarchism, actually embodied a 'rather orthodox liberalism',[4] in which musician subjects are given the illusion of choice while the restrictions on the frame within which these choices are made are so extensive that the actually existing freedom is paltry. Moreover, Piekut argues, Cage, in trying to advance 'a model of utopian social systems that we do not yet have', relied on 'the threat of discipline' in order to bring this new model into reality: the New York Philharmonic's music director Leonard Bernstein and its general manager Carlos Moseley 'castigated the orchestra' and the labour contract issued by the Philharmonic to its musicians made it clear that the musicians had to 'obey Cage's demands'.[5] Foucault is present but unmentioned in this chapter: Piekut relies primarily on Wendy Brown to introduce his understanding of liberalism and neoliberalism, and her understanding, in turn, is heavily influenced by Foucault.[6] Meanwhile Piekut's usage of 'discipline' appears to derive from Foucault's famous analysis of discipline, in *Discipline and Punish*, as a modern technique of power that coerces subtly compared with a pre-modern technique of power that relied on highly visible displays of torture and execution. The thrust of Piekut's argument is that while Cage purports to be advancing a gentler form of government, he actually, in a classical liberal manner, merely conceals his mechanisms of control.

I find the critical aspect of Piekut's account valuable, but I think it exaggerates Cage's role in the lives of the New York Philharmonic musicians. Cage, after all, had only one two-and-a-half-hour rehearsal with the group before a run-through rehearsal that included four other pieces. More importantly for present purposes, Foucault's characterisation of liberalism in *Security, Territory, Population*, offers decidedly different insights than those of *Discipline and Punish*, above all calling into question the association of disciplinary techniques with liberal governance by proposing a third technique of power, which he calls security. Foucault thus alters his apparent historical schema here, and moreover, he suggests that this schema should not be taken too strictly, insofar as all three techniques of power he identifies – juridico-legal, disciplinary, and security – have actually been present throughout ancient, modern, and contemporary periods.[7] His characterisation of security offers, in my view, a compelling parallel to Cage's peculiar authorial role within some of his purportedly liberating music. Meanwhile I propose to make explicit Piekut's implication that discipline functions within Cage's practice, as well as his implication that, on the other hand, Cage also at times resists the historically accumulated effects of disciplinary power. In sum, I am proposing that Cage's practice does two different things, at different moments: it resists the effects of discipline, yet in a manner consistent with the principles of discipline; and it embodies security.

Throughout the first three lectures of *Security, Territory, Population*, originally given in Paris on 11, 18, and 25 January 1978, Foucault conveys the significance of security mechanisms by differentiating them from disciplinary mechanisms. In the process, he makes it clear that security, in distinction to discipline, is part of a larger strategy of government that includes laissez-faire economic policies. Foucault first distinguishes apparatuses of security, however, by articulating their particular orientation towards space, dubbing spaces determined by such an orientation 'spaces of security'. Cage's methods in the 1952 Black Mountain College event enabled him to create sonic spaces that differ slightly from those created by another work of his from the same period, *26'1.1499" for a String Player* (begun in 1953, returned to and completed in 1955). I believe we can identify two distinct modalities of power in these two works from the early 1950s. Foucault's characterisation of security and discipline as distinct from one another can illuminate this comparison.

Piekut again provides a starting point for such an analysis. His discussion of Charlotte Moorman's performances in the 1960s and 1970s of *26'1.1499" for a String Player* draws explicitly on *Discipline and Punish*. Piekut explains that the unique notation system of this extremely difficult piece 'requires considerable effort to understand, let alone master'.[8] Each of the several rows of notation instructs the player on a different aspect of playing. One row indicates how to articulate notes (for example, with bow hair, bow wood, finger, fingernail; near or far from the instrument's 'bridge'); another prescribes how hard to press with the bow; there are rows unconventionally representing what to play on each of the instrument's four strings; and a row is devoted to noises that may issue from 'entirely other sources, e.g. percussion instruments, whistles, radios, etc.'[9] Altogether the instrumentalist must attend to seven rows of instructions at once.[10] Piekut refers to Foucault's notion of 'subjectivation' (*assujettissement*) in order to articulate the opportunity for self-reconstitution that Cage's piece affords a string player: 'Because Cage's piece so denaturalized the "normal" ways of playing a cello, it pulled off the layer of disciplinary efficiency that customarily managed and administered the relationship between body and instrument, returning that interaction to a clumsier encounter among flesh, metal, and wood'.[11] In Piekut's reading, then, Cage's composition mounts a kind of resistance to the 'disciplines' responsible for constructing the Western classical musician subject. I am in agreement with Piekut here. I would just add that in resisting the training that is constitutive of classical musicians' subjecthood, this composition adopts the same posture as that which it resists. Cage's novel music notation resists tradition, but it too 'leaves its trace directly on the body, its behaviors, and its habits'.[12] His tools for breaking history and tradition take what Derek Hook calls, paraphrasing Foucault in *Psychiatric Power*, the ' "somatic singularity" of the body as their target',[13] just as disciplinary mechanisms do. Security mechanisms, in Foucault's account, have a different target: not the body, but the population. Although Piekut discusses Foucault's later writings in his chapter on Charlotte Moorman – in particular he cites 'The Ethics of the Concern of the Self as a Practice of Freedom', an interview conducted in January 1984 – he does not engage with the concept of security. I wish to extend his utilisation of Foucault in the context of Cage's practice by doing so here.

When Foucault introduces security as a 'mechanism of power' in the first of his 1978 lectures at the Collège de France,[14] he emphasises a principle of aleatoric govern-ance that I argue could equally well describe Cage's posture as a composer in many of his best-known works.[15] This particular connection between Foucault's thought and Cage's practice has not been theorised. It is worth mentioning that despite the two men's shared personal acquaintance with composer Pierre Boulez, and Foucault's long-term romantic relationship in the 1950s with Boulez's colleague, composer Jean Barraqué,[16] there is no evidence that Foucault knew Cage's work, and Foucault's brief writing on Boulez suggests that he did not feel equipped to comment on contemporary art music.[17] In January 1978, however, this music may well have been on Foucault's mind; the following month he would participate in a debate on contemporary music, chaired by Boulez, and including Gilles Deleuze and Roland Barthes, at the Institut de Recherche et Coordination Acoustique/Musique (IRCAM) in Paris.[18]

At any rate, Cage utilised a principle of aleatoric governance in the 1952 event at Black Mountain College, thereby arguably providing a sonic and theatrical parallel to what Foucault calls spaces of security. In this event, often referred to as the first 'happening', Merce Cunningham danced, Robert Rauschenberg exhibited paintings and played a Victrola, Charles Olson and M. C. Richards read their poetry from the tops of ladders, David Tudor played piano, and Cage read a lecture that included silences from the top of another ladder.[19] The performers all used stopwatches to keep track of time and Cage prescribed when each performer was allowed to be active. For this event, Cage eschewed the usual composerly tasks of constructing an artificial space – a sonic imaginary space – characterised by melodies or motifs, accompanimental fig-ures or noises, that musicians must materially produce with their trained bodies – and instead adopted the responsibility of regulating a collection of individual performers in their independent movements by giving structure to a series of simultaneities: two, three, four, five, or six people performing at once. The structure Cage provides, in this somewhat managerial role, thus takes the form of a particular progression of densities of activity (the more people doing things, the denser), in a particular set of proportions (for example, one minute of a trio followed by two minutes of a quintet, and so on), all of which is determined by his time brackets for each performer.[20] In taking on this role, Cage relinquishes the usual composerly role of intervening on matters of taste pertaining to the minutiae of sonic material. He simply and fully accepts the individual performers' personal inclinations, abilities, limitations, and peculiar performative work. Cage does not presume to tell the performers of this particular work what to do, only when they may do it. Yet he does not fail to make a distinctive authorial mark on the performance. For Cage his willingness to accept what performers are inclined to do is representative of his anarchism. For Piekut, the fact that Cage nonetheless controls the overall situation links the work with discipline and liberal governance.

Yet Cage's regulation of time here, I would argue, is of a different sort than that promoted by a disciplinary modality of power. I suggest we might instead understand the innovations of the Black Mountain event in terms of a parallel conceptual shift that we find in Foucault. 'Discipline', Foucault says, preparing to distinguish between the modern technique of power he analysed at book-length in 1975 in *Discipline and Punish*[21] and the technique that he had come to see as more relevant at that moment,

> works in an empty, artificial space that is to be completely constructed. Security will rely on a number of material givens. […] Security will try to plan a milieu in terms of events or series of events or possible elements, or series that will have to be regulated within a multivalent and transformable framework.[22]

It is an elusive distinction, which concerns both a relationship with space and an approach to managing events in time. As I've argued above, in the Black Mountain event Cage indeed relied on material givens instead of constructing an artificial space. Moreover, Cage's concern with time in this 1952 event was similarly on the order of a 'series of possible elements'. I would like to stress that this modality of timekeeping does not evidence any kind of parallel with the disciplinary mechanisms that Foucault articulated in *Discipline and Punish*. It is not the regulation of people's time, per se, that defines disciplinary techniques of power. That existed already in earlier modalities of power. What Foucault draws our attention to in *Discipline and Punish* is the rise, during the eighteenth century, of a particular *kind* of attention to time, of precisely timed instructions that aim to constitute bodies as individuals with particular specialised abilities, and to extract the maximum possible forces out of these bodies. Foucault articulates this somewhat repetitively in the following passage:

> Discipline […] poses the principle of a theoretically ever-growing use of time […]; it is a question of extracting, from time, ever more available moments and, from each moment, ever more useful forces. This means that one must seek to intensify the use of the slightest moment, as if time, in its very fragmentation, were inexhaustible or as if, at least by an ever more detailed internal arrangement, one could tend towards an ideal point at which one maintained maximum speed and maximum efficiency.[23]

The statement contains several variants of the same principle. Foucault's overall concern is with two actions: the extraction of forces and the intensification of the brief moment. It is worth recalling that workers and soldiers are the target of this disciplinary control, and that Cage is operating in a radically different, if potentially parallel, realm. My argument here is that in *26'1.1499" for a String Player*, this kind of extraction of forces and intensification of the brief moment is part of Cage's work, but that in the Black Mountain event, it is not. Unlike a Wagner or a Stravinsky or a Gershwin composing an opera or ballet, Cage temporally choreographs the Black Mountain performers on a broader structural level, indicating only starting and stopping times, in minutes and seconds, for an overall performance time of 45 minutes – enacting the opposite of disciplinary mechanisms' heightened attention to ever-briefer moments.

Cage scholars commonly call this approach to musical time, which is associated with a particular method of music notation, the 'time-bracket method' or 'time-bracket technique'. This technique basically means that each performer has an independent score telling him or her, in terms of minutes and seconds, when he or she may be active. Radically, the musicians do not have to adjust their playing to the playing of their fellows; instead each musician is encouraged to ignore the others and to focus on their own playing. Cage connected many of his later pieces that use the time-bracket technique, with anarchism.[24] He wrote forty-three works in the last eleven years of his life whose titles are all simply the number of performers required[25] – for example, *One* for solo piano (1987); *Five* for any five voices or instruments (1988); and *108* for orchestra (1991).[26] All of these pieces – commonly referred to as the 'Number Pieces' – use the time-bracket technique. Unlike Cage's instructions for the Black Mountain event, the time brackets here are flexible: each period of activity is given a window of time, in minutes and seconds, for example [0'45"-1'30"], within which to begin, and another time window within which to end, for example, [2'15"-2'45"]. In addition, rather than leave the decision of what to do entirely up to the performer, Cage indicates a single note, or a few notes, to play within each time bracket (see Figure 1). Rob Haskins has analysed Cage's intended evocation of anarchic communities in detail, noting aspects of the works that would seem to contradict it – a fixed sequence of pitches for specific instruments; a fixed duration for the overall work; a reduced quantity of pitches; and so on.[27] At the same time, Haskins elaborates reasons nonetheless to see them as 'anarchic societies of sounds': the time brackets allow players a degree of choice over when to start and stop playing; players may also choose 'to play short, loud sounds or long, quiet ones'; and, in a somewhat less self-evident argument, 'the restricted pitch material suggests the virtue of poverty', an assertion that Cage implied.[28]

Haskins' assessment is inconclusive, which further supports the attempt here to explore the political nature of Cage's work through other lenses. While I will not attempt to judge whether the Number Pieces embody anarchist utopias, I would like to examine the means with which Cage attempted to lend them that allegorical meaning. Haskins reports that Richard Kostelanetz 'identifies six elements that make [Cage's] work specifically anarchistic.'[29] The conjunction of all six elements, as Haskins argues, only appears in a handful of Cage's works, but it is useful for the present argument to note a couple of them here, insofar as all of them, when they do appear, are supported by Cage's withdrawal from the moment-to-moment composerly control over time. The first element that Kostelanetz names is: 'the presence of all participants as equals.'[30] In the majority of Number Pieces, Cage aims to support egalitarianism in the rehearsal and performance process by making the individual parts easy to play. There are, at most, a few notes each minute, and it is not necessary to start playing at a precise time. The fact that participants need not have any particular training has a levelling effect. Meanwhile, in the process of creating easy parts for everyone, Cage omits to exploit each moment of musical time for expressive potential. Again, his control of time is distinctly different from a disciplinary one as might be derived in relation to Foucault's analysis of discipline based on the extraction of forces and the intensification of the briefest moment.

Other 'anarchistic' elements, including 'the formal expression of chaos' and 'a tendency toward levity',[31] cannot be said to apply to the Number Pieces in general. Kostelanetz's sixth element, however, contains a strikingly literal resonance with Foucault's characterisation of apparatuses of security. This element pertains to Cage's

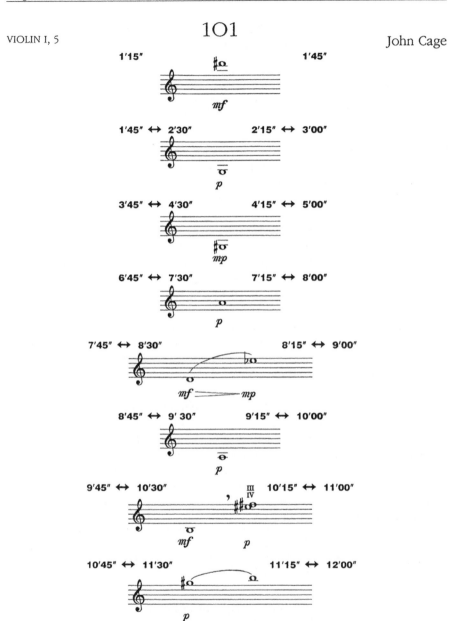

VIOLIN I, 5   101   John Cage

Figure 1 Extract from '101' by John Cage (EP67265)

style of hosting a performance: 'the desire not to hold the audience prisoner, but to give them the opportunity to leave whenever they wish'.[32] Here a reading of Foucault affords a forceful critique of Cage's desire to link this style of hosting to anarchism. Foucault associates the freedom to circulate – around town, from countryside to town, across jurisdictional borders – not with anarchism, but with a modern kind of 'government of men'.[33] Near the end of his lecture on 18 January 1978 he says,

> an apparatus of security, in any case the one I have spoken about, cannot operate well except on condition that it is given freedom, in the modern sense [the word] acquires in the eighteenth century: no longer the exemptions and privileges attached to a person, but the possibility of movement, change of place, and processes of circulation of both people and things.[34]

Freedom of circulation – posited by Kostelanetz as anarchistic – is interpreted by Foucault instead as a necessary element of liberal government and 'the correlative of the deployment of apparatuses of security'.[35] What Foucault then goes on to describe, I would argue, aptly defines Cage's creative thrust: 'a power thought of as regulation that can only be carried out through and by reliance on the freedom of each'.[36]

To encapsulate the argument at this stage: like Foucault's 'spaces of security', Cage's Number Pieces (1981–92), as well as the 1952 Black Mountain event, are defined at the level of a milieu of possibilities, rather than a totally constructed sound-world. The Number Pieces, like the Black Mountain event, rely on a series of possible elements – in some cases a less motley crew than at the Black Mountain event, but in the larger-number pieces, such as *101* for orchestra (1988), a very diverse ensemble indeed. Cage dictates specific instrumental sounds in the scores, but Cage's creative intervention is, so to speak, at a greater distance than normal for a composer – he does not compose phrases, only individual notes whose articulations are not fixed in time. Crucially, he also does not compose counterpoint – that is, he does not fix instrumentalists' parts to one another in time.

The lack of counterpoint signals another important departure from the way that disciplinary mechanisms aim to exert control in the context of music. As Foucault writes in *Discipline and Punish*, the time of workers and soldiers, each composed of the individual's own pace and prescribed tasks, must be combined to form a composite time. The efficiency of this combination is a crucial element within larger systems of production and domination.[37] His description, in terms of the time and forces of a multiplicity, is at a level of abstraction that is equally suggestive of musical counterpoint as of workplace division of labour:

> The various chronological series that discipline must combine to form a composite time are also pieces of machinery. The time of each must be adjusted to the time of the others in such a way that the maximum quantity of forces may be extracted from each and combined with the optimum result.[38]

The kind of combination of timelines Foucault describes is aimed at maximising forces, and it requires that each individual adjust the timing of their productive articulations to the timing of their colleagues. To a musician's ears, Foucault's terminology may seem already musical here. It is striking that he felt he had so little to say about musical form.[39] In a short piece on Pierre Boulez in 1982 he acknowledged that he felt perplexed regarding contemporary art music, despite learning about it through personal relationships with France's most illustrious practitioners. At the same time he acknowledged that the concern with radically reinventing musical form that occupied many composers in the mid-1950s was absolutely central to broader twentieth-century culture as well.[40]

At any rate, Foucault's statement regarding the composite time of disciplinary mechanisms appears to have a specific parallel in the realm of Western art music (circa 1600–1910). In this musical era, broadly encompassing Baroque, Classical, and Romantic music, individual voices produce momentary dissonances with one another in such a way within a system of consonances and dissonances, that tension is created in an ever increasing manner, until a final dissonance of maximum possible force eventually resolves to a consonance, dissipating the energy that has been built up over the course of a musical work.[41] Composers in the early twentieth century had already rejected the aim of increasing force – Debussy is a frequent canonical example – but Cage goes a step further by removing the stipulation that the time of each player should be adjusted to the time of the others. The relaxation of this requirement represents a new way of constructing a musical work. The mechanism that produces the work, that generates the work's integrity as a work, thus cannot be found at the moment-to-moment level, where this integration of elements is worked out, but must be found on another level.

For Cage, it is clear that when you remove counterpoint, you get superimposition.[42] Yet Foucault's distinction between discipline and security offers an instructive analogy. In *Security, Territory, Population*, he analyses the 'disciplinary' strategy of urban planning as one of combining elements: discipline structures a space hierarchically by placing residences in broader portions of the grid of streets, and commercial activities in denser parts of the grid, and also crucially placing the latter in close proximity to the former.[43] So, there is what I would call a spatial counterpoint of areas differentiated, as well as related to one another, by their respective functions. Security, in contrast, takes the grid and its surrounding natural elements as given and focuses instead on organising circulation, attempting to maximise the 'good circulation'[44] of goods and the people who are trading those goods, while diminishing the 'bad circulation' of unwanted people from outside – 'beggars, vagrants, delinquents, criminals, thieves, murderers, and so on'.[45] Individual flows, under the framework of this tactic of power, would remain determined in part by the well-worn paths belonging to the contrapuntal formations of disciplinary power, but attention would now be focused elsewhere. Foucault is not entirely clear about what security does to organise circulation without reconstructing any part of an urban space, but he alludes to the possibility of intervention in matters of taxes and public health – water cleanliness, air temperature, the presence of trees, the health of the soil – all of which influence populations to live or to be active, in certain areas rather than in others.[46]

The analogy between Cage's work and the apparatus of security may seem stretched here: after all, can it be said that Cage is interested in allowing people freedom yet managing the conditions that influence what people would do with that freedom? Furthermore, can it be said that he is interested in creating conditions to exclude certain types of people from taking part in his performances? Is he interested in producing some sort of overall effect at the level of the population? In fact, I would argue, the answer is 'yes' to all three of these propositions. That Cage worked on managing the conditions within which musicians could act while embodying his image of freedom, and that these conditions effectively excluded types of people, has been argued by numerous others.[47] Cage notoriously condemned Julius Eastman's sexualised rendition of *0'00"*.[48] And, as Rob Haskins reminds us, Cage wrote after early performances of his *Concert for Piano and Orchestra* (1958): 'I must find a way to let people be free without their becoming foolish. So that their freedom will make them noble … My problems have become social rather than musical'.[49] That Cage was interested in producing an effect at the level of the population is borne out by his statements endorsing Buckminster Fuller's project to improve humankind by developing global utilities while doing away with politics.[50] Still, we might wonder, is this the same sort of effect that Foucault has in mind when characterising the will of the eighteenth-century liberal economists?

In at least one further respect Cage's time-bracket pieces seem to resemble what Foucault calls 'spaces of security', and that is their relationship with a material given. These pieces work, so to speak, 'on site with the flows of water, islands, air, and so forth';[51] they are not akin to cities constructed from scratch. Other well-known works by Cage illustrate the point even more clearly – for example, his famous silent piece, *4'33"* (1952), whose soundscape is defined entirely by the environment in which it is performed. The piece is not site-specific – it can be performed at any site – and yet the piece's content is unusually dependent on the environment in which it is performed; its authorial intervention consists in drawing attention to the performance site as it already exists.

Of course, what is understood as 'given' varies depending on the context. In order to be more specific about what Foucault means by 'a given' in the context of 'spaces of security', it is necessary to refer to his contrasting characterisation of disciplinary spaces. This also allows us to attend to an important point: the meaning of 'spaces of security' for Foucault arises in part through their differentiation from disciplinary spaces. That is, a constituent vector of security's will-to-power is its very difference from disciplinary mechanisms. This differential component of meaning also has a counterpart in Cage's work. In the Number Pieces Cage continues to practice an evasive swerve, shunning the power of his own taste to determine an aesthetic world.

This impulse was present in Cage's practice already in the early 1950s, a period during which Cage largely discussed his work in technical musical terms. Even then, he made it clear – as he did in more explicitly political terms later in his career – that whatever he worked through in the medium of musical technique also afforded resonances with other realms of life. In 1952 he writes, '[i]t is thus possible to make a musical composition the continuity of which is free of individual taste and memory (psychology) and also of the literature and "traditions" of the art'.[52] This bold statement provides an elegant summary of his project at that time, characterised by his creation of rules for compositions that allowed musical content (number of performers, choice of instruments, durations, pitches), to be decided by chance (dice throws, consulting the *I Ching*).[53] Relying on these 'chance procedures' enabled him to bypass his own habits to some extent. As a composing method it stands out as a rejection not only of a cultivated sense of taste but of an inherited 'self'; it seeks to undo, through making, that self which has been constituted by myriad influences and conventions, and to remake its affective orientation, to open it up to liking things it hitherto found ugly or boring.

Discipline *and* security

As I've suggested, Cage's approach in *26'1.1499"* is dissimilar to his posture in the Black Mountain event and the Number Pieces. Here not only is the sonic space completely constructed – and Cage constructs it with exaggerated clock-precision down to the ten-thousandth of a second – the performer has to be constructed, as well – in a sense, dissolved and, through this dissolution, reconstructed. And she is not simply passive in this process; she also constructs herself. The deeper the reconstitution goes, the more successful any performer's engagement with *26'1.1499"* is.[54] This sort of reconstitution is, however, not an aim of the Black Mountain event or the Number Pieces, which instead take the performer's body and bodily training as material givens.

This inconsistency in Cage's methods – within the same period – could not be accounted for if we relied on the political metaphors with which his work is usually described. Neither anarchy nor liberal government properly describes the ambivalent relationship with control that exists within his *œuvre*. A statement of Cage's about his time-bracket pieces supports a reading in other terms:

> Each musician is a soloist. To bring to orchestral society the devotion to music that characterizes chamber music. To build a society one by one. To bring chamber music to the size of orchestra. *Music for -----* [1984, revised 1987]. So far I have written eighteen parts, any of which can be played together or omitted. Flexible time-brackets. Variable structure. A music, so to speak, that's earthquake proof.[55]

What is an earthquake-proof music? In the context of Cage's utterance, the possibilities he seems to be accounting for, in making sure that a music would go ahead – would survive, would continue to be itself – even if certain unforeseen events transpired, could quite literally include performers' incapacitation due to injury or death from earthquake. But it is important to note that the designation 'earthquake proof' does not apply to any physical structure. Buildings and bridges are at best earthquake-resistant: built to minimise damage in a natural catastrophe, their designers acknowledge that it is not possible to entirely prevent such damage. Meanwhile, humanity does not have the ability to prevent earthquakes from occurring.

Cage's time-bracket pieces are 'so to speak' earthquake proof, because they have flexible structures. They are ductile – they can undergo significant plastic deformation before rupturing. This ductility is not a material property; it metaphorically describes a temporal structure written into the scores. Again, I contend that Foucault's characterisation of security offers a striking parallel. Following his description of security's particular relationship with spaces, in his second lecture of *Security, Territory, Population*, he articulates security apparatuses' particular relationship with 'the event'. Foucault is not concerned with music but with how governments deal with unwanted events like grain scarcity or theft. A transformation in European techniques of government takes place for him with the eighteenth-century French physiocrats:

> Abeille, the physiocrats, and the economic theorists of the eighteenth century, tried to arrive at an apparatus (*dispositif*) for arranging things so that, by connecting up with the

very reality of these fluctuations [of grain's abundance and cheapness], and by establishing a series of connections with other elements of reality, the phenomenon is gradually compensated for, checked, finally limited, and, in the final degree, canceled out, without it being prevented or losing any of its reality.[56]

The apparatus that Abeille tried to arrive at allows all sorts of fluctuations (for instance, of land quality and climatic conditions, as well as rising grain prices) to take place, without trying to prevent them, and by allowing a bit of scarcity, a bit of hunger, it is able to contain the negative effects, to prevent these fluctuations from exploding into a catastrophe. Cage's work flirts with governing a span of performance time in an analogous manner – accepting the hypothetical undesirable event at face value while trying to contain any negative consequences. His time-bracket pieces are ductile so that such fluctuations as mistimed entries, errant noises, and a player playing too fast or too slow relative to other players, are held within a generous structure that cancels out the phenomena – that is, these fluctuations do not appear as mistakes at all. This general aesthetic economy, like Foucault's characterisation of security, is centrifugal, possessing the constant tendency to expand, constantly integrating new elements – this is both what is newest in Cage's œuvre and what is most familiar to us in performance practices today, thanks in part to Cage's influence.

Thus we have seen three aspects of the distinction between disciplinary and security mechanisms: discipline constructs a space while security relies on material givens; discipline controls the minutiae of time in order to extract greater forces while security eschews both the small-scale control of time as well as counterpoint in favour of achieving effects at a global level; and discipline tries to prevent negative events while security tries to situate undesirable events in a larger context in which they never erupt although they never disappear either. Discipline is characterised in *Discipline and Punish* as a gentler form of power that is nonetheless blatantly controlling. Discipline 'regulates everything' and 'allows nothing to escape'. Security, in contrast, 'lets things happen'.[57] Foucault associates both mechanisms with eighteenth-century liberalism, and although security exercises control more subtly, at a greater distance from its targets, both mechanisms continue to differentiate themselves from the highly visible older form of juridico-legal power, which Foucault famously illustrated in the opening of *Discipline and Punish* via a brutal scene of public torture and execution.

The relative visibility of figures of power

One of the reasons Foucault gives for emphasising the distinction between security and discipline, as we've seen already, is to evade the simplistic assertion of power as something monolithic and centralised in a 'master' figure: 'Neither power nor master, neither Power nor the master, and neither one nor the other as God'.[58] In other words, Foucault's analysis of discipline, in *Discipline and Punish*, understood as a gentler yet still brutal power, is to be distinguished from the sovereign power over death only because it does not take the same form. What is insinuated here is that this centralised sovereign power continues to operate, only in cloaked form. By introducing a third term he aimed to buttress his position against the possibility of this insinuation. In the remainder of this chapter, I will focus firstly on how both security and discipline, in forgoing visible forms of power, differ from an older model of legal power. This will bring forward questions regarding the relationship between politically conceived music and governance conceived in terms of the control of time and space. At stake is the primacy of the aesthetic or the domain of legislative policy, in political life.

Both security and disciplinary mechanisms of power work as they do in part because they are invisible. Though social hierarchies persist, these mechanisms of power operate not through a monarch or any form of personal directorship but on an entirely other dimension. Western classical music offers a compelling illustration of the highly visible figure of power, as well as the complicated history of its attempted removal. Elias Canetti writes in *Crowds and Power*:

> There is no more obvious expression of power than the performance of a conductor. [...] The conductor [...] is the only person who stands. In front of him sits the orchestra and behind him the audience. [...] Quite small movements are all he needs to wake this or that instrument to life or to silence it at will. He has the power of life and death over the voices of the instruments; one long silent will speak again at his command. Their diversity stands for the diversity of mankind; an orchestra is like an assemblage of different types of men. The willingness of its members to obey him makes it possible for the conductor to transform them into a unit, which he then embodies. [...] The complexity of the work he performs means that he must be alert. Presence of mind is among his essential attributes; law-breakers must be curbed instantly. The code of laws, in the form of the score, is in his hands.[59]

For Canetti the conductor is such a strong imago of power that he seems to forget the person behind the creation of the score. He doesn't mention the composer, but we can infer from his family of analogies that the composer is a legislator – the writer of laws. This writer is an invisible power. Meanwhile, the conductor figure Canetti speaks of is particular to the Western European orchestral tradition. It is an unusual figure in the history of music insofar as he or she leads a group from outside it, without also playing. Historically the figure arose in Western Europe in the late eighteenth and early nineteenth centuries. Around the same time, according to Foucault's account in *Discipline and Punish* – that is, from around 1760 to around 1840 – a shift in the power to punish, away from theatricality and towards invisibility, is decisive in Western Europe. I find the coincidence notable. Why should the conductor – this visible figure of power – emerge in Western European societies during the same period that the power to punish goes into hiding? Does the conductor embody the sublimation of a pre-classical form of power? Does the conductor represent the preservation of a form of power that is dormant but not yet – perhaps never – passed? This notion would in fact be consistent with Foucault's thesis in *Discipline and Punish* that while the post-revolutionary decades overturned the way that punishment worked by getting rid of public torture, a trace or sediment of torture [*un fond 'suppliciant'*] remained within the corporal nature of imprisonment.[60] The conductor, sediment of monarchical power, survived, even grew in strength until the early twentieth century. We could speculate that the emergence and survival of the conductor figure in the nineteenth century either supplements the trace of monarchical power or embodies the possibility of the monarch's return.

What has happened to the conductor figure since then has many twists and mutually contradictory tendencies, and there is not scope to go into it here. However, it is worth noting that conductorless orchestra projects began in the early days of the Soviet Union with the Moscow-based 'Persimfans' (*Pervïy Simfonicheskiy Ansambl' bez Dirizhyora* – literally, the first conductorless orchestra), and have been enjoying a resurgence in the past decade, in the United States, Russia, and around Europe. The majority of Cage's works for orchestra after 1951 are written such that a conductor is not needed. No conductor is needed to perform the Number Pieces because precise synchronisation is not needed. If we can speak of a general aesthetic economy of security in the twentieth-century neo-avant-garde, it is curious that in political thought and practice this mechanism of power emerged 150 years earlier. Can it be that music praxis is, in at least this one sense, mirroring a society that has ceased to exist?

Discipline as mere fun

On 2 October 1954, David Tudor and John Cage set off from New York City on the *Maasdam* ship, bound for a European tour. The next day the ship collided with a French freighter, crumpling the *Maasdam*'s stern, and the two ships had to return to Hoboken for repairs.[61] Cage's plan had been to write a lecture, to be given in London later that month, while crossing the Atlantic. Instead, after he and Tudor banded together with other passengers to get the Holland-America line to charter a flight to Amsterdam, he wrote the lecture 'on trains and in hotels and restaurants' while on tour.[62] His anticipated expanse of uninterrupted, contemplative time at sea was thus replaced by bitty intervals broken up by the distractions involved in moving between places.

The lecture that Cage wrote under unanticipated time pressure, *45' for a Speaker*, was originally intended to be *39'16.95"*. Cage used a pre-determined 'rhythmic structure' (a sequence of whole numbers), which he had also used for the two piano pieces, and a multiplier, which he obtained through a chance procedure, in order to decide this length.[63] However, he subsequently composed the text using chance procedures as well, and when he completed it he found he 'was unable to perform it within that time-length'. So he made it longer. He reports that it remained difficult to read, 'but one can still try'.[64] Cage indicates ten-second increments every six lines, along the left side of the page (0'10" … 0'20" … 0'30" … etc.) (see Figure 2). The indication is vague enough that the speaker may take some extra time – on the order of a few seconds – with the denser passages while shortening the silent passages in compensation. Once again an 'earthquake-proof' security mechanism seems to be at play. Yet the speaker's attempt to stay 'with the clock' creates tautness in the performance – a dramatic tension for the performer, which is conveyed to the spectator/auditor. For the performer it can be fun – a kind of game. Yet if we analyse this structure, it appears cruel – tension is

6'00"   the course
        of the
        performance.

10"   The principle called mobility-immobility is this:
        every thing is changing
        but while some things
        are changing
        others
        are not.
20"
        Eventually those

        that were

        not
30"
        changing

        begin suddenly

        to change
40"
        et vice versa ad infinitum.

        A technique to be useful (skillful, that is)

        must be such that it fails
50"   to control
        the elements subjected to it. Otherwise
        it is apt to become unclear.
        And listening is best
        in a state of mental
        emptiness.

154/SILENCE

Figure 2 Excerpt from '45' for a Speaker' in *Silence: Lectures and Writings*

created through a differential between time expected for a task and time that ultimately materialises for that task. It mirrors the workplace dynamic wherein the boss requires his or her workers to produce more than they previously had been able to within a given timeframe, to 'perform or else' as McKenzie aptly puts it, in order to produce outputs at the efficiency rate that has been 'benchmarked' in an unrelated field. Clearly, the moral value of this general aesthetic economy is hugely variable, depending on who creates the tension, and for whom it is created.

This leads to a final set of questions. It is not just the mirroring of a political strategy that should interest us in Cage. The greater mystery is the relationship between his aesthetic economy and the political mechanism it appears to double – why did this doubling take this particular form? As previously noted, Foucault had little to say about contemporary art music, but a remark of his, made in conversation with Pierre Boulez in 1983, seems apposite here. Foucault posed the question regarding twentieth-century art music: 'this music which is so close, so consubstantial with all our culture, how does it happen that we feel it, as it were, projected afar and placed at an almost insurmountable distance?'[65] If an artform that doubles society feels nonetheless distant from that society, what else is hidden in the doubling relationship? Is this disjunction between music and broader culture not reason to suspect that whatever Cage's practice appears to resemble, it cannot be reduced to a 'political rationality'? That would be altogether too tidy.

Conclusion

In my view, we are not finished with critical appraisals of Cage's practice in relation to political imaginaries. I have tried to use a particular moment in Foucault's thought to extend some of the links that Benjamin Piekut made between Cage's practice and liberal governance, and to revise others of these links. Foucault's conceptualisation of security must be understood not simply as a new concept, but as a complex moment in his thought during which his characterisation of modern societies as 'disciplinary' was displaced by a more complex account involving three distinctive mechanisms of power. Two of these mechanisms – security, which functions through the application of pressure to aspects of a broadly conceived environment in which human life freely moves, and discipline, which focuses on forming certain kinds of subjects – are broadly associated, in Foucault's account, with modernity, although he insists that the apparent historical alignment in his account is not absolute. They both differ from an older model of juridico-legal power, but the latter does not disappear entirely in modernity. This complex tripartite account is designed in part to make it difficult to place greater value on one or the other form of power over the others. By identifying parallels between John Cage's practice and both security and discipline, we can move beyond current scholarship's tendency to seek ultimate judgement on his practice by exaggerating one or another evaluation of its power dynamics – either praising its anarchistic vision as Rob Haskins has done, or cautioning against its liberalism as Piekut has done.

And, at the same time, by using Cage's work to exemplify the conceptual development in Foucault's own thought, I suggest that we are conversely better able to think how Foucault moved beyond the impasses of disciplinary power.[66] Foucault's thought is often erroneously cited in order to suggest that a singular thing called disciplinary power, which appears to be gentle and innocuous, is actually coercively responsible for the order of our world. By introducing the term security, Foucault aimed to complicate our understanding of the locations of power and to rein in the impulse simply to condemn the functioning of power. He clarifies his position in his 1984 interview, 'The Ethics of the Concern of the Self as a Practice of Freedom':

> The idea that there could exist a state of communication that would allow games of truth to circulate freely, without any constraints or coercive effects, seems utopian to me. This is precisely a failure to see that power relations are not something that is bad in itself, that we have to break free of. I do not think that a society can exist without power relations, if by that one means the strategies by which individuals try to direct and control the conduct of others. The problem, then, is not to try to dissolve them in the utopia of completely transparent communication but to acquire the rules of law, the management techniques, and also the morality, the *ēthos*, the practice of the self, that will allow us to play these games of power with as little domination as possible.[67]

Notes

1 According to Michel Senellart, editor of the original French edition of Foucault's lectures at the Collège de France, 'Foucault distinguishes security mechanisms from disciplinary mechanisms for the first time in the final lecture (17 March 1976) of the 1975–1976 course "*Il faut défendre la société*" p. 219; "Society Must Be Defended" p. 246'. Michel Foucault, *Security, Territory, Population: Lectures at the Collège de France, 1977–1978*, ed. Michel Senellart, gen. eds. François Ewald and Alessandro Fontana, English series ed. Arnold I. Davidson, trans. Graham Burchell (New York: Picador, 2007 [2004]), p. 24n5.

2 Jon McKenzie, *Perform or Else: From Discipline to Performance* (London: Routledge, 2001), p. 175.

3 Ibid., p. 175; and Gilles Deleuze, 'Postscript on the Societies of Control', *October* 59 (1992), 4–7.

4 Benjamin Piekut, *Experimentalism Otherwise: The New York Avant-Garde and Its Limits* (Berkeley: University of California Press, 2011), p. 61.

5 Ibid., p. 63.

6 Wendy Brown, 'Neo-Liberalism and the End of Liberal Democracy', *Theory & Event* 7.1 (2003), n.p.

7 Foucault, *Security, Territory, Population*, pp. 6–9.

8 Piekut, *Experimentalism Otherwise*, p. 145.

9 Ibid., p. 145.

10 An excerpt of the score can be seen on James Pritchett's website, *Rose White Music*, http://rosewhitemusic.com/piano/wp-content/uploads/2013/10/Fig6–2.png, accessed 31 December 2017.

11 Piekut, *Experimentalism Otherwise*, p. 172.

12 Ibid., p. 148.

13 Derek Hook, *Foucault, Psychology and the Analytics of Power* (Basingstoke: Palgrave MacMillan, 2007), p. 8.

14 'Introduces', that is, within the context of the 1977–78 lecture series. See note 1 above.

15 Foucault, *Security, Territory, Population*. Foucault declares near the beginning of his first lecture of 1977–78 that he will be continuing an 'analysis of these mechanisms of power' that he began years ago. Midway

through the lecture, he outlines four 'general features of [...] apparatuses of security', the second of which is its 'treatment of the uncertain, the aleatory' (p. 11).

16 For Foucault's relationship with Barraqué, see Didier Eribon, *Michel Foucault*, trans. Betsy Wing (Cambridge, MA: Harvard University Press, 1991), pp. 64–8.

17 Michel Foucault, 'Pierre Boulez, Passing Through the Screen' (1982), in *Aesthetics, Method, and Epistemology*, ed. James D. Faubion, Vol. 2, *Essential Works of Foucault, 1954–1984* (New York: New Press, 1998), pp. 241–4. See also Edward Campbell, *Boulez, Music and Philosophy* (Cambridge: Cambridge University Press, 2010), pp. 138–40. There are many near-misses linking Foucault with Cage's aleatoric music, but none of them are very helpful: Boulez had a well-publicised correspondence with Cage, in which the two spoke extensively about their individual conceptions of what sort of freedom should be involved in 'aleatoric music'. After a number of letters back and forth they appear to have realised that they disagreed fundamentally about this. It's probably fair to say that Cage's conception was much more daring and as such has provoked more extensive artistic repercussions. Even so, and despite Cage's fame, it is not necessarily the case that Foucault would have known his work.

18 David Macey, *The Lives of Michel Foucault* (London: Vintage, 1993), pp. 398–9. Macey explains that Foucault, in his contribution, 'concentrated on a brief analysis of the musical culture of the Parisian intelligentsia, noting with some surprise that few of his colleagues or students took any serious interest in contemporary music and commenting on the anomaly between their philosophical and musical tastes: people who were passionately interested in Heidegger and Nietzsche followed the fortunes of mediocre rock groups rather than the experiments of IRCAM'. See also David Macey, *Michel Foucault* (London: Reaktion, 2004), pp. 41–3.

19 John Cage, 'An Autobiographical Statement', *John Cage.org*, http://johncage.org/autobiographical_statement.html, accessed 1 January 2018.

20 Arnold Aronson, *American Avant-Garde Theatre: A History* (New York: Routledge, 2000), pp. 38–40.

21 Michel Foucault, *Discipline and Punish: The Birth of the Prison*, trans. Alan Sheridan (London: Penguin, 1991 [1977]); orig. *Surveiller et punir: Naissance de la prison* (Paris: Gallimard, 1975).

22 Foucault, *Security, Territory, Population*. The first part of the quotation is from p. 19; the second from p. 20.

23 Foucault, *Discipline and Punish*, p. 154.

24 Rob Haskins, 'John Cage and Anarchism', http://terz.cc/print.php?where=magazin&id=264, accessed 26 December 2017.

25 James Pritchett, *The Music of John Cage* (Cambridge: Cambridge University Press, 1993), p. 199.

26 Cage, *John Cage.org*, http://johncage.org/pp/john-cage-works.cfm, accessed 2 January 2018.

27 Haskins, 'John Cage and Anarchism'.

28 Ibid.

29 Ibid.

30 Ibid.

31 Ibid.

32 Ibid.

33 Foucault, *Security, Territory, Population*, p. 49.

34 Ibid., pp. 48–9.

35 Ibid., p. 48.

36 Ibid., p. 49.

37 Foucault, *Discipline and Punish*, pp. 164–5.

38 Ibid.

39 Foucault, 'Pierre Boulez, Passing Through the Screen'. It is interesting to note that Gilles Deleuze and Félix Guattari, in A *Thousand Plateaus: Capitalism and Schizophrenia*, trans. Brian Massumi (Minneapolis: University of Minnesota Press, 1987), name Cage's practice as emblematic of a particular kind of temporality, which 'affirms ... floating time above pulsed time or tempo' (p. 267). The interconnectedness of all topics within this book may suggest that their concern with temporality has some relation to their concern with Foucault's disciplinary society, mentioned elsewhere in the book (pp. 67, 224). But their discussion is too ambiguous to be helpful here.

40 Michel Foucault and Pierre Boulez, 'Contemporary Music and the Public', trans. John Rahn, *Perspectives of New Music*, 24.1 (1985), 6–12. The original appeared in *CNAC Magazine*, 15 (May–June 1983), 10–12.

41 Edward Aldwell and Carl Schachter, *Harmony and Voice Leading*, 3rd edn (Belmont, CA: Thomson, 2003).

42 John Cage, '45' for a Speaker', in *Silence: Lectures and Writings* (Middletown: Wesleyan University Press, 1961), p. 164. Deleuze and Guattari allude to Cage in a discussion not unrelated to superposition in *A Thousand Plateaus*, pp. 267, 269.

43 Foucault, *Security, Territory, Population*, p. 16.

44 Ibid., p. 18.

45 Ibid.

46 Ibid., pp. 22–3.

47 On the latter point see Ryan Dohoney, 'John Cage, Julius Eastman, and the Homosexual Ego', in Benjamin Piekut (ed.), *Tomorrow is the Question: New Directions in Experimental Music Studies* (Ann Arbor: University of Michigan Press, 2014), pp. 39–62. On the former see Sharon Williams, 'Uncaged: John Cage and Conceptual Approaches to Participatory Music-making', *Malaysian Music Journal*, 2.2 (2013), 90–103.

48 Dohoney, 'John Cage, Julius Eastman, and the Homosexual Ego'.

49 Cited in Haskins, 'John Cage and Anarchism'. Original: John Cage, 'How to Pass, Kick, Fall, and Run', in *A Year from Monday: New Lectures and Writings* (Middletown: Wesleyan University Press, 1969), p. 136.

50 See Cage, *A Year from Monday*, pp. 4–5, 19, 162. See also Piekut, *Experimentalism Otherwise*, p. 60.

51 Foucault, *Security, Territory, Population*, p. 19.

52 John Cage, 'To Describe the Process of Composition Used in Music of Changes and Imaginary Landscape No. 4', in *Silence*, p. 59; initially published as part of 'Four Musicians at Work' in *trans/formation*, 1.3 (1952).

53 Much has been written about Cage's use of 'chance techniques'. See Pritchett, *The Music of John Cage*.

54 Piekut's discussion highlights cellist Charlotte Moorman's creative relationship with her own subjecthood in her performances of Cage's piece.

55 John Cage, 'An Autobiographical Statement', *John Cage*, http://johncage.org/autobiographical_statement.html, accessed 30 December 2017.

56 Foucault, *Security, Territory, Population*, p. 37.

57 Ibid., p. 45.

58 Ibid., pp. 55–6.

59 Elias Canetti, *Crowds and Power*, trans. Carol Stewart (1962) (New York: Continuum, 1981 [1960]), pp. 394–5.

60 Foucault, *Discipline and Punish*, p. 16. See also Stuart Elden on the translation of this passage at *Progressive Geographies*, https://progressivegeographies.com/2014/01/22/beyond-discipline-and-punish-is-it-time-for-a-new-translation-of-foucaults-surveiller-et-punir/, accessed 3 August 2017.

61 Peter C. Kohler, 'The Atlantic's "Great Little Liners": "Ryndam" and "Maasdam"', www.halpostcards.com/unofficial/kohler.html, accessed 29 December 2017; *The Suffolk County News* (Sayville, NY), 8 October 1954, p. 7, http://nyshistoricnewspapers.org/lccn/sn84031477/1954-10-08/ed-1/seq-7/, accessed 29 December 2017; Henrik Ljungström, Maasdam (IV)/Stefan Batory/Stefan, www.thegreatoceanliners.com/maasdam4.html, accessed 30 December 2017.

62 Cage, *Silence*, p. 147.

63 Ibid., p. 146.

64 Ibid.

65 Foucault and Boulez, 'Contemporary Music and the Public', pp. 10–12.

66 Foucault, *Security, Territory, Population*, pp. 55–6.

67 Michel Foucault, 'The Ethics of the Concern of the Self as a Practice of Freedom', in *Ethics: Subjectivity and Truth*, ed. Paul Rabinow, Vol. 1, *Essential Works of Foucault, 1954–1984* (New York: New Press, 1997), p. 298.

PART III

Governmentality and power

10

Foucault and the Iranian Revolution: reassessed

Tracey Nicholls

A decade ago, just out of graduate school, I published an article exploring questions of the politics of representation in jazz criticism in which I argued that, in some contexts, 'the death of the author' actually promotes the abuse of cultural power that Michel Foucault objected to in his 1969 lecture *Qu'est-ce qu'un auteur?*, later published as 'What Is An Author?'[1] The inconsistency I identified in Foucault's theorising was his inattention to the ways in which *écriture*'s celebrated erasure of an author's authority can fail to liberate meanings and interpretations. Specifically, I worried that this erasure can in fact entrench both the dominance of socially legitimated viewpoints and the continued marginalisation of social commentaries and critiques which oppose dominant threads of discourse. I illustrated my concern about the warping and subverting effects of social privilege through a discussion of how saxophonist John Coltrane's 'free jazz' improvisations of the 1960s were represented by critics unwilling to take notice of issues of identity and social positioning – both their own, and Coltrane's – and I concluded that theorising a socially unequal world as if it were an abstract play of power relations made Foucault's aesthetic commitments seem politically irresponsible.

In the time between that article and the invitation to contribute to this volume, Foucault scholarship has continued to inform my thinking about power, and has continued to encourage me to see a more nuanced Foucault than the one I remember trying to take on in that early work. In particular, I was recently struck by the concept of 'political spirituality' that Drucilla Cornell and Stephen D. Seely offer as a complex ideological viewpoint from which to understand Foucault's later thinking about 'care of the self'.[2] Their discussion of Foucault's attempt to think beyond secular politics, to think about spirituality as a site – or perhaps, as a constitutive attitude? – for revolutionary solidarity, emphasises the centrality of Iran's theocratic revolution within Foucault's later political thought, a connection they noted is the central focus of Janet

Afary and Kevin B. Anderson's translation and analysis of Foucault's writings on the Iranian Revolution.[3] When invited to contribute to a volume on Foucault and performance, I hoped that examination of Afary and Anderson's arguments, informed by the 'political spirituality' Cornell and Seely had drawn from their reading of Foucault and his critics, would support a revisiting of my early engagement, in which Foucault might emerge as a more cross-culturally careful thinker than I thought I had found in my 2006 article.

I found myself reading two very different accounts of the Iranian Revolution and Foucault's engagement with it: the one presented within Afary and Anderson's *Foucault and the Iranian Revolution* (2005), and the critical corrective to that book that is Behrooz Ghamari-Tabrizi's *Foucault in Iran* (2016).[4] Both books, despite their disagreement on points crucial to understanding Iran, convinced me that what Foucault saw in Iran – immersed himself in – was crucial to his thinking about possible political futures, even as I felt simultaneously completely unequipped to mediate the interpretive controversies generated by reading these two books together. The net effect of trying to explore how this political phenomenon that I do not know well enough to understand had shaped the thinking of someone so robustly committed to asking every interesting question, regardless of the likely answers, is my deep appreciation for Foucault's willingness to throw himself into new fields of possibilities. The Foucault who appears to dismiss feminist concerns about a revolution's potential for human rights violations does not seem to me any more nuanced a cultural interlocutor than the one whose concern about the abstract authority of 'the author' trumped appreciation of the variety of ways in which privilege and racism might congeal in evaluations of cultural products. The Foucault whose thinking has inspired feminist philosophising about power, authority, oppression, and abuse[5] is, on the other hand, an intellectually generative figure who articulates a commitment to asking questions and opening up discourses that would otherwise be dismissed as pointless, as teleologically unwarranted. In ways I am just starting to recognise, the very questions I began with in 2006 were 'askable' because Foucault is an instructive guide in matters of how to think differently and where to speak freely.

Recapitulating 'dominant positions'

My 2006 discussion of Foucault's theorising, through analysis of Coltrane's performing, stressed that evaluation of works (in my illustration, journalistic criticism) can take place in a context in which power, including the power to assert meaning and value, is in the hands of the critic/theoriser, not the author or artist.[6] In this kind of case, the author has, socially speaking, either no authority or an anomalous, deviantly accessed authority,[7] and erasing him or her from the artwork does not liberate meaning or proliferate interpretation in the way Foucault hopes it will. The impetus of this criticism of Foucault's desire to celebrate 'the death of the author' was not an interest on my part in defending the primacy of authorial intentions, but a commitment to aesthetic pluralism that, in the realm of interpretation of artworks, looks for and debates the widest array possible of persuasive and plausible interpretations. Foucault and I both share an interest in proliferating stories; my concern, and my departure from him with respect to 'What Is an Author?', is on the question of power- and privilege-differences that determine whose interpretations get taken seriously and whose get dismissed. As I see it, all too often, power limits our articulation of our (aesthetic) experience to the conventions licensed by the arbiters of a given subculture, and silences voices that are already ignored. Although I make much of this concern in my 2006 paper, I do think that Foucault's injunction to celebrate intertextuality has a lot of merit in contemporary European literature, that is, within the tradition from which he speaks. And certainly one could argue that entire artforms – hip hop comes instantly to mind – exist precisely because of, and in, the erased author and proliferated (separated, truncated, reintegrated) parts of multiple, multiply-author-functioned texts. That is undeniable, and it makes 'What Is An Author?' perennially interesting. But it remains also true, I think, that application of an aesthetic worldview like *écriture* in contexts of privilege disparity will have effects diametrically opposed to what Foucault wants to champion. What most concerned me in my early reading of 'What Is An Author?' was the obvious worry that if the theoretical lenses used in critical theoretical assessments are being warped by privilege disparities, then the audience whose knowledge and aesthetic experiences are being shaped by these critics' reviews will not be able to determine whether the theoriser has done justice to the artist's project.

In the case of my John Coltrane example, radical musical innovation was dismissed by some influential white music critics of the 1960s as 'anti-jazz', giving rise to a representation of Coltrane's experimentation as 'unlistenable' and 'inaccessible' that persists to this day.[8] Coltrane was (mis)represented, in his words, as not knowing 'the first thing about music [despite] really trying to push things off'.[9] This evaluation was, of course, taking place in a systemically racist society, one in which white voices were (and still are) typically accorded greater authority than black ones. Even when the black voice is famous, as Coltrane was when the denunciations began, and revered, as he has been in the intervening decades. An editor's dismissive review could end the career of a lesser-known artist, and even had the power to render Coltrane's experimentalism as an aesthetic defect. That could and did happen because the jazz critics – not the artist[10] – had the cultural power to choose the theoretical lens through which Coltrane's project was interrogated, and they chose to reduce music that was overtly dialogical, meant to be experienced in live performance, to formalist discussion of its sonic properties.[11]

While the 'anti-jazz' marginalisation of Coltrane was couched in formalist terms, my point in bringing Foucault's 'What Is An Author?' discussion into the paper was to demonstrate that even a more context-sensitive consideration of the artwork is not necessarily going to avoid the pitfall of congealed privilege disparities. The interplay of texts Foucault endorses *is* context-cognisant, but did not appear to be power-cognisant. And this is the issue that I now realise I was struggling to articulate in my earlier engagement with Foucault: I wanted the insights of the Michel Foucault who wrote *Discipline and Punish*,[12] a Foucault more thoughtful and careful about the potential dark side of the liberatory permissiveness he thinks we get from casting aside the author function.

Considering 'political spirituality'

Challenging a standard reading of Foucault as pessimistic about our possibilities for liberation, Cornell and Seely argue that when the call for care of the self and for new arrangements of 'bodies and pleasures' in his later work is considered alongside his commentaries on the Iranian Revolution of 1979, Foucault emerges as passionately and thoughtfully engaged with a new, non-commodified conception of the erotic.[13] Foucault, they argue, is not rejecting revolution and its emancipatory possibilities so much as he is rejecting the way that revolution has been discussed in European political philosophy, with its over-attention to the nation-state.[14] From the standpoint of their thesis – that the revolutionary politics which might save humanity demand a robust spirituality and 'nothing less than the complete reconfiguration of erotic relations'[15] – Foucault is clearly an indispensable voice in discourses around the construction of sexuality and, in his Iranian writings, discourse around what spirituality might be like in more public performances than those licensed by a secular 'West'. As they present his interest in the Iranian Revolution, it was about 'a different way of thinking about social and political organization'[16] such that revolution is more than a political activity, or perhaps, that it is an immersion of epistemological commitments into the crucible of politics: 'not only fighting for another world [...] but rather fighting for a *new truth* and for how to be a different subject in *this world*'.[17]

Observing with Foucault that we, as products of European modernity, relate to ourselves as objects of knowledge rather than objects of care, Cornell and Seely read him as wanting to shift our thinking towards 'an ethics of pleasure and an art of living' as a way of resolving the sex/care split in European modernity's cultural attitudes.[18] But this call is not a mere and simplistic urging to choose a different conception of human sexuality, or to choose 'care' over 'knowledge'. Cornell and Seely quote Foucault explaining why his investigation of sexuality in the ancient world (which he analyses extensively in volumes two and three of *Histoire de la sexualité*)[19] does not consti-tute an argument that we should return to those conceptions as an alternative to our contemporary worldview: 'My point is not that everything is bad, but that everything is dangerous, which is not exactly the same [... i]f everything is dangerous, *then we always have something to do*'.[20]

This willingness to make/see everything as dangerous seems helpful to me insofar as we think that a confrontation-positive attitude (fighting for new truths and how to be different subjects) might open up social space to talk about dangers. Having lived all my life in explicitly secular societies, and having been taught a history of human wars whose subtext was a close connection between violence and religiosity, it is easiest for me to see most clearly the danger that the theological dissident faces in a public sphere characterised by political spirituality. We are each private in our beliefs as a way of accommodating different belief systems, says my 'raised by lapsed-Protestants' worldview. And yet, the allure I see in the idea of political spirituality that Cornell and Seely adopt from Foucault is its powerful capacity to forge a collective identity, powerful enough even to provide the stabilising force that holds together a society during revolutionary transition. Foucault is right insofar as he is endorsing (identi-fying) the need for a shared worldview in times of great social upheaval, and he is reasonable and responsible insofar as he is willing to take up the project of considering the dangers of the brave new world he wants. There are, however, empirically answer-able questions to be considered with respect to the framework shift Foucault urges upon us: does confrontation nurture 'dangerous' conversation or foreclose it? Does moving away from consideration of what is 'bad' and turning to questions of what is 'dangerous' help to move us, as societies, away from juvenile and insecure moralising about others' lives and into the task of a more 'adult' awareness that our world is indeed full of risks and trade-offs that we can only navigate if we first acknowledge them?

If we consider this idea – that seeing a world of danger is more politically useful than seeing a world of bad – as informing Foucault's desire to recast as public the spirituality that Western secularism (France's *laïcité*; the United States' constitutional commitment to separation of church and state) thinks of as deeply personal and indi-vidually variable,[21] what does this mean we can expect of Foucault with respect to these questions? Perhaps a publically performed spirituality functions like the 'public space' of artistic practices ruled by intertextuality? If so, from Foucault's vantage point, it might be that removing the assumption of the spiritual/religious as neces-sarily personal – relocating from private to public a set of practices we think char-acteristic of human civilisation – is a way of finding the 'outside' of (disciplinary) power-knowledge matrices in which our thinking gets enmeshed to the detriment of our capacities to transform and develop. Taking Foucault seriously on either political spirituality or intertextuality obligates us to engage with him in sustained discussion of what risks 'we' are taking, the harms that might result (particularly those that happen to people/entities that are not 'us'), and an at least plausible rationale for what we gain by relocating what is now private/privileged back into the public sphere.

(Not) listening to who is speaking

Extending my 2006 concern about theoretical lenses, and the ways they might be warped by perspective disparities, to Foucault's account of the possibilities he saw in the Iranian Revolution can open up for us some important questions about what he might have been able to see as a francophone outsider to the political battles being fought in Paris (the city from which Ayatollah Khomeini left his exile to lead the revo-lution) and in Tehran. As I noted in my introduction, Foucault's interposition has been assessed in very different ways, due in large part to divergent views of the revolution itself.

In their assessment of Foucault's Iranian writings and those of his interlocutors, what emerges most clearly from Afary and Anderson's analysis is a Foucault whose rejection of Western social narratives was constructed through overly simplistic binaries of East and West, modernity and pre-modernity, that might reasonably be considered Orientalist.[22] They foreground a romanticisation and objectification of 'the

East' – the singularity Foucault praised in the Iranian Revolution, the sexual tourism he would have been exposed to as a visiting professor in Tunisia in the late 1960s[23] – but leave undigested a more interesting Foucauldian move in his Iranian dispatches: the 'meta-narratives' they see as privileging pre-modern social orders over modern ones by eliding the violence of the pre-modern are being constructed in order to draw our attention to the 'social control' of our apparently more humane modernity.[24] They charge that '[a]t a more general level, Foucault remained insensitive toward the diverse ways in which power affected women, as against men' to the point of dismissing warnings by French and Iranian feminists about gender relations in theocratic states and dismissing news reports of anti-gay violence directed by Khomeini in the early days of postrevolutionary government.[25] In essence, they claim, 'Foucault made an abstraction of Islam and Shi'ism, never exploring the fact that a group of opposition clerics and intellectuals [the Islamists he supported] had adopted a particular reading of Shi'ism' and never acknowledging that what he had championed was 'a carefully staged and crafted version of Shi'ism'.[26]

This account is robustly contested, if not denounced, in Ghamari-Tabrizi's account of the Iranian Revolution: for him, Afary and Anderson betray their outsider bias through their misreading of both the revolution and Foucault, and their uncritical dichotomisation of secular democracy and religious autocracy.[27] The oversimplification is not in Foucault, but in themselves. Ghamari-Tabrizi argues that Foucault saw, and remained committed to, the Iranian Revolution as an unexpected, 'antiteleological' political moment that revealed not 'his fascination with death or his absorption in the aesthetics of violence, [but] the inexplicability of the man in revolt'.[28] The pure possibility of something that erupts outside 'the normative progressive discourses of history' captured Foucault's imagination, Ghamari-Tabrizi asserts, and did so precisely because it did not adhere to the logic of the secular, Enlightenment-shaped West that Afary and Anderson set up as the unimpeachable discursive sphere of universal human rights.[29]

Ghamari-Tabrizi correctly observes that 'whether a revolution is a failure or a success within itself is an ideological question', and I am reminded by current events occurring before this volume goes to press[30] that resisting the temptation to weigh in on things about which one has only read is frequently the mark of a thoughtful scholar.[31] It is simply not clear to me to what extent Afary and Anderson might be misreading the centrality to the revolution of clerical-Islamic political agency, or even to what extent they miss or misidentify key moments in the historical record.[32] It is also, for me, less interesting than the significance of Iran in Foucault's thought, and whether indeed he did engage in a deliberately chosen silence when called to account for having endorsed a revolution that subsequently engaged in violence against gay men and restriction of women's social freedoms, as we in the West might understand them.[33] Both books acknowledge that these abuses happened, and the Afary and Anderson book helpfully reproduces English translations of Foucault's writings and the critical commentary they received.

The concept of political spirituality that Cornell and Seely found so fruitful for their theorising of the humanity we need to become is presented in Afary and Anderson's analysis as infused by Foucault's under-informed and romanticised belief that the Islamist revolutionary society constituted by Ayatollah Khomeini's deposing of the shah would contain pockets of freedom or permissiveness in which male homosexuality could flourish. This is a framing of Foucault that gives credence, I think, to Ghamari-Tabrizi's charge of misreading: Foucault's analytic tendency, which is not acknowledged in Afary and Anderson's reading of him, is to brush past concerns that are already being articulated by others – in this case, Western and Iranian feminists and women's rights activists – in order to point to an unappreciated virtue that is being overlooked.[34] For Foucault, Iran emerges not as a slippery slope towards repression,[35] but as a template for the capacity of Islam to generate resistance internal to a society. Essentially, he saw in this particular spirituality a political 'outside' to the secular, liberal, democratic 'failure' of the French Revolution.

Unwillingness to give up the alluring possibility of another way is, for Afary and Anderson, the explanation for Foucault's public silence when the regime began in March–April 1979 to execute gay men and demand that women veil themselves in public.[36] And it is this perceived refusal to speak out during the protests over compulsory veiling that Afary and Anderson identify as instigating the public criticism of his earlier utopianism, in articles written from September through December 1978.[37] The endorsement Foucault issued in one of his most criticised 1978 dispatches, 'What Are the Iranians Dreaming [Rêvent] About?', and is charged with never having publicly retracted, was called out in the early days of postrevolutionary repression of March–April 1979 by (then-)leftist/post-Maoist journalists Claudie and Jacques Broyelle in a Le Matin opinion piece titled 'What Are the Philosophers Dreaming About?'[38] In it they urge Foucault to admit that he had misjudged Khomeini's revolution: 'When one is an intellectual', they write, 'then one also has some obligations [… among which] is to take responsibility for the ideas that one has defended when they are finally realized'.[39] Foucault's apparent failure to anticipate the brutality of the regime and his apparent lapse into silence in the face of that brutality (which had been predicted and denounced by Iranian and French feminist voices), are subsequently characterised by Afary and Anderson as his recognition of failure in 'the most significant and passionate political commitment of his life' apart from his prison reform work of the early 1970s.[40]

Ironically, in this book that commits itself so thoroughly to a thesis of Foucauldian silence, Afary and Anderson reproduce the very response from Foucault that they charge him with not making. It is difficult to imagine how Foucault's May 1979 page-one essay from Le Monde, translated into English as 'Is It Useless to Revolt?', can be read as anything other than a weary reiteration of who he is, what he is looking at, and from what perspective.[41] He begins by pointing out that there is no contradiction – and therefore no apology or repudiation required – in first being inspired by a revolutionary moment and then being horrified by subsequent repression.[42] He then proceeds to summarise the particular insight he drew from the revolution – the irreducibility and inexplicability of 'the man in revolt' – and invites us to consider a view of humanity in which our concepts of rights and freedoms are more grounded in revolution than they are in nature.[43] His response to the Broyelles's demand that he take responsibility, as a public intellectual, for his words is to affirm that he is as opposed to the brutal repression of postrevolutionary Iran as he was to the shah's repression, and to simultaneously reject the posture of an 'intellectual' harassed into public recantation by what we would today call the 'virtue-signalling' of others.[44] He is not refusing to take responsibility – his final sentences are: 'this is my work. I am neither the first nor the only one to do it,'[45] – but he is refusing the abstraction and the public theatre that these demands impose upon him. One of Foucault's points that inspired me so long ago, in my graduate school reading of 'What Is An Author?', was his quotation of Samuel Beckett's question, 'what does it matter who is speaking?'[46] And this, ultimately, is the point to which I return as my own assessment of Foucault's Iranian writings: it *is* Foucault who is speaking, and we must either listen to him speak his own views in his own voice or risk missing his point utterly.

Thinking new ways

To return in conclusion to the question of how we ought to regard Foucault's endorsements of intertextuality and public/political spirituality, I would argue that consideration of his Iranian writings should indeed transform the ways we play with our ideas. The messy, empirical questions of what happens, and to whom, when power and privilege intersect without scrutiny or disclosure remain a pressing challenge for us all. But, for all that Foucault does not say the things others might want him to, does not conduct himself as 'a public intellectual', his thinking on power remains provocative. The response he makes to his critics in 'Is It Useless to Revolt?' reveals, in his suggestion that rights and freedoms might emerge from revolution (uprising, revolt, death-defying resistance to power), a political philosopher with a radical focus on human agency.[47] Of all the writings about the Iranian Revolution, by Foucault and by his critics, this short essay on the unquenchability of the human spirit and the impossibility of permanent suppression of our humanity strikes me as the most important for scholars of improvisation theory and theatre studies who are interested in performativity. We have Foucault's conceptual tools, and a host of dangerous questions to be asked. In helping to stir up these questions and challenging us to concern ourselves with what is dangerous instead of what is bad, Foucault has indeed ensured that 'we always have something to do'.[48]

Notes

1 Tracey Nicholls, 'Dominant Positions: John Coltrane, Michel Foucault, and the Politics of Representation', *Critical Studies in Improvisation/Études critiques en improvisation*, ed. Ellen Waterman, 2.1 (2006), http://journal.lib.uoguelph.ca/index.php/csieci/issue/view/25; Michel Foucault, 'What Is an Author?', in *Aesthetics, Method, and Epistemology*, ed. James D. Faubion, trans. Josué V. Harari (New York: New Press, 1998), pp. 205–22.

2 Drucilla Cornell and Stephen D. Seely, *The Spirit of Revolution: Beyond the Dead Ends of Man* (Cambridge: Polity Press, 2016).

3 Janet Afary and Kevin B. Anderson, *Foucault and the Iranian Revolution: Gender and the Seductions of Islamism* (Chicago, IL: University of Chicago Press, 2005).

4 Behrooz Ghamari-Tabrizi, *Foucault in Iran: Islamic Revolution after the Enlightenment* (Minneapolis: University of Minnesota Press, 2016).

5 Even a cursory search of feminist philosophy referencing Foucault turns up an enormous body of work. The feminist-Foucauldian work that springs immediately to my mind are the analysis of gender identity/ performance as 'regulative discourse' shaped by Foucauldian disciplinary power that Judith Butler offers in *Gender Trouble: Feminism and the Subversion of Identity* (New York: Routledge, 1990); the account of the dangers and normalisation processes to which sexual identities are subjected in Ladelle McWhorter's *Bodies and Pleasures: Foucault and the Politics of Sexual Normalization* (Bloomington: Indiana University Press, 1999); and the ongoing work by Chloë Taylor on sex crimes, for example, 'Foucault, Feminism, and Sex Crimes', *Hypatia*, 24.4 (2009), 1–25.

6 Nicholls, 'Dominant Positions'.

7 In this reference to authority as something that can be 'deviantly accessed' I intend to identify one way that people can (socially speaking) 'transcend' the privilege/marginalisation categories they would otherwise be sorted into, through remarkable achievement of some sort. In the context of African-American experiences of the social world of the United States, I am thinking of athletic achievement and the arts and entertainment world (for example, Michael Jordan, Spike Lee, Oprah). Because of his position as the most famous soprano saxophone player of his day, John Coltrane was able to speak back against his representation by white music critics in a way that, say, his much more openly politically radical and politically outspoken contemporary Archie Shepp was not.

8 This label is attributed to then-associate editor of *Down Beat*, John Tynan, who has been identified as 'the first to take a strong – and public – stand' against Coltrane, and against alto sax player Eric Dolphy's tour with Coltrane's quartet. See Don DeMicheal, 'John Coltrane and Eric Dolphy Answer the Jazz Critics', in Carl Woideck (ed.), *The John Coltrane Companion: Five Decades of Commentary* (New York: Schirmer, 1998), pp. 109–17 (p. 110), which was originally published in *Down Beat*, 12 April 1962. Tynan's 1961 review of one of those performance dates describes 'a horrifying demonstration of what appears to be a growing anti-jazz trend […] a good rhythm section […] go[ing] to waste behind the nihilistic exercises of the two horns' (quoted in ibid., p. 110).

9 Quoted in Frank Kofsky, *Black Nationalism and the Revolution in Music* (New York: Pathfinder, 1970), p. 242.

10 To be clear, I am not arguing here that Coltrane's account of his project should be privileged as the definitive interpretation because he is the author. I do think authors'/artists' accounts of what they are doing *should* always be one of the accounts considered in any interpretive debates about their works, but I reject the idea that any voice has a prima facie claim to delimit the meanings or values relevant to the work's assessment. My insistence on (author) Coltrane's voice in this example and my desire to engage with the voices of (author) Foucault's critics in the later section on his Iranian Revolution writings are united by my concern – which I believe I share with Foucault – to hear voices that are being dismissed by those who have the power to direct our cultural thinking.

11 Another early example of this ideological choice of aesthetic theory is Ira Gitler's profile 'Trane on the Track' (originally published in *Down Beat*, 16 October 1958), which offers an account of Coltrane's then-current style in purely formal terms: the much-quoted description of Coltrane's multinote playing as 'sheets of sound'. Ira Gitler, 'Trane on the Track', in Woideck (ed.), *The John Coltrane Companion*, pp. 3–7 (p. 6). The context that prompts me to categorise this putatively neutral choice of theoretical constructs as 'ideological' is a longstanding debate in the world of jazz criticism about whether jazz is a 'black' music (and therefore an inferior cultural product) or 'America's artform' (in which case, not uniquely a product of *African*-American culture). Both sides of this debate, conscientiously analysed in Frank Kofsky's history of the free jazz movement (see Kofsky, *Black Nationalism*), are making racist arguments; the appeal to formalism comes from the view that if jazz is truly an art music, it can and should be discussed in the (formalist) language of Western art music. This assumption that one can evaluate a cultural product that comes from outside one's cultural traditions, using only the concepts of one's own traditions, is precisely

the cultural myopia that Kofsky calls out as racist in jazz criticism, and that I see also at work, harmfully, in Foucault's endorsement of *écriture* without considering the subverting effects of an artist's social marginalisation or a critic's social dominance.

12 I am thinking in particular of the discussion of 'docile bodies' in which Foucault describes methods ('disciplines') of self-regulation that transform individual bodies into interchangeable units, obedient to the power structures in which they exist. Michel Foucault, *Discipline and Punish: The Birth of the Prison*, trans. Alan Sheridan (New York: Vintage/Random House, 1995), pp. 135–69. If Foucault had looked at the workings of the 1960s jazz world Kofsky describes, I think he would have to have seen disciplinary practices throughout. For example, *Down Beat* rankings of 'best saxophonist' and 'best album' functioned to produce a competition towards conformity just as exercises and examinations motivate the student and the soldier of Foucault's examples to 'normalise' themselves through calibration to a social ideal. But, as I read 'What Is An Author?', I saw no consideration of how erasing the author might have varying effects in different cultural contexts, and that seemed a disappointing lapse of observation and analysis coming from a thinker who has elsewhere demonstrated remarkable awareness of power's effects on individuals.

13 Cornell and Seely, *The Spirit of Revolution*, pp. 54–5.

14 Ibid., p. 56.

15 Ibid., pp. 9–10; 15.

16 Foucault quoted in ibid., p. 59.

17 Ibid., p. 66, original emphasis.

18 Ibid., p. 71. This is the key argument in Michel Foucault, *An Introduction*, Vol. 1, *The History of Sexuality*, trans. Robert Hurley (New York: Vintage/Random House, 1978).

19 Michel Foucault, *The Care of the Self*, Vol. 3, *The History of Sexuality*, trans. Robert Hurley (New York: Pantheon/Random House, 1986), p. 273. Michel Foucault, *The Use of Pleasure*, Vol. 2, *The History of Sexuality*, trans. Robert Hurley (New York: Vintage/Random House, 1985).

20 Foucault, quoted in Cornell and Seely, *The Spirit of Revolution*, p. 72, original emphasis. This same quotation is rendered more completely in Ghamari-Tabrizi's investigation of Foucault's engagement with the Iranian Revolution: 'My point is not that everything is bad, but that everything is dangerous, which is not exactly the same as bad. If everything is dangerous, then we always have something to do. *So my position leads not to apathy but to a hyper- and pessimistic activism*'. Foucault, quoted in Ghamari-Tabrizi, *Foucault in Iran*, p. 70, original emphasis.

21 Further informing Foucault's desire to trouble Western-secular notions of spirituality, perhaps, is its very sectarian (partisan?) understanding of religious life and spiritual experience: that there are distinct and identifiable places individuals can go to worship; that there are badges of affiliation (hijabs, confirmation crosses); that 'the afterlife' is a reality for many, which it is important for the rest of us not to mock. This is a point I had not fully appreciated until pressed by the editors of this volume on the question of Western secularism's implicit Christianity. The observation strikes me as an astute and necessary clarification; even for those of us who do not identify as Christian, conceptions of religious space and what counts as sacred or profane are indeed tempered by the Christian pasts of our societies, while simultaneously being presented to us as neutral concessions to tolerance. From a North American perspective, I think most notably of the rhetoric required of American presidents: despite the much-vaunted separation of politics and religious ideology in American life, it has always seemed quite obvious to me that a president cannot be (openly) atheist, that he must finish important speeches, for instance, with the phrase 'God bless America'.

22 Afary and Anderson, *Foucault and the Iranian Revolution*, p. 21. The reference here is to Edward Said's theorising of European and American tendencies – in politics, in art and literature, in academic scholarship – to reduce disparate cultures across that part of the world designated 'East' to a caricatured unchanging, inscrutable 'other' which exists for and is subordinate to the fully agentic 'West'. See Edward W. Said, *Orientalism* (New York: Vintage/Random House, 1979).

23 Afary and Anderson, *Foucault and the Iranian Revolution*, pp. 203–9, 140–4.

24 Ibid., p. 22.

25 Ibid., pp. 5, 6.

26 Ibid., p. 39.

27 Ghamari-Tabrizi, *Foucault in Iran*, pp. 109–10.
28 Ibid., p. 189.
29 Ibid., pp. 189, 111.
30 At the beginning of 2018 there are protests across Iran which appear to be met by the conservative leaders of the theocratic government with stricter censorship, tightened control over candidates for political office, and further repression of liberalisation and globalisation efforts. See Ray Takeyh, 'The Islamic Republic of Iran is Doomed', *Politico.com*, 2 January 2018, www.politico.com/magazine/story/ 2018/01/02/the-islamic-republic-of-iran-is-doomed-216210, accessed 25 March 2018.
31 Ghamari-Tabrizi, *Foucault in Iran*, p. 111.
32 Ibid., pp. 75–111.
33 Afary and Anderson, *Foucault and the Iranian Revolution*, pp. 129–32.
34 Basically, I think Ghamari-Tabrizi's account shows us that we can read Foucault's identification of the Iranian Revolution as a singular moment that ushered in a new spirituality, in the same way Foucault speaks of the cultural evolution from madness to mental illness in 'The Birth of the Asylum'. Foucault does not want to argue that people were better treated when we imprisoned 'the mad' instead of hospitalising the ill; he does want to draw our attention to a very specific way in which that earlier, harsher treatment did at least offer 'the mad' the respect of being listened to (in case their ravings were the word of God). Likewise, here, he can, I think, be understood as saying that there is something important in this 'political spirituality' being articulated in Iran without being committed to an outright disregard for the possibilities of revolution going badly wrong.
35 This was the concern voiced by Atoussa H., an Iranian leftist living in Paris, whose criticism of Foucault's embrace of Khomeini warned of tyranny (Afary and Anderson, *Foucault and the Iranian Revolution*, pp. 91–4). The full text of her response to Foucault is part of the reproduction of (translated) primary sources appended to Afary and Anderson's analysis (ibid., pp. 209–10). Feminists in both France and Iran warned in 1978 against the curtailing of rights and gender equality they feared from a theocratic regime, and many women planned and participated in protests in Iran the following year against the growing exclusion of women from public life and the growing violence against homosexual men, even when that protest risked violent reaction against female protestors (ibid., pp. 113–14).
36 Afary and Anderson, *Foucault and the Iranian Revolution*, pp. 129–32. According to Afary and Anderson, the only response Foucault ever issued, on 11 May 1979, after the Iranian theocracy had embarked on its brutal repression, made a single mention of 'subjugation of women' and made no mention of the summary executions of gay men (ibid.). From that point until his death in 1984, they claim, he made no further statements about his previously enthusiastic endorsement of Khomeini's revolution (ibid., p. 133). This is another interpretive point that Ghamari-Tabrizi contests, arguing that Foucault's later critical engagement with Western political thought through a response to Immanuel Kant's 'What is Enlightenment?' is in fact his continued endorsement of and engagement with the 'outside the Enlightenment' epiphany he gleaned from the example of Iran (*Foucault in Iran*, p. 185).
37 Afary and Anderson, *Foucault and the Iranian Revolution*, p. 108. Notable in this discussion of women's rights in cultures traditionally associated with the veiling of women in public is their acknowledgement that there is ongoing debate about what veiling means: whether, in a given society, it necessarily indicates the subordination of women or whether it might be a freely chosen expression of solidarity. Ibid., p. 109.
38 Ibid., p. 118.
39 Reproduced in ibid., 249.
40 Ibid., p. 8. I must note here that this claim about the importance of the Iran writings is considered by some Foucault scholars to be exaggerated, and it is this consideration, not the indictment Ghamari-Tabrizi offers, that has made the Afary and Anderson book controversial within Foucauldian scholarship. The view of those who charge Afary and Anderson with inflating the significance of Foucault's time in Iran is that this was merely an interlude – a desire to break free from depression and writer's block – as he worked his way through rethinking the trajectory of his three-volume *History of Sexuality*. While I find myself personally persuaded by the overlap in Afary and Anderson's and Ghamari-Tabrizi's arguments, respectively, on the significance of the Iran writings, I am grateful to Chloë Taylor for bringing to my attention how controversial a thesis this is.
41 In Afary and Anderson, *Foucault and the Iranian Revolution*, pp. 263–7.

42 Foucault in ibid., p. 263.
43 Foucault in ibid.
44 Foucault in ibid., p. 266.
45 Foucault in ibid., p. 267.
46 Foucault, 'What Is an Author?', p. 205.
47 Foucault in Afary and Anderson, *Foucault and the Iranian Revolution*, p. 263.
48 Quoted in Cornell and Seely, *The Spirit of Revolution*, p. 72, original emphasis.

11

Sightlines: Foucault and Naturalist theatre

Dan Rebellato

Foucault wrote frequently about theatre. He described his encounter with Beckett's *Waiting for Godot* in 1953 as a key moment in his intellectual development;[1] his writings make use of theatrical examples from tragedy to farce, Socrates to Artaud; thematically, the theatrical and the dramatic play an important conceptual role right across his work.[2] Strangely though, he wrote nothing substantial about Naturalist theatre. I say 'strangely' for two reasons: first, in his first academic appointment in Uppsala in the late 1950s, he taught a course on modern theatre, focusing particularly on the first and perhaps most influential of the Naturalist theatres, Antoine's Théâtre Libre;[3] second, less than five years later, Foucault would publish a book that shares some of the intellectual obsessions and historical sources of Naturalism, such that one might even see the book as a secret analysis of Naturalist theatre. That book is *The Birth of the Clinic* (1963).[4]

This is not one of the more celebrated of Foucault's works. One of his first books, it is sometimes suggested that its historical methodology was superseded by the more systematic archaeology of the late 1960s, the Nietzsche-influenced genealogy of the 1970s, and finally the ethical turn of the 1980s.[5] In addition, the book is not an easy read, for several reasons. First, the engagement with historical sources and Foucault's subtle interpretive parsing of fine distinctions within them is sometimes dense to the point of impenetrability. Second, the book exists in two editions: the first, in 1963, is couched in a structuralist vocabulary of signifiers, signifieds, myths, codes, and differences; the second – now the standard – edition, a decade later, removes quite a lot of this vocabulary, but not all of it,[6] leaving the book as most people read it caught between methodologies; third, the only English translation so far has a number of errors and infelicities and, in addition, is a translation neither of the 1963 nor of the 1972 edition but a perplexing mixture of the two;[7] finally, Foucault's style in the book switches continually and without warning between historical commentary and a kind of historical enactment, where he ventriloquises, perhaps in slightly parodic form, the historical ideas whose emergence he is tracing. Stylistically, this 'indirect free style' may be traced back to its most influential exponent, Gustave Flaubert, himself a key inspiration on literary Naturalism.

This is a pity as the book rehearses some of Foucault's more radical political and historiographical moves in the 1970s, as I shall show. But more particularly, the book is invaluable as offering a crucial analysis of the context for the emergence of Naturalist theatre. Foucault's book is an account of the development of clinical medical practice at the turn of the nineteenth century. I will discuss this history in a moment, but it is important to mark the ubiquity of doctors, surgeons, and medical images in Naturalism, both in literature and the theatre.[8]

To the second edition of his first major novel, *Thérèse Raquin*, Émile Zola added a famous preface in which he sought to make his intentions clear against accusations of immorality: 'my objective was first and foremost a scientific one. [...] I simply carried out on two living bodies the same analytical examination that surgeons perform on corpses'.[9] To those who claimed he had an unhealthy interest in moral and human decay, he retorted that he had become 'engrossed in human rottenness, only in the same way as a doctor lecturing to students about disease'.[10] These medical images persist right through his accounts of his own work; over twenty-five years later, he would say of *Doctor Pascal* (1893), the last volume of his epic Rougon-Macquart novel sequence, '[i]t is a scientific work, the logical deduction and conclusion of all my preceding novels', adding that his aim has always been '*to show all so that all may be cured*'.[11] The protagonist of that novel, Dr Pascal, is clearly modelled on Zola himself, from his obsessive tracing of the Rougon and Macquart families' genetic inheritance to his passionate relationship in middle age with a much younger woman. Doctors play pivotal – and generally positive – roles in *A Love Story* (1878), *Nana* (1880), *Pot Luck* (1882), *The Bright Side of Life* (1884), *The Earth* (1887), and *The Debacle* (1892).[12] When Zola publishes his collection of essays arguing for Naturalism, his title *The Experimental Novel* (1880) refers not to artistic but to medical experiments.

Doctors regularly appeared on the Naturalist stage. This is unsurprising, given, as Stanton Garner has helpfully noted, the medical experience of many of the major Naturalist playwrights: Ibsen spent six years as a pharmacist's assistant and Strindberg studied medicine for a couple of years but failed the chemistry component.[13] Chekhov was, of course, a successful doctor whose medical work was of some local and historical importance.[14] Naturalism's stage doctors are less uncomplicatedly benevolent than in the novels. Dr Rank in *A Doll's House* (Royal Danish Theatre, Copenhagen, 1879) is a physician unable to heal himself. Dr Stockmann in *An Enemy of the People* (Christiania Theater, 1883) begins the play as the scientific hero but after proving himself unable to heal his town, retreats into a sociopathic individualism. *The Wild Duck*'s Dr Relling (National Theatre, Bergen, 1885) seems sceptical of whether people should be cured at all. In Georg Hauptmann's *Before Sunrise* (Freie Bühne: Lessingtheater, 1889), Dr Schimmelpfennig seeks to alleviate the suffering he sees around him but perhaps contrasts unfavourably with the more high-minded Alfred Loth. Chekhov's short stories throng with doctors (enough for a substantial collection focusing entirely on them)[15] and so do his plays. Chekhov's doctors, however, are increasingly detached from the task of providing medical care. Dr Dorn prescribes Valerian drops that even he doesn't think do any good while Dr Chebutykin casually admits to accidentally killing a patient, responding not with guilt but self-pity.[16]

Questioned or not, the medical model runs through Naturalism and from there into the bloodstream of European Modernism. Although much Modernist work responded in hostile fashion to Naturalism's theatrical choices, it often secretly adopted the art-theatre model pioneered by Antoine, as well as taking on its spiky confrontation of the audience, and its determination to represent reality (however that reality was defined). Positively and negatively, Naturalism shaped the twentieth century and remains a touchstone of our own theatre.

The Birth of the Clinic does not merely offer a history of the medical practice that forms the background to all this Naturalist enthusiasm; rather, Foucault is attempting to offer what he calls the 'concrete a priori'[17] of a wholly new attitude to bodies, the living and individuality. By this phrase, Foucault seems to mean the materially instantiated conceptual shifts that made a new mode of thought possible and reshaped the imaginary of nineteenth century Europe. I want to insert Naturalism into that story and show that it, too, is caught up in the conceptual faultlines and contradictions of this imaginary, in a way that, I argue, will transform how we understand this originating theatrical moment, particularly its engagement with the secret and the human. Given Naturalism's shaping importance even in our own theatre, there has rarely been a more pressing candidate for a 'history of the present'.[18]

The medical gaze

Between the middle of the eighteenth century and the middle of the nineteenth, it is generally agreed that medical practice experienced a profound change. The standard story is that the medical profession finally threw off superstition and embraced objectivity about the body and disease. Foucault's picture is more complex than that, suggesting not that medicine somehow emerged from falsehood into truth, but that a series of profound shifts changed the very meaning of disease, the patient's body, the role of the doctor, and the relations between them.

The dominant mode of medical practice at the start of that period was nosology, a classificatory approach to disease. Still very much in thrall to the Ancients, doctors relied on pre-existing taxonomies of disease connected by complex interrelations and hierarchies; consultations were a matter of establishing those symptoms that allowed the doctor to place the patient's illness within the established classificatory system. By the end of that period, the doctor is required purely to observe the patient without the intervention of theory or language. The body becomes a transparent vessel through which disease can be observed and thus eliminated. To use Zola's language, the nineteenth-century clinic was a means to show all so that all may be cured.

The passage from nosology to the limpid purity of the medical gaze has several stages. The first is to remove disease from its location in the space of classification. In the nosological era, it is in classification that disease has its purest reality;[19] if it has any material location at all, illness is confined to the family home. This was disrupted by concerns about standards of private practice, which demands that 'medicine becomes a task for the nation […] integrated into the social space in its entirety'.[20] The classificatory system is retained, but now it is mapped onto a new system of institutions, the hospitals.[21] In the enforced spatialisation of the hospital, the disease is for the first time forced to yield itself up to the gaze, or, as Foucault puts it, 'in the hospital, disease finds its rightful place, under the house arrest of its own truth'.[22]

During the Revolutionary period, a contradiction opened up that demonstrated the hospital's weakness as a mechanism of the gaze. The Jacobin ascendancy insisted on the openness of the hospital, in which all were permitted to be treated and all permitted to treat, freed from the privileges given by esoteric and exclusive knowledge. The problem this raised was: what to do about quacks and charlatans? Who could guarantee the health of healthcare?[23] The hospital's organisation seemed merely to enshrine already-existing forms of knowledge, to reify the old nosology in architectural form.

The answer was the clinic. In the one-to-one clinical encounter between the doctor and the patient, the disease would 'formulate of itself an unchanging truth, offered, undisturbed, to the doctor's gaze'.[24] This spontaneous gaze was freed of the *a priori* classification of diseases, its apparent directness also bypassing both secrecy and writing: secrecy, the occult knowledge of a previous generation of doctors, and writing, with its intervals and ambiguities, together meant the 'dissociation of the immediate relationship which had neither obstacle nor limits between Gaze and Speech'.[25] The clinic was a place of direct perception in which disease delivered itself up to the gaze, prior to any system or theory.[26] As Jean-Nicholas Corvisart, lecturer in Medicine at the Collège de France, noted in 1806, '[t]heory is silent or most often vanishes by the patient's bedside, giving way to observation and experiment'.[27] Speech itself is stripped of all friction, becoming a perfectly neutral medium.

This was supposedly restoring what had been the original essence of medicine, the timeless transparency of knowledge from patient to doctor: 'the clinic was a universal relationship of mankind with itself'.[28] This transparency, this immediacy, this freedom from theory and writing were, of course, concepts designed to efface their own conceptuality, a discourse that concealed the 'discursive structure in which, in fact, it originated'.[29] Clinical experience was, in fact, 'an isomorph of ideology'.[30]

As the clinic develops, the nature of the medical object changes: in the eighteenth century, disease was inferred from the symptom that 'gradually gropes its way into the dimensions of the hidden';[31] under the medical gaze, in which everything is immediate, this temporal and spatial interval is eliminated by understanding the disease to *be* its symptoms, or, as Foucault says in semiological mode, 'henceforth the signifier (sign and symptom) would be entirely transparent for the signified, which would appear, without concealment or residue, in its most pristine reality'.[32] Even what had been the least localised, more generalised of illnesses, fevers, were eventually subjected to the new gaze, ontologically reduced, identified with, and dispersed into 'a certain complex movement of tissues in reaction to an irritating cause'.[33] Everything becomes visible in itself and everything becomes itself by being visible.

At first, the clinic excluded the study of corpses because of its interest in observing diseases at work in the living, but soon the needs of 'a more genuinely scientific empiricism'[34] requires that diseases be pursued beyond death and a campaign insists on lifting the taboos against post-mortem examinations. Thus the body becomes a full three-dimensional object of the gaze, its tissues subject to a new 'invisible visibility',[35] whereby, as Xavier Bichat, chief physician at the Hotel-Dieu Hospital in Paris, writes, all tissue is a 'transparent veil'[36] through which one could direct the gaze at and through the entire interiority of the human body.

The Birth of the Clinic prefigures Foucault's more celebrated work in the 1970s, particularly Discipline and Punish, the first volume of The History of Sexuality, and the power/knowledge writings. He does not do so particularly in terms of their contents; prisons are only mentioned in passing, sexuality only alluded to, and the political ramifications of his analysis are only vaguely indicated. Nonetheless, like Discipline and Punish, The Birth of the Clinic is a book precisely about the way in which the gaze is deployed as a weapon of institutional power that controls and constitutes its object. To observe is always, to some extent, to invent what you see.

It is in this sense that Foucault is beginning to develop a theory of the way in which power and knowledge are brought together; this is not the banal observation that 'knowledge is power' but rather that a potent means of exercising power is to control what counts as knowledge. In The Birth of the Clinic, Foucault makes at one point a key distinction between savoir and connaissances,[37] both words that mean 'knowledge' in French, but while the latter denotes a body of knowledge (as one might have connaissances of the workings of the human body), the former is 'epistemic knowledge': that is, the meta-discursive view of what knowledge is, how it may be found, how it may be expressed. The clinic operates as a locus of power in the sense that it deploys particular forms of both connaissances and savoir: it establishes a new understanding of the body and its diseases, but it also establishes the savoir that legitimises this body of connaissances and delegitimises others. The medical gaze was a system that reconstituted what it was to be a body, an individual, even a human.

Naturalism and the clinic

It may already be apparent what affinities medical practice, as Foucault describes it, has with Naturalism. Certain passages outlining the new medical discourse could equally well describe the Naturalist project. Listing the ideas that underlay the campaign for anatomy, Foucault could be Zola describing the Naturalist novel: 'progress in observation, a wish to develop and extend experiment, an increasing fidelity to what can be revealed by sense-perceptible data, abandonment of theories and systems in favour of a more genuinely scientific empiricism'.[38] The Naturalist project and the medical gaze similarly demanded it should be able to observe – in the words of François-Joseph

Double, the founder of the Académie Royale de Médecine, without 'false modesty' or 'excessive restraint'[39] – absolutely everything in the world. 'The questions to be asked are innumerable', says Foucault, 'the things to be seen infinite'.[40]

That there should be affinities is not surprising, given Foucault's observation that some of the most basic conceptual distinctions of the new medicine spread through the 'science of man'.[41] Indeed, he notes that the medical gaze is reproduced in various ways in art and literature – in Sade, Hölderlin, and Nietzsche, among others.[42] Naturalism is not mentioned, but connections abound. In the early development of the clinic, Foucault explains that health became a responsibility of the state, such that the state of the nation's health became a key indicator of the health of the state; it is hard not to read that without thinking of precisely the same literal and metaphorical connection being made by Ibsen in *An Enemy of the People*. At one point, Foucault summarises the change from the eighteenth to the nineteenth-century as a move from 'what is the matter with you?' to 'where does it hurt?'[43] The Naturalists similarly moved away from the metaphysics of tragedy to the socialisation and localisation of moral crisis. To the question, where does it hurt?, the Naturalist will answer, in the mines and laundries, in the Senate and the seminaries, in the brothels and boardrooms, and above all in the bourgeois home.

Medical ideas and imagery spread rapidly through French life in the last third of the nineteenth century. Naturalism was a phenomenon of the Third Republic, the system of government brought into being by the collapse of the Second Empire in the Franco-Prussian War of 1870. The humiliation of that defeat and a recognition that France was falling behind the scientific advances being made in Germany and Britain, spurred new investment in medical research. The growth of literacy and the spread of cheap printing assisted the growth of interest in science.[44] It is noteworthy that even Zola's fiercest critics themselves resorted to medical imagery in criticising him: 'Ferragus', the pseudonymous author of the first major attack on Naturalism, argued that the writer's territory was 'everything, right up to the epidermis' but 'remove the skin, and it is no longer observation, but surgery' yet even so resorts to criticising Zola in the language of medical diagnosis, detecting 'sickly spasms' in the work.[45] Max Nordau in the 1890s, devoted a whole chapter to Zola's work, concluding that 'Zola's novels do not prove that things are badly managed in this world, but merely that Zola's nervous system is out of order'.[46]

Naturalism was part of a wider movement that placed a new emphasis and value on observation through the nineteenth century. We see it in the mid-century fashion for the panorama, cyclorama, and diorama,[47] for the international expositions that promised to make the world visible in a single installation,[48] and of course in the development and spread of photography.[49] Jonathan Crary notes these were the symptoms and not the cause of this desire to observe, suggesting, in Foucauldian style, that the technology was 'dependent on a new arrangement of knowledge about the body and the constitutive relation of that knowledge to social power',[50] which was then embodied in the development of new visual prostheses like the camera obscura and stereoscope. When the surgeon and lecturer at the University of Lyon, Marc-Antoine Petit, wrote in 1797 that '[o]ne must, as far as possible, make science ocular'[51] he set a tone for the wider culture of the nineteenth century.

The double silence

The connections between clinical medicine and Naturalism are not merely shared metaphors, but precisely shared practices. Foucault describes the medical gaze as constituted by a 'double silence': the silence of theory and the silence of language.[52]

By the silence of theory, Foucault means that nothing can intervene between the gaze and its object. Patterns may be found but they may not be looked for, for fear of imposing a prior structure on the gaze and its objects. Naturalism's 'method' placed particular emphasis on observation: the Goncourt brothers 'descended into the abyss of charity hospitals, working-class funerals, cheap eating houses and dance halls, the studios of unsuccessful painters, the compositors' rooms of popular newspapers'[53] and Zola went down a mine, rode the footplate of a steam engine, visited the battlefields of Sedan, and observed the workings of the Bourse to write the Rougon-Macquart.

To ensure that a pattern is not imposed on observation, clinical practice 'plunges into the marvelous density of perception, offering the grain of things as the first face of truth,'[54] creating an exhaustive verbal account of the observed phenomena, a 'completely scanned multiplicity of individual facts'.[55] This is precisely Naturalism's approach. Zola's Rougon-Macquart's twenty-volume novel sequence intends to be a *complete* account of a family and a nation in both the immense architectonics of the whole and the meticulous granularity of each description, the density and intensity of the way a department store or a coal mine are evoked. Several of Zola's novels themselves contain taxonomic structures: *Pot Luck*'s tenement block is a kind of visual structure where Zola can display all classes and social types to the reader's imaginative gaze; *The Belly of Paris* presents the stalls and storerooms of Les Halles, with the protagonist as market inspector, Zola's Virgil, taking us systematically through the meat, fish, vegetable, and cheese stands.

Foucault notes that patterns can be derived from observation through a series of processes: complexity of combination, the principle of analogy, perception of frequencies, and the calculation of certainty.[56] These vast novels and novel sequences, with their vast casts of characters and innumerable locations, offered multiple opportunities for the novelist and the reader to find patterns by accumulating detail, which seems, through its teeming abundance, to generate its own shapes and systems. It is unsurprising to find the structure of Zola's novel sequence echoed almost immediately in projects that move even further towards the sociological like Ali Coffignon's *Paris Vivant* series in the 1880s or Armand Dubarry's *Les Déséquilibres de l'Amour* in the 1890s.

The theatre fits less comfortably into this structure. The necessarily restricted casts and settings of nineteenth-century theatre precluded some of that descriptive abundance. But what the theatre could do, perhaps more easily than the novel, was to supply kinds of descriptive density in the form of putting real objects on stage. When Antoine staged Fernand Icres's *The Butchers* at the Théâtre Libre in October 1888, perhaps inspired by the script's reference to 'hooks showing here and there scraps of torn-off meat',[57] he hung an entire side of beef on the stage. The density of colour, texture, shape, and no doubt smell would have been more intense than any verbal description could be (reality always exceeding its linguistic representation). Similarly, there is in this kind of representational surplus what Barthes calls a 'reality effect', a signifying excess that overflows the functional control of narrative and operates as a 'resistance to meaning' which Barthes explains in terms of a 'mythic opposition of the *true-to-life* (the lifelike) and the intelligible'.[58] In other words, the theatre's capacity for semiotic intensity can create an experience of the real as an asystemic, atheoretical immediacy, the first part of the medical gaze's double silence.

The second silence is the silence of language and here the theatre is a more fertile ground. The real anxiety about language concerned writing, which introduces a spatial and temporal interval into the gaze. Speech is to be preferred as the immediate form in which the discoveries of the gaze can be communicated. This speech neutrally reproduces what is seen, in 'a language that is the very speech of things [...] a language without words'.[59] This language is frictionless, silent, without remainder. The nineteenth-century novel was – Dickensian public readings aside – almost inevitably an experience of writing, but the theatre was a matter of speech. Further, it is striking that Naturalist theatre makers were prolific writers of manifestos, commentators on their work and the work of others, but one thing they hardly ever did was offer advice on how to write a play. It is clear, I think, that to do such a thing would be to impose a prior structure on what is meant to be a reflection of pure exteriority. Many critics have noted that Naturalism in fact tended to reproduce certain conventional structures, devices, and motifs,[60] but in principle Naturalism was a literary and theatrical movement expressly without formal rules.[61]

This phonocentricity (to use an unFoucauldian word) does not prevent speech from being affected by the same problematics as writing, so it is also important that it adopts a 'clear, ordered language'.[62] We can see this in the demotic, everyday language of Naturalist novels and plays, quite different from the clotted intricacies of the Symbolists in the 1890s. This is how Zola could be a genuinely popular novelist, his language offering an experience of immediacy without reserve. The new conception of disease also offers a new conception of language; as explained above, nineteenth-century medicine treated symptoms as part of the disease, not clues to its hidden existence. The patient's body is a text, but it is entirely without subtext. No play can be without subtext, but Naturalist theatre pushes towards this in various ways, by placing onstage everything that would previously have been hidden, inferred, alluded to, or offstage.[63] In addition, Naturalists are keen to stamp out metaphor whenever they see one spring up; in *An Enemy of the People*, no sooner than the audience has noted that the poisoned water network feeding the town might be a metaphor for its political corruption than Dr Stockmann voices this thought himself: 'You see, it isn't just a question of the water system and the sewer. This whole community's got to be cleansed and decontaminated'.[64] Ibsen decontaminates metaphor by drawing its effects back into the world of representation, rather than letting it trouble the edges of the text, opening it to an interminable play of significations.

Another kind of troubling linguistic excess is generalisation. Philippe Pinel, Chief physician at Salpêtrière, argued for 'a strict exactitude of description, precise and uniform in its terminology, a wise reserve in rising to general views without lending reality to abstract terms.'[65] The requirement to observe without remainder means not seeing the patient as an 'example' or the disease as the basis of a generalisation. We see this in Naturalism's insistence on specificity. As Roland Barthes notes, Zola's realist predecessor Balzac is given to statements 'made in a collective and anonymous voice originating in traditional human experience,'[66] which propose a generality of experience to which we are invited to assent.[67] It is striking how rarely Zola indulges in that 'cultural code', preferring to describe and observe without generalising. While audiences have often generalised Naturalist plays – such that Nora 'stands in for' all bourgeois wives, for example – these are generally plays that represent particular individuals and do not pitch character at an archetypal level, as does, say, Racinian tragedy.

Naturalism and the secret

'To destroy one rhetoric', wrote Emile Zola in *Naturalism in the Theatre*, 'it was not necessary to invent another.'[68] He was describing Romanticism's replacement of Classicism with its own endless variations on its new clichés, but the implausible implication is that Naturalist writing would be entirely free of rhetorical structure. Even stranger is Zola's insistence that he makes nothing up when he writes his works of fiction: 'I don't invent; the novel matures, emerging all by itself from the [research] materials.'[69] In these affirmations, Zola is aligned with the discursive presentation of nineteenth-century medicine which forbade all 'obstacles to reason by theories and to the senses by the imagination.'[70] It would be easy to indulge in what E. P. Thompson famously called 'the enormous condescension of posterity' and scorn the Naturalists for naivety. But that would fail to learn Foucault's lesson, that we must not blunder ahistorically through the past approving or condemning ideas and actions, but instead understand the conditions that made those comments possible.

A common criticism of Zolian Naturalism, made at the time, is that the novel or a play is not scientific, because the novelist or playwright has invented the objects he or she is claiming to study.[71] Foucault weakens this critique by noting that the medical gaze does the same thing. The object of the gaze is constituted by the gaze itself, which it transforms conceptually and as an object of experience. The diseased body in 1750 was a quite different thing in 1850.

Foucault twice describes the emergence of the medical gaze as a process of detheatricalisation. In eighteenth-century clinical training, when students were asked to diagnose, they were simply being trained to repeat already-existing knowledge; this training 'grouped all experience around the play of a verbal unmasking that was simply its form of transmission, *theatrically retarded*.'[72] The suggestion is that, like a cheap theatrical or dramaturgical trick, the information is artificially hidden before being revealed with a flourish. Elsewhere he describes the eighteenth-century view of disease (as something hidden inside the body and only visible as symptoms) as both 'natural and dramatic.'[73] By placing everything before the gaze, the medical gaze eliminates this theatrical playfulness.[74] But in doing so, ironically, the medical gaze has to theatrically reconstitute medicine's recent past; the medical gaze retrospectively inserts disease deep in the dark recesses of the body, where nosological practice had supposedly hidden it, only now to release it to the gaze; 'knowledge', writes Foucault, 'invents the Secret'.[75] In other words, the medical gaze constitutes its new knowledge and then insists that it was hidden before revealing it (precisely the eighteenth-century structure of theatrically delayed revelation).

Naturalism partakes of this medical anti-theatricality in its apparent wish to eliminate all artifice, all *form*, in favour of an unmediated presentation of social content. To do so, it must invent its new objects and assert their secrecy. In fact, many of the topics that Naturalism dealt with – divorce, adultery, corruption, violence, lust – were common subjects on the European stage. Farce deals with many of them, but where farce places us within the pleasures of the secret and promises to conceal even as it threatens to reveal, Naturalism constitutes the secret in order to abolish it. It favours an aggressive exposure of hidden things. When Foucault describes the gaze as employing 'the majestic violence of light',[76] one is reminded of the way that Naturalism reinvents the relations of theatrical experience, placing the secret under stage lights, but simultaneously placing the audience in darkness.[77]

Naturalism and the human

Foucault's project in *The Birth of the Clinic* is not entirely historical. He wrote about the birth of the modern individual in the early 1960s because he believed he was witnessing the death of the modern individual. The clinic was an idea, he wrote, from which we are 'just beginning to detach ourselves'.[78] In this sense, this book is pointing towards the high watermark of Foucault's anti-humanism, the famous conclusion to *The Order of Things*: that if the discursive arrangements that made the modern individual possible were to disappear, 'then one can certainly wager that man would be erased, like a face drawn in sand at the edge of the sea'.[79] Roger Paden has argued that Foucault doesn't seem to mean all actual human beings but rather the epistemological arrangements that underpin a particular understanding of who we are,[80] but there is some ambiguity here. For one thing, the radical discursivity of Foucault's thinking in the late 1960s makes it difficult to distinguish between 'actual human beings' and their appearance in discourse. Further, when we trace this anti-humanism back to *The Birth of the Clinic*, we find an association between the end of man and actual corporeal human death. Death haunts Foucault's work, even as he seems to move away from the full discursive relativism of *The Order of the Things* by embracing politics and a developing a fuller theory of power in the early 1970s,[81] but it has always been there. Death stalks the corridors of the clinic and the wings of the Naturalist stage.

To understand *The Birth of the Clinic* – and, I suggest, Naturalism – it is important to recognise that the disappearance or transcendence of the individual and the human is already there in the individual's birth. The emergence of the clinic was a moment, in which the individual became an 'object of positive knowledge'. That marked 'the possibility for the individual of being both subject and object of his own knowledge'.[82] Naturalism has often been criticised, particularly from the left, for its bourgeois individualism; for Brecht, while it marked 'the breakthrough of realism into modern literature', in Naturalism 'the inessentials of historical development overgrow everything'.[83] What Brecht means by this may be elucidated by looking at Lukács's critique of Zola; he argues that Zola's scientific conception of realism leads him to 'identify mechanically the human body and human society'.[84] The problem for Lukács is that a human body is a more or less harmonious system working together, while capitalist society is a site of contradiction, division, and class struggle. Two things are worth underlining here: first, Lukács is suggesting that Zola has based his theory on precisely that vision of the individual human body that was produced in European culture by the clinic; second, Lukács evidently shares this conception of the body, even if he criticises its metaphorical extension to social life. As with the medical imagery in the critics of Naturalism, it's a sign of the pervasiveness of the clinical model that it is shared equally by Zola and his critics.

But are these critics correct in identifying Naturalism with bourgeois individualism? *The Birth of the Clinic* can perhaps help us answer this question. The stages in the development of the medicalised individual take us from the classificatory stage where the doctor's attention was focused on 'the essential truth *beneath* the sensible individuality',[85] to the doctor grasping 'that visible whole, that positive plenitude that faces him – the patient'[86] and finally to the 'three-dimensional space'[87] of the patient's body.

In a Zolian spirit, one might map this onto the successive French theatrical phases of Classicism, Romanticism, and Naturalism, particularly its presentation of character; in Classicism, the detail of individual characters is superficial compared to the fundamental qualities of heroism and *hamartia* that drive the character's path through the tragedy. Romanticism sees the emergence of a splendid individualism, but still pitched at a somewhat metaphysical level. In Naturalism, the individual character is no longer a mere bearer of attributes but a complex combination of qualities and aspects, none of which is *a priori* more important than any other. In his preface to *Miss Julie* (Students Union, University of Copenhagen, 1889), Strindberg relishes the constellation of qualities that make up Julie's character: 'my motivation of the action is not simple [...] there is no singular point of view'.[88] Simple motivations he associates with mainstream bourgeois theatre and the stock character. 'So I don't believe in simple theatrical characters, or the summary judgments authors make of their characters – this one's stupid, that one's a brute, this one's jealous, that one's miserly – which should be challenged by the Naturalists, who know the rich complexity of the human soul'.[89] Instead, he mentions at least a dozen motivations for Julie's actions[90] and declares that his characters are 'assemblages of past and present culture, snatches of books and newspapers, scraps of once-fine clothing now in rags, just as a human soul is patched together'.[91] Character is not meant to be looked *through* in Naturalism. It's not a structured hierarchy of factors, but a composite of forces all acting equally to produce action. Everything is equally available to the gaze which 'establishes the individual in his irreducible quality'.[92]

Naturalist characters are therefore not 'typical', in the sense of referring outward to some larger category. Certainly, Zola's or Ibsen's characters might be verifiable in certain sociological aspects (*there are people just like this*) but they are not themselves mouthpieces for a particular ideology or allegories of a class. If collectively the characters amount to a larger picture of society, they do that through their accumulation across numerous scenes and novels. Naturalism, like medicine, 'was faced with the task of observing, and to infinity, the events of an open domain'.[93]

This infinitude would push the medical gaze beyond the human. In the metaphysical reduction on which Naturalism prided itself, humans were difficult to grasp as humans: 'I set out to study, not characters, but temperaments', wrote Zola of his aims in writing *Thérèse Raquin*. 'Therese and Laurent are human animals nothing more. In these animals I set out to trace, step by step, the hidden workings of the passions, the urges of instinct, and the derangements of the brain which follow on from a nervous crisis'.[94] Zola's language equivocates: first, briefly, they are 'characters', then 'human animals', and then, silently, the human drops away and they become 'animals'. The title 'Naturalism' has its philosophical origin in the idea that humans should be considered entirely part of the natural world, and anything that might hitherto have distinguished humans from animals (soul, spirit, free will) is excluded. 'There is', says Zola, 'a total absence of soul'.[95] But this attempt to grasp the human, freed of metaphysical abstraction or religious superstition, also risks erasing the boundary between human and animals, perhaps also between human and machine, individual actions being explained beyond the individual in the mechanical determinism of impersonal forces.

Perhaps even more disturbing is the erasure of the distinction between life and death. Foucault calls the emergence of pathological anatomy, in which the autopsy had particular importance, 'the technique of the corpse'.[96] The ability to open up dead bodies completed the omniscience of the gaze and allowed the whole human to be viewed. But in doing so, medicine acknowledges the continuity of life and death (cutting open a body is only valuable if the dead and the living are continuous). The principle of localisation, that all physical phenomena must have a visible location in the body, created a problem for the distinction between life and death; in the moments before and after death the organic structure of the body is identical, so where is 'being alive' to be located? This required death to be understood not as a clear moment but a process. Bichat 'volatized [death], distributed it throughout life in the form of separate, partial, progressive deaths, deaths that are so slow in occurring that they extend even beyond death itself'.[97] Thus life can only be understood by embracing death, accepting the continuity between the two and so: 'At this epistemological level, life is bound up with death, as to that which positively threatens to destroy its living force'.[98]

In a passage I have already cited, Zola seems to glimpse something of this intertwining of the living and the dead, writing, 'I simply carried out on two living bodies the same analytical examination that surgeons perform on corpses',[99] a description that oscillates undecidably between the two. Zola's contemporary critics register this disturbance between the boundaries of life of death. 'Ferragus', for example, repeatedly uses cadaverous metaphors to describe the effect of the novels; the words 'pourriture' and 'putride', meaning 'rottenness' in the sense of decomposition, are scattered through the text, culminating in the horrifying claim that reading the book 'is like you are stretched out beneath the tap of one of the slabs in the morgue and, right up to the final page, you feel dribbling onto you, drip by drip, the water running off the corpses'.[100]

Despite its repudiation of classical tragedy, a great many Naturalist plays end in a death.[101] In doing so, some of these plays are showing the consequence not of *hubris* or a metaphysical destiny, but of a biological force or a social contradiction. The death of Oswald in (or just after) *Ghosts* (Aurora Turner Hall, Chicago, 1882), Hedvig in *The Wild Duck*, Thérèse and Laurent in *Thérèse Raquin* (Théâtre de la Renaissance, 1873), Helen in *Before Sunrise*, Konstantin in *The Seagull* (Aleksandrinsky Theatre, St Petersburg, 1896), Louise in *The Enchantment* (Swedish Theatre, Stockholm, 1910), the eponymous protagonists of *Miss Julie* and *The Father* (Casino Theatre, Copenhagen) can all plausibly be discussed in these terms. The deaths mark the finitude of the plays and their 'scientific' analysis, retrospectively justifying the action we have seen, while the action then explains the conclusion; the life illuminates the death and the death illuminates the life. But as we have seen, grasping the individual in Naturalist non-metaphysical terms opens up new apertures in the individual, to the animal, the machine, and to death. 'Nineteenth-century medicine was haunted by that absolute eye that cadaverizes life and rediscovers in the corpse the frail, broken nervure of life'.[102] There is something in Naturalism, too, that cadaverises life.

In February 1865, Zola reviewed the newly published Naturalist novel *Germinie Lacerteux* by the Goncourt Brothers. He begins by describing his reviewing technique, with a familiar metaphor: 'Scalpel in hand, I perform an autopsy on this newborn, and I am delighted to discover in him a previous-unknown creature, a distinct organism'.[103] Observe the moves in this curious passage: he is observing an allegory of the newly created nineteenth-century whole human ('a distinct organism'); but then on this newborn, mysteriously, Zola plans to conduct an autopsy. In doing so, we have the perfect image of the medico-Naturalist discourse of the later nineteenth century; the birth of the individual must be requited by the death of the individual.

Foucault's interest in the clinic is to trace not just the beginning of the modern individual but also its end. Naturalism, like the clinic, emerges from the moment of bourgeois ascendancy but it is marked and haunted, like Thérèse and Laurent, by the death that its success makes necessary. While the specific conditions in which Foucault was led to imagine the erasure of humanity may themselves have faded away, there is something wholly contemporary in Foucault's seeming attempt to imagine the world outside the imaginary of the anthropocene. Perhaps too this is the world that Naturalism conjures, its bourgeois men and women preparing for their own dissolution into a world of animals, machines, and the dead. Seeing Naturalist theatre through Foucault's gaze shows us that it is truly the modern theatrical origin of not just the human, but also the post-human.

Notes

1 James Miller, *The Passion of Michel Foucault* (London: Harper Collins, 1993), pp. 64–5.
2 Arianna Sforzini, *Les Scènes de la Verité: Michel Foucault et le Théâtre* (Lormont: Le Bord de l'Eau, 2017).
3 Ibid., p. 21.

4 Michel Foucault, *The Birth of the Clinic: An Archaeology of Medical Perception* (London: Tavistock, 1976 [1963]).

5 See Hubert L. Dreyfus and Paul Rabinow, *Michel Foucault: Beyond Structuralism and Hermeneutics* (Hemel Hempstead: Harvester Wheatsheaf, 1982), pp. 64, 67, 113.

6 For example, in 1963s preface Foucault writes:

> By definition, to speak of the thought of others, to try to say what they have said, has been to analyse the signified. But must the signified only ever be treated as content, as a sequence of themes present more or less implicitly to each other? Is it not possible to undertake a structural analysis of the signified that would escape the fatality of commentary by leaving the signifier and signified in their original balance?

Michel Foucault, *Naissance de la Clinique: Une Archéologie du Regard Médical* (Paris: Presses Universitaires de France, 1963), p. xiii, my translation. But in 1972, Foucault has distanced himself from the structural language, holding it at arm's length:

> Traditionally, to speak of the thought of others, to try to say what they have said, has been to analyse the signified. But must the things said, at other times by other people, be treated exclusively according to the play of the signifier and signified? Is it not possible to undertake an analysis of discourses that would escape the fatality of commentary by supposing no remainder, no excess in what was said, only the fact of its historical appearance?

Michel Foucault, *Naissance de la Clinique* (Paris: Presses Universitaires de France, 1972), p. 15, my translation. The structural analysis that seemed axiomatic ('by definition') in 1963 is by 1972 merely a tradition. While he is arguing in the early 1960s for an analysis that pays attention to the form of the utterance as well as its meaning, by the early 1970s the gesture is to reject the semiological method altogether. Confusingly, though, he still retains the language of signifier and signified elsewhere (particularly in Chapter 6, 'Signs and Cases' where the language is embedded throughout).

7 For example, Alan Sheridan translates the second sentence of the passage in Note 6 as: 'But must the things said, elsewhere and by others, be treated exclusively in accordance with the play of signifier and signified, as a series of themes present more or less implicitly to one another?'; the first half of the sentence is from 1972, the second from 1963. Foucault, *The Birth of the Clinic*, p. xvii.

8 Naturalism in the theatre would eventually become a pan-European and then global phenomenon, but its origins are in Paris of the 1870s and 1880s. It emerged out of and in dialogue with literature, particularly the novel. To discuss Naturalism's emergence, then, it is artificial to ignore the continuities with literature and I will make frequent reference to the literary context.

9 Émile Zola, *Thérèse Raquin*, ed. Andrew Rothwell (Oxford: Oxford University Press, 1992), p. 2.

10 Ibid., p. 3.

11 Émile Zola, *Doctor Pascal: Or, Life and Heredity*, trans. Ernest A. Vizetelly (London: Chatto & Windus, 1894), p. xi, original emphasis.

12 For consistency, I am using the titles of the Oxford World's Classics editions, since they are the most recent translations of these novels.

13 Stanton B. Garner, Jr., 'Introduction: Is There a Doctor in the House? Medicine and the Making of Modern Drama', *Modern Drama* 51.3 (2008), 311–28 (pp. 313–14).

14 See Kenneth Dewhurst, 'Anton Chekhov (1860–1904) – Pioneer in Social Medicine', *Journal of the History of Medicine and Allied Sciences* 10.1 (1955), 1–16. and Doris Vidaver and Maynard M. Cohen, 'Vocation: Dr. A. P. Chekhov', *The American Scholar* 55.2 (1986), 227–33.

15 Anton Chekhov, *Chekhov's Doctors: A Collection of Chekhov's Medical Tales* (Kent, OH: Kent State University Press, 2003).

16 Anton Chekhov, *Five Plays*, trans. Ronald Hingley (Oxford: Oxford University Press, 1980), pp. 84, 211.

17 Foucault, *The Birth of the Clinic*, p. xv. Despite problems with the translation, for ease of reference, I shall mostly quote from the existing English edition, noting problems as they appear.

18 Michel Foucault, *Discipline and Punish: The Birth of the Prison* (Harmondsworth: Allen Lane, 1977), p. 31.

19 Foucault, *The Birth of the Clinic*, p. 9.

20 Ibid., pp. 19–20.

21 Ibid., p. 42.

22 Ibid., p. 42, translation amended. The translator of this English edition Alan Sheridan renders this as '[i]n the hospital, disease meets, as it were, the forced residence of its truth', which is a clumsy approximation of Foucault's admittedly mixed metaphor 'La maladie rencontre là son haut lieu, et comme la résidence forcée de sa vérité'. Foucault, *Naissance de la Clinique*, 1972, p. 69.

23 Foucault, *The Birth of the Clinic*, pp. 50–1.

24 Ibid., p. 51.

25 Ibid., p. 55.

26 Ibid., p. 56.

27 J[ean]-N[icolas] Corvisart, [Léopold] Avenbrugger, and [Pierre] Bayle, *Essai sur les maladies et les lésions organiques du coeur et des gros vaisseux; nouvelle méthode pour reconnaître les maladies internes de la poitrine par la percussion de cette cavité; recherches sur la phthisie pulmonaire* (Paris: Delahays, 1855), p. 181, my translation.

28 Foucault, *The Birth of the Clinic*, p. 55. These passages are good examples of Foucault's Flaubertian 'indirect free style'.

29 Ibid., p. 52.

30 Ibid., p. 96.

31 Ibid., p. 90.

32 Ibid., p. 91.

33 Ibid., p. 189.

34 Ibid., p. 136.

35 Ibid., p. 165, original emphasis.

36 Quoted in ibid., p. 166.

37 Ibid., p. 137.

38 Ibid., p. 136.

39 Quoted in ibid., p. 118.

40 Ibid., p. 111.

41 Ibid., p. 36.

42 Ibid., pp. 58–60.

43 Ibid., p. xviii.

44 See Robert Fox, *The Savant and the State: Science and Cultural Politics in Nineteenth-Century France* (Baltimore, MD: Johns Hopkins University Press, 2012), chapters five and six.

45 Ferragus, 'Lettres De Ferragus III: La Littérature Putride', *Le Figaro*, 23 January 1868, p. 1, my translation.

46 Max Nordau, *Degeneration* (Lincoln: University of Nebraska Press, 1993), p. 499.

47 Ralph Hyde, *Panoramania! The Art and Entertainment of the 'All-Embracing' View* (London: Trefoil & Barbican Art Gallery, 1988).

48 Alexander C. T. Geppert, *Fleeting Cities: Imperial Expositions in Fin-De-Siècle Europe* (Basingstoke: Palgrave Macmillan, 2010).

49 Shelley Rice, *Parisian Views* (Cambridge, MA: MIT Press, 1997).

50 Jonathan Crary, *Techniques of the Observer: On Vision and Modernity in the Nineteenth Century* (Cambridge, MA: MIT Press, 1990), p. 17.

51 Quoted in Foucault, *The Birth of the Clinic*, p. 88.

52 Ibid., p. 108.

53 Anita Brookner, 'Introduction', in *Sister Philomène* (London: Chatto & Windus, 1989), pp. 1–5 (p. 3).

54 Foucault, *The Birth of the Clinic*, p. xiii.

55 Ibid., p. 101, original emphasis.

56 Ibid., pp. 99–104.

57 Fernand Icres, *Les Bouchers: Drama en un acte en vers* (Paris: Tresse, 1888), p. 1, my translation.

58 Roland Barthes, 'The Reality Effect', in *The Rustle of Language* (Oxford: Blackwell, 1986), pp. 141–8 (p. 146), original emphasis.

59 Foucault, *The Birth of the Clinic*, pp. 95, 68.

60 See, particularly, David Baguley, *Naturalist Fiction: The Entropic Vision* (Cambridge: Cambridge University Press, 1990).

61 Possibly the most famous exception to this is 'Chekhov's gun', the advice that '[i]f in Act 1 you have a pistol hanging on the wall, then it must fire in the last act'. Quoted in Donald Rayfield, *Anton Chekhov: A Life* (London: Harper Collins, 1997), p. 203. This is a curious piece of advice since it represents precisely the kind of playwright that Chekhov is not; his work is so often about subverting such mechanical plotting.

62 Foucault, *The Birth of the Clinic*, p. 95.

63 Pre-production censorship was still in operation in the French theatre (and would be until 1906), so there were still restrictions on what could be shown. The Théâtre Libre was a private club theatre so technically did not have to submit plays to the censor, though Antoine felt it would be unwise to test this freedom too radically. Foucault, in fact, notes that the medical gaze was compatible with modesty and discretion, doctors allowing patients to disrobe behind screens and so on. Indeed, the stethoscope, he says, was invented to permit continued investigation while preserving modesty. 'The stethoscope – distance solidified – transmits profound and invisible events along a semi-tactile, semi-auditory axis'. Foucault, *The Birth of the Clinic*, p. 164, translation modified. Perhaps we might think of the theatre as a similar kind of prosthesis.

64 Henrik Ibsen, *An Enemy of the People*, in *Plays: One* (London: Methuen, 1980), p. 165.

65 Philippe Pinel, *Nosographie philosophique ou la méthode de l'analyse appliquée à la médicine*, 4th edn (Paris: Brosson, 1810), pp. iii–iv.

66 Roland Barthes, *S/Z*, trans. Richard Miller (Oxford: Blackwell, 1990), p. 16.

67 Barthes is commenting on the first sentence of Balzac's short story 'Sarrasine': 'I was deep in one of those daydreams which overtake even the shallowest of men, in the midst of the most tumultuous parties'. Ibid., p. 221.

68 Émile Zola, *Le Naturalisme au Théâtre* (Brussels: Complexe, 2003), p. 33, my translation.

69 Émile Zola, 'Enquête Sur Le Langage Intérieur', *Archives d'anthropologie criminelle* 9 (1894), 102–5 (p. 104), my translation.

70 Foucault, *The Birth of the Clinic*, p. 107.

71 See, for example, Ferdinand Brunetière, 'Le Roman Experimental', *Revue des Deux Mondes* 37 (15 February 1880), 935–48; Henri Houssaye, 'Le Roman Contemporain', *Journal des débats politiques et littéraires*, 26 April 1884, p. 3.

72 Foucault, *The Birth of the Clinic*, p. 62, my emphasis, translation amended. Sheridan wrongly translates 'qui n'en est que la simple forme de transmission' (Foucault, *Naissance de la Clinique*, 1972, pp. 94–5) as 'that was not simply its form of transmission', thus reversing its sense.

73 Foucault, *The Birth of the Clinic*, p. 91.

74 This is perhaps where Foucault reveals his reading of Antoine in an identification of theatre with artifice. Antoine, like Zola, would beat away at this drum so often that it becomes possible to imagine that he believes himself not to be making theatre at all. This anti-theatricality in *The Birth of the Clinic* would give way, later, to a more positive use of the theatrical metaphor. In a late series of lectures, he refers to the 'dramatic' as 'the analysis of these facts of discourse, which show how the very event of the enunciation may affect the enunciator's being'. Michel Foucault, *The Government of Self and Others: Lectures at the Collège De France 1982–1983*, ed. Frédéric Gros, gen. eds. François Ewald and Alessandro Fontana, English series ed. Arnold I. Davidson, trans. Graham Burchell (Basingstoke: Palgrave Macmillan, 2008), p. 68. In this he is very close to offering an Austinian theory of performativity (although he insists that it is different, he seems actually to have misunderstood how performative utterances are thought to work). Now the 'dramatic' is used to suggest the way a whole person may be involved in certain kinds of ethico-political speech (confession, truth-telling, *parrhesia*, etc.). Similarly, when he discusses how Cynic practices found their way into traditions of mendicant Christian asceticism, he find in those actions 'The choice of life as scandal of the truth, the bareness of life as a way of constituting the body itself as the visible theater of the truth', the theatre now associated not with deceitful trickery in revealing the truth, but with the transformative power of truth telling, an extreme kind of display of unadorned truthfulness. Michel Foucault, *The Courage of the Truth (the Government of Self and Others II): Lectures at the Collège De France 1983–1984*, ed. Frédéric Gros, gen. eds. François Ewald and Alessandro Fontana, English series ed. Arnold I. Davidson, trans. Graham Burchell (Basingstoke: Palgrave Macmillan, 2011), p. 183.

75 Foucault, *The Birth of the Clinic*, p. 163. This structure unmistakeably prefigures what he will call 'The Repressive Hypothesis' in Michel Foucault, *The Will to Knowledge*, trans. Robert Hurley, Vol. 1, *The History of Sexuality* (London: Penguin, 1998), pp. 15–49.

76 Foucault, *The Birth of the Clinic*, p. 22.

77 Antoine first dimmed lights in the auditorium for the final scene of *The Death of the Duke of Enghien* by Léon Hennique in December 1888, something already practised at Bayreuth and the Meiningen. Jean Chothia, *André Antoine* (Cambridge: Cambridge University Press, 1991), p. 64.

78 Foucault, *The Birth of the Clinic*, p. 3.

79 Michel Foucault, *The Order of Things: An Archaeology of the Human Sciences* (London: Tavistock, 1970), p. 387.

80 Roger Paden, 'Foucault's Anti-Humanism', *Human Studies* 10.1 (1987), 123–41 (p. 123).

81 Stuart Elden, *Foucault: The Birth of Power* (Cambridge: Polity, 2017).

82 Foucault, *The Birth of the Clinic*, p. 197.

83 Quoted in Geoffrey A Baker, *The Aesthetics of Clarity and Confusion: Literature and Engagement since Nietzsche and the Naturalists* (Basingstoke: Palgrave Macmillan, 2016), p. 133.

84 Georg Lukács, *Studies in European Realism: A Sociological Survey of the Writings of Balzac, Stendhal, Zola, Tolstoy, Gorki and Others* (London: Merlin, 1972), p. 86.

85 Foucault, *The Birth of the Clinic*, p. 98, my emphasis.

86 Ibid., p. 8.

87 Ibid., p. xviii.

88 August Strindberg, *Fadren/Fröken Julie/Fordringsägare*, Samlade Verk, 27 (Stockholm: Almqvist & Wiksell, 1984), p. 103, my translation.

89 Ibid., p. 104.

90 Ibid., p. 103.

91 Ibid., p. 105.

92 Foucault, *The Birth of the Clinic*, p. xiv.

93 Ibid., p. 98, translation amended.

94 Zola, *Thérèse Raquin*, pp. 1–2.

95 Ibid., p. 2. I have explored the plausibility of this idea in some detail in my essay Dan Rebellato, 'Is the Theatre a Zombie? On the Successful Failures of Émile Zola' *Anglia*, 136.1 (2018), 100–20.

96 Foucault, *The Birth of the Clinic*, p. 141.

97 Ibid., p. 144.

98 Ibid., p. 155, translation amended.

99 Zola, *Thérèse Raquin*, p. 2.

100 Ferragus, 'Lettres De Ferragus III', p. 1, my translation.

101 For example (and acknowledging that there might be debates about how far some of these are strictly Naturalistic) Zola's *Thérèse Raquin*, Ibsen's *Ghosts*, *The Wild Duck*, *Rosmersholm*, Strindberg's *The Father*, *Miss Julie*, *Creditors*, Hauptmann's *Before Sunrise*, *The Weavers*, Chekhov's *The Seagull*, *Three Sisters*, *The Cherry Orchard*, Benedictsson's *The Enchantment*, Gorky's *The Lower Depths*, Robins and Bell's *Alan's Wife*.

102 Foucault, *The Birth of the Clinic*, p. 166.

103 Émile Zola, *Zola Journaliste: Articles et Chroniques* (Paris: Flammarion, 2011), pp. 69–70, my translation.

12

Theatre of poverty: popular illegalism on the nineteenth-century stage

Tony Fisher

Images of poverty saturate the cultural landscape of the nineteenth century. As the forces of industrialisation progressed, so those images proliferated – just as did the poor. No doubt representations of the poor enabled the middle classes to discover their 'social conscience'; no doubt, also, they incriminated them. Thus did bourgeois society learn to distinguish itself from its victims, as though, in encountering the poor, it encountered itself 'through a glass darkly'. Not only were the poor of uppermost concern for government legislators and social reformers throughout the period, but poverty permeated its literary and artistic imagination. Workhouses, prisons, 'northern powerhouses', and slums, as well as the itinerancy of urban street life – all were vividly described by writers such as Charles Dickens and Henry Mayhew, depicted with sentimental pathos in paintings by artists such as Luke Fildes and William Frith, and were documented in stark monochromatic prints through the efforts of amateur photographers. The destitute condition and plight of the labouring classes – of the new 'proletarianized plebeian'[1] – thereby attained an unprecedented degree of publicity during the century. It was thanks to that publicity, articulated around the representational matrix of the poor, the distressed, and the disenfranchised, that a society, scarred by human misery, and confronted with the bitter realities of industrialisation, came to constitute itself in the general form of a 'theatre of poverty'.

It is hardly a surprise, then, to discover that the nineteenth-century stage also gave expression to the public's growing consciousness of poverty and its disturbing effects. What it produced on that stage might be described as a kind of sub-genre of the melodrama. Often social reformist in outlook, frequently didactic, occasionally politically adversative – sometimes dangerously so – the 'poor play' aimed to make poverty thematic by speculating on its causes, consequences, and possible remedies. The poor play did not simply reflect public concerns over poverty, however, as though the stage really were a 'mirror'. It constituted a point of visibility, forming a kind of theatrical apex for the articulation of a more dispersed discourse, one that originated elsewhere, far away from the splendid illuminations of the theatrical stage, in the gloomier and rather soberer sphere of political economy. It is in relating theatre to this wider field of discourse that the present task can be articulated. My aim is to 'localise', as Foucault might have put it, the 'poor play' by tugging on the threads that situate theatre's representations indiscernibly yet inescapably within the context of a murkier historical genealogy – that of the concept of poverty and the social construction of the poor. To determine the *discursive* locality of the poor play is to set it not just within its 'historical' context but – more specifically – to situate it 'genealogically', in relation to the wider derivation of a specific discursive formation, in which a general theatre of poverty first became discernible.

Taking the poor play as an object of genealogical analysis (understanding genealogy in Foucault's sense to be a critical endeavour that 'refuses the certainty of absolutes'[2] and which understands history as an 'endlessly repeated play of dominations')[3] entails that it should not be treated as being irreducibly one thing; it is plural. The treatment of the poor in British theatre during the period of radicalism and popular insurgency prior to the Great Reform Act of 1832 betrays quite distinct motives to those that were written and performed in the later period of growing bourgeois dominance, following the eventual suppression of Chartism between the 1840s and 1860s. An early example of the poor play is John Walker's radical and highly agitational *The Factory Lad* – performed to the lower-middle-class and artisanal audiences who attended the Surrey Theatre in 1832, a year before the Factory Act was passed – in which a band of hand loom weavers are persuaded to burn down the factory from which they have just been made redundant following the introduction of steam-powered machinery. A much later example, by contrast, aimed at producing a wholly different set of effects in its audience: Dion Boucicault's *The Streets of New York* sought to evoke a sense of charity in the spectator by pricking their conscience. Adapted from the popular French play, *Les Pauvres de Paris*, and later performed in London as *The Streets of London* (1864), Boucicault's drama examined the effects of impoverishment among the petit bourgeoisie following a banking crisis, and in doing so identified poverty with a social class quite distinct from Walker's factory workers.[4]

These plays were not without a degree of sensationalism, as is to be expected of the melodrama. Some bore lurid titles such as *The Beggar of Brussels; or, the Mendicant Murderer*, first performed at the Royal Pavilion theatre in 1831; others took a more sentimental approach to the subject – *Fatherless Fanny; or the Fair Mendicant and the Spirit of the Rock*, performed on 21 April 1834, also at the Royal Pavilion, or Charles Webb's depiction of unemployed silk weavers at the mercy of unscrupulous landlords in *The Vagrant, His Wife and Family*, at the Royal City of London Theatre, in September 1838.[5] Many of them aspired to reproduce the poor through a form of theatrical reportage, professing to show poverty as it 'really is'. According to Frederick Burwick, they testified to poverty's truth with 'stark documentary fidelity'.[6] They shone a light on its dire social consequences; revealed its devastating human face by revelling in the depiction of its individual tragedies. Theatre thus drew audiences by speculating on poverty's fatalities and incited the viewer's pity at the plight of the indigent.

One play bears particular mention at this point, and not least because it articulates a point of historical distinction, a moment of mutation, important to the genealogy of the poor play: Moncrieff's immensely popular (and controversial) *Tom and Jerry*, presented at the Adelphi Theatre in 1821. Moncrief aimed at producing precisely the effect of pity in the audience, or so *The Literary Chronicle* recounted in its review of his play:

> The object of this piece is to represent faithfully, the varied scenes which the metrop-
> olis presents [...] exhibiting life in all its varieties [... its] last scene presented a group of
> beggars, as well dressed for the purpose of exciting pity and operating on the feelings of the
> humane, as the Mendicity Society itself could collect: even the costume and the names of
> the most notorious of the London mendicants were preserved in this facsimile of a Beggar's
> Opera in St. Giles's.[7]

And yet the play, in many ways, belongs to an earlier period of dramatic representation, and a different genealogy, prior to that which would see the emergence of the
poor play. Although in some respects it anticipated the poor play, it essentially looked
back to a rather more bucolic and charming image of the beggar: to 'their wild free
life, their careless revelry',[8] as depicted in earlier dramatic representations of the poor
such as Beaufort and Fletcher's *Beggar's Bush* (1612) or Richard Brome's *A Jovial Crew,
or the Merry Beggars* (1641). On the other hand, as a dramatisation of Pierce Egan's
Life in London – an episodic and, as Jacky Bratton describes it, 'exuberant' depiction of the metropolis and the vivacity of its people, illustrated with plates by George
Cruikshank – it indeed established a degree of documentary fidelity that no poor play
would subsequently match.[9] Not only did it employ the actual slang or 'flash', as spoken
by the poor inhabitants of transpontine London, it directly referenced several individuals who populated the 'Back Slums' of St Giles and public houses on Church Lane –
Creeping Jack, Little Jemmy, Ragged Dick ... – and in at least two instances, it put
them actually on the stage.[10] It was precisely due to this 'fidelity' that *Tom and Jerry*
cannot be seen as a 'mere representation' but, in Bratton's words, as the intrusion of
'real life' in its 'fleshy presence' on the stage.[11] What that presence invoked, insofar as it
was performed in the public space of the theatre, was immense alarm among the more
'respectable' part of the audience at the spectre of London's great unwashed, appearing
for the first time *in propria persona* rather than as a sanitised object of representation; but that is not the only reason why Moncrieff's bold experiment would not be
repeated. What foreclosed that possibility were political and social forces that would
soon oversee the 'segregation of the vulgar' from the theatre, which would henceforth
be reserved only for the 'serious drama' – forces whose power to reshape the theatrical
landscape would eventually be consolidated with the passing of the Theatres Act of
1843.[12] Behind that act lay an extensive discursive realignment of economic thinking
that had been taking place over the previous decades, structured around an emergent
liberalism, at the heart of which can be found the question of how the poor should be
represented, and specifically as an object of governmental knowledge.

Viewed in terms of the poor play, this problem of representation might be stated in
the following terms: what exactly was being staged through theatre's faithful representation of poverty? – a question rendered all the more poignant by the fact that the poor

of the nineteenth century belonged to that peculiar social group for whom the poverty of representation was a defining characteristic. Denied political representation, in other words, the poor found themselves represented all the same – on the stage. Doubtless, the desire to excite through theatrical means the 'feelings of the humane', produced not only laudable or commendable but sincere representations; that at times the theatre, through the poor play, was able to express its solidarity with those whose miseries it sought to preserve in the form of a facsimile, as being 'true to life'. All the same, it should be remembered that theatre's representational structures are by no means self-evident, as though these plays displayed their motives as plainly as a shop window displays its wares. Through the fabrication of theatre's simulacra, the nineteenth-century stage increasingly presented an image of the poor that owed as much if not more to the symbolic structures of discourse than it did to the liberal imaginary that proclaimed itself to be the eternal friend of the poor. The more the theatre professed its solidarity with the poor, the more the danger arose that the poor play merely ventriloquised the poor, while insisting, at all costs, that the poor must not speak for themselves. Thus, when considering how the poor came to speak through the medium of the theatre during the period of the poor play, it is obligatory to ask: what did that theatre say in speaking through them?

These are the questions that preoccupy me in this chapter. In seeking to address them, I would like to show how, purporting at times to represent the poor in 'their own words', the nineteenth-century's theatre of poverty produced a peculiar and indeed paradoxical effect on the poor themselves: it deprived them of their own capacity for speech; it encoded the way they would appear according to the circumscribed spaces made available to them by its modes of visibility. It determined how the poor should be represented, and how they should be heard. In short, it procured a stage for the poor, but it was a stage that rendered its protagonists the puppets of permissible discourse, which would govern their actions and speech. At the same time, I would also like to indicate, even if briefly, how 'discourse' incited forms of resistance: that a distinction should be made between the space of representation ordered by discourse and the spaces of reception in which discourse intersected with non-discursive practices. This conflict is perhaps nowhere more visible than in the diverse theatrical spaces of the nineteenth century, in which discourse exposed itself to the fluid and at times volatile social dynamics of London's theatre audiences – theatre, a space of immense ambiguity, would pose this problem to government throughout the century.[13]

To show that the poor play belonged to a wider discursive field, I turn first to Michel Foucault's work on nineteenth-century political economy, drawing also on later Foucauldian scholarship that emerged in response to the influential theme of governmentality, developed by Foucault during the lecture courses held at the *Collège de France* in Paris in the 1970s and 1980s. For this, and for a multitude of other reasons, which will soon become apparent, I would like to begin with a few methodological pointers before proceeding to the analysis. One lecture course, delivered by Foucault between 3 January and 14 March 1973, which acted as a precursor – a kind of dry run – to *Discipline and Punish*, has a particular bearing on what comes next. What is notable about this lecture course, whose themes of punishment, discipline, and the 'punitive society', from which it derives its title, is the way it both predates those themes of the later courses (associated with biopolitics, security, and governmentality) and anticipates them (in focusing on the problem of the government of population).[14] Of specific interest to me is Foucault's analysis of political economy in England and France insofar as it converges around a notion of 'societies of moralization'.[15] What is to be understood by a society of moralisation? Moralising discourse is not simply, as Marx suggested at one point, a means of blaming the problems of poverty on the 'evil dispositions of the poor';[16] rather, it had – beyond the explicit formulations of what was said about the morals of the poor – both strategic and tactical functions. These 'moral' functions were operative within the social and political dimension. Ordered around a fundamental guiding ethical principle – that of *ascesis* – they were determined by the economic need to impose self-discipline on the population. The aim of moralising discourse is the transformation into a productive resource of what is unruly, disruptive, or unproductive within the social body. Here Foucault follows Marx in associating that resource with 'labour-power'; in contrast to Marx, however, labour-power for Foucault is not a pre-given human essence: it must be constituted through disciplinary techniques. Accordingly, moralisation, while it sought to produce 'docile bodies', as is famously asserted in *Discipline and Punish*, was in fact developed concretely and specifically through a complex of what Foucault termed 'capillary' techniques. Through a 'micro-physics of power', these techniques circulated at a local level, in relative autonomy from centralised authority, within the interstices of social practices, permeating life as so many procedures – modes of subjectivation, practices of coercion, and systems of control.[17] Societies of moralisation were established on the basis both of inculcative forms of moral correction, as well as through more repressive controls – through the imposition of penalties and sanctions associated with the mechanisms of disciplinary power, such as the penitentiary. Foucault will put the point as follows, '[the] primary function of these societies is not so much to detect and punish crime as first to attack moral faults, and even before this, psychological propensities, habits, manners, and behavior such as idleness, gambling, and debauchery'.[18] What moralisation takes aim at in targeting these behaviours – what it seeks to disturb, thwart, or disrupt – are activities that Foucault describes, in the lectures of 1973, as 'popular illegalisms' (*illégalisme populaire*).[19]

Illegalisms are to be found in all strata of society. They describe a continual zone of tactical circumventions, avoidances, evasions – even direct confrontations – in relation to law, norms, and rules of conduct (morals and mores). With illegalisms, as Bernard E. Harcourt describes the phenomenon, one has the 'idea that law is a constant contestation over its boundaries and serves primarily to manage the margins of legality'.[20] There are the illegalities of the rich and privileged that are more or less tolerated, overlooked, or forgiven; and then there are the illegalities that circulate within the dimension of common life: popular illegalisms. At the dawn of the nineteenth century, popular illegalisms had inevitably begun to intensify in response to the new economic context, as novel forms of depredation that preyed on or explicitly resisted the development of industrialised capital. New illegalisms emerged that challenged, on the one hand, the emergent conditions of modern labour – the rights of the new proprietors, the expansion of working hours, the lowering of wages, factory regulations, and so on (for instance, through illegal practices of 'combining', or through absenteeism, idleness, and general dissipation). On the other hand, the new conditions of wealth directly exposed bourgeois property to the threat of plunder by workers on a vast scale (with massively increased vulnerability of property to theft or sabotage arising from the development of industrial modes of factory production, with its networks for transportation and shipping of goods and materials). Foucault remarks, at 'a certain point [...] wealth, in its materiality, is spatialized in new forms, and runs the risk of being attacked frontally by a popular illegalism that, henceforth, would not clash with the system of laws and regulations of power, but with its goods themselves in their materiality'.[21] It is for this reason that threats to the new economic structures, taking the form of popular illegalisms, required not only a whole raft of measures, punishments, and innovative practices of discipline, but came to define the punitive society, which they shaped. I shall return to this problem of illegalism later, specifically in relation to the poor play, but for now, with this new society of moralisation in view, I would like to explore in more detail the discursive context that informed the emergence of the theatre of poverty, within which the poor play is situated.

The theatre of poverty and the discursive construction of the poor

In the first place, the 'theatre of poverty' signifies a general structure of representation: a general 'optics' that makes poverty manifest or visible in certain ways. For the nineteenth century, it constituted what Foucault termed a 'grid of intelligibility', enabling certain objects to appear, while suppressing others.[22] It was a discursive construction that shaped and presented, with its spaces of appearance, the images of poverty and the poor. As discourse, it belonged to a larger strategic field, which aimed at producing a set of tactical effects, influencing the dimension of social existence and its forms of life, as determined by the discursive statements that governed them; correlatively, as a representational and iterative practice, it circulated and reproduced those statements, amplifying at the same time as dispersing and redistributing them in subsidiary forms.[23] The representational field in which the 'theatre of poverty' originated did not belong, in other words, to a particular sphere of representations – the theatre, for example, or even to culture in general. It belonged, rather, to representational structures whose origins can be traced back to wider discourses, particularly to economic discourses, which emerged towards the end of the eighteenth century; it is through those discourses that poverty, and how it came to be understood as a social category – how it came to be signified in the nineteenth century – underwent a radical alteration.

This is to say that the theatre of poverty was constituted in the first instance through the discourse of political economy. It was a discourse that was essentially preoccupied with the problem of wealth, which is why the fact of poverty was of less importance to it than how it related to the central question that it posed. That question can be framed in the following terms: what is the *real* of the discourse of wealth? – this is what political economy wished to understand. Now, if every discourse has its 'real', which it both constitutes and around which it is reciprocally constituted, for the discourse of wealth that real was, evidently, not prosperity, affluence, riches – which would indicate a purely circular and vacuous discourse. On the contrary, the real that determined what wealth is (that makes wealth possible and that explains it) was the condition of poverty. Political economy naturalised the condition of poverty in the form of an economic law. Patrick Colquhoun in his *A Treatise on the Wealth, Power and Resources of the British Empire*, written in 1814, would assert:

> every state is supported *by the poverty of the community* composing the body politic. Without a large proportion of poverty there could be no riches in any country; since riches are the offspring of labour, while labour can result only from the state of poverty.[24]

Notable here is Colquhoun's definition of poverty, where the discourse of wealth is not primarily concerned with 'the poor' as such, but precisely with poverty viewed as a necessary component in the production of social labour. Poverty simply designates the *necessary condition* of labour in respect of the *natural state* of the labourer. Productive labour arises out of the fact of poverty for the simple reason that it is poverty that compels the poor to work; that impels those with 'no property or means of subsistence but what is derived from the constant exercise of industry in the various occupations of life'. And it is for this reason that Colquhoun proclaims poverty to be, not a social ill, but 'a most necessary and indispensable ingredient in society'. It is, he says,

> the lot of man. It is the source of wealth, since without poverty there could be no labour; there could be no riches, no refinement, no comfort, and no benefit to those who may be possessed of wealth [...] without a large proportion of poverty, surplus labour could never be rendered productive in producing either the conveniences or luxuries of life.[25]

There is more at play here than simply the description of an economic law governing the possible conditions of wealth production: to understand these statements as belonging to political economy is to grasp them as *political* arguments, at the centre of which lay the opposition of political economists to the old poor laws – the system of poor relief that was established in Elizabethan England, and which had operated through the parish system ever since. In 1798, the terms of the debate over how to provide relief for the poor were to be radically transformed with the publication of Thomas Malthus's (in)famous essay on population. Malthus argued that the poor laws 'create the poor they maintain'.[26] But the Malthusian account of poverty did not simply rest on moral arguments; it was distinguished by his innovative 'scientific' treatment of the question. Poverty must be gasped, he argued, first and foremost, in relation to the principle of population. The principle of population asserted that the development of population is founded upon a natural process whose fundamental tendency leads to a state of *disequilibrium* between the means of subsistence (food production) and the number of mouths to feed, leading (in turn) to the necessary presence of the poor within any population. What was radical in Malthus, as Mitchell Dean has suggested, was the idea that at the 'heart of the natural order [there is] an insurmountable situation of scarcity'.[27] There are only two 'checks' on this process of population growth. The first of these Malthus called 'misery', whose symptoms are disease, epidemics, famine, wars, and various other immiserating pathologies of what is in fact *ungoverned* poverty; the second means of checking poverty is enacted *through* government; through education, sobriety, industry, prudence, and self-discipline – in a word, through 'moral restraint'.

The influence of Malthus over the development of poor policy cannot be overestimated. Malthus crystallised in the starkest terms the principal demand of political economy: the need for the liberalisation of the price of labour through the wholesale reform of the poor laws. The system of poor relief simply ran at odds with the basic doctrines of emergent economic liberalism. David Ricardo was to put it as follows, in one of the most influential tracts of political economy: 'the clear and direct tendency of the poor laws is in direct opposition [to the principle that like] all other contracts wages should be left to the fair and free competition of the market, and should never be controlled by the interference of the legislature'.[28] What did the poor laws do, then? Two things: first, they perverted the price of labour by subsidising it through taxation, paid out in the form of relief; but, second, they perverted the disposition of labour itself – they corrupted labour by rendering it *dependent* on charity. The combined effect of these economic and moral tendencies would lead to economic disaster – in Ricardo's now famous prognosis, 'instead of making the poor rich, [the poor laws] are calculated to make the rich poor'.[29]

Ricardo's solution was soon taken up by the government with the Reform Act of 1832, which established a new principle of government for the poor. Ricardo argued that one must impress upon the poor 'the value of independence'; that it should therefore be the policy of government to 'teach' the poor, by whatever means, 'that they must not look to systematic or casual charity, but to their own exertions for support'.[30] Labour must be made 'independent' of the state and of charity, of the forms of dependence generated by the poor laws, if it is to function productively – if its proper disposition is not to be corroded and if it is to be attuned, temperamentally, to the production of wealth. The first annual report of the Poor Law Commission showed just how much it owed to Ricardo and Malthus when it stated, in 1834:

> It has never been deemed expedient that the provision [of poor relief] should extend to the relief of *poverty*: that is, the state of one who, in order to obtain a mere subsistence, is forced to have recourse to labour.[31]

The principles behind the (liberal) government of the poor were now firmly established and accepted: first, poverty should be made productive through policies designed to ensure the independence of labour; and, second, it was the responsibility of government to guarantee that 'dependent' labour, wherever it arose, would never be paid more than the natural price labour finds on the open market. Indeed, it would be paid far less – as the Poor Law commissioners asserted in 1834: 'the condition of the independent labourer is taken as a standard, and the condition of the pauper purposely kept below it'.[32]

Now this distinction within the discourse on poverty – between the state of independent labour and the condition of the pauper, who is dependent on state charity – testifies to a series of discursive alignments, subject positions, and theoretical affiliations, designed to associate two things, to indelibly fix them, through the power of economic discourse according to its distinctive enunciative functions: independence is to be attributed to productive poverty, while dependence identified with 'the condition of the pauper'. And it is this twofold distinction, within the discursive formation of political economy, which brings me to the heart of the problem of the 'theatre of poverty', and to the way in which poverty will take on, at the commencement of the nineteenth century, multiple ways of being characterised and distributed; multiple ways of appearing – producing, within its configuration of the social, a whole typology of characters, inscribable into any melodrama: the honest poor, deserving victim, undeserving mendicant, beggar, and, of course, the pauper – the latter signifying the principal evil to be eliminated: pauperisation. As Thomas Walker put it, in his *Observations on the Nature, Extent, and Effects of Pauperism* in 1831, '[p]overty in its simple sense signifies a deficiency of means: pauperism is a mode of poverty, of which improvidence is the essence'.[33]

A complex determination of poverty now began to remould the way the poor would be perceived according to a new economic, political, and moral rationality, which thoroughly permeated the representation of poverty in the nineteenth century. A new horizon of visibility began to open up, coming into being with political economy and which provided the discursive topology whereby the theatre of poverty could henceforth be constituted as a more general cultural formation. It is quite literally 'topological' because, as Giovanna Procacci rightly asserts, what political economy represented was 'the economic conquest of a new continent',[34] whose landscape was quite unfamiliar, with its unchartered regions and savage peoples, and whose impenetrable interiority, sealed off from the world of the civilised bourgeois, just as surely as Conrad's imagined Africa in the *Heart of Darkness* was to Marlow, appeared deeply disturbing – even menacing. In his tracts on the *Poor Laws and Pauper Management*, Jeremy Bentham would provide a name for this new continent. He called it 'pauper-land'. In order to render pauper-land visible, Bentham proposed to establish what would, in effect, become a new science – a science of the working population. A sociology of the poor, founded on the development of statistics, would provide a 'general Map of Pauper-Land, with all the Roads to it'. It would, according to Bentham, lead to the making of a 'pauper population table'[35] and the devising of improved systems of 'pauper-management'. Better management required more exact documentation, precise forms of classification, clear methods of categorisation, which would render perceptible pauper-land in all its divisions and branches. Not only could the condition of pauperism be comprehensively tabulated, to do so would be of immense use to both economist and government official. The expense of maintaining the poor, for instance, could be offset against their potential profitability. Thus, for Bentham, a 'pauper population table' was essentially a means of detailing the social accountability of the value of poverty through its profits, losses, earnings, and costs. It would be able to procure from that hitherto unknown and shady part of the population a 'permanent stock of pauper hands'.[36] But the pauper population table would do more than provide economic data: it would illuminate crepuscular poverty in distinguishing the various forms of poverty; in permitting the multiple forms of indigence, with which it is associated, to emerge into the purifying light of economic reason. Above all, it would render visible the 'degraded classes', as Bentham called them: 'those whose condition shuns the light; reputed *thieves*, and other *depredators – deserters – beggars – prostitutes*'.[37] This is the part of the pauper community from which 'no general returns could reasonably be expected' and where government must be prepared to make use of coercive powers to compel the class of the degraded poor to work.[38]

It was in this way that a generalised 'theatre of poverty' came to be constituted through (and disseminated by) economic discourse. It aimed to make the poor visible by transforming the *topos* of poverty from something impervious to light into a surveyable social geography. It subdivided, classified, and redistributed the poor by entering them into the documentary space of a nascent social science. Nowhere was this more starkly illustrated than in Colquhoun's work and no one did more than he to illuminate the dark recesses of poverty – to penetrate the disposition, temperament, behaviour, and 'conduct' of the poor.[39] In so doing he sought to demonstrate that indigence signalled a kind of mortal danger to civil life because 'it generates', as he expressed it, 'every thing that is noxious, criminal, and vicious in the body politic'.[40] For Colquhoun, however, the point was not to condemn indigence on moral grounds; his aim, rather, was to reverse poverty's abstruse forms of appearance, by mapping the phenomena of indigence, comprehensively and systematically, according to its causes:

1   The 'Innocent Causes of Indigence irremedial' – or poverty caused by disability, insanity, 'incurable madness', weakness of the intellect, old age, and infirmity; in short, the hopeless but innocent poor, deserving of charity.

2   'Remedial Indigence' – comprising temporary unemployment, economic stagnation, the itinerancy, and homelessness that arises when the unemployed go in search of work – go 'tramping' – these are broadly forms of temporary dependence caused by economic failure of one kind or another, but which, with government intervention, can be transformed once again into 'independent Poverty', i.e., paid labour.

3   The class of 'culpable causes of indigence' – the class of the prodigal poor; those who have brought indigence upon themselves through chaotic and disordered lifestyles. It is by far the most difficult form of poverty to govern since it inhabits the margins of visibility, and constitutes the penumbra of poverty, where the disobedient, insolent, defiant, recalcitrant, insubordinate, and rebellious exist. Colquhoun lists 25 causes of prodigal poverty – to name a few: idleness, indolence, thoughtlessness, improvidence, prodigality, dissipation, habitual drunkenness, bankruptcy, 'female prostitution', and systematic criminality.

These are, of course, the popular illegalisms described by Foucault. Consequently, if governing the disposition of labour will henceforth be the foremost concern for government, the greatest problem will be associated with this third class of poor and the illegalities to which they are prone. Colquhoun's advice to government was to devise 'restraints as shall improve the morals, and produce industry among this noxious class of the community'.[41] One must deploy the 'whole force of law [...] against culpable indigence'.[42] The *whole* force of the law did not mean that the poor were to be explicitly criminalised, but that they were to be subject to coercive forms of power, designed to modify their behaviour (for instance, through fear of the workhouse, with its casual and systemic brutality). This would require devising a 'department of *general and internal police*',[43] which would be 'aided by a *thorough knowledge of the facts*'.[44] This new 'science of police' would be able to monitor and evaluate the success of policies – the education of poor children; the 'progress of morals'; the causes of indigence, and so on. All of this data, produced by a vast governmental network, would be returned to the 'pauper department' where it was to be 'systematised' and digested, so that, at long last, government policies would finally be informed by 'the facts thus disclosed'. What is glimpsed here, in Colquhoun's work on the poor – and indeed why he is of such immense importance to Foucault – is nothing less than the fundamental ideal of modern government, whose aim was to render transparent the entire social field; this is what the 'discourse on poverty' dared to imagine in constructing its 'theatre of poverty'.[45]

The poor play – a discursive interpretation

There is an obvious objection to the argument I began to propose at the outset, and to which I would now like to return: that the poor play owed as much to the discourse of poverty that it disavowed – to this general discursive 'theatre of poverty' – as it did to the genuine desire of reformers to represent the interests of the poor in the face of the social war that political economy waged against them. After all, the movement for social reform, which emerged in the 1830s in response to the new poor laws, and which included socially liberal playwrights such as Douglas William Jerrold, by no means endorsed the crude dictates of the 'punitive society', which dominated the first part of the century. On the contrary, what motivated liberal reformers and social commentators, in particular from the mid-1830s onwards, was the abhorrence felt amongst the middle classes at the state of poverty that benighted the lives of the labouring poor and their families. Their efforts, if anything, resisted the theatre of poverty. Jerrold's own sardonic picture of Malthus painted him as a 'moralist of a gloomy creed [… who] put his icy hand upon the very human heart of Pauperism'.[46] Accordingly, care must be taken not to simply conflate the moralism of political economy with the moral concerns of social reformers. Nevertheless, as Foucault pointed out, discourse is by no means to be conceived as though it were constituted by a coherent and unified underlying set of propositions, whose consistency – once fully revealed – would dispel all internal contradictions as being merely apparent: if the theatre of poverty embodied precisely this contradiction, it is because of the way in which the system of wealth had already begun to constitute a 'surface of emergence' for social liberalism, anticipating the mutation of *political* economy into a *social* economy.[47] This occurred because economic liberalism, as a governmental project, was compelled to confront the social and moral problems that grew out of industrial modes of production; it emerged precisely because poverty, in the form of pauperism, had – as Procacci suggests – 'intensified to the level of *social danger*'.[48] Rather than marking a break with the 'society of moralisation', social liberalism articulated itself on the same discursive surface, even as it sought to transform the terms of that discourse: it did not constitute a precise or clean break with it. This is not to say that it was not characterised by distinct and different concerns – notably, that it signals a shift away from moralising remedies to issues of education, and its social uses in controlling the popular classes. Hence Jerrold will write that it is not immorality but 'ignorance' that makes the 'poor man [...] into a brute';[49] while elsewhere, expressing the paternalistic approach of government, Sir James Kay-Shuttleworth, in his *Minutes of the Committee of Education, 1840–41*, advocated education as a means of 'teaching the poor man his political position in society, and the moral and religious duties attendant upon it'.[50] In other words, liberal reformers, in the process of challenging, should nevertheless be seen as *extending* the intellectual, cultural, and social reach of the 'society of moralisation'. Indeed, very few social reformers of the period rejected the idea that morality should be deployed as an instrument of intervention; most took it for granted.[51]

There are, then, a number of ways of complicating the representations of those who sought to ameliorate the conditions of the working class. It is well known, for example, that while Dickens was a fierce opponent of the New Poor Laws, introduced with the Poor Law Act of 1834 (going so far as to remark in the postscript of *Our Mutual Friend* that no law had been 'habitually so ill supervised [...] the illegality is quite equal to the inhumanity'),[52] this fact did not prevent him from being profoundly mistrustful of plebeian radicalism. In the *Old Curiosity Shop*, he would describe the Chartists as 'bands of unemployed labourers [who] paraded on the roads or clustered by torchlight round their leader, who told them in stern language of their wrongs, and urged them on to frightful cries and threats'.[53] Similarly, in *Hard Times* the union leader, Slackbridge, is drawn as a self-important figure – his oratorical style: 'gnashing and tearing'[54] – who is ludicrously wrong-headed, while the members of his union are hopelessly credulous.[55] To discover ambiguities in social reformers such as Dickens is hardly surprising. Laced into the fabric of the social consciousness of bourgeois reformers was also an underlying fear of a vengeful, wronged class, whose members nursed profound grievances; a class consumed by resentments that were socially dangerous and whose conditions of existence placed them in a state of virtual civil war. One contemporary of Dickens was to write: 'The Dangerous Classes in England, no less than in France, consist of those whom vice or poverty, or ignorance – generally all three – have placed in a state of warfare with social order'.[56]

But there is also something more complex going on here, located at the level of the discursive statements governing the representational logic of the theatre of poverty, beyond the ambivalences and misgivings of liberal reformers, which points to a structural complication. The wider point is to understand how the poor came to enter the space of representation, whether as victims or as the enemies of society; and it is this complexity which merits some consideration insofar as it indicates a deep, discursive ambiguity that circulated in the way images of the poor were constituted on the stage. This ambiguity is explicitly proclaimed on the playbill for the Strand Theatre's production of *The Pride of Poverty; Or, The Real Poor of London*, by Benjamin Barnett – which like Boucicault's play was also adapted from *Les Pauvres de Paris* – in which the question is posed: 'who exactly are the "real" poor?' The bill goes on to elaborate further by stating the aims of the play, that in it '[an] attempt is made to bring before the Public notice, the trials and sufferings, not of the professed Mendicant, but of those whose Pride and Self-respect induce them to preserve appearances – in fact, the real poor of London'.

If the question is, then, 'who are, in actual fact, the real poor?' it is instructive to observe how Boucicault's version of the play, *The Poor of New York*, answers it – and does so unequivocally:

> The poor! – whom do you call the poor? Do you know them? Do you see them? They are more frequently found under a black coat than under a red shirt. The poor man is the clerk with a family, forced to maintain a decent suit of clothes, paid for out of the hunger of his children. The poor man is the artist who is obliged to pledge the tools of his trade to buy medicines for his sick wife. The lawyer who, craving for employment, buttons up his thin paletot to hide his shirtless breast. These needy wretches are poorer than the poor, for they are obliged to conceal their poverty with the false mask of content – smoking a cigar to disguise their hunger – they drag from their pockets their last quarter, to cast it with studied carelessness, to the beggar, whose mattress at home is lined with gold. Those are the most miserable of the Poor of New York.[57]

The poor are not the labouring poor, those who are easily identified on any busy street corner by the red shirts they wear: the 'common labourer [...] has no fears, no care, beyond his food and shelter'.[58] Nor are the poor the class of people reduced to beggary – the mendicants, who are the secret hoarders of appropriated wealth. No, the real poor are the professional classes – the artists, lawyers, tradesmen, and clerks – who suffer the most when financial crises deprive them of their livelihood. In short, the real poor belong to the class most likely to be watching the play; and indeed this is what the play is reminding them of: that each has cause and reason to fear the spectre of poverty. What makes their poverty all the more real – more real than the poverty of the labouring poor – is that where the latter are naturally accustomed to a life of deprivation, the former are not. This lack of attunement, which makes poverty all the more vivid 'because unnatural for those who are unused to it', is asserted in a further rendition of the play, *Fraud and its Victims*, this version by J. Stirling Coyne, performed at the Surrey Theatre in 1857, when one of the few working-class characters in the play reflects – no doubt with a degree of irony:

> It's hard times for 'em, Patty; but when people are born poor of course they're used to it – and don't mind a little starving and perishing. I pity most those poor gentlefolks who have been at the top of the ladder, and have fallen to the bottom, and can't bring down their pride to their poverty.[59]

It is here, precisely in these ambiguous distinctions, in which the question of who really are the poor, that the social reform drama of the nineteenth century reveals itself as belonging to the more general structure of representation of the theatre of poverty. It is a structure that enables the victim to appear precisely as a *victim*: they are victims because they have been robbed of their *independence* and thrust into the agonies of humiliation that are associated with dependent poverty. Lucy – one of Boucicault's victims – proclaims at one point: 'I would beg, yes – I would ask alms';[60] and yet the affective prohibition that mendicancy brings with it, what *Punch* called the 'blight and the disgrace of pauperism', prevents her from doing so.[61] She thus does not, or so she laments, have the 'courage to beg'.[62] The poverty experienced by Boucicault's cast of characters is therefore of the order of 'remedial indigence', to employ Colquhoun's terms; and it is precisely because these good folk are not the congenital or habitual poor, that they are so vulnerable to different sorts of unscrupulous men, when they fall on hard times – depredators who prey on those who are essentially decent and honest: the rapacious landlord, the greedy factory owner, or (as is the case in the various versions of *Les Pauvres*) the corrupt banker and swindler.

By contrast, there is a different distribution of the poor at play in the 'temperance' reform drama, where it is not remedial indigence that is a central concern to the dramatist, but blameworthy or culpable indigence. This class of poor play, blending sensationalism with abjurations against the effects of vice, showed poverty to arise as a consequence of reckless and dissipated life choices. Jerrold's *Fifteen Years of a Drunkard's Life*, written in 1828, exemplifies the basic objective of this kind of play, whose moral – that is to say, whose *strategic effect*, as Jerrold's son was to pronounce in his biography of his father – was 'written with excellent purpose, for a popular audience, the moral being shown, of course, in the destitution and disgrace which intemperance induces'.[63] The play interweaves two stories of intemperance. The first, and principal plot, describes a wealthy gentleman, Vernon, whose drunkenness results in his being swindled out of his family fortune, leading to destitution for his family and dishonour for him; the second depicts a peasant farmer, Copsewood, who having lost the money gained from selling his grain, on his way home from the tavern, is compelled to confront the consequence of his action – the eviction of his family: 'Tomorrow the rent's due and I – that money – lost – and instead of seeking it – I must go to yonder inn, and – father, mother, sister, all turned out, houseless beggars – and I – I the cause'.[64] The play thus shows that all ranks of men are susceptible to the perils of intemperance; that destitution, crime and poverty are its inevitable consequences, whatever one's background. At the end of the play, Copsewood has become 'an old, decrepit pauper – name and health lost',[65] while Vernon has fared no better. He is a 'wretched man – some poor traveler o'erwearied in his journey', reduced to begging for brandy and wine, who eventually commits murder.[66] As he laments: 'The drunkard has no son, no wife, no friend; with one frantic grasp he tears from his heart all ties of blood and honour. Oh! That I had ne'er been born – ne'er had life to crawl a wretched outcast, hateful to the world, loathsome to myself'.[67]

There are two things to remark on here. First, the poor play must not be reduced to mere moralism, but is to be understood in terms of the instrumental effects for which it was intended, namely the reform of the conduct of its audience; and, second, that insofar as its discursive effect is directed to what Foucault termed the 'conduct of conducts'[68] – its objective is to transform or correct the 'different forms of conduct [...] not amenable to the project of socialization'.[69] In other words, what the temperance drama targets are nothing less than the anti-social, unproductive, and delinquent behaviours associated with poverty and, in particular, with the plebeian poor: the class of popular illegalisms that require social marginalisation or, if necessary, absolute exclusion and ostracism. T. P. Taylor's play, *The Bottle* of 1847, based on the graphic illustrations of George Cruikshank, explicitly directed itself at working-class men and an illegalism to which they were particularly disposed: their tendency to embrace Colquhoun's vice of 'habitual drunkenness'. Drunkenness is an illegalism not just because it leads to a disorderly existence but because it undermines the effective use of the worker's body; the only thing he has to sell as his own productive capital is thus 'wasted' in failing to look after himself.[70] This 'pest of the humble house'[71] was, of course, nothing new. As early as the 1770s, Adam Smith had warned that the poor man's 'hatred of labour' and 'love of present ease and enjoyment'[72] must be viewed as a specifically economic problem – something which led him to advocate imposing '[upon] the sober and industrial poor, taxes upon such commodities [as] act as sumptuary laws'.[73] Smith's acknowledgement of the new social hazards that materialised with the development of the capitalist market, spoke of temptations to be stringently guarded against – specifically, those that induced 'bad habits' among workers such as intemperance; that led to imprudent and improvident life styles (where – for instance – instead of saving their wages, workers would spend them in the public houses). As the *Select Committee on the Irremovable Poor* minuted in its report of 1860, '[i]t is a very common practice, with the improvident class of people, to give their wives a certain sum of money to provide for the house for a week, and they go to the public houses and spend the rest'.[74] And, it is precisely in seeking to warn of the dangers of this kind of 'improvident and imprudent' lifestyle that *The Bottle* was written – from the very outset, the play's central character, Richard Thornley, is forewarned: 'Your conduct has been noticed […] from being one of the most sober and industrious men, you are becoming – / I know – a drunkard!'[75] Thornley is a factory worker, where the blight of drunkenness among the workforce has led its owner to announce to his men 'that intoxication had spread to so great an extent in the factory, that he should put a stop to it, by discharging those who had given way to this fatal vice'.[76] Thornley attempts to conceal his drinking from his wife, but he knows that his 'discharge [is] threatened – and it may come, and with it poverty, ruin, and disgrace'.[77] Later in the play, now reduced to utter penury by her husband's addiction to beer, Ruth, his wife, reflects on Richard's descent into a life of dissipation:

> Go back to the days when industry brought content and every face in our humble dwelling wore a smile, for love and esteem were deeply implanted in the hearts of its inmates; and so years rolled on, and then came, like the mildew of the corn, the fatal drink. Slowly but surely was its progress. The man from whose lips a cross word had never fallen, grew angry and excited – the children, whose caresses ever met with smiles, received harsh treatment, and at length blows, and the broken-hearted wife neglect. So, steeped in poverty, the home became a wreck, and the streets at length their refuge. Happy! look at the boy who clung to your knee, the girl who fondled you, the mother who reared them – and read an answer in their rags.[78]

When, in a drunken stupor, Richard finally murders Ruth – the dismal conclusion to Taylor's drama – he at last discovers enough clarity of mind to comprehend the truth of his predicament: 'The bottle', he laments, 'has done its work'.[79]

There is one further class – or at least element – of poor play that I would like to briefly examine before concluding. What it brings to the fore is the ambiguity that haunts theatre's attempt to represent the poor within the 'society of moralisation';

moreover, it draws out what was profoundly ambiguous in the way these plays were encountered by different social classes and constituencies within nineteenth-century spectatorial practices. In this version of the poor play, it is neither the blameless victim nor the dissolute wretch, whose poverty is self-inflicted, that constitutes the principal object of interest for the dramatist or audience. Rather, it is criminal depredation itself, embodied in the figure of what Foucault terms the 'criminal-social enemy',[80] which induces the poor play not only to represent the very limits of culpable indigence, but to cross the threshold of permissible discourse – to become a kind of illegality itself or at least to act as a spur to popular illegalism within the audience. What arises with this class of plays, in other words, is the suspicion that theatre may not simply amplify the moral effects of discourse but that it might corrupt or undermine the order of discourse as such, and that it might do so by encouraging its audience to indulge in depredatory forms of spectatorship. When, for instance, Boucicault's *Streets of London*, was revived in 1891, at the Olympic Theatre, an alarmed observer noted that of the play's two villains, despite being morally inseparable, one was 'execrated' by the audience, 'because he wears a black coat', while the other was 'applauded [...] because he is in rags'.[81] That working-class audiences responded sympathetically to poor characters is not, however, the issue here; what is at issue is the thought that in so doing they identified with the popular illegality itself. It is the thought that those 'poor half-starved dirty devils' who attend plays such as Jerrold's might disregard the intended moral of the play; that instead the theatre might provoke the predatory instincts of the poorest of the audience – it is this thought that constitutes the limit on what can and cannot be tolerated within the space of theatrical representation.[82] What, after all, is it that the poor man enjoys about the theatre? In *London Labour and the London Poor*, Henry Mayhew asked this question of the costermongers who frequented minor theatres such as The Surrey, The Victoria, and Astley's – their response: 'Love and murder suits us best, sir'.[83] Even worse were those popular theatres that, according to Caroline Cornwallis, indulged the delinquent tastes of juveniles: the penny gaffs of the East End, where 'the subjects are chosen from the adventures of thieves &., and the language is suited to the subject of the hearers'.[84] Although it is hard to know what exactly was performed in the gaffs, Cornwallis claimed to have witnessed the following stage improvisation being acted for the amusement of its young audience:

Tom: I say, Harry, will you lend me a tanner (six pence) till tomorrow.
Finch: I would if I could, but blow me tight if I've got one.
Tom: I say, chaps! as we are all poor alike, what do you say to agoin' a robbin some old rich fellows?[85]

It is this sort of theatre, with its emphasis on 'ruffians, villains and assassins', entirely free of the controls of the censor, that led Cornwallis to the certain conviction that 'these places are no better than so many nurseries of juvenile thieves'.[86] A Report of the Inspectorate of Prisons confirmed her view, when young inmates confessed to having been inspired to commit robbery after frequenting the theatre where a play dramatising the life of the notorious thief Jack Sheppard was playing: 'A few weeks after I saw the play, I committed the first robbery'.[87] *Jack Sheppard* was suppressed by

the Lord Chamberlain, along with George Almar's dramatisation of *Oliver Twist* which
had opened at the Royal Surrey Theatre in January 1839. Almar's play, which depicted
scenes of street robbery, housebreaking, and ruthless violence, caused a great amount
of controversy, with the theatre compelled to defend itself by issuing a statement
designed to reassure the public:

> The stage is never devoted to a more noble or better purpose than when it lends its powerful
> aid to improve the morals and correct the vices of the ages. It is this conviction which has
> led to the adaptation of the impressive work upon which this drama is founded, opening
> one of the darkest volumes of life, and revealing facts that must startle more strongly, from
> the previous total ignorance of their existence.[88]

The moral intention of the play is asserted by Nancy, moments before Sikes murders
her: 'let us lead better lives, and forget how we have lived ... It is never too late to
repent – never!'[89] But this was not enough to prevent suspicion that the play's actual
effect was to encourage predation in its audience, as the *Pall Mall Gazette* later reflected:

> [*Oliver Twist*] came to be classed with 'Jack Sheppard' and other dramas glorifying dishon-
> esty and of doubtful moral purpose, and further representation of it was strictly prohibited.
> There was a danger, it was assumed, of the novel's intentions being misconceived by some
> of the audience. These scenes of criminal conduct which distinguished the story might, it
> was apprehended, allure rather than repel – be regarded less as warning of what to avoid
> than an example for imitation.[90]

Besides the obvious worry that instead of combatting popular illegalism the theatre
is in danger of encouraging delinquent behaviours, by providing exemplars for depredatory spectators, there is a deeper ambiguity which, although it should be said is
not explicitly asserted, nevertheless both inhabits and disturbs the representation of
poverty in the poor play. The point, I think, becomes rather less ambiguous once one
reviews what has so far been established. First, it is clear that within the discourses of
nineteenth-century victimology, which circulates in the poor play, one finds a liberal
tolerance for an acceptable poor – represented by those characters who have, in one
way or another, been defeated by forces beyond their control. In this instance, the poor
play rallies to the defence of society's victims – Boucicault's play even goes so far as to
encourage its audience, on leaving the theatre, to give to charity: 'Have the sufferings
we have depicted [...] touched your hearts and caused a tear of sympathy to fill your
eyes? [... W]hen you leave this place, should you see some poor creatures, extend your
hands to them'.[91] Second, and conversely, the poor play offers an appropriate object for
condemnation to its audience in representing characters whose ruin is entirely self-
inflicted, and it acts as a social warning for those who may be so tempted as to pursue
a similar path. But what of the depredatory figure who appears in the poor play – the
thief, the pickpocket, the burglar, or the smuggler? These figures, I think, must be seen
as being quite distinct from the typical villain of the melodrama. What is specifically
problematic about these figures is that they present an image of poverty which enacts
a refusal on the part of the poor to play the role of obliging supplicant, by their very
pursuit of a popular illegality that is thoroughly criminal. Rather than being defeated,
the depredatory character, in the poor play, proclaims their defiance of the law: and
it is likely that for this very reason his depredation becomes interpreted – at least by

a certain section of the audience – as potentially admirable, as something to applaud and cheer on. Theatre's images of depredation thus present a means, not so much of escaping poverty, but of resisting the conditions of industrial labour and its forms of subordination.

Given this, it is no surprise that John Walker's *The Factory Lad* – despite only being performed six times, and never being revived – nevertheless found an alternative audience through amateur working-class theatre and reading groups, during the nineteenth century, after it was published in Duncombe's *British Theatre* and *Dick's Standard Plays*.[92] At the centre of the drama, one finds the peculiar figure of Rushton, who has been driven insane by the cruel ravages of poverty. Described as 'crazed, heart-broken, a pauper',[93] it is Rushton who finally incites the gang of unemployed men to destroy the factory that has ruined them. 'Revenge, revenge! Come, revenge!' he cries, before goading them on to '[break], crack, and split into the thousand pieces these engines of your disgrace, your poverty, and your ruin!'[94] Rushton is not simply a pauper but the harbinger of a dangerous insurgent class antagonism. Thus, for anyone alarmed at what Rushton represents, and no doubt many would have been, perturbation of pauperism betrays a rather more profound apprehension of those dangerous classes who refuse to be absorbed into the body of the docile but industrious poor.

Who or what is a pauper, then, and how does the poor play represent him? The pauper is not simply someone who is dependent on state relief, and thus a burden on the taxpayer; he is also, within the cultural imagination of the nineteenth-century bourgeois, a rather mysterious, shadowy figure – like the vagrant, he exists at the margins of society. For Thomas Walker, the 'habits of deceit and self-abasement' define the 'very essence of pauperism';[95] he is an 'arch-hypocrite'[96] defined by '[idle] and lawless habits and abandoned principles'[97] – the 'whole life of a pauper is a lie'.[98] The pauper, in this sense, is the very embodiment of the 'criminal-social enemy'. In George Dibdin Pitt's quite remarkable domestic tragedy, *The Beggar's Petition: or, a Father's Love and a Mother's Care*, first performed at the City Theatre on 18 October 1841, the criminal-social enemy appears in the mysterious figure of Dick Darkly, a foundling child, 'born in a wood, and found under a tree'[99] – who is called 'darkly' because he was 'found in the evening'. He is a man with no family background, thus no origin; unbaptised, he is a man with no history – and having no origin and no affiliation or attachment is profoundly unsettling; his occupation, or so he testifies before a magistrate, is 'travelling' – so he belongs to the race of men, defined by Mayhew, as nomadic – the wandering classes, as he calls them, 'comprised of paupers, beggars and outcasts, possessing nothing but what they acquire by depredation from the industrious, provident, and civilized portion of the community'.[100] What characterises these nomads is 'an indomitable "self-will" or hatred of the least restraint or controul – an innate aversion to every species of law or government, whether political, moral or domestic [and] a stubborn, contradictory nature – an incapability of continuous labour'.[101] Finally, Darkly's criminality is inscribed, as though it were an occult signature, into his very behaviour and appearance – he is 'swarthy, bold and reckless'. In fact, Darkly is the exemplary depredator, who exists at the periphery of society – but also at the margins of the play, where he lurks in the shadows of the stage wings; his very appearance thereby seems to disturb his representational function since he has no discernible role in the plot, except to act as a kind of counterpoint to the play's hero, Brightwell, whose poverty we are to pity. Brightwell may be a beggar, but he is a victim of circumstance, who – after his daughter is seduced by a wealthy villain – is reduced to 'Acts of Mendicity – his begging at the Gates of the Proud and the Unfeeling'. By contrast, when Darkly appears on stage, once again, towards the end of the play, he is depicted on a desolate heath, bearing a 'pair of pistols and bludgeon'; alongside him a companion, who is equally 'starved, wretched, thin and fearful'.[102] It is hard to know whether one should pity, fear or despise the pair of robbers – or simply laugh at them – for rather like Samuel Beckett's clowns, in *Waiting for Godot*, they are grimly comic. Their natural habitat is likewise a no-man's land, where they wait for their victim, who may or may not arrive; similar to Estragon and Vladimir, they too can be found beneath a fatal tree. In Pitt's play, however, it takes the form of a gibbet, from which is suspended the corpse of a fellow-depredator, of whom Dick opines:

> Oh, that's black Will, an old friend of mind, a regular devil-may-care go-your-hardest fellow. He robbed the mail on the heath here, and shot a passenger through the body – they hanged him in chains. Poor Will! I see there's only his head and ribs and one arm left! I always nod as I pass, and I am blessed if the jaws didn't chatter as I passed under him just now, as he used to laugh![103]

There is, I think, in this fleeting moment of gallows humour, which I imagine the audience greatly appreciated in what is an otherwise forbidding play, a peculiar acknowledgement of the limits of discourse. In the burlesquing of the pauper-clown, the threat contained in this depredatory figure appears to be both revealed and simultaneously neutralised – as if burlesquing Darkly had the power to return the spectator to the safe haven of ordered discourse. While Pitt's play suggests that there is nothing outside the law for the depredator but death, nevertheless, Darkly's humour inadvertently lets something else slip, I would suggest: that in the very attempt to represent this space of nothingness, which exists somehow beyond the law, the play cannot but introduce a subtle incommensurability into the society of moralisation. It is the idea that freedom outside the law is an impossibility that is nonetheless a possibility. What it discloses, in the very act of burlesquing the most extreme depredation, is the exteriority of the law itself – not the ground of legitimacy upon which it supposedly rests, but rather the space within which, rather like black Will's gallows, illegality subsists: a space defined by anomie and antagonism to law. It is anomie – lawlessness – which appears fleetingly on Pitt's stage, and which, however momentarily, is conjured spectrally in order to defy the logic of the society of moralisation, disquieting the moral universe of the poor play.

A brief postscript on genealogical methodology

There is a moment in *Discipline and Punish* when Foucault, interrogating his own motives, reflects on what it means to write a history of the prison: is it simply out of an interest 'in the past', an antiquarian interest in the history of penal reform? Foucault's answer is instructive for the way it begins to reveal the strategic purpose and aims of genealogical historical methodology: 'No, if one means by that writing a history of the past in terms of the present. Yes, if one means writing a history of the present'.[104] What is asserted here is already, to a certain extent at least, well-rehearsed within Foucault scholarship: genealogical research rejects any progressivist implication that historiography can be used to justify the present, as though the present could, in some way, be said to be the culminating locus of an underlying rationality; that history – in the sense of *res gestum* – develops, however surreptitiously, however clandestinely, as the cunning of reason. But what is implied by Foucault's affirmation that one should, instead, write a history of the present? Here, the work of the genealogist is rather more elusive – as he would later develop the theme elsewhere: it is to develop an 'ontology of present reality [...] an ontology of ourselves'. And he goes on to elaborate that this would be a 'critical thought which takes the form of an ontology of ourselves, of present reality'.[105] What is involved in that critical thought are two commitments: in the first instance it implies that the practice of writing history must itself be a *critical* practice, which takes its orientation from the problematisation of the present; and in the second place, that insofar as it involves problematising the present, the task of critique can only develop in a space of estrangement or defamiliarisation – in other words, genealogy conceives historiography as simultaneously a means of displacing the present and of opening up a distance from the present reality in which the genealogist is otherwise immersed. Admitting that there can be no 'escape from history', no adoption of an Archimedean point beyond or outside it, the genealogist can nonetheless deploy history as a means of approaching the present in a critical attitude; genealogy stands in an immanental and critical relation to the present.

It is, of course, easy to show that what I have described throughout this chapter as the nineteenth-century 'theatre of poverty' – rooted in a discourse on poverty that was first developed by the political economists of the late eighteenth-century – has enjoyed something of a resurgence in the early part of the twenty-first century. And indeed one of the lessons to be drawn here is how 'discourse' – or at least certain aspects of discourse – can be effectively reanimated, even in the radically altered circumstances of our own present reality, almost two centuries later. In contemporary Britain, for instance, one need look only to the steady rise of TV programmes pathologising poverty – a pathology located in the disposition of the poor themselves rather than as a consequence of the failure of government and economic policy – such as Channel 4's *Benefits Street* and the even more egregious *The Great British Benefits Handout*, on Channel 5, in which unemployed families are given a lump sum of cash in return for signing off welfare for a year (provided they agree to being filmed to see how well they fare – or fail). These programmes might well be seen to have an affinity with the more voyeuristic aspects of the melodramas of the Victorian stage – yet significant differences emerge: where the poor play no doubt elicited a degree of prurient interest on the part of theatre-goers, the ambition of the poor play was rather less concerned with revelling in sordid stories of dissipation, and had nothing at all to do with delegitimising the idea of a welfare state, which had yet to come into existence. If anything, its concern was with changing public attitudes in ways that would eventually see the rise of the social state, albeit over a century later. True, in doing so, it re-victimised the poor; its tendency was dominated either by a charitable middle-class sentimentalism or by moralising caricatures of an 'improvident' and undeserving mendicant class.

This is also to say that while we are at some distance from the nineteenth-century 'society of moralisation', we can hardly claim to have escaped the matrices of moralising discourse, or the effects of the punitive society. Indeed, it is perfectly easy to show how the contemporary modes of discursive identification by which the poor come to enter the field of social visibility possess more than a passing resemblance to ideas once advocated by men such as Colquhoun. Not only can one recognise it in the crude form of numerous tabloid front pages – 'War on Scroungers'[106] or 'Disabled Benefit? Just Fill in a Form',[107] etc. – it can be discerned in speeches of politicians – notoriously, in the repetitive mantra that distinguished 'strivers and skivers',[108] from the former Chancellor of the Exchequer, George Osborne, during the years of the Liberal Democrat and Tory Coalition government, but also in political justification for developing contemporary 'poor laws': Iain Duncan Smith, the former Secretary of State for Work and Pensions (2010–16), would explicitly invoke the discourse on poverty in announcing the consolidation of all welfare benefits in Britain into the single form of a 'universal credit and work programme'. This policy would not only challenge 'entrenched and intergenerational worklessness and welfare dependency', it would help the poor 'move from dependence to independence [...] a journey to independence through work'. And in a gesture that invoked the punitive spirit of the Poor Law Commissioners of 1834, he would proclaim: 'No matter how the different benefits add up, claimants will not receive more than average earnings'.[109]

Thus one finds an order of discourse, a political, economic, and cultural system of thought, whose contours can be discerned not only historically but more precisely as *effectual* history – as continuing to exert an influence over the present state of economic reality. Yet to problematise present reality in this way, as Foucault advocates, is not simply to show that the order of discourse within which we find ourselves already located is always instantiated by knowledges and practices that operate over the 'longue durée' – that ongoing historical reality is determined by epistemic patterns that, however contingent they may be, nevertheless remain necessary for contemporary economic or political forms of intelligibility. On the contrary, it is to challenge the apparent necessity of those systemic discursive patterns. Thus when Foucault asks, as he does: 'What is the present field of possible experiences?'[110] what he is proposing, through this kind of genealogical work, is a 'twist', as Judith Revel has recently expressed it – a 'problematisation of the way in which we can or cannot instantiate a discontinuity in respect to that which we historically belong to'.[111] This 'critical ontology of ourselves', Foucault would write, 'has to be conceived as an attitude, an ethos, a philosophical life in which the critique of what we are is at one and the same time the historical analysis of the limits that are imposed upon us and an experiment with the possibility of going beyond them'.[112] In this sense, to conduct a history of our own ontology is not simply to ask the question: who are we? It is to announce at the same time a novel 'transgressive' thought: that we might be otherwise.[113]

Notes

1 Michel Foucault, 'Confining Societies', *Foucault Live: Collected Interviews, 1961–1984*, ed. Sylvère Lotringer, trans. Lysa Hochroth and John Johnston (New York: Semiotext(e), 1996), pp. 83–94 (p. 91).

2 Michel Foucault, 'Nietzsche, Genealogy, History', in *The Foucault Reader*, ed. Paul Rabinow (London: Penguin Books, 1986), pp. 76–100 (p. 87).

3 Ibid., p. 85.

4 It was also performed in Dublin and Liverpool – the title of the play adapted according to the city in which it was played. A further adaptation of the play appeared in 1860 – this time in the form of a novel – *Hard Cash* by Charles Reade that had an identical plot. A rival version of the play by Benjamin Barnett was called *Pride and Poverty*, performed at the Strand.

5 Frederick Burwick, *British Drama of the Industrial Revolution* (Cambridge: Cambridge University Press, 2015), see chapter 7, pp. 180–207.

6 Ibid, p. 193.

7 *The Literary Chronicle and Weekly Review for 1821, Forming an Analysis and General Repository of Literature* (London: Limbird, 1821), p. 765. The 'Beggar's Opera' referred to here is not John Gay's play, but the public house, The Rose and Crown – a notorious drinking den for London's 'mendicant' class.

8 William Moncrieff, 'Tom and Jerry; or, Life in London', in *Selection from the Dramatic Works of William T. Moncrieff* (London: Hailes Lacy 1851), pp. 12–142 (p. 115).

9 Jacky Bratton, *New Readings in Theatre History* (Cambridge: Cambridge University Press, 2003), p. 155.

10 See ibid., p. 167.

11 Ibid., p. 160.

12 Ibid., p. 169. The Act would extend the licensing of plays to all 'minor' theatres, as long as they conceded to the authority of the censor. Bratton also points to the emergence of the musical halls. See also, section 3 of Tony Fisher, *Theatre and Governance in Britain, 1500–1900: Democracy, Disorder and the State* (Cambridge: Cambridge University Press, 2017).

13 For a more extensive analysis of this problem of theatrical government, see Fisher, *Theatre and Governance in Britain*.

14 What this signals, nevertheless, is the historical shift, in Foucault's analysis, from the disciplinary societies of the eighteenth and early nineteenth century to contemporary 'societies of control', as Gilles Deleuze calls them; from one mode of capitalism, based on a logic 'of concentration, for production and for property' to another, whose form is rather more 'dispersive' or networked, in which disciplinary institutions such as the factory, the prison, and the school are in crisis. See Gilles Deleuze, 'Postscript on Societies of Control', *October*, 59 (Winter 1992), 3–7 (p. 6).

15 Michel Foucault, *The Punitive Society, Lectures at the College de France, 1972–1973*, ed. Bernard E. Harcourt, gen. eds. François Ewald and Alessandro Fontana, English series ed. Arnold I. Davidson, trans. Graham Burchell (Basingstoke: Palgrave Macmillan, 2015), p. 139.

16 Karl Marx, *Selected Writings in Sociology & Social Philosophy*, ed. T. B. Bottomore and Maximilien Rubel (London: Penguin, 1975), p. 222.

17 Michel Foucault, *Discipline and Punish: The Birth of the Prison*, trans. Alan Sheridan (London: Penguin 1991), p. 139.

18 Foucault, *Punitive Society*, p. 105.

19 Ibid., p. 140.

20 Bernard E. Harcourt, 'Course Context', in *Punitive Society*, pp. 265–310 (p. 281).

21 Foucault, *Punitive Society*, p. 108.

22 The *theatre* of poverty is not reducible to 'the theatre', but equally nor does it exclude the theatre from its radius of influence. In this sense, the term 'the theatre of poverty' is not simply meant to invoke theatre as a metaphor for 'seeing'; rather, its aim is to connect the concept of 'theatre' methodologically to theoretical practices aimed at making phenomena visible within a specifically delimited range of possibilities – staging them, as it were, insofar as it constitutes them as objects of knowledge, caught within a 'tightly woven' 'epistemic web' comprised of both technical and discursive knowledges and practical techniques

of inspection, surveillance, reconnaissance, observation, and exhibition. Michel Foucault, *Society Must Be Defended, Lectures at the Collège de France, 1975–1976*, ed. Mauro Bertani and Alessandro Fontana, gen. eds. François Ewald and Alessandro Fontana, English series ed. Arnold I. Davidson, trans. David Macey (London: Penguin Books, 2004), p. 208.

23 Foucault, *Punitive Society*, p. 166.

24 Patrick Colquhoun, *A Treatise on the Wealth, Power, and Resources of the British Empire in Every Quarter of the World* (London: Joseph Mawman, 1814), p. 110, original emphasis.

25 Ibid.

26 Thomas Malthus, *An Essay on the Principle of Population* (Cambridge: Cambridge University Press, 1798), p. 100.

27 Mitchell Dean, *The Constitution of Poverty: Toward a Genealogy of Liberal Governance* (Oxon: Routledge, 2011), p. 75.

28 David Ricardo, *On the Principles of Political Economy and Taxation*, 3rd edn (London: John Murray, 1821), p. 57.

29 Ibid.

30 Ibid., p. 58.

31 *Report from His Majesty's Commissioners for Inquiring into the Administration and Practical Operation of the Poor Laws* (London: n.p., 1834), p. 227, original emphasis.

32 Ibid., p. 232.

33 Thomas Walker, *Observations on the Nature, Extent, and Effects of Pauperism* (London, J. Ridgway, 1831), p. 17. See also Edwin Chadwick's *An Article on the Principles and Progress of the Poor Law Amendment Act* (London: C. Knight, 1837): poverty 'is the nature, the primitive, the general and unchangeable state of man; that as labour is the source of wealth; so is poverty of labour. Banish poverty, you banish wealth. Indigence, therefore, and not poverty is the evil'. Quoted in Dean, *The Constitution of Poverty*, p. 175. Likewise, the *Report of the Committee on the Subject of Pauperism in New York*, in 1818 asserted: 'Indigence [...] and not poverty is the evil to be guarded against'. Quoted in ibid., p. 5.

34 Giovanna Procacci, 'Social Economy and the Government of Poverty', in *The Foucault Effect, Studies in Governmentality, With Two Lectures by and an Interview with Michel Foucault*, ed. Graham Burchell, Colin Gordon, and Peter Miller (Chicago, IL: University of Chicago Press, 1991), pp. 151–68 (pp. 153–4).

35 Jeremy Bentham, 'Tracts on Poor Laws and Pauper Management', 1797, in *The Works of Jeremy Bentham*, Vol. 8 (Edinburgh: Bowring, 1843), pp. 359–439 (p. 361).

36 Ibid., p. 365.

37 Ibid., p. 365, original emphasis.

38 Ibid., p. 370.

39 A clarification: the 'real of discourse' is not the 'real' Real, inaccessible to the symbolic dimension of discourse and which forever evades the order of signification. It is rather that upon which discourse projects its fantasy of the Real, which nevertheless is supported by certain evidentiary facts and pragmatic effects – facts being, in any case, a description of the world, not the world as it is 'beyond' discourse: the real of discourse, in other words, consists of *how* 'reality' is imagined *outside* of discourse, and *for which* it serves as a symbolic and pragmatic ground for discourse's production of 'truth' effects.

40 Colquhoun, *A Treatise on the Wealth, Power and Resources of the British Empire*, p. 111.

41 Ibid., p. 115.

42 Ibid., p. 113.

43 Patrick Colquhoun, *A Treatise on Indigence* (London: J. Hatchard, 1806), p. 89.

44 Ibid., p. 90, original emphasis.

45 According to Foucault, it is not Kant but Colquhoun whose work will 'determine the history of morals' in Western societies; and it is thus Colquhoun who is 'fundamental for our morality'. Foucault, *Punitive Society*, p. 108.

46 Douglas William Jerrold, 'Time Versus Malthus – The Last Verdict', *Douglas Jerrold's Shilling Magazine*, Vol. 3, London, January–June 1846, pp. 441–3 (pp. 441–2).

47 Describing the method of 'archaeological analysis', Foucault asserts: 'An intrinsic archaeological contradiction is not a fact [... it] is a complex phenomenon that is distributed over different levels of the

discursive formation'. Michel Foucault, *The Archaeology of Knowledge*, trans. A. M. Sheridan Smith (New York: Pantheon Books, 1972), p. 154.

48 Procacci, 'Social Economy and the Government of Poverty', p. 158, original emphasis.

49 Jerrold, 'Time Versus Malthus', p. 444.

50 Kay-Shuttleworth cited in David Lloyd and Paul Thomas, *Culture and the State* (London: Routledge, 1998), p. 99.

51 Procacci, 'Social Economy and the Government of Poverty', p. 158.

52 Charles Dickens, *Our Mutual Friend* (London: Penguin, 1998), p. 894. A further example is the play *The Chimes, a Goblin Story, of Some Bells that Rang an Old Year Out and a New One In*, adapted for the stage from a short story by Dickens by his friends Gilbert Abbott à Beckett and Mark Lemon, which played in December 1844 at the Adelphi theatre. The play offers a trenchant critique of Malthusian principles, depicting the deleterious consequences that follow from Malthus's advice that the poor should not indulge in 'improvident marriages'. See Gilbert Abbott à Beckett and Mark Lemon, '*The Chimes, a Goblin Story, of Some Bells that Rang an Old Year Out and a New One In*', in *Dickensian Dramas, Volume 1: Plays from Charles Dickens*, ed. Jacky Bratton (Oxford: Oxford University Press, 2017 [1844]).

53 Charles Dickens, *The Old Curiosity Shop* (London: Chapman and Hall, 1841), chapter 44, p. 240. See for further discussion: Michael Sanders, 'Politics', in Sally Ledger and Holly Furneaux (ed.), *Charles Dickens in Context* (Cambridge: Cambridge University Press, 2011), pp. 235–42.

54 Charles Dickens, *Hard Times* (London: Bradbury & Evans, 1854), p. 168.

55 'Then Slackbridge, who had kept his oratorical arm extended […] as if repressing with infinite solicitude and by a wonderful moral power the vehement passions of the multitude, applied himself to raising their spirits'. Ibid, p. 170.

56 Caroline Frances Cornwallis, *Philosophy of the Ragged School* (London: William Pickering, 1851), p. 22.

57 Dion Boucicault, *The Poor of New York* (New York: Samuel French, 1857), p. 18. For J. Stirling Coyne's version, see '*Fraud and its Victims, A Drama in Four Acts Preceded by a Prologue*', in *Lacy's Acting Edition of Plays, Dramas, Farces and Extravaganzas as Performed at the Various Theatres*, Vol. 29 (London: Thomas Hailes Lacy, 1857), pp. 25–6.

58 Boucicault, *Poor of New York*, p. 18.

59 Coyne, *Fraud and its Victims*, p. 18.

60 Boucicault, *Poor of New York*, p. 31.

61 'The Reconciliation', in *Punch*, Vol. 8, London, 1845, p. 122.

62 Boucicault, *Poor of New York*, Act IV, pp. 47–8.

63 W. Blanchard Jerrold, *The Life and Remains of Douglas Jerrold* (London: Boston, Ticknor, and Fields, 1859), p. 78.

64 Douglas Jerrold, *Fifteen Years of a Drunkard's Life, A Melodrama in Three Acts* (New York: Happy Hours Company, publication date unknown).

65 Ibid., p. 32.

66 Ibid.

67 Ibid., p. 33.

68 Michel Foucault, 'The Subject and Power', in *Michel Foucault: Power, Essential Works of Foucault, 1954–1984*, trans. Robert Hurley and others (New York: The New York Press, 2000), pp. 326–48 (p. 341).

69 Procacci, 'Social Economy and the Government of Poverty', p. 161.

70 See, Foucault, *Punitive Society*, p. 187; see also p. 173.

71 T. P. Taylor, 'The Bottle', in *Dicks Standard Plays* (London: John Dicks, 1847), p. 3.

72 Adam Smith, *An Inquiry in the Nature and Causes of the Wealth of Nations*, Vol. 2, 2nd edn (London: Dent, 1778), p. 316.

73 Smith, *Wealth of Nations*, p. 487.

74 'Irremovable Poor', *Report from the Select Committee on Irremovable Poor in Reports from Committees*, Session 24 January to 28 August 1860, Vol. 17, London, p. 189.

75 Taylor, *The Bottle*, p. 4.

76 Ibid.

77 Ibid.

78 Ibid., p. 11.

79 Ibid., p. 18.
80 Foucault, *Punitive Society*, pp. 32–4.
81 'The Licensed Victualler's Mirror', 12 May 1891.
82 From a review of Jerrold's play *The Factory Girl* in *Figaro*, London, 13 October 1832.
83 Henry Mayhew, *London Labour and the London Poor: The London Street Folk*, Vol. 1 (London: n.p., 1861), p. 34.
84 Cornwallis, *Ragged School*, pp. 27–8.
85 Ibid.
86 Ibid., p. 31. For a more extended analysis of popular audiences during the period, see Marc Brodie's 'Free Trade and Cheap Theatre: Sources of Politics for the Nineteenth-Century London Poor', *Social History*, 28.3 (2003), 346–60.
87 Cited in Cornwallis, *Ragged School*, p. 31. See also for more extensive reporting of the influence of theatre on juvenile crime, *Reports from Committees, Thirteen Volumes, Criminal and Destitute Juveniles, 3 February–1 July, 1852*, Vol. 7, 1852 – one such testimony reads: 'I got a great love for the theatre, and stole from people often to get there. I thought this "Jack Sheppard" was a clever fellow for making his escape and robbing his master [...] I have seen "Oliver Twist" and think the Artful Dodger is very like some of the boys here. I am here for picking a pocket of 25.*l*', p. 421.
88 Management, Surrey Theatre, 1838 republished in George Almar, *Oliver Twist, The 1838 Theatrical Adaptation* (London: Theatre Arts Press, 1838).
89 Ibid., p. 52.
90 *Pall Mall Gazette*, 15 April 1868.
91 Boucicault, *Poor of New York*, p. 68.
92 See, James L. Smith, *Victorian Melodrama: Featuring Seven Sensational Dramas* (London: Dent, 1976), p. 41.
93 Ibid., p. 50.
94 Ibid., pp. 55–6.
95 Walker, *Observations on the Nature, Extent, and Effects of Pauperism*, p. 17.
96 Ibid., p. 27.
97 Ibid., p. 28.
98 Ibid., p. 22.
99 George Dibdin Pitt, *The Beggar's Petition: Or, a Father's Love and a Mother's Care* (London: Thomas Hailes Lacy, 1840), p. 10.
100 Mayhew, *London Labour*, p. 3.
101 Ibid., p. 228.
102 Pitt, *Beggar's Petition*, p. 40.
103 Ibid.
104 Foucault, *Discipline and Punish*, p. 31.
105 Michel Foucault, *The Government of Self and Others: Lectures at the Collège de France 1982–1983*, ed. Frédéric Gros, gen. eds. François Ewald and Alessandro Fontana, English series ed. Arnold I. Davidson, trans. Graham Burchell (Basingstoke: Palgrave Macmillan, 2010), p. 21.
106 Tracey Boles and Ravender Sembhy, 'War on Scroungers', *The Sunday Express*, 28 August 2013, www.express.co.uk/news/uk/267673/War-on-scroungers, accessed 27 March 2018.
107 Kirsty Walker, 'Disabled Benefit? Just Fill in a Form', *The Daily Mail*, 11 November 2011, www.dailymail.co.uk/news/article-2060067/Disabled-benefit-Just-form-200–000-got-handouts-year-face-face-interview.html, accessed 27 March 2018.
108 George Osborne: 'Where is the fairness, we ask, for the shift worker, leaving home in the dark hours of the early morning, who looks up at the closed blinds of their next-door neighbor sleeping off a life on benefits?' quoted in Juliette Jowitt, 'Strivers v Shirkers: The Language of the Welfare Debate', *Guardian*, 8 January 2013, www.theguardian.com/politics/2013/jan/08/strivers-shirkers-language-welfare, accessed 5 January 2018.
109 Iain Duncan Smith, Speech to Ways and Means Committee, House of Congress, *Department for Work and Pensions*, 27 June 2012, www.gov.uk/government/speeches/ways-and-means-committee-house-of-congress, accessed 5 January 2018.

110 Foucault, *The Government of Self and Others*, p. 20.
111 Judith Revel, '"What Are We at the Present Time?": Foucault and the Question of the Present', in Sophie Fuggle, Yari Lanci, and Martina Tazzioli (eds), *Foucault and the History of the Present* (Basingstoke: Palgrave Macmillan, 2015), pp. 13–25 (p. 22).
112 Michel Foucault, 'What is Enlightenment?', in Michel Foucault, *The Politics of Truth*, trans. Catherine Porter, ed. Sylvère Lotringer (Los Angeles: Semiotext(e), 2007), pp. 97–119 (p. 118).
113 I would like to thank Jacky Bratton and Gilli Bush-Bailey for their critical reading of an earlier draft of this chapter, and for their helpful comments and insights.

Foucault speaks: interview with Moriaki Watanabe

13

The philosophical scene: Foucault interviewed by Moriaki Watanabe

(Conducted 22 April 1978 and first published in *Sekai*, July 1978, 312–32. New English translation by Robert Bononno, 2018.)

A specialist in French theatre and literature, Moriaki Watanabe, who introduced Foucault to Japanese theatre, was in the process of translating *The Will to Knowledge* at the time of the interview.

Moriaki Watanabe: Why do the themes of the gaze and the theatre occur so insistently in your writing that they appear to govern the general economy of speech [*discours*]?

Michel Foucault: It's a very important question. Western philosophy has rarely shown any interest in theatre since its condemnation by Plato. We had to wait until Nietzsche for the question of the relation between philosophy and theatre to be asked again of Western philosophy in all its acuity. I feel there's a connection between the diminishment of theatre in Western philosophy and a specific way of presenting the question of the gaze. Since Plato, and even more so since Descartes, one of the most important philosophical questions has been to understand what it means to look at things or, rather, to know whether what we see is true or illusory; whether we're in the real world or the world of lies. To disentangle the real from illusion, to disentangle truth from lies, is the function of philosophy. But the theatre is something that absolutely ignores these distinctions. It makes no sense to ask if the theatre is true, if it's real, or if it's illusory or deceitful; the simple fact of asking the question obscures the very reality of the theatre. To accept the lack of difference between the true and the false, between the real and the illusory is the very premise of theatre. Although I'm not like you a well-known theatre specialist, and haven't looked deeply into the problems inherent in theatre as you have, there is something that interests and fascinates me. What I'd like to do is describe the way in which Western man has looked at things without ever asking the question of whether it was true or not, to try to describe the way in which the West established the spectacle of the world through the play of the gaze. At bottom I don't care very much whether psychiatry is true or false; in any event, it's not the question I want to ask. I don't care very much whether medicine makes claims that are erroneous or truthful; it means a great deal to those who are ill, but from my viewpoint, as an analyst, that's not what interests me, even more so since I'm not competent to discriminate between what's true and what's false. But I would like to know how illness has been staged, how madness has been staged, how crime has been staged, that is, how they have been perceived, how they have been received, what value has been given to madness, to crime, to illness, what role have we made them play. I would like to write a history of the *theatre* in which we tried to distinguish truth from falsehood; but that's not the distinction that most interests me, it's the constitution of what is staged and the constitution of theatre. It's the theatre of truth that I would like to describe. How did the West construct a theatre of truth, a stage for truth, a stage for the rationality that has now become a sign of Western man's imperialism, because its economy, Western economy, may have arrived at its apogee? The essence of the West's way of life and its political domination have no doubt come to an end. But there is something that has remained, which the West has left to the rest of the world, and that is a certain form of rationality, a particular perception of truth and error, a theatre of the true and the false.

MW: Concerning the relationship between your language and the theatre, the pleasure I experience in reading you – Barthes would say the 'pleasure of the text' – is certainly associated with the way you write: your writing is organised very dramatically, whether in *Discipline and Punish* or the *Will to Knowledge*. Reading certain chapters in *The Order of Things* provides a pleasure equal to that found in reading the great political tragedies of Racine, *Britannicus*, for example.

MF: That's very flattering.

MW: It's not entirely incorrect – and I hope you don't mind my saying so – to consider you the last great classical writer. It's not so much because I practise Racine, if I can put it that way, that I'm particularly sensitive to this stylistic aspect of your books, but simply because it responds to a certain way of writing, a certain conception of writing, when you describe the lines of force that intersect the great epistemological and institutional mutations of the Western world. For example, in the special issue of the review *Arc, La crise dans la tête* – it was initially intended to be devoted to Michel Foucault, which you rejected, saying that a special issue is a burial – there's an interview with Fontana, initially published in Italy. In this interview you speak of the need to 'distinguish events, to differentiate the networks and levels to which they belong, and to reconstruct the threads that join them and cause them to reproduce one another'. You insisted on the 'rejection of analyses that refer to the symbolic field or the domain of signifying structures', in favour of 'the use of analyses based on the genealogy of power relations, of strategic developments, of tactics'. What we should refer to is not 'a grand model of language and signs' but 'of war and battle', for 'the historicity that matters and determines us is bellicose', it is not 'linguistic'. What we must seek out are not 'relations of meanings' but 'power relations'. Yet, as analysed by Barthes, Racine's tragedy is governed by power relations. Those relations are a function of the relations of passion and power. The strategy of Racinian passion is entirely bellicose. It's probably because of a certain realism in such dramatic and bellicose confrontations that I find a genealogical relationship between your discourse and Racine's writing.

In Western culture, theatre, as a dramatic representation, constructed an exemplary confrontation on the stage, this being the 'field of battle', the space of strategies and tactics par excellence. In your books, your focus could be compared to the great genius of classical French dramaturgy because it is able to bring to life large-scale historical confrontations that have remained unnoticed or unrecognised.

MF: Yes, you're absolutely correct. And if I'm not a philosopher in the conventional sense of the term – maybe I'm not a philosopher at all, in any event, not a good philosopher – it's because I'm not interested in the eternal, I'm not interested in what doesn't move, I'm not interested in what remains stable when exposed to the shimmer of appearance. I'm interested in the event. The event has hardly been considered a philosophical category, except maybe for the Stoics, for whom it was a problem of logic. But once again it was Nietzsche who was the first, I believe, to define philosophy as an activity that helps us to determine what is going on and what is going on now. In other words, we are crisscrossed by processes, movements, forces. We do not know what these processes and forces are, and the philosopher's role is to diagnose those forces, to diagnose actuality.

The questions 'Who are we?' and 'What is going on?' are very different from traditional questions – such as 'What is the soul?' or 'What is eternity?' Philosophy of the present, philosophy of the event, philosophy of what is going on, in a sense it's a way of using philosophy to grasp what theatre addresses, for theatre always concerns itself with an event. The paradox of theatre is that this event is repeated, repeated every evening, because it is acted, and is repeated in eternity or, in any case, for an indefinite period of time, because it is always a reference to a certain repeatable prior event. Theatre takes hold of the event and puts it on the stage.

And it's true that in my books I try to grasp an event that seemed to me, that seems important for our daily life, although it's something that has already taken place. For example, in the case of madness, there was, at a given moment in the Western world, a division between madness and non-madness; and at a different moment, there was a way of grasping the intensity of crime and the human problem posed by crime. And we repeat those events. We repeat them in our day-to-day life, and I try to identify the event that characterises our birth and the nature of the event that continues to affect us.

So the books, as you correctly state – I flatter myself in speaking with so much indulgence, but anyway – are dramaturgies. I realise that this presents certain problems and I risk wrongly presenting as a significant or dramatic event something that might not have had the importance I attribute to it. Which is my weakness – it's important to speak of one's weaknesses along with one's projects – that is, a kind of intensification or dramatization of events that should perhaps be discussed with less ardour. Nonetheless, it's important to provide as much opportunity as possible to those secret events that scintillate in the past and continue to have an effect on our present.

MW: Your comments about secret events strike me as being very important, especially given that the inflation of events or their overdramatization by the mass media risks disqualifying the event as an event. We experience a kind of suspicion about events, which are only representations carried by the networks of mass media. You attempt to grasp events as true agents of mutation. The themes of the gaze, the stage, dramaturgy, and the event are connected, as if through some logical process, to that of space. Already, in the preface to *The Birth of the Clinic*, you write 'it is a question of space, of language and death', adding 'it's a question of the gaze'. It seems to me, if you'll allow me to put it this way, that the paradigm of your analysis and your discourse is composed of a certain number of terms or themes such as 'space', 'language', 'death', 'gaze', and that the theme of death is replaced, depending on the subject of the analysis, with 'madness', 'crime', or *episteme*.

Of those key themes, space, which is preeminent, maintains a very close relationship with theatre. Your analysis and your discourse, until *Discipline and Punish*, are presented as objects of investigation, the genesis and production of a space enclosed in its specificity. Clinics, psychiatric asylums, prisons – these were closed spaces, instituted for isolation from the rest of the social body, while remaining topologically inside the city. The large-scale sequestration of the insane in the seventeenth century, as you analysed it in *The History of Madness*, is a typical example.

Your analysis then addresses – as you discussed yesterday during the seminar at Tokyo University – the mechanics of power in legal institutions. Allow me to take a small detour around another case of isolation, the use of speech in Mallarmé, for it represents the fundamental poetic experience of Western modernity. You yourself noted in the interview we did eight years ago that modern literature since Hölderlin has been constructed around madness for the purpose of radically detaching itself, as essential language or *other* language, from ordinary language seen as a kind of currency. And this language, isolated by its very status of social exclusion, ended by resembling another excluded form of speech, the language of madness, which you once called, in referring to Blanchot, as the 'part of fire'. I bring up this episode simply to say that your early admirers in Japan were people who read your work on modern Western literature – Mallarmé, Bataille, Klossowsky.

Consequently, your analysis doesn't examine the content of those isolated, enclosed, excluded spaces but the mechanics of power that relies on them, although fully aware of the limits of their effectiveness. In that sense, it's a question not so much of the dramaturgy that takes place in those spaces, whose value increases with their isolation and exclusion, but of the staging or positioning of the mechanism that makes such dramaturgy of space possible.

The beginning of *Discipline and Punish* strikes me as being typical: the great ceremonial and blood-saturated theatricality of the torture of Damiens shifts without transition to the meticulous and cold rules of a correctional establishment for young delinquents. The very rejection of theatricality or, at least, its invisibility

in the disciplinary records, is on a par with the process of internalising the theatrical viewpoint in the mechanism of power, as conceived by Bentham for his
panopticon. In any event, in your books, the division and reorganisation of social
space are perceived as essentially strategic elements of the mechanism of power.

MF: Yes, exactly. When I was a student, a kind of latent Bergsonism dominated French
philosophy. Of course, Bergsonism was not necessarily the reality of Bergson, far
from it. The emphasis was on temporal analysis at the expense of space, considered
to be something dead and rigid. Later, as I recall – I think it's a relevant anecdote
for the renewed Bergsonism in which we were still living – I recall being at a con-
ference in a school of architecture and speaking about the forms of differentiation
among spaces in a society like our own. At the end, someone began speaking, and
their tone of voice was very violent. They cl aimed that to talk about space was to be
an agent of capitalism, that everyone knew that space was death, was rigidity, was
the immobility that bourgeois society wanted to impose upon itself, and that to
talk about space meant failing to recognise the great movement of history, failing
to recognise revolutionary dialectics and dynamism. It was quite clear how a kind
of Bergsonian emphasis on time at the expense of space initiated, developed a
very, very simplistic notion of Marxism. The story isn't that important, but what is
important is the way in which a given Hegelian and Marxist conception of history
picked up and repeated a Bergsonian emphasis on time.

MW: That's the story you describe in the introductory discussion in the reprint edition
of the French translation of the *Panopticon*.[1]

MF: Yes. I felt it was important to examine how space was a part of history, how a
society arranged its space and established power relations. There's nothing original about this; historians of agriculture have shown how spatial distribution
did nothing more than translate as well as support, inscribe, and anchor power
relations, economic relations. I felt it was important to show how, in industrial
society, the type of capitalist society that developed after the sixteenth century,
there was a new form of social space, a distinct way of distributing spaces socially
and politically, and that we can write the history of a country, a culture, or a
society based on the way in which space is valued and distributed. The first space
that seemed to raise the question and manifest this strong social and historical differentiation in society was the space of exclusion, of exclusion and imprisonment.

In Greco-Roman societies, Greek especially, when they wanted to get rid of
someone – you see this clearly in Greek theatre – they exiled him. There was always
a space around them. There was always the possibility of going to a different place,
one the polis was unable to recognise or, in any case, one in which the polis had
no intention of introducing its laws and values. The Greek world of the time was
divided into autonomous cities and was surrounded by barbarians. So there was
always a *polymorphism* or *versatility* of space, a distinction between space and
emptiness, of the outside, the indefinite. It is clear that the world we now live in is
full: the Earth has become round, it is overpopulated. For a long time, the Middle
Ages maintained the habit, like the Greeks, of simply getting rid of bothersome
individuals by exiling them. We shouldn't forget that the most common punishment used in the Middle Ages was banishment. 'Get lost. We don't want to see you

around here anymore'. And they branded people with a hot iron so they wouldn't return. The same thing for the mad. But, from the seventeenth century on, we had a relatively dense population – nothing at all like our current population density – which led to the conclusion that the world was full. And when space had begun to be organised within the State or within Europe – Europe as a political and economic entity began to take shape at the end of the sixteenth and beginning of the seventeenth century – at that moment, it was no longer possible or acceptable to simply get rid of someone. This led to the need to create spaces of exclusion that no longer took the form of banishment and exile, and which were, at the same time, spaces of inclusion: they got rid of someone by locking him up. The practice of imprisonment seems to me to be one of the consequences of the existence of a world that is full and a world that is closed. Imprisonment is a consequence of the Earth's fecundity, in short.

A whole series of spatial mutations arose. Contrary to what we customarily believe, the Middle Ages was a period when individuals moved around continuously; borders didn't exist, people were completely mobile; monks, scholars, merchants, and sometimes even peasants moved when they had no more land to which they were attached. Long-distance travel didn't begin in the sixteenth century, far from it. But the social space began to stabilise in Western societies beginning in the sixteenth and seventeenth centuries with the organisation of cities, new forms of ownership, surveillance, networks of roads. At this time vagrants began to be arrested and the poor locked up, begging was forbidden and the world solidified. But this could only happen if different types of space were institutionalised – spaces for the sick, for the mad, for the poor – and if neighbourhoods for the rich were differentiated from those for the poor, unhealthy neighbourhoods from comfortable neighbourhoods. This differentiation of space is part of our history and one of its shared elements.

MW: In Japan we have had a historical experience that is both similar and very different. The *shogunate* of the Tokugawa in the seventeenth century decided to enclose the red-light district and the theatre district in a space on the outskirts of the city, a spatial distinction and topological separation maintained until the Meiji Restoration. Social discrimination was materially inscribed in the urban space. I'd also like to mention the fascination exerted by spaces outside the Western world on artists, especially those in Western theatre. From Claudel to Artaud and Brecht, and more recently from Grotowski to the Théâtre du Soleil, we find that from the late nineteenth century, various forms of traditional Oriental theatre began to attract Western playwrights and directors as something closer to its origins, which had escaped the Western historical mould. In a way it was the Rousseauian quest for origins that turned to spaces outside Europe, becoming a search for the *other*, for something *outside* Western civilisation. We can't reduce this entire movement to a simple cultural variant of the imperialism of Western power. What is certain is the attraction of a space in which another time holds sway, different from the theo-teleological time of the West. And, contemporaneous with these developments, from Durkheim to Mauss, ethnology inaugurated a divergent space as its field of investigation.

The resurgence of the great theme of space in the years 1950 to 1960 was certainly one of the most interesting moments in the history of ideas; from Maurice Blanchot's *The Space of Literature* to Jean-Luc Godard's *Pierrot le fou* (1965), in the fields of literary criticism, experimental creativity, and the human sciences, the re-evaluation of space took its revenge against the all-powerful domination of univocal time and history.[2]

It is probably superfluous to add that it was during this period that a series of theoretical discourses came into existence to which the name of structuralism was given – rightly or wrongly. Lévi-Strauss is a typical example. It was necessary to liberate the field of investigation and the domination of Hegelian time, theo-teleological time, to ensure the autonomy of research in structural anthropology. That act of liberation was only possible because there arose the idea of a plurality of spaces and their difference from Western space.

MF: Yes, structuralism, what was called structuralism, never really existed outside of a handful of thinkers, ethnologists, historians of religion, and linguists. But what was called structuralism was characterised by a liberation or emancipation, a shift, if you will, away from the Hegelian concept of history.

MW: But at the same time it is incorrect to confuse the rejection of the Hegelian concept of history with the re-evaluation of events, of their 'event-ness'; is that what you mean?

MF: Well – I can't speak for Lévi-Strauss, of course, he can speak for himself and has, in fact, come here to do so – for me it was a way of bringing the event into focus and to do historical analysis. It has been said that I'm a structuralist and antihistorian, whereas I have nothing to do with structuralism and I am a historian. But I take as the subject of history, that is, of an analysis that unfolds over time, I try to take as a somewhat privileged subject, those events formed by the organisation, the arrangement of cultural spaces. That's my first subject of analysis.

This was the source of the confusion. You know, French critics – I don't know how things are in Japan – are always a bit hasty, they very easily confuse what one is talking about and what one has said. So, you simply have to speak about space for them to believe that you're a spatio-centrist and that you detest history and time. These are absurd ideas.

MW: There are direct echoes of this in Japan.

MF: Well, during the fifties, it's true that there was a way of avoiding, of stepping away from a particular way of doing history without also denying history, rejecting history, or criticising historians, by writing history differently. Barthes, for example, is a historian in the way I understand the term. It's just that he doesn't do history as it's been done until now. This has been interpreted as a rejection of history.

What's interesting is to see how that has been experienced as a rejection of history by philosophers. The historians, they weren't fooled; the historians saw the work that was being done, what the so-called structuralists were doing, and they began to read them as historical works. They accepted them, they appreciated them, and they criticised them as historical works.

MW: You often refer to the historian Ferdinand Braudel and his work on the Mediterranean world.

MF: Yes, precisely. All the great historians of what is called the Annales school in France, not all of them but most of them. But the greatest of them all and one of the founders, Marc Bloch, was interested in rural space, whose history he tried to write. It's important that structuralism, what we call structuralism, attempted to bring to light a kind of different time; in other words, there is not just one time, as understood by Hegel and Bergson, some great flow that carries everything with it; there are different histories, which are superimposed on one another. Braudel did some very interesting work on these different periods: you have elements that remain stable for very long periods of time, while others break away, and finally there are events whose effects or whose records have very different values and scopes; so a short time span and very long periods of time; the problem is to analyse this interplay from within time.

MW: I don't know if it's simple coincidence or historical necessity but this resurgence of the problem of space corresponded with the end of French colonialism.

MF: Yes, that's something I hadn't thought about, but we could relate them to one another. In the first place, European space is not space in its entirety, the kind we experience in a series of polymorphous spaces, and second, the idea that there isn't just a single history, that there are several, several time periods, several durations, several speeds, which are intertwined with one another, which cross one another and form events. An event is not a segment of time, it's the point of intersection between two durations, two speeds, two evolutions, two lines of history.

MW: After all, imperialist colonisation was the transcription of the obsession with univocal time on a different space, which had to be transformed according to the Western model.

MF: The subject of my history is, to some extent, imperialist colonisation within European space itself. In what way are forms of domination over individuals or on a certain category of individual established and how have they allowed Western societies, modern societies, to function.

There's an example, which hasn't been studied very closely but which fascinates me and has been useful to me as a guide, even though I haven't analysed it closely. This is the problem of the army, the army in Europe. Before the modern period, Europe had never been established along the lines of the military state. Feudalism wasn't exactly a military system, it was a complex legal system in which, at certain times, certain categories of individual had to carry out the function of warfare. But they weren't soldiers. Although their particular function was warfare, they weren't professional soldiers. And society wasn't organised as a large army and didn't follow the model of a permanent army. Something like the Roman legion, which had served Rome as a model of colonisation, whose organisation we find in the spatial distribution of Roman colonies that had been set up along the Danube, in Romania, or on the shores of the Rhine, none of that existed. The spatial organisation of feudalism was not organised along military lines, even if society's leading players, even those who held power, were at the same time warriors. European armies were always somewhat transitory. There came a moment, a season, always the summer, when wars were fought. People were assembled and then disbanded when the war had ended, often even before the war had ended, the battle lost or won, the campaign concluded. People were always at war, always at peace; there were moments of war, but there was no military space. The armies dissolved then reformed, then dissolved again.

From the seventeenth century on we had standing armies and, once they were permanent, they had to be located somewhere in the country. There were specific weapons, canons and especially rifles, that required that manoeuvres, the location of armies, the spatial arrangements troops assumed before going into battle, be subject to calculation, to very precise speculation. So you had a twofold spatialisation of the army: it existed permanently and it was distributed across the countryside; it had to be organised so that its movements, its deployment, the way it fought, obeyed very precise spatial rules. It's at this point that army discipline became an issue, and training was required to manage the front, to transform the line into a front.

The army became a kind of spatial model; the checkerboard arrangement of military camps, for example, became the model for cities, for the urban grids that appeared during the Renaissance in Italy, then in the seventeenth century in Sweden, France, and Germany. There was a strong temptation, expressed clearly by builders in the seventeenth and eighteenth centuries, especially the eighteenth, to construct a society on the model of an army, entirely framed by the army. People dreamt of a military society, of which the Napoleonic state was an expression, the Prussian state as well. This presents us with a real problem in the history of space.

MW: There's a wonderful article by Deleuze on your book, *Discipline and Punish*, entitled 'Écrivain, non, un nouveau cartographe'.[³] Deleuze insisted on a kind of mutation that took place between *The Archaeology of Knowledge* and *Discipline and Punish*. Until *The Archaeology of Knowledge*, your analysis focused on utterances or things said, but with *Discipline and Punish* your analysis looked at space or the ground on which those utterances were connected, the surface on which they appeared – within the confines of language, space, ground, and surface, which they divided like a diagram. Not only what was said at a given moment in history but what was done at that moment became the subject of your analysis; and this was directed at exposing the immanence of the relationships of power that had made possible the production of those utterances.

MF: Yes, exactly. We could say that my point of view, my initial subject was the history of the sciences. This didn't present a problem for phenomenology. You don't find any analysis of the make-up of scientific knowledge in Sartre or even in Merleau-Ponty. This isn't a criticism, it's simply a fact.

I was a student of historians of science, Canguilhem, for example, and my problem has been to find out if it was possible to write a history of the sciences that attempted to grasp the birth, development, and organisation of a science not so much on the basis of its internal rational structures but through outside elements that may have served it as a support mechanism.

So, I've always gone back and forth, rather, for a certain period of time, I've gone back and forth between the internal analysis of scientific discourses and the analysis of their external conditions of development. In *The History of Madness*, I tried to show how psychiatry had developed, what topics it had addressed, what subjects it had covered, and the concepts it made use of. At the same time, I tried to grasp the historical ground on which all of that transpired, that is the practice of imprisonment, the change in social and economic conditions in the seventeenth century. Then, in *The Order of Things*, I tried to return to the problem, but the problem of scientific discourse itself, without taking into account the historical context in which it had operated; in *The Order of Things*, the analysis is essentially an analysis of things said, the rules of formation of things said.

But there was something else that hadn't been addressed – it was mentioned to me a number of times, and I was always aware of it – and that is the analysis of the external conditions of the existence, functioning, and development of that scientific discourse. Simply put, the explanations provided at the time, those that were suggested to me, those I was reproached for not having used, didn't satisfy me. It seems to me that it's not by making reference to the relations of production or the ideology of a ruling class that we can settle this problem. In fact, the examples of madness or illness – psychiatry and medicine – seem to indicate that we had to look at the relations of power within society if we were to discover the point where the organisation and development of a body of knowledge were externally rooted.

Since I'm slow, it took me a long time to figure this out, but, in the end, it was obvious that we had to examine the relation between knowledge and power if we were to investigate the history of this staging of truth, the history of this theatre of truth you mentioned. What is it that staged the history of truth in the West? I think that it's not so much power understood in the sense of a State apparatus but the relations of power, which, clearly, are themselves tightly connected to economic relations, to relations of production; it is essentially relations of power that established this theatre in which Western rationality and the rules of truth have been performed.

MW: In the first volume of *The History of Sexuality*, *The Will to Knowledge*, you make a distinction between utterance and discourse. Discourse, especially when it is theoretical, assumes and entails something that surpasses the utterance.

MF: Yes, at the time, attempting to write the history of scientific discourse, I studied Anglo-American philosophy, analytic philosophy a bit more closely. Analytic philosophy has made a series of remarkable analyses about utterances and statements that are fairly clear. But my problem was somewhat different. I wasn't trying to find out how a given utterance was formed or under what conditions it could be true, but to look at units larger than utterances – although looking at larger units doesn't mean being less rigorous. The problem was to determine how a type of discourse might come into existence and why, within that type of discourse, there are rules that operate and that are such that, if the utterance isn't formed according to those rules, well then, that utterance cannot belong to that type of discourse.

Let's look at a simple example. Until the late eighteenth century in France, there wasn't much difference between the discourse of a charlatan and medical discourse. The differences were found in their success or failure, in the research conducted or not conducted by the subject; the nature of the things they said wasn't all that different: the type of discourse was, more or less, the same. Then there came a time when medical discourse was organised around certain norms and rules such that we can immediately recognise not whether a doctor is good but whether he's a doctor or a charlatan. Because he didn't talk about the same things, he didn't appeal to the same kind of causality, he didn't use the same concepts. Once again, this doesn't mean that someone couldn't fully imitate medical discourse, avoid making erroneous statements, and still not be capable of being a good doctor and, in fact, might be a charlatan. But the discourse he employed, taken by itself, would obey norms other than those used by the charlatan. What should a discourse talk about – medical discourse, for example – in order to be considered scientific discourse, or recognised as medical discourse? What concepts does it have to have, what type of theory should it refer to? Those were the problems I tried to resolve in *The Order of Things*, at least, those were the questions I asked in *The Order of Things* and in *The Archaeology of Knowledge*.

MW: We spoke of space and power, and discourse and power. But between the two terms of each series of questions there arises the problem of the body. Ever since the sixties we have witnessed a reevaluation of the body in theatrical practice, in avant-garde theatre, which emphasised the body and work with the body, a questioning of the actor's body, and the phenomenon assumed a worldwide dimension. In this reevaluation of the body, theoreticians recognise a strategic antithesis to Western logocentrism. In Japan we still have a cult of physical practice in traditional areas of culture, a cult that some avant-garde theatrical practitioners took to be an essential anchorage from which to denounce the many forms of political and cultural alienation that the Japanese experienced during the three-quarters of a century of modernisation and Westernisation the country underwent.

I don't want to repeat what I've discussed with you previously but the technology of the body in traditional cultural practices, from martial arts to kabuki theatre, must have prepared the way for the modern training of the body, for the introduction of a whole series of disciplinary guidelines centred on what you refer to as the 'political technology of the body'. Paradoxically, in Japanese avant-garde theatre, the fascination with the body and physical competence was even greater because the military's exploitation of the political technology of the body had been pushed to the point of absurdity.

In your books, the body has been present from the start: widescale incarceration entailed the physical presence of the mad and the clinic concerned itself with the bodies of patients. But prior to *Discipline and Punish*, the body appeared, if I can put it this way, like a watermark, and it is with this book on crime and correctional discipline that the body made its spectacular entrance.

MF: I felt that there was something important not only in the political and economic history but also in what I would call the metaphysical and philosophical history of the West. How did I end up attempting to retrace this history of the social sciences from the point of view of relations of power? How, in Western societies, did mankind become a subject of uneasiness, of concern – a traditional question – as well as the subject of sciences that saw themselves as specifically focused on determining the nature of mankind, what he was made of, how his behaviour could be predicted. So, where does one look for this?

That's where the problem of space came in, and it seemed to hold the key. In a feudal society, of course, the body of individuals is important. Political, economic, and religious power over the body was exercised in three ways. First, the subject's body was required to furnish, produce, and put into circulation signs: signs of respect, signs of devotion, signs of humility and servility. These signs were provided through gestures, through clothing. Second, the body was subjected to power in the sense that one had the right to treat it violently, up to and including death. Not always, and certain rules had to be followed, but the right over life and death was one of the marks of sovereignty. Third, it could be made to work.

This being said, power in a feudal society is indifferent to everything else. That is to say, whether or not people are in good health or whether or not they have children. It is indifferent to the way in which people live, how they behave, how they act, how they work.

From the seventeenth century on, in Western societies, a series of techniques were developed for training and monitoring the individual's physical behaviour. This is very clear, for example, in school. What did school consist of back then? It taught people a certain number of things. Up to the early nineteenth century, students huddled around the teacher, who was in the centre; the students, their eyes open and alert, formed a small tight group around him, catching what they could of the teacher's words. From the sixteenth to the nineteenth century, techniques were developed for teaching people to be still, to behave in a certain way, and the school simultaneously became a place of physical indoctrination. Students were required to place themselves in rows, to line up before the teacher, so that the supervisor could see what they were doing at every moment, if they were distracted, if they were listening, if they were writing their dictation – an entire programme of physical indoctrination. The same thing took place in the army. Previously, it was enough to be able to shoot a bow and arrow, for better or worse. Then soldiers had to learn the types of manoeuvres we spoke about earlier, how to shoot, how to aim. The same for the worker. You had an artisanal tradition of skill, of methods of production, and then came a moment when the terrorism of the assembly line was imposed on people.

It was discovered – and this is what is so surprising – that political power, economic power, cultural power in Western societies, from the seventeenth century, took an interest in the physical body that was completely novel. This took the form of training, of continuous surveillance and performance, and the intensification of performance. You always had to do more, always more in increasingly less time. The acceleration of the productivity of the body was the historical condition that allowed for the development of the social sciences – sociology, psychology. From this there arose an entire technology of the body, and from this psychiatry became one of the aspects of modern medicine.

This revaluation of the body, from a political and economic rather than a moral perspective, was one of the fundamental characteristics of the West. What is strange is that this political and economic revaluation, this importance we

attached to the body, is accompanied by an increasingly greater moral devalu-
ation. The body wasn't simply nothing, the body was evil, the body was the
thing that had to be concealed, the thing we had to learn to be ashamed of. This
culminated, in the nineteenth century, before the so-called Victorian period, in a
kind of dissociation, a break that must have been the origin of a number of individual psychological disturbances, and possibly even larger collective and cultural
disturbances: a body that was economically overvalued and morally undervalued.

MW: As you discussed yesterday in your seminar at the University of Tokyo, the negative attitude toward the body was not the invention of Christianity, as is often
thought – it's a common belief in fact – it already existed among the Roman stoics.
Christianity introduced and generalised a technology of power centred on the
body and sex, which you call 'pastoral power'.

MF: Yes.

MW: Your remarks about school remind me of Wedekind's *Spring Awakening*, which
I saw a few years ago at the Odéon Theatre. Isn't Wedekind's play a kind of cari-
cature of the Philanthropinum, which you analyse in *The Will to Knowledge*?[4]

MF: Absolutely. In German theatre there's a tradition, not very well known, of pedagogical theatre. The scene takes place in a school. *The Tutor* by Lenz[5] is directly
related to the Philanthropinum. Lenz wrote his text based on eighteenth-century
educational experiences and, unfortunately, French directors who produced the
play were unaware of this. The play was directly connected with an almost technical reality, namely, educational reform. Wedekind's *Spring Awakening*, a century
later, continues to pose the same problem.

MW: Since you've brought up Lenz, I'd like to mention a young French director who
got his start about fifteen years ago with Lenz's *The Soldiers* – it seems like we
can't get away from the army and discipline tonight – I'm referring to Patrice
Chéreau. You said that last year you went to see a production of *The Ring* put on
by the Chéreau-Boulez team at Bayreuth. In *Spring Awakening*, which I referred
to earlier, there were bits of Wagner in there as elements of the stage presentation.
Maybe it's time that our dialogue, converging on the *Götterdämmerung*, hastens
toward its conclusion. But before getting to Wagner, would you mind talking
about your friends? For example, you mentioned Gilles Deleuze at the beginning
of our interview. But what about Pierre Klossowski, Georges Bataille, and Maurice
Blanchot, who appear throughout your work like a kind of magic constellation?
Or Claude Mauriac, who, even in private life, in *Et comme la espérance est violente*,
referred to the unexpected presence of certain Parisian intellectuals, especially
their political activities – the research you conducted on the illegal arrest of immi-
grant workers or the work of the Groupe d'information sur les prisons – these are
important personal records of your work as a militant.

MF: So let's talk about friends, but I won't talk about friends as friends. Maybe I belong
to a somewhat old-fashioned generation for whom friendship is something both
very important and mysterious. And I admit that I've always had difficulty fully
superimposing or integrating friendships with certain types of organisations or
political groups or schools of thought or academic circles. Friendship, for me, is
a kind of secret freemasonry. But it has visible elements. You mentioned Deleuze,

who is obviously someone very important to me; I consider him the greatest contemporary French philosopher.

MW: 'The next century will be Deleuzian?'

MF: Allow me to make one small correction. We have to imagine the polemical climate in Paris at the time. I remember very clearly the way in which I used the expression. But the expression arose as follows. At the time – this was in 1970 – very few people knew about Deleuze, other than a handful of initiates who recognised his importance. But a day may come when 'the age will be Deleuzian', that is 'age' in the Christian sense of the term, shared opinion rather than elite opinion. I'd also say that this does not prevent Deleuze from being an important philosopher. I used the word 'age' in its pejorative sense. Yes, Deleuze is someone very important to me. Klossowski, Bataille, Blanchot have been very important to me. And I fear that I didn't sufficiently emphasise the importance of their influence in my writings. I think I did it more out of timidity than from ingratitude. I say timidity because I consider their literary or philosophical work to be so much more important than what I am able to do, that I feel it's in bad taste to emphasise the little I've attempted by placing it beneath the sign, beneath the inscription of their names, as if seeking the protection of some divinity, and I don't want to protect myself, especially not with people I regard too highly to enlist as my sponsors.

Now, I occasionally meet students who ask me who Blanchot is when I mention him.

MW: That's really scandalous!

MF: Klossowski, they know somewhat, Bataille too, but I felt that, when all is said and done, for myself and others, maybe we didn't do such a good job showing how much we owe them. These are the people who, in the 1950s, were the first to get us away from the fascination with Hegel in which we were trapped, in any case, that stood over us. And they were the ones who first called attention to the problem of the *subject* as a fundamental problem for philosophy and for modern thought. So, from Descartes to Sartre – I'm not being polemical here – the subject was considered to be something fundamental but something we couldn't touch: it was the thing we didn't question. It's most likely for that reason – as Lacan pointed out – that Sartre never accepted the unconscious in the Freudian sense. The idea that the subject is not the fundamental and originary form but develops out of a number of processes that are not encompassed by subjectivity but something much more difficult to identify and bring into view, something even more fundamental and more originary than the subject itself, had not yet come into view. The subject has a genesis, the subject has an education, a history; the subject is not originary. But who said this? Freud most likely, but we needed Lacan to express it clearly, which is why he's so important. Bataille in a sense, Blanchot in his own way, Klossowski too, also helped to explode the originary evidence of the subject and exposed forms of experience in which the rupture of the subject, its annihilation, the recognition of its limits, and its projection outside those limits, clearly revealed that it wasn't the originary and self-sufficient form that philosophy traditionally assumed it to be.

This non-fundamental, non-originary aspect of the subject is shared by those known as structuralists. And it created, on the part of the previous generation or its representatives, tremendous irritation – it's true for Lacanian psychoanalysis, for Lévi-Strauss's structuralism, Barthes' analyses, for Althusser, for what I myself have tried to do, in my own way. We were all in agreement on this one point: we shouldn't begin with the subject, the subject in the Cartesian sense as the originary point from which everything came into being; the subject itself had a genesis. And this led back to a dialogue with Nietzsche.

MW: I started our interview within the context of theatre, not only with reference to the theatre as it is currently practised but also thinking of Nietzsche, whose shadow hovers over any contemporary considerations of theatre. You yourself, in your beautiful text, 'Nietzsche, Genealogy, History', just as Deleuze and Klossowski in their own writings on Nietzsche, insist on the importance of theatre in Nietzsche's thinking.[6]

In this context, I'd like to get back to the Chéreau-Boulez *Ring*, which you've seen. I had the opportunity to see it and hear it during the hundred-year anniversary at the Festspielhaus in Bayreuth and I'm planning to go back this year. We spoke about Chéreau's work, mostly with respect to his staging of Marivaux's *La Dispute*, a completely absorbing work, which situated Marivaux's play in the historical and philosophical context of the eighteenth century, within a context, if I can put it this way, in which Rousseau and Sade exchange their ideas on education, the training of the body and the soul, and on the violence of the pedagogical gaze. If my memory is correct, the author of the prologue that Chéreau added in his staging was someone you know very well. It was François Regnault, who also worked on the anniversary production of the *Ring*.

MF: Yes, François Regnault. I've known him for ten years.

MW: Isn't he the brother of Anne Delbée, the director of Claudel's *L'Échange*?

MF: Yes.

MW: And what did you think of the *Ring*?

MF: I've known Boulez for a long time, we're the same age, and I met him when we were twenty-two, twenty-three years old. At the time I was very interested in music. I was at this Wagner cycle because Boulez invited me, but that's not the only reason. Chéreau's work and Boulez's work were interesting for several reasons. First of all, there has always been a misunderstanding of the theatrical values of the *Ring* in Western culture – and a reduction of the theatrical aspect of Wagner's work, limiting it to the musical dimension alone. We listened to Wagner, we didn't see Wagner. The very beautiful staging by Wieland Wagner served primarily to exalt the music and as a kind of visual support for the music, which Wagner had wanted to be spatially beneath the visuals.

MW: Whether it's called opera or musical drama, it has to be seen: it's theatre.

MF: Exactly. Even though the music was below, it had to come from the stage on which visible characters appear. There shouldn't be this screen between the audience-listeners and the stage like there is in classical opera.

Chéreau understood this and, you could say, that that's his job, he did what the work required of him. But what was really wonderful is that Boulez, as great a musician and as great a conductor as any around, agreed to play the game.

This is the problem with the anti-Hegelians of the nineteenth century – Wagner, Nietzsche – who, ever since they appeared in Western culture, have always played an ambiguous role. Hegelianism had become so linked to leftist thought that to be anti-Hegelian was to be on the right! We are finally beginning to figure out that this wasn't the case with Nietzsche; although he wrote things that were anti-Semitic, his ideas cannot simply be called right-wing ideas, we can see that now. Nor Wagner for that matter. Regardless of his disagreements with Nietzsche, Wagner was at bottom essentially an anarchist, in any event, his political thinking was quite different. And I think that Chéreau did something very important by understanding this and allowing us, through his staging, to go back to Wagner's texts, which are very interesting. Wagner's theatre is not simply a somewhat retrograde mythological declamation that serves to support and accompany beautiful music. These are important dramas that have a historical dimension, which Chéreau clearly showed.

And Wagner, like Schopenhauer and Nietzsche, is one of the few people who raised the question of the subject in non-Cartesian terms. He wanted to find out why the Western conception of the subject was so limited, and show that it couldn't serve as the unconditional foundation of all thought; this came from his study of the Orient. And this dissolution of European subjectivity, of the limiting subjectivity that we have imposed on our culture since the nineteenth century, is still there, and is one of the elements of our current struggles. That's why I'm interested in Zen Buddhism.

MW: I've heard that you're going to spend a few days in a Zen monastery; we'll have to return to the problem of the body.

MF: In the history I'm working on about the technology of power in the West, technologies that affect the body, individuals, conduct, the souls of individuals, I had to devote significant space to Christian disciplines, to Christianity as formative of Western individuality and subjectivity, and I would like to be able to compare these Christian techniques to those of Buddhist spirituality or the spirituality of the Far East. I'd like to compare techniques that, up to a certain point, resemble one another; after all, Western monasticism and Christian monasticism were marked by, copied from Buddhist monasticism, but with a completely different result because the precepts of Buddhist spirituality have to tend toward deindividualisation, to desubjectivation, in effect to push individuality to its limits and beyond its limits in order to liberate the subject. My project would involve my own initiation and to learn how, through apparently very similar techniques of asceticism and meditation, through this global similarity, we come to entirely different results. No doubt because the techniques were for things that were necessarily different. That's the first point and, in truth, the second point would be to locate, in a country in the Far East, people who are also interested in this type of problem so we might, if possible, engage in research projects that, if not exactly parallel, would at least intersect and bounce off one another with respect to the disciplining of the body and the construction of individuality.

MW: As you know, Japanese spirituality always involves the body and its language is very different than that of Christian spirituality. That's one thing. And in modern Japanese society, which was formed on the nineteenth-century Western model – modernisation meant Westernisation following the political, economic, social, and cultural norms of nineteenth-century Western society – the Japanese were primarily concerned with the establishment of the Western, Cartesian subject. After the retrograde exploitation of physical practise by the fascist regime, the construction of the modern subject based on Western models was considered to be a release from imperial subjugation, an essential component of the democratisation of the country. This led to the success of existentialism, which had a longer life in Japan than in France. But there was also the question of the most important gap in the construction of modern individuality, which is that of Christianity. The problem you raise would throw light on this discrepancy, which is not simply historical in nature but also cultural. You began your seminar yesterday at the University of Tokyo with a comment on the two-part phenomenon found in the nineteenth-century West in the field of sexuality: the rejection of one's own desire, which manifests itself as hysteria, and the overabundance of sexual knowledge, which made it possible for the sexual sciences to come into existence. In *The Will to Knowledge*, you stress that we shouldn't overlook the positive aspects of the political technologies of the body and sexuality; we had to undo the myth of what you have called the 'repressive hypothesis'. Between the absence of discourse or the silence about sex and the encouragement of discourse about sex, it's the second phenomenon that serves as the key element of the mechanism of power.

   Unfortunately, we don't have the time to discuss this encouragement of sexual discourse and censorship, which has a long history as a characteristically Japanese phenomenon. All the same, in a society that sees itself as being saturated with information and knowledge, what role do you assign to intellectuals?

MF: That's what I would like to talk about tomorrow in Asahi. Briefly, I'd say that the intellectual, at this time, doesn't seem to play the role of telling truths, of revealing prophetic truths about the future. Maybe as a diagnostician of the present, as I mentioned earlier, he could try to point out to people what is going on in those areas where intellectuals might be competent. By the small gesture that consists in shifting our attention, he makes visible what is visible, brings into focus things that are close, that are immediate, so intimately part of us that we don't see them. His role is much closer to what was known as a 'philosopher' in the eighteenth century.

MW: Someone you refer to as the specific intellectual compared to the universal intellectual.

MF: Yes. Currently, things are going on in the organisation of health, censorship, sexual liberation, the environment, and ecology. You have a whole series of events in which I believe the intellectual is competent. The atomic physicist, the biologist for the environment, the physician in medical practice, they have to intervene to tell us what is happening, by making diagnoses, by revealing current dangers, not simply to present some systematic, unconditional, global critique.

I believe that knowledge in our societies is now something so broad and so complex that it truly becomes the unconscious of our societies. We don't know what we know, we don't know what the effects of knowledge are. But the intellectual can help make us conscious of this knowledge, which serves as the unconscious of our society.

MW: With this shift of the gaze and the ethical role assigned to it, our dialogue comes to an end, after a long, spiralling finale, back to where we started from, to our questions about the gaze in philosophy and the gaze in the theatre. Thank you very much.

Notes

1 Michel Foucault, 'Preface', Jeremy Bentham, *Le Panoptique* (Paris: Belfond, 1977). Translation author's own.

2 Maurice Blanchot, *The Space of Literature*, trans. Ann Smock (Lincoln: University of Nebraska Press, 1989).

3 Gilles Deleuze, 'Écrivain, non, un nouveau cartographe', *Critique*, 343 (December 1975), 1207–77.

4 Allusion to a festival of sexual education organised by Basedow in 1776 in his philanthropic school.

5 Jakob Michael Reinhold Lenz (1751–92), German poet and dramatist. Translation author's own.

6 See *The Foucault Reader*, ed. Paul Rabinow (New York: Pantheon, 1984). Translation author's own.

14

After words, afterwards: teaching Foucault

Ann Pellegrini

> I am an experimenter and not a theorist. I call a theorist someone who constructs a general system either deductive or analytical, and applies it to different fields in a uniform way. This isn't my case. I am an experimenter in the sense that I write in order to change myself and in order not to think the same thing as before.[1]

Foucault's 1975–76 lectures at the Collège de France, 'Society Must Be Defended', open theatrically with a kind of meta-commentary on the activity of teaching. 'I would like us to be a bit clearer about what is going on here, in these lectures,'[2] he begins. The Collège 'is not exactly a teaching institution', but 'a research institute'.[3] This does not mean teaching cannot happen, but if it is to happen, it will take a specific form. Foucault will offer 'public reports' on the work he is doing, and the audience are 'free to do what you like with what I am saying'.[4] His research can become the audience's own 'starting point'.[5] This is pedagogy as point of departure, as restless movement of thought, not some final word passed down from on high.

But Foucault's pedagogical ambition is brought to a 'standstill' by the physical circumstances of his speech.[6] He found himself lecturing – performing, really – to over-flow audiences. Such was the demand to hear Foucault speak that a large portion of his audience would be channelled into another room, there to listen to Foucault's voice, powered by a mike, but unable to see him, nor he them, a lost co-presence he laments: 'I've found myself faced with an audience made up of people, with whom I had strictly no contact because part of the audience, if not half of it, had to go into another room [...] It was turning into something that wasn't even a spectacle, because we couldn't see each other'.[7] No 'masked philosopher' here,[8] or, at least, this is not the masking Foucault wishes for. He wants 'the possibility of the exchange and contact that are part of the normal practice of research or teaching'.[9] Confronted with this over-sized audience, Foucault began 'really preparing these lectures, putting a lot of care and attention into it, and [...] spending a lot less time on research in the real sense of the word if you like, on the interesting but somewhat incoherent things [he] could have been saying'.[10] These more heavily scripted lectures, with their loss in room to improvise, were an offering to the divided and distanced audience, lest he 'bore people too much'.[11] His smooth, prepared speech may polish away boredom, but it also cleans *out* the research. 'The reason for my presence here', he says, in words initially written to be heard (and now packaged to be read), 'and the reason for your presence here, is to do research, to slog away, to blow the dust off certain things, to have ideas'.[12]

And so, an exasperated or cunning Foucault tries to reduce attendance by moving his lectures to a 9:30 am start-time; an unnamed source had told him 'students are no longer capable of getting up at' that hour.[13] A large number still were. Nevertheless, apologising to those he may have gotten out of bed early, and 'to those who can't be with us', Foucault pivots to the question at hand – 'So what was I going to say to you this year?'[14] – as if the opening meditation on teaching and its frustrations were off to the side of the main thing, the lecture course proper? (Indeed, the first English-language publication of this lecture starts just after this question,[15] leaving out all Foucault's opening musings on the style of the lecture course – and 'the' lecture more generally – and why forms of speaking and listening matter.) But this is Foucault, after all, whose research methods and public personae, no less than his pedagogy, are propelled by détournements, stutter steps, and cuts, a point brought wonderfully home by several essays in this volume (Gotman, Pauker, Wiame). As he will tell another lecture class, in another year, 'I am like the crawfish, and advance sideways'.[16]

This sideways move befits what Kélina Gotman terms (this volume) Foucault's 'anarchaeological manner of doing intellectual work'. We can see it and hear it in the stutter steps and 'stumbles' of Foucault's published texts, as much as in his 'live' interviews and lectures, where he stages an encounter of thought with itself. This is a choreography of riff and revision; knowledge and truth, far from being settled affairs, are shown to emerge in the wake of accident. Like Oedipus at the crossroads, we are charged to ask what and where next?

There is so much in this opening episode that fascinates and, even, delights. First, there is Foucault's hyperbolic self-dramatisation: 'The problem for me was – I'll be quite blunt about it – the fact that I had to go through this sort of circus every Wednesday was really – how can I put it? – torture is putting it too strongly, boredom is putting it too mildly, so I suppose it is somewhere between the two'.[17] And then there is his 9:30 am 'guerrilla method' to restore a space for exchange and contact.[18] Here we have further evidence of how keenly space matters to Foucault, how its physical arrangements materialise or block avenues for thought (Robson, Tompkins).

But what most arrests me in this opening gambit is Foucault's sense of what goes missing in the bifurcated space of his oversubscribed lecture course: namely, embodied exchange and contact and the disruptive, improvisatory force of inter-embodiment. It would be bad enough, he implies, if his lectures were reduced to mere spectacle (though Foucault persistently shows us that there is nothing 'mere' about spectacle). But even that much is blocked, 'because we couldn't see each other'. It is as if, without the capacity to see each other – to engage in the action or play of the gaze? – Foucault could not do research, teach, or even hear himself think. Thought cannot reflect on itself. The reciprocal and theatrical experience of teaching (arguably, reciprocal precisely to the extent it is theatrical) is reduced, even as Foucault's authority is enlarged. As amplified voice in a box, heard but not seen by half his audience, he is inflated into the very role of disembodied authority and master of truth he constantly rejects for himself, as in his distinction between the specific and universal intellectual.

Foucault's 'philosophical theatre' of teaching derives in large part from 'a corporeal interruption of reflection' (Twitchin), in the double sense that reflection is both interrupted by intercorporeality and enabled by it. Put somewhat differently, to no small degree the more Foucault seeks to script his lectures to stave off his audience's boredom (and his own), the less he is teaching. 'Detheatricalization' turns the classroom into a clinic (Rebellato), and is the death of research, teaching, and the space for transformation as opposed to transmission.

Foucault's theatrical thinking and writing (Jordan, Wiame) aims not only at his own transformation, as in: 'I am an experimenter in the sense that I write in order to change myself and in order not to think the same thing as before'.[19] It aims as well at creating the possibility of another transformation – that of his readers, listeners, students – and with a 'minimum of domination'.[20] Teaching, no less than other human relations, unfolds within relations of power. Power 'cannot *not* play there', he says, but 'it is not evil in itself'.[21] Here, we might take a cue at once from Steve Potter's discussion of John Cage's 'conductorless' works (and the question how undetermined are they, really) and Foucault's observations, in *Security, Territory, Population*, and elsewhere, about 'revolts of conduct' and the right to be governed ('conducted') differently.[22] As teacher, Foucault may conduct lessons, may transmit knowledge, but this does not make him the final arbiter of what comes next, of what and how things get played, where playing is always a re-playing because there is no originary truth. The philosopher 'himself' never speaks from nowhere. To restate an earlier point: the philosophical theatre of Foucault's teaching is experimental. Tony Fisher glosses this experimental attitude well in his chapter for this volume: 'to conduct a history of our own ontology is not simply to ask the question: who are we? It is to announce at the same time a novel "transgressive" thought: that we might be otherwise'. Among the many pleasures of this exciting volume, *Foucault's theatres*, are the prospective ones of experimenting with it in the classroom and teaching Foucault anew.

Foucault's 1980 *Le Monde* interview, 'The Masked Philosopher', in which Foucault chose to appear without name, makes multiple appearances in this volume. Asked by his interviewer why the masking, Foucault replies: 'a name makes reading too easy'.[23] This answer playfully echoes his own much earlier invocation (in 'What Is An Author?') of Beckett's question: 'what does it matter who is speaking?'[24] The long Beckettian shadow over Foucault's work is explored in this volume by Mark Robson, and in her chapter in this book, Tracey Nicholls takes up the author function anew by asking what does it matter that *Foucault* was speaking about the Iranian Revolution. 'The Masked Philosopher' is also notable for Foucault's call for a de-institutionalised, undisciplined teaching:

MF One of the main functions of teaching was that the training of the individual should be accompanied by his being situated in society. We should now see teaching in such a way that it allows the individual to change at will, which is possible only on condition that teaching is a possibility always being offered.

CD Are you in fact for a society of scholars [*société savant*]?

MF I'm saying that people must be constantly able to plug into culture and in as many ways as possible. There ought not be, on the one hand, this education to which one is subjected, and, on the other, this information one is fed.[25]

The figure of the masked philosopher and of philosophy as masking provides deeply generative hooks for getting a-hold of the profoundly theatrical character of Foucault's thought. 'What is philosophy', Foucault-as-masked-philosopher asks, 'if not a way of reflecting, not so much on what is true and what is false, as on our relationship to truth?'[26] Philosophy's task, according to this line of reasoning, is not to unmask ideology, appearance, artifice so as to arrive at capital-T Truth. It is rather to reveal the play of masks, of the 'theatre of truth'.

This phrase appears in a 1978 interview with Moriaki Watanabe (reprinted in this volume). There, Foucault describes his over-arching intellectual project as an attempt to 'describe the way in which the West established the spectacle of the world through the action of the gaze [*par le jeu de leur regard*]. I would like to know how illness has been staged, how madness has been staged, how crime has been staged, that is, how they have been perceived, how they have been received, what value has been given to madness, to crime, to illness, what role have we made them play.'[27] As chapters in this volume make clear (Elden and Gotman), Foucault turns to specific theatrical examples (Shakespeare's Lear and Sophocles' Oedipus) to illuminate questions of madness, truth, and sovereignty's failures. But still more centrally, this volume as a whole brilliantly brings to the fore the extent to which theatricality – the staginess and performativity of 'true' and 'false' – serves as both metaphor and method for Foucault's diverse investigations of Western regimes of truth.

So much of Foucault's work is suffused with the language of 'struggle', 'force', 'war'. The question when 'war' became a model of intelligibility for politics, and with what effects, is at the centre of the *'Society Must Be Defended'* lecture course. But perhaps the theatrical opening to those lectures hints at another grid for thinking and doing power: theatre. Is it going too far to suggest that theatre provides the grid of intelligibility for reading with Foucault and thinking relations of power? If so, there is a wonderful irony in this possibility. War and theatre have a long history, of course. The oldest extant play in the Western theatrical tradition is Aeschylus's *The Persians*, which dramatises the Athenians' surprising victory over a much-superior Persian force at the Battle of Salamis just eight years earlier. Aeschylus's play is both a shout-out to Athens and a warning: don't let the victory go to your head.

In more Foucauldian terms, '[m]y point is not that everything is bad, but that everything is dangerous, which is not exactly the same as bad. If everything is dangerous, then we always have something to do'.[28] This is the bad news-good news of Foucault's thought. He tells us that 'power is everywhere', but so too is resistance. Theatre – including the philosophical theatre of teaching – is among the places we can 'plug in', learn how things have been played, and practice playing them, playing ourselves, otherwise.

Notes

1 Michel Foucault, 'Interview with Michel Foucault', in James D. Faubion (ed.), *Power*, Vol. 3, *The Essential Works of Foucault, 1954–1984*, trans. Robert Hurley and others, 3 vols (New York: New York Press, 2000), p. 240.

2 Michel Foucault, *'Society Must Be Defended': Lectures at the Collège de France, 1975–1976*, ed. Mauro Bertani and Alessandro Fontana, gen. eds. François Ewald and Alessandro Fontana, English series ed. Arnold I. Davidson, trans. David Macey (New York: Picador, 2003), p. 1.

3 Ibid.

4 Ibid., p. 2.

5 Ibid., p. 1.

6 Ibid., p. 2.

7 Ibid.

8 Michel Foucault, 'The Masked Philosopher', in Paul Rabinow (ed.), *Ethics*, Vol. 1, *The Essential Works of Foucault, 1954–1984*, trans. Robert Hurley and others, 3 vols (New York: New Press, 1997), pp. 321–8.

9 Ibid., p. 3.

10 Ibid., p. 2.

11 Ibid.

12 Ibid.

13 Ibid.

14 Ibid.

15 Michel Foucault, 'Two Lectures', in *Power/Knowledge: Selected Interviews and Other Writings, 1972–1977*, ed. Colin Gordon (New York: Pantheon Books, 1980), p. 78.

16 Michel Foucault, *The Birth of Biopolitics: Lectures at the Collège de France, 1978–79*, ed. Michel Senellart, gen. eds. François Ewald and Alessandro Fontana, English series ed. Arnold I. Davidson, trans. Graham Burchell (New York: Picador, 2008), p. 78.

17 Foucault, *'Society Must Be Defended'*, p. 2.

18 Ibid.

19 'Interview with Michel Foucault', p. 240.

20 Michel Foucault, 'The Ethic of Care for the Self as a Practice of Freedom', in *The Final Foucault*, ed. James Bernauer and David Rasmussen (Cambridge, MA: MIT Press, 1994), p. 18.

21 Ibid., emphasis added.

22 See, in particular, lectures six and eight of *Security, Territory, Population: Lectures at the Collège de France, 1977–1978*, ed. Michel Senellart, gen. eds. François Ewald and Alessandro Fontana, English series ed. Arnold I. Davidson, trans. Graham Burchell (New York: Palgrave Macmillan, 2007), pp. 135–61, pp. 191–226.

23 Foucault, 'The Masked Philosopher', p. 321.

24 Michel Foucault, 'What Is an Author?', in *Aesthetics, Method, and Epistemology*, ed. James D. Faubion, trans. Josué V. Harari (New York: New Press, 1998), p. 205.

25 Foucault, 'The Masked Philosopher', pp. 326–7.

26 Ibid., p. 327.

27 Michael Foucault, 'The Philosophical Scene: An interview with Moriaki Watanabe' (this volume).

28 Michel Foucault, 'On the Genealogy of Ethics: An Overview of Work in Progress', in *The Foucault Reader*, ed. Paul Rabinow (New York: Pantheon, 1984), p. 343. See Nicholls's discussion of this passage in this volume.

INDEX